SECOND EDITION

Life in Schools

An Introduction to Critical Pedagogy in the Foundations of Education

PETER MCLAREN

University of California, Los Angeles

Longman

**Life in Schools: An Introduction to
Critical Pedagogy in the Foundations
of Education, Second Edition**

Longman, 10 Bank Street, White Plains, N.Y. 10606

Associated companies:
Longman Group Ltd., London
Longman Cheshire Pty., Melbourne
Longman Paul Pty., Auckland
Copp Clark Pitman, Toronto

This book is dedicated to my friend and colleague
Henry Giroux, my wife Jenny, my daughter Laura and
my son-in-law Marcelo, my son Jon, and to the memory
of James Montgomerie and Jake Dale. I also wish to
dedicate this book to Joe Kincheloe and Donald Macedo.

Acquisitions editor: Stuart B. Miller
Development editor: Virginia L. Blanford
Production editor: Linda Moser
Cover design: Joseph DePinho
Production supervisor: Anne Armeny

 This book is printed on recycled paper.

Library of Congress Cataloging-in-Publication Data

McLaren, Peter, 1948–
    Life in schools : an introduction to critical pedagogy in the
foundations of education / Peter McLaren.—2nd ed.
        p.   cm.
    Includes bibliographical references (p.).
    ISBN 0-8013-0638-8
    1. Education—Social aspects—United States.   2. Critical
pedagogy—United States.   3. Education—United States—Philosophy.
4. Educational equalization—United States.   I. Title.
LC191.4.M38   1994
370.19'0973—dc20   93-17627
                                                                            CIP

3 4 5 6 7 8 9 10-MA-97969594

Contents

Foreword to the First Edition

Life in Schools brilliantly combines theory and practice. McLaren integrates a moving description of his own teaching experiences with an analysis of current social problems and a clear, understandable statement of a theory that allows us to analyze and formulate solutions to modern educational problems.

The centerpiece of the book is McLaren's autobiographical journal—the narrative of a teacher struggling to make a difference in the lives of children of immigrant and minority-group parents stuck in the netherworld of the economic and social underclass. These children constitute the major social problem for American public schools in the 1980s and 1990s. The new immigrant population of the 1980s confronts educators once again, as did the immigrant population of the early twentieth century, with the task of teaching children from a variety of cultural, language, and socioeconomic backgrounds. At the same time, other groups of students seem destined to join the permanent underclass, of which sociologists include a growing segment of the United States population.[1] McLaren provides both a powerful portrayal of his students and his efforts to reach them, and a theoretical context in which to begin thinking about the challenges they represent.

Critical theory is one of the most important methods available to us for understanding modern social problems. Applied to education, critical theory helps students and teachers understand the political, social, and economic issues underlying classroom practices and the social world of the school, and it points the way to possible solutions. In *Life in Schools,* Peter McLaren makes critical theory accessible and understandable to the reader by applying its methods of analysis to his vivid description of school life.

---

[1] Isabel Wilkerson, "New Studies Zeroing in on Poorest of the Poor," *New York Times,* Vol. CXXXVII, No. 47,359 (December 20, 1987), p. 26.

Life in Schools is a thought-provoking introduction to the real world of modern schools, to the social problems confronting educators, and to a theory that provides both insight and hope.

Joel Spring
University of Cincinnati

Foreword to the Second Edition

In April of 1992, many white Americans were surprised by what they perceived to be a violent overreaction by the black and Latino communities of Los Angeles to the acquittal of police officers for the beating of Rodney King. Many students I spoke with, although skeptical of media interpretation of the rebellion, still floundered for an alternative analysis. Like most mainstream media coverage, their questions tended to be limited to the beating and acquittal itself, decontextualizing these acts from the history of relations between African-Americans and white-controlled police forces and vigilante groups. They also decontextualized what happened from the growing poverty and hopelessness in many large urban areas as jobs have been exported to Third World nations and as white middle- and upper-class communities have reinforced their own physical and social distance from urban poor people. They tended to view the aftermath of the acquittal as a self-contained event, taking place in a particular time and location that has little connection with their own world.

The discourse most readily available to students, as well as to the wider society, questions the motives and morals of individuals, placing everyone on a fictitious equal plane that is buttressed by the words "equal opportunity," "democracy," "progress," and "individualism." How can educators engage students in a process of analyzing social issues with reference to unequal and unethical social structures and processes that they see every day but have learned to take for granted? And how can educators do this in a way that affirms students' ability to grasp concepts, while at the same time challenging them to place particular events in a wider context?

Critical pedagogy directs educators toward a teaching process that does this but that often enmeshes us in an ethical and pedagogical dilemma. Critical pedagogy is about power and empowerment. Although this assertion may seem straightforward, in the classroom it often plays itself out in contradictory ways.

On the one hand, the critical educator invites students to construct their own analysis of social phenomena and to appropriate for themselves the process of theory-building. But on the other hand, the critical educator wants students to situate social phenomena in broader structural relationships and to ask questions, such as who benefits from these relationships, how are unequal relationships being reproduced, and how do individuals interpret their situatedness in a system of unequal economic, racial, and gendered relations? For some students, these kinds of questions support their own analysis of social phenomena; for others, they do not. In the latter case, the critical educator often finds herself or himself caught in a dilemma: how to support students' questioning and meaning-making while at the same time teaching students to critique power relations that contextualize schools and place limits on lives.

Life in Schools offers the critical educator an excellent resource for addressing precisely this dilemma. In the first half of the text, readers travel with Peter McLaren through four years of teaching in the inner city, by way of a journal he kept. Although the journal does not pretend to be a repository of systematically collected ethnographic data, it does provide a wealth of relatively uninterpreted vignettes of the students, the school, and McLaren's experiences. I say "relatively uninterpreted" because McLaren did decide what to write about and what not to write about. Nevertheless, the journal is extensive enough to present a rich picture, and one that readily connects with my own experiences in inner-city schools, as well as that of many other educators.

The journal invites students to ask questions and begin to theorize about conditions of life in schools that serve poor students and racial and ethnic minority students. It provides a concrete referent around which students can begin to generate interpretations and analyses of why youth tend to leave school prepared to follow in their parents' footsteps despite the rhetoric of schools serving as avenues for social mobility. A class might stick to analysis of the experiences in the journal itself, or explore local and current experiences in urban areas that are similar to those recorded in the journal.

In the next section of the text, students then engage with McLaren in his own analysis of schooling, which was written several years after the journal. Here, the text stretches students to consider life in schools through the theoretical framework of critical pedagogy and to ask how teachers can engage children in inner-city schools in ways that actually empower them to gain more control over their own lives. After introducing students to the main concepts of critical pedagogy, McLaren uses it to analyze the content of the journal and, more broadly, the failure of most inner-city schools (and other urban institutions) and to suggest a vision for doing schooling differently.

The text then offers students a rare opportunity to engage with other students in their examination of the journal and McLaren's application of critical pedagogy to its analysis, and to "hear" (from Kelly and Portelli) their teachers' rationales for choosing the text and reactions to students' ideas. In Portelli's discussion, for example, students can see their own feelings and reactions to the text reflected in the writings of other students, providing a mirror for both affirmation and reflection. Is his account "too negative"? Inapplicable to here and now? These are reactions my own students commonly have to critical analyses of schooling. The second edition of *Life in Schools* permits students to ask their own questions, placing them on the table for examination.

Excellent teachers grow; their analysis of issues expands and their vision for the possible becomes richer. The final section of *Life in Schools* presents Peter McLaren's most recent reading of his own journal and earlier analysis of ideas. Over a period of years, he grapples with a broader array of issues and theoretical perspectives. Here, he critiques his own earlier thinking and recasts and extends issues raised in the journal through a critical postmodern perspective. In so doing, he challenges students to think, grow, and allow themselves to self-reflect and self-critique, just as he did. Some students will be tempted to target their criticisms solely toward McLaren, but by making himself vulnerable, he directs their questions back to them and challenges them to examine their own ideas.

Students need not agree with McLaren, but they must engage with him. The text, in fact, welcomes their engagement, and presents them with multiple layers of analysis. *Life in Schools* is not bounded by its cover. The text also invites the critical educator to apply additional theoretical analyses that interrogate unequal power relations, to the issues raised by the journal, such as postcolonialism and socialist feminism. *Life in Schools* offers a rare opportunity for students, critical educators, and a leading educational theorist to dialog, disagree, question, and stretch each other's thinking and action around ethical issues involving schooling and democracy in a capitalistic, patriarchal, and racist society.

Christine Sleeter
University of Wisconsin—Parkside

Preface

This book is an attempt to bring together two worlds that the poet William Blake once called "songs of innocence" and "songs of experience." Within the context of this writing, these worlds represent, respectively, the intuitive, practical knowledge of the beginning classroom teacher and the domain of critical educational theory. I bring them together in this book to shed a more critical light on the issue of why disadvantaged students generally don't succeed in school, despite the efforts of well-meaning and enthusiastic educators and teachers. The tradition of critical pedagogy from which grew the challenge of this book represents an approach to schooling that is committed to the imperatives of empowering students and transforming the larger social order in the interests of justice and equality. My central task is to develop a language through which educators and others can unravel and comprehend the relationship among schooling, the wider social relations which inform it, and the historically constructed needs and competencies that students bring to schools.

Every book constitutes for its author a struggle with the past; each page testifies to a place somewhere in the writer's own sedimented history. This book represents for me a particular crossroads in time, an historical juncture in which I remain poised pedagogically between the innocence and naivete of a young man's sudden introduction to teaching and the reflections of a social theorist privileged with the power of hindsight and research. *Life in Schools* is an attempt to reconstruct a set of past experiences in the light of my current research efforts, in order to give some pedagogical hope to the tension they embody and the story they tell.

The story begins in 1980, with the publication of the journal documenting my teaching experiences in an inner-city elementary school in Toronto's Jane-Finch Corridor. The book became a controversial best-seller in Canada in the wake of heated public debate. Like so many public school teachers, I survived the classroom by drawing upon a mixture of practical knowledge and relatively untutored pedagogical instinct. This got me through five years of teaching and under the circumstances I felt that I had fared quite well. But a troublesome feeling that I had not made a real difference in the chances of my students to acquire a qualitatively better future began to shadow my personal and intellectual life. With few theoretical resources to help me better understand my students, their families, and the nature of the schooling process, I had failed to see how all of these were related to the larger socioeconomic context and technologies of power of the wider society. I was blind to the most damaging effects of exercising my professional duties among the children of the disaffected, the disadvantaged, the disenfranchised, the dispossessed. I let slip an important chance to develop a pedagogy that would have been more effective in both empowering my students and transforming conditions in the existing community.

My purpose in publishing my journal was neither to create scholarly discourse for an academic audience, nor to transform schools into communities of risk and resistance; quite simply, my purpose was to draw public attention to the social conditions of the disaffected students who lived in the nearby public housing units under terribly oppressive circumstances. I also wanted to address the immediate needs of inner-city teachers, many of whom felt desperate and helpless in their overcrowded classrooms, which lacked both necessary material resources and an ethos conducive to learning.

Unfortunately I couldn't then avail myself of the conceptual tools that might have given my journal a necessary theoretical depth. I had little or no familiarity with the tradition of critical pedagogy and the writings of Paulo Freire, Henry Giroux, Maxine Greene, Jane Gaskell, Michael Apple, Roger Simon, Joel Spring, Paul Willis, Tom Popkewitz, and others. But I did have an important story to tell of the lives and struggles of children. In the triumphal manner of a young frontier-style muckraker, I set off an educational debate through the publication of my classroom diary. My immediate goal in publishing my journal was not to embrace despair but rather to convince school board members to decrease the pupil-teacher ratio, to develop new programs that were more sensitive to the needs and experiences of disaffected students, and to funnel more curriculum resources and equipment into inner-city schools. As it turned out, the board felt pressured enough to transfer a few hundred thousand dollars into the schools in my area, thanks in part to the efforts of the Canadian media, who reported the contents of my book on a national scale, and to the growing advocacy of grass roots groups and popular constituencies who took full advantage of the publicity brought on by the efforts of investigative journalists and by the publication of my journal. But the real roots of the problems remained inexorably entangled in the everyday lives of the students and their families. Once the publicity ceased, the Board of Education reneged on its plan for school reform.

Since the journal's publication, I have grown increasingly dissatisfied with my attempt to understand and communicate my classroom experiences. My journal was primarily description, without a theoretical framework that could help the reader better understand the conditions I was attempting to portray. On the advice of a prominent journalist, I had reluctantly removed the few theoretical insights that I had initially included in the early drafts of the manuscript. My theoretical formulations—which admittedly were, at the time, crude stabs in the dark—"slowed down" what was otherwise a good "crisp" read; forget theories, I was advised, and let the vignettes "speak for themselves." In those days, that advice sounded almost profound. After all, who was I to impose an analysis or set of recommendations on the lived culture of the disadvantaged?

I realize now that observations of events—whether in the classroom or the laboratory—*never* speak for themselves. Every description is ideologically loaded, codified, and intertextually related to larger interpretive contexts. Nothing that can be observed or named is ideologically neutral or innocent. No thoughts, ideas, or theories are transparent, autonomous, or free floating; to say that they are is a middle-class mystification that seeks to disguise the social interests being served. Ideas are always and necessarily tied to particular interests and enciphered in particular relations of power, and tied to particular power/knowledge configurations. Absolutely nothing is of unmediated availability to human consciousness. To "know" anything is always an effect of power/knowledge relationships. The crucial question is: Who has the power to make some forms of knowledge more legitimate than others? By failing to set my classroom journal within a critical theoretical context, I could not adequately reveal how power and knowledge work in the interests of certain groups over others. Consequently, I ran the risk of allowing readers to reinforce their stereotypes of what schooling was like in the "blackboard jungle" and what constituted the behavior of economically disadvantaged students. I also was in danger of portraying impoverished communities as crucibles of violence and hatred, devoid of humanity and dignity. This book is an attempt to provide the reader with the necessary theoretical framework for initiating a critical interpretation of the classroom episodes included in the journal.

I tried to convey in the journal both my concern for my students and their strength and perseverance in the face of their oppression. Looking back from my present vantage point, however, I see the author of that journal as a young, liberal teacher both fascinated by and fearful of the marginalized, the disaffected, the disenfranchised, and the indigent—fascinated because their poverty and behavior seemed to be born of defiance rather than despair; and fearful because their anger, pain, and hate had clearly been constructed out of the neglect and greed of a democratic society. The full horror of the situation struck me only when I realized that my students were essentially spitting in the eye of a ruling ideology, and in many ways I represented that eye.

The perspective of that young journal writer represents one moment in my understanding of inner-city teaching. That moment has now been put in context by an excursion into the theory of schooling's "deep structure," from which I have drawn a new theoretical figuration. The project that began as *Cries from the Corridor* has now become part of a larger work which provides a critical analysis of schooling and classroom culture.

Shortly after the publication of the journal I left teaching to enroll in graduate studies. In my attempt to understand how schooling "really" works, I was soon struck by the range of sociological theories that explained how schools can and do disempower, delegitimate, and disconfirm the lives of disadvantaged students.

I discovered as well that schools operate through a "hidden curriculum" which incarcerates students in the "semiotics of power" and works against the success of racial minorities, women, and the poor. Yet I was also made aware of how schools could work in emancipatory ways to empower students to accomplish, in the words of Paulo Freire, "reading the word and reading the world." This book does not attempt to answer fully the question of *how* to construct a critical pedagogy within the constraints of an educational system whose character and structure are firmly established by the state. Rather, this book asks: *Why* is a critical pedagogy so necessary? Part of the answer is that mainstream pedagogies generally avoid or attempt to obscure the question that should be central to education: What is the relationship between what we do in the classroom and our effort to build a better society?

Apart from the obvious need for a theoretical introduction to critical pedagogy, it has occurred to me that educators are rarely encouraged to seek connections that would link their personal brand of pedagogy to wider social processes, structures, and issues. One of the purposes for writing this book has been to respond to the failure of North American education to provide prospective teachers with the critical skills, conceptual means, and moral imperatives to analyze critically the goals of schooling. This book attempts to present ways of understanding schooling in terms generally unfamiliar to teachers and prospective teachers. The terminology and frames of reference that I shall be using are drawn from an educational tradition known as critical pedagogy. The book is organized with the intention of introducing readers to some general perspectives that make up this tradition while at the same time providing them with an opportunity to make informed decisions regarding the overall purposes and day-to-day realities of schooling in the United States. More specifically, the problem this book attempts to address is how critical educators can create a language that enables teachers to examine the role that schooling plays in joining knowledge and power. Critical pedagogy is designed to serve the purpose of both empowering teachers and teaching for empowerment. Within this perspective, pedagogy and culture are seen as intersecting fields of struggle, and the contradictory character of teaching as it currently defines the nature of teacher work, everyday classroom life, and the purpose of schooling is subjected to more critical forms of analysis.

Part One documents the nature of the present crisis in schooling and society in this country. Part Two attempts to present the day-to-day struggles of teachers and students in an inner-city school through the inclusion of sections of my elementary school journal. In Part Three I offer a broad overview of the tradition of critical pedagogy and introduce you to an array of general terms associated with the critical educational tradition. Since many of the terms and theoretical formulations within this tradition are presently being debated, refined, and extended, I discuss only the more fundamental categories, and only in the briefest possible fashion. This fits well with the purpose of this book, which is to provide those of you who are virtually unacquainted with critical pedagogy or the critical social sciences with an overview of some of the more basic socio-pedagogical formulations. After reading this part, you are encouraged to return to the journal in Part Two in order to reevaluate my experiences as a beginning teacher. I also encourage you to consider the classroom journal and new theoretical categories in terms of your own experiences as teachers and as students. Some questions have been provided at the end of Part Three to help you get started. Part Four presents additional categories and theoretical perspectives from the critical tradition and concludes with a short essay on the role of the teacher as social agent. Part Five is comprised of two essay reviews of the first edition of *Life in Schools* and my response to these reviews. Part Five provides me with the opportunity both to respond to the strengths and weaknesses of the original volume and to address questions that are often raised with respect to my own history and intellectual and political development. It also provides a unique context for furthering the analysis of critical pedagogy with respect to my more recent analyses of schooling and social and political struggles. The two reviews, by Ursula Kelly and John Portelli, have been previously published in the *Journal of Education* and my response was published in the same issue. I have modified and extended my response for this edition of *Life in Schools*.

The purpose of the book is to provide a theoretical framework that will enable readers to interrogate critically my own ideological formation as a white Anglo male and a middle-class teacher. Reading my journal after so many years is always a painful experience, especially when I see my early development as a teacher as complicitous in the reproduction of dominant systems of intelligibility that position minorities and working-class students and parents in relations of subordination.

This book is an invitation to interrogate the liberal humanist discourse of progressive and well-intentioned teachers—including my own early teaching practices—and uncover its complicity in dominant myths about people of color and working-class people from a new, critical perspective. This perspective is the result of my work in critical pedagogy over the last ten years. This new perspective appears in Parts Three and Four of the book, and it is greatly extended in the new Part Five.

I hope that this book might prove to be not just a book *about* education, but an *educational book* that will promote an understanding of teaching in cultural, political, and ethical terms. This book will have failed if it merely presents an alternative or opposing view and does not provoke you to begin to examine seriously the assumptions that underlie your own teaching. I do not pretend that this book represents a scholarly advancement of the fundamental issues in critical pedagogy. If my book serves its purpose as an introductory text, then it should leave you with a desire to move beyond the theoretical parameters that I have constructed within these pages.

ACKNOWLEDGMENTS

I am grateful to Henry Giroux for graciously permitting me to include throughout this book ideas from his research as well as sections from our co-authored works. I want to make clear at the outset that many of the perspectives presented in the first edition were inspired by his writings, especially *Theory and Resistance in Education, Education Under Siege* (with Stanley Aronowitz), *Teachers as Intellectuals: A Critical Pedagogy for Practical Learning,* and *Schooling and the Struggle for Public Life: Critical Pedagogy in the Modern Age.* I would be remiss if I failed to credit him for developing many of the categories and concepts used in this work. I would also like to thank him for his spirited encouragement and critical support, and for providing me with perceptive lines of inquiry which I might otherwise have overlooked. I especially want to thank him for providing me with comradeship and shelter during a time of exile and for being such a good friend and colleague. I an grateful, too, for the friendship and support of Jeanne Brady, whose work as a mother and educator offers concrete evidence that critical pedagogy can empower the lives of young people. I am deeply grateful to Jenny McLaren, whose unyielding support for this project was truly a labor of love. Her intelligence and strength are a continual source of inspiration. I wish to thank Methuen Publications (Canada) and PaperJacks (Canada) for their assistance in reprinting Part Two of this book, which appeared in Canada under the title *Cries from the Corridor: The New Suburban Ghettos.* I should mention that I have edited sections of *Cries from the Corridor* for reasons of length and style and in so doing I trust that I have not shifted the original context of the book nor altered the meaning of the diary entries.

I owe a debt of thanks to the editors of the following journals who have agreed to let me print material from previous publications: *The Harvard Educational Review, Metropolitan Education, Philosophy and Social Criticism, Boston University Journal of Education, Educational Policy, Insights, Canadian Woman Studies, Educational Studies, The Canadian Journal of Sociology, The Ontario Public School Teachers' Federation News, Social Education, Review of Education, The University of Toronto Review,* and *Educational Theory.*

David Llewellyn and Nikki Raeburn deserve acknowledgment for their editorial suggestions and advice. David Llewellyn provided me with excellent editorial assistance from the very outset of this project and deserves a heartfelt thanks, especially with respect to the revised format of *Cries from the Corridor.* A thanks also to Richard Smith and Anna Zantiotis, my good friends from Australia, and to Stanley Aronowitz. I want to express my gratitude to Lourdes Lugo Lopez, whose work with the Puerto Rican community, and whose courage and intelligence, inspire hope and faith in the struggle for liberation. Richard Quantz and the late Laurie McDade, friends and colleagues at the Center for Education and Cultural Studies, and Donaldo Macedo of the Department of English, University of Massachusetts, were sources of wisdom throughout the project. Khaula Murtadha and Marcia Moraes gave me critical advice. Rhonda Hammer's intelligent suggestions were welcome, as were those of Gary McCarron. I greatly appreciate the efforts of Beth Eldridge and Tammy Huntsman, who corrected proofs of the original version. I want to add a special note of gratitude to Joel Spring and Naomi Silverman for encouraging me to undertake this project and for seeing it through to its completion. Their critical comments greatly helped improve the volume. Thanks to Naomi Silverman too for encouraging me to undertake a second edition of *Life in Schools* and for offering some initial suggestions. I want also to thank Ginny Blanford of Longman for her excellent editing of the first edition, which helped make some very complex ideas clearer and more accessible. The second edition required the coordinated efforts of a number of people. I am especially grateful for the assistance of Linda Sinsheimer Moser, Ginny Blanford, Mary Bucher Fisher, and Jude Patterson. I would like to thank Jan Kettlewell and Nelda Cambron-McCabe for creating a welcome atmosphere at the School of Education and Allied Professions at Miami University of Ohio for those who wish to undertake critical work in education. I would like to thank my undergraduate and graduate students for their reactions to drafts of this book, and for making the initial suggestion that an introductory text on critical pedagogy be made available for classroom study. I should mention too, that Barry Kanpol's sage suggestions have been invaluable. I want to thank Stuart Miller of Longman for his guidance and support in getting the second edition of *Life in Schools* into production. I also want to thank Sonia Nieto for providing me with some criticisms of my work. I hope I have been able to respond to those in this second edition. A new colleague of mine, Dennis Carlson, deserves thanks for his many insights into the politics of urban schooling.

There are many other individuals whose work has provided me with ideas and insights. I want to thank Siebren Miedema, Alice de Alba, Christie Sleeter, Gert Biesta, Adriana Puiggrós, Edgar Gonzalez, Ira Shor, Bertha Orozco Fuentes, Nize Maria Campos Pellanda, Tom Popkewitz, Mike Peters, Nick Burbules, Jim Giarelli, John Novak, Bill Pinar, Tom Oldenski, Mike Apple, Michelle Fine, Stanley Aronowitz, Joe Kincheloe, Shirley Steinberg, Valerie Scatamburlo, Antonia Darder, Barbara Flores, Phil Carspecken, Bill Tierney, Carlos Alberto Torres, Doug Kellner, Cathy Walsh, Kris Guttierez, Concepcion Valadez, Colin Lankshear, Don Dippo, Richard Smith, and Paulo Freire. Of course, I take full responsibility for what appears within these pages.

I should note I have tried to use the term ''Latinos'' rather than Hispanics'' wherever possible (the reason will be made clear in Part Five). However, when reporting on other researchers' work, this was not always possible. I have also used the term ''minority'' while recognizing people of color are in the minority only in North America. I have talked about ''Anglo Americans'' as a counterpart to ''Latin Americans'' while recognizing ''Americans'' as a term meaning people from the Western hemisphere rather than solely from the United States. I use the term ''Third World'' while recognizing it cannot be used monolithically since characteristics associated with Third World countries are proliferating in many so-called ''First World'' contexts.

PART I

Broken Dreams, False Promises, and the Decline of Public Schooling

INTRODUCTION

Schooling in general, and teacher education in particular, have rarely occupied a critical space in contemporary culture. Such endeavors as presently exist are damagingly bereft of both social conscience and social consciousness. The political space that education occupies today continues to de-emphasize the struggle for teacher and student empowerment; furthermore, it generally serves to reproduce the technocratic and corporate ideologies that characterize dominant societies. It is, in fact, reasonable to argue that education programs are designed to create individuals who operate in the interests of the state, whose social function is primarily to sustain and legitimate the status quo. This is not to suggest that critics have not put forth proposals for reforming education programs. The problem has been that when such proposals appear, teaching is often viewed as nearly synonymous with "executing" prefashioned methodologies and "delivering" prepackaged curricula. The absurdity of this position is most evident in the development of programs that some school boards glowingly describe as "teacher-proofed." Teaching thus becomes stripped of its decision-making potential, including its ethical imperative to analyze and remediate existing societal and institutional practices. Teachers are reduced to what Henry Giroux calls "clerks of the empire," whose dreams, desires, and voices are often silenced in order to remove any distractions to industry's call for more entrepreneurial savvy among its future workers, and its desire for a more compliant, devoted, and efficient work force. This image of the teacher is frighteningly similar to the one promulgated in our colleges of education. There, an undue emphasis is placed on training teachers to be managers and implementers of preordained content,

---

Moments in America

Every 35 seconds an infant is born into poverty.

Every 2 minutes an infant is born to a mother who received late or no prenatal care.

Every 2 minutes an infant is born at low birthweight (less than 5 pounds, 8 ounces).

Every 11 minutes an infant is born at very low birthweight (less than 3 pounds, 8 ounces).

Every 14 minutes an infant dies in the first year of life.

Every 31 seconds an infant is born to an unmarried mother.

Every 55 seconds an infant is born to a mother who is not a high school graduate.

Every 21 seconds a 15- to 19-year-old woman becomes sexually active for the first time.

Every 32 seconds a 15- to 19-year-old woman becomes pregnant.

Every 64 seconds an infant is born to a teenage mother.

Every 5 minutes an infant is born to a teenage mother who already had a child.

Every 74 seconds a 15- to 19-year-old woman has an abortion.

Every 14 hours a child younger than 5 is murdered.

Every 5 hours a 15- to 19-year-old is murdered.

Every 2 hours a 20- to 24-year-old is murdered.

Every 2 seconds of the school day a public school student is suspended.

Every 4 seconds of the school day a public school student is corporally punished.

Every 10 seconds of the school day a student drops out of school.

SOURCE: Children's Defense Fund, *The State of America's Children 1991*, Washington, D.C., p. 5.

---

and on methods courses that rarely provide students with an opportunity to analyze the ideological assumptions and underlying interests that structure the way teaching is taught.

When teachers, in their acceptance of the role of technicians, fail to challenge the ways in which educational curricula correspond to the demands of industry or the means by which schooling reproduces existing class, race, and gender relations in our society, they run the risk of transmitting to disadvantaged students the message that their subordinate roles in the social order are justified and inviolable. We are unable, then, to assist students in determining how certain individuals, because of their race, class, gender, or social status, come to be positioned favorably or unfavorably within larger sociopolitical relations. For teachers of students who inhabit subordinate positions within society, and for teachers of economically disadvantaged students especially, this apolitical approach to teaching reflects an inability to take a stand on matters of equality and social justice. Such a pedagogical absence turns many inner-city schools into prisons for those students whose parents can't buy them into learning institutions for the more socially privileged. And it turns more affluent schools into educational enclaves for the few, guardians of the status quo (Carlson, 1992).

THE ILLUSION OF EDUCATION
IN AN AGE OF DECLINE

As I write on the anniversary of the birth of Martin Luther King, Jr., a state holiday rescinded by the governor of Arizona,[1] reports of growing racial unrest rattle the airwaves. Images of violence in Howard Beach, New York, and the shrouded spectres of Ku Klux Klansmen leading demonstrations in Forsyth County, Georgia, appear ominously across the television screens of America. For me, these scenes have a sense of déjà vu. I am startled by a news clip showing six camouflaged Tennessee Army National Guardsmen breaking from the bowels of a U.S. Army chopper and charging, rebel-style, into a local high school auditorium during a student assembly, mounting a platform near the stage, wild tongues of fire flicking from their M–16s. Surprised by the mock raid and the near deafening gunfire (which turned out to be blank rounds), the students nevertheless respond with unflinching enthusiasm to the Sergeant Major's crisp address:

> This morning, shortly after dawn, as we lifted off from Eagle Support Base deep in our territory, we received orders directing us to this location. It seems that an airborne aggressor force had plans to attack this auditorium at 10:00 this morning. And I guess you heard what happened outside just a moment ago. Guys and girls, this is just a scenario; its not for real. The weapons are real, the uniforms are real, the helicopter is real, the soldiers are real, but the bullets are not real. . . . Almost every continent has war. Almost every continent has people destroying governments. . . . Today the ball is in your court. If you are not willing to . . . pick up the weapons of war and defend . . . this American way of life . . . then the future America may be like other nations in Central America, South America, the Orient, the Middle East, the Far East. We cannot let that happen in America![2]

The speech was followed by a terse, "Bravo Company" style command to all those who love America to raise their fists and shout "Hurrah!" Perhaps this event seems too isolated—if not too ludicrous—to be viewed with the same concern as racism and violence in the streets; the Guardsmen had staged their mock raid "lesson" on patriotism, with its portentous millenarian pitch, in only eighteen schools. Yet I cannot divorce such cold-war ideology from other forms of "entertainment" so prevalent here in the theaters of this Midwestern town where I now live and teach. Here, as in so many other university towns, sizable numbers of students swaddled in Greek insignia flock to see the likes of *Rambo, Iron Eagle, White Nights, Top Gun, Born American,* or a karate-chopping Chuck Norris rescuing America from hirsute mobsters or Viet Cong infidels. The confluence of patriotism and market strategy occurs in such an orgy of self-assertion that students are unable to evaluate the implications of their ideological allegiance. Here, students inhabit a world of designer identities and regimented desire that transforms forms of difference and improvised community into indicators of deviance.

My conscience obliges me to contrast this situation and the peremptory, authoritarian, and cultural despotism it reflects, with a recent report by the Children's Defense Fund that claims that the United States is one of the worst places to be born in the industrialized world, with 10.8 infant deaths for every 1,000 live births in 1984.[3] One cannot help but morally recoil upon reading that "A black infant born within five miles of the White House . . . is more likely to die in the first year of life than an infant born in Third World countries like Trinidad."[4] Could it be that the most dangerous enemies of America are the gods of expansion, progress, and accumulation, and not some dark and scheming superpowers surreptitiously poised to strike from a distant hemisphere?

We inhabit a perilous course in history in which democracy is in retreat. Many of the gains made during previous decades in social and educational reform have been abandoned or at the very least have demonstrably waned. Not only have we sadly witnessed the delegitimization of the egalitarian impulses of the last two decades, but we have seen an inordinate stress placed on career motivation and school/business partnerships in efforts to link youth to the corporate imperatives of the international marketplace.

In this age of historical amnesia, endlessly deferred hope, and a retreat from civil rights, the concepts of social struggle and civic courage have congealed around politically accommodating forms of liberal humanism and an ideological shift towards the conservative New Right. As the pillars of our democratic temple wobble in current reactionary winds, we can only glimpse through the cracks of history an uncertain future.

The civil rights marches in Selma, Alabama, and other parts of the South, and the fight for day-care programs and community schools, now seem consigned to a museum of memories, historical artifacts of a strange and uncomfortable past. Little has been accomplished beyond the palliative to build upon the democratization of our schools and to ensure the welfare of our nation's youth. Freedom and equality have become dust-covered relics in history's warehouse. Since the aborted cultural revolution of the 1960s, we seem more like curators of old dreams, archivists of history who arrange the past in glass-enclosed dioramas. We have turned into disembodied repositories of reformist visions, shelved in moments of cynical despair, rather than active agents of new communities of risk and resistance.

It is symptomatic of the present crisis that a new public philosophy has emerged along with the rise of the new Christian Right, a philosophy whose moral charter celebrates the virtues of the nuclear family, defends at all costs America's God-fearing cultural tradition, and interprets world events according to a literal reading of the Bible; this burgeoning revival of "born again" Christianity—especially the televangelistic variety—represents a jingoism of the spirit whose lay equivalents include the hyper-patriotism of "resurgent America," the importance of the patriarchal family as the Promethean embodiment of a righteous life-style, the prevailing rhetoric about consensus enemies such as Iraq and Nicaragua, and the moral terrorism of shuttle diplomacy. The ideological conservatism of the New Christian Right enshrines a masqueraded version of the Christian faith, a parody of its originating source, a form of tyrannical surrogacy whose dogmatic intolerance of feminists, gays, radicals, and non-Christians has militantly invaded what could ideally be a considerate, compassionate, and loving community of faith.

The ideological shift that characterizes schooling in the last fifteen years has hardly been subtle. We need only witness attempts in the mid-1980s by New Right reformists to construct an unproblematic view of history in which schools are called upon to assume their roles as the gatekeepers of society by passing on the great tradition of old-fashioned "republican virtues" embodied, for example, in books such as the McGuffey readers and in the old Latin classics curriculum. In fact, the image of the public school put forward by exponents of the New Right approximates a mixture of the fundamentalist Sunday school, company store, and "old West" museum.[5] The dominating logic of this agenda is bolstered by arguments put forward by individuals such as Gary L. Bauer, former Under-secretary of Education, who blames America's "youthful fling with self-indulgence" during the 1960s and 1970s for the current malaise in American Society.[6] This view was less than convincing when promulgated by representatives of a government that was performing terrorist acts against governments in Central America, trading in arms with Iran, and eroding the call for civic courage and critical citizenship in our public schools.[7]

Today's students have inherited an age in which liberty and democracy are in retreat. Ironically, existing criticisms of schooling and the agenda for educational reform themselves constitute part of this retreat. On the one hand, neoconservatives have defined the school as an adjunct of the labor market, couching their analysis in the technocratic language of human capital theory. On the other hand, liberals have provided a more comprehensive critique of schooling, but so far have been incapable of addressing the major problems that schools face within a race-, class-, and gender-divided society. The resulting prescriptions for school reform are severely restricted.

In the present rush towards accountability schemes, corporate management pedagogies, and state-mandated curricula, an ominous silence exists regarding the ways in which new attempts to streamline teaching represent an attack on both the democratic possibilities of schooling and the very conditions that make critical teaching possible.

Framed in the language of hypernationalism and supply-side economics, the current conservative attack on schools represents, in large part, a truncation of the democratic vision. Underlying the new reform proposals set forth by the recent coalition of conservatives and liberals is an attack on schools for producing a wide-ranging series of national crises, ranging in scope from the growing trade deficit to the breakdown of family morality. Not only does such an attack misconstrue the responsibility schools have for wider economic and social problems, but it is characteristic of a dangerous ideological shift that has been taking place regarding the role that schools should play in relation to the wider society.

At the heart of the ideological shift is an attempt to define academic success almost exclusively in terms of capital accumulation and the logic of the marketplace. The authors of the "blue ribbon" committee reports have cast their recommendations in a language that reflects the resurgence of chauvinistic patriotism and have reformulated their goals along elitist lines.[8] In doing so, they have attempted to eliminate a social concern for nurturing a critical and committed citizenry. They have passively surrendered educational reform to a fetishism of procedure rather than demonstrating a concern with social goals. Furthermore, the increasing adoption of management-type pedagogies has resulted in policy proposals that promote the deskilling of teachers and the creation of a technocratic rationality in which planning and conception are removed from implementation, and the dominant model of the teacher becomes that of the technician or white-collar clerk. At the same time, the model of the school has been transformed, in Giroux's terms, into that of the "company store." In general, the new efficiency-smart and conservative-minded discourse encourages schools to define themselves essentially as service institutions charged with the task of providing students with the requisite technical expertise to enable them to find a place within the corporate hierarchy.

This New Right ideology of school reform provides only a sterile and truncated range of discourses and conceptions which undermines what it means to be a critical citizen. Under the logic of the reforms, students are taught to link citizenship to the profit imperative and to the norms of market relations and brokerage politics wherein the vested interests of the individual, the corporation, or one's country are always valued over the collective interests of humanity. Rarely is the concept of profit maximization considered immoral, even when it is discovered to be at the expense of the poor or minority groups, or, further afield, at the expense of the social and educational development of Central American and Third World populations. Absent from this discourse is any recognition of the importance of viewing schools as sites for social transformation and emancipation, as places where students are educated not only to be critical thinkers, but also to view the world as a place where their actions might make a difference.

Some statistics may help guide the reader's attention to the full seriousness of the decline of this particular epoch. In their book, *On Democracy,* Joshua Cohen and Joel Rogers provide some startling statistics which at the very least call into question—if not effectively shatter—the larger-than-life braggadocio of pro-American apologists and the quiescence surrounding some long-standing myths of American life. For instance, the common assumption that the American standard of living is the highest in the world has been repeatedly challenged by The Organization for Economic Cooperation and Development who claim that in 1980 the United States ranked eleventh, behind Switzerland, Denmark, Sweden, Germany, Iceland, Norway, Belgium, Luxembourg, the Netherlands, and France. Diminished expectations exist where once there were endless possibilities. In 1950 nearly 70 percent of all American families could afford to buy a house. By 1980, first time purchase of a home was impossible for 80 percent of those who did not already own a home. This means that, unless the situation reverses itself, only about two out of every ten students in our classrooms can look forward to eventually owning their own homes, let alone realizing the dream of the paneled recreation room and the two-car garage. Worker benefits lag far behind those in the rest of the industrialized West. And social planning? As a percentage of the GNP, social spending in America constitutes less than half what it is in Germany and Sweden. Virtually all advanced nations, including the Netherlands, the United Kingdom, Japan, and France, spend more on social services than does the United States.[9]

In addition to the crisis of social planning and services, there are serious concerns today regarding issues such as the safety of our citizens. Urban dwellers now live in the frightening hypertrophy of an urban frontier populated by gunslingers (usually the exploited poor and ethnic minorities). In fact, in some of our major cities we are in peril of being murdered at a rate eight or nine times greater than in other advanced industrial nations. In fact, if one was born and remains a resident of a major city in the United States, one's chances of being murdered are greater than the threat of death in combat experienced by American soldiers in World War II, and it may come as little surprise to minority groups that the probability of being murdered for nonwhite men in the United States is six times as great as the probability for white men.[10] For those of us who have actually grown up believing in a free and equal America, the grim news is staggering: with the exception of the former Soviet Union and South Africa, the United States has a larger percentage of its citizens behind bars than any other country. In fact, a new handgun is sold every thirteen seconds in this country. Homicide, coupled with suicide, constitutes the sixth leading cause of death.[11] Teenage homicide is up more than 200 percent since 1960; arrests of eighteen to twenty-four-year-olds are up from 18 percent in 1960 to 34 percent in 1980, and young people under twenty-one account for more than half of all arrests for serious crimes. School vandalism has been estimated by a Senate subcommittee to cost $500 million a year.[12] In 1983, approximately 46 percent of all persons sent to prison were black, even though blacks make up only 12 percent of the population.[13] Most of the victims of their crimes were black.

There is little question that American life continues to produce an underclass among many black, Puerto Rican, Chicano, West Indian, and Central American communities concentrated in urban ghettos (the South Bronx, Spanish Harlem, Roxbury, Watts, and West Town, Chicago, for example) where the violent impact of ghetto conditions is suffered most cruelly. It is here where gang life proliferates. For instance, Los Angeles is home to over 200 gangs, with 187 gang-related homicides in 1986.[14] We also know that there has been an explosion of white suburban gangs in places like California, whose middle-class members engage in fights, robberies, and killings. The Los Angeles County Sheriff's Department estimates that there are 1,200 members of white street gangs in Los Angeles County alone.[15]

We are all familiar with the ecological crisis, having witnessed smog levels in our cities growing by 1000 percent between World War II and the early 1970s. Environmental hazards are, we grudgingly admit, getting worse, as safe drinking water standards are constantly violated and toxic waste dumps continue to leak poisonous chemicals. But we are equally inattentive and inactive when it comes to the estimated 2 to 6 million students and 100,000 to 300,000 teachers who still attend and work in schools with asbestos surfaces.[16]

Increasingly we face reports about widespread drug and alcohol abuse, with the number of alcoholics and problem drinkers in the United States numbering approximately 13 million, and one in every forty residents of New York City addicted to heroin.[17] The media has good copy here. Journalists wearing pastel colors and accompanied by television crews join secret vice squad raids on cocaine pushers in a Hollywood-style attempt to add excitement and glamour to the epidemic. Total arrests for drug abuse violations among those under eighteen years of age increased sixty-fold between 1960 and 1980.[18]

As poverty, inequality, and drug addiction blight the nation, we direct our anger not at government policies or the social conditions that manufacture human suffering, but at the arch villains of communism and socialism. We forget that the lowest fifth of our own population receives a smaller percentage of total after tax income than is true in Japan, Sweden, Australia, the Netherlands, Germany, the United Kingdom, Norway, Canada, and France. In fact, the gap in real-income level between the bottom quintile of American families and the top 5 percent has nearly doubled over the past forty years. On the one hand, the percentage of wealth held by the top 1 to 2 percent of the population is greater in the United States than in most industrial nations; on the other hand, it remains the case that one in every seven Americans and more than one in every five children under the age of six lives in poverty.[19]

Appearing in tandem with the decimation of low-income housing, growing unemployment, the deinstitutionalization of mental patients, and the rise of alcohol and drug-related abuse is the new class of urban homeless. The housing shortage across the United States, coupled with the substantial increase in the poverty population of the cities, has created a new and growing group of vaga-bond city dwellers who report a wide range of social and personal pathologies.[20] Many homeless are teenagers coming directly out of foster care and precipitously dumped into the streets without follow-up community support.[21]

There is an epidemic of teenage pregnancies (500,000 births to girls under twenty in 1983).[22] In 1982, nine out of ten babies born to black women under the age of twenty were outside of marriage. Teenage pregnancy is up 109 percent for whites and 10 percent for nonwhites since 1960.[23]

These are only a few of the available statistics and reports on the crisis in American society, but they should be sobering enough to most Americans to make us aware that we live in a time of drastic social upheaval. Regardless of how we wish to characterize the crisis, the familiar adage seems to hold true: the rich get richer while the poor get poorer.

Other statistics related to youth and schooling have been made available by the authors of the highly acclaimed book, *Choosing Equality.* Unfortunately, these statistics do not give us cause to rest any easier. Our school system is revealed as inexorably multitiered, with the children of the working poor held to the lower rung and suffering the most. For example, the authors of *Choosing Equality* report that 50 to 80 percent of all inner-city students drop out of high school (Chicanos and Puerto Ricans use the more appropriate term ''pushed out''); 1 million teenagers cannot read above the third-grade level; 13 percent of all seventeen-year-olds are functionally illiterate; 28 percent of all students fail to achieve high school diplomas; 50 percent of all college entrants drop out in their freshman year; and 33 percent of all adults are described as functionally or marginally illiterate.[24]

It is becoming clear that the consequences of schooling are increasingly dependent on the social class of the child. Radical educators argue that the structural constraints that characterize schooling and the wider society reinforce inegalitarian stratification—that schools are reduced to credentializing mechanisms, protected enclaves that favor the more affluent. The ''best'' schools nurture cocoons of yuppie larvae, facilitating entry of certain students into more privileged locations in the labor market; the worst simply lock the doors to those privileged locations for students already disproportionately disadvantaged. In all, the schools constitute a loaded social lottery in which the dice fall in favor of those who already have money and power.

One index of the persistent refusal of schools to develop a means to empower minority and disadvantaged groups is the widespread practice of tracking students into ability groups. Tracking assumes that schools play a part in meritocratic selection and allocation based on ability. In fact, however, tracking fosters the *illusion* of meritocratic competition while in reality functioning as a ''ranking'' system that legitimates differences based on race, gender, and social power and locks students into positions of limited opportunity. Tracking thus perpetuates social class inequalities through selection and allocation procedures.[25]

Tracking in the United States can be traced to the birth of the comprehensive high school in the early 1900s.[26] This new type of schooling, made necessary by the influx of unskilled immigrants from southern and eastern Europe and the enforcement of child labor and compulsory education laws, abandoned the principle of presenting a common core of learning to build a cohesive nation. Instead, it emphasized curriculum differentiation in the form of tracking and homogeneous grouping. Social Darwinism provided legitimacy to the notion that ethnic minorities and the poor were lower on the evolutionary ladder and less fit in moral development than the dominant Anglo-Protestant majority. Coupled with a growing concern for preserving the Anglo-Saxon culture against the ''depravity'' of the expanding immigrant population, Social Darwinism thus provided a foundation for the trend toward ''Americanization,'' which eventually came to dominate the school curriculum.

American industry provided the logic for this new kind of education by presenting schools with the factory model of learning. Production and efficiency became the guiding ideological principles in establishing vocational education as an appropriate alternative for students not bound for college. The development of IQ tests provided a statistical base with which to classify students, although these tests simply reinforced the original classification by racial, ethnic, and economic background. Educational testing, undertaken in the spirit of scientific efficiency, was viewed as meritocratic, since it helped sort students into specialized programs where they would receive what was thought to be the best possible education, given their abilities and the opportunities available to immigrants in the industrial workplace.

Jeannie Oakes's study *Keeping Track* illustrates how tracking in American schools alienates students and undermines their social aspirations and feelings of self-worth. Oakes argues that students at the bottom of the social hierarchy adjust their aspirations downward as a result of tracking without being aware that schools are treating them unjustly. In essence, schools play a major role in the legitimization of inequality; that is, in socializing students to accept the unequal features of the larger society. Oakes argues that students who are poor and from a minority background are the most disempowered and disenfranchised by school tracking procedures. This effect derives in part from the way in which school knowledge is distributed within high-track and low-track groups. Students in low-track groups are more likely than others to be from poor and minority backgrounds and to be taught behaviors that will make them suitable for low status jobs. In other words, low-track students are taught low status knowledge, which has little exchange value in a social or economic sense.

Oakes's data on tracking reveal that students in high-track groups enjoy distinct educational advantages over those in low- and middle-track groups: for the high-track groups, more time is set aside by teachers for learning; more actual class time is spent on learning activities; more attention to homework is expected; fewer students are permitted to be off-task; and more instructional practice is given. In short, for high-track students, learning takes place in an environment that confirms the students' high-track identity, where time, activity, and place are structured so as to encourage their sense of self-esteem and achievement.

For low-track students, time in school may be more a burden than an asset. Such students often view knowledge as unrelated to their lives and instruction as an assault on their time. School becomes a place for enduring "dead time" rather than using it in the interests of self and social empowerment. If such students learn anything, it is *in spite of* the degradation they endure.

It is safe to assume that the degradation students experience in the lower tracks significantly contributes to the growing instances of dropping out of school. In the United States there are presently 1.1 million sixteen- to nineteen-year-olds and 3.3 million twenty- to twenty-four-year-olds with less than a high school diploma who are not currently enrolled in school. The proportion of seventeen- to eighteen-year olds who were not high school graduates increased from about 24 percent in 1972 to about 28 percent in 1982. Dropping out is not evenly distributed racially, economically, or geographically. Among twenty- to twenty-four-year-olds, the dropout rate proportion for Latinos is 40.8 percent;

for blacks, 23.2 percent; for whites, 14.6 percent. Despite the lower dropout rate for whites, this pattern can be better explained by income than race. For instance, Michael W. Sherridan cites a 1977 study of families with incomes under $10,000 that reveals the proportion of white fourteen- to seventeen-year-olds who were not enrolled in school to be nearly twice as high as for blacks.[27] High school dropouts are more likely to require a wide range of social services, including welfare, medical assistance, and unemployment assistance. They are more likely to engage in crime, have poorer health, have lower rates of intergenerational mobility, and have lower rates of political participation. As early as 1972, estimated costs throughout the country of providing social services and fighting crime associated with dropping out was $6 billion per year.[28]

School systems in the inner city are usually the hardest hit by dropouts for it is here that the last remnants of real education have been driven out of the process of schooling. Consider the case of New York City. An independent study of public high school dropouts claims that 66 percent of all students who attend high school in New York fail to graduate. For Hispanic students, the rate is 80 percent; for blacks, 72 percent; and for whites, 50 percent. Equally alarming is the news that 80 percent of teenage mothers and 90 percent of all special education students fail to achieve their high school diplomas.[29]

The case of Chicago schools is equally as grim. A recent survey of forty-four nonselective, four-year high schools, each with over 50 percent black and Hispanic enrollment, revealed that only 39 percent of entering freshmen were still in school in their senior year. Of that 39 percent, 41 percent were below the ninth grade reading level (the minimum proficiency level), 41 percent were at or above ninth grade proficiency but were below the national median for seniors, and only 18 percent were finishing high school at or above the national median. In urban school systems in general, only 7 percent of those who enter high school graduate with achievement levels equal to 50 percent of their peers nationwide.[30]

The chilling reality is that poor and minority youth who are already receiving substandard schooling are likely to be left entirely outside the job market. The authors of *Choosing Equality* point out that:

> Working-class youth, who have no particular advantage in their schooling, will not have compensating job or income opportunities as adults. And schools will be increasingly hard-pressed to motivate their students through career aspirations or goals.
>
> Given the disjuncture between economic and educational rewards, the effort to link school reform to the market value of education threatens to abandon large segments of American youth. If one argues that schools should reflect the logic of a polarizing labor market, the necessary conclusion is that we must reinforce competitive schooling—raise elitist barriers, add new stratification mechanisms, reward only the most exceptional or advantaged.[31]

The emerging generation with its attendant familial, racial, ethnic, and socioeconomic characteristics does not give teachers much cause for optimism. A demographic portrait made in the mid-1980s suggested that teachers face a prospect of grimly enormous proportions and ever greater social implications. By September of 1987: 25 percent of the childhood population were from families who were living in poverty; 14 percent were children of teenage mothers; 15 percent were physically and/or mentally handicapped; another 15 percent were non-English-speaking immigrants; 14 percent were children of unmarried parents; 40 percent lived in broken homes before they reached 18; and 10 percent had illiterate or nearly illiterate parents. And finally, up to 33 percent were latchkey children who had no one to look after them during lunch and during the late afternoon, and 25 percent of them were not expected to finish high school.[32]

The United States is facing a growing immigrant population with school systems exceedingly hard-pressed to meet their needs. In the 40 years since *Brown* vs. *Board of Education of Topeka* in 1954, schools in the United States have enrolled more linguistic and cultural minorities than ever before. Forty percent of all legal immigrants to the United States are Asian.[33] The steadily expanding population of Asian Americans, now at 5.1 million, represents 2.1 percent of the total population of the United States. Happily, immigrants from Taiwan, the Phillipines, South Korea, Japan, Hong Kong, India, and Vietnam—whose native cultures have been credited with highly valuing education as a means to success—have become the country's most upwardly mobile minorities. Asian students average higher on the Scholastic Aptitude Test math scores than any other ethnic group. Furthermore, they take more math, science, and foreign language courses, and spend more hours on homework assignments.[34]

For some time the dominant culture has portrayed Asian immigrants as the "model minority"—a homogeneous community that is uncomplaining, hard-working, highly educated, family-oriented, and financially successful. Although this depiction has partly been true, it also masks the complexity of the reality many Asians presently face in American society. Undoubtedly the dominant culture would like other oppressed minorities to link success to the virtues of self-sacrifice and competitiveness, rather than to struggle politically for the redress of social injustices and institutionalized racism. But the face of the Asian minority is changing. The majority of current Asian immigrants are impoverished refugees fleeing war and repression. Unlike the ethnic Chinese from Vietnam, China, Hong Kong, and Singapore, many of whom came from privileged backgrounds in their own countries and arrived in the United States before 1976, southeast Asian refugees are not urban people, have little or no formal education or previous contact with western culture, and have no pre-established communities to join.[35] The immigrants enter the United States, as other immigrants have before them, on the lowest rung of the socioeconomic ladder. In California, approximately 50 percent of Indochinese immigrants are on welfare, and a 1980 census revealed more than 35 percent of Vietnamese families in the United States living below the poverty line. The dropout rate for southeast Asian students increased from 14.4 percent in 1982 to 26.5 percent in 1985.[36]

While Asians are the second fastest growing minority population in the country, and while the mean family income for Asian-American families according to the 1980 U.S. census is $26,456 (nearly $3,000 higher than for white families), more recent immigrants such as the Hmong, Laotian, Kampuchean/Cambodian, and Vietnamese arriving after 1976 do not mirror the success stories so widely proclaimed in the nation's press.

The stereotyping of Asian students as successful due to the virtues of passivity, industriousness, and conformity not only exhorts other minorities to adopt these nonresistant values and behaviors, but also has prompted a backlash against Asian-Americans. There has been a dramatic rise in acts of violence against Asian immigrants, and there is increasing evidence that select universities are designing "hidden quotas" to exclude qualified Asian applicants.

For another 40 percent of all legal immigrants—those from Mexico, Central and South America, and the Caribbean—success is less often secured.[37] These are the students most clearly devalued by intelligence tests that continue to be culturally and linguistically biased in favor of middle-class Anglo-Saxon students. Since the tests are usually administered before the student has had a chance to adapt to North American life, many students understandably score poorly. Yet these scores often become the basis for tracking students into basic level courses and for sending them to the school psychologist's office. It is wrong to accept the stereotype that every Asian youth is a predestined Merit Scholar, just as it is wrong to consider all blacks and Latinos irrevocably trapped on the lower rungs of the socioeconomic order. There are Asian youth gangs, and Asian students are by no means immune to illiteracy. There are also high-achieving black, Chicano, and Puerto Rican students. Nevertheless, when considering factors such as intelligence, creativity, motivation, and economic prosperity, it remains the case that socioeconomic status is the greatest predictor of academic success in the United States.[38]

By 1980, 27 percent of all public school students in the United States were nonwhite, and the immigrant population has grown substantially since that time. By 1986, California had a "majority of minorities" in its elementary schools, while Texas had 46 percent black and Latino students.[39] Many of these minority families were supported by a single parent. Nearly every large city school system has predominately minority enrollments and large numbers of students whose first language is not English. One study estimates that by the year 2000, fifty-three major cities will have predominantly immigrant populations.[40] In 1985, however, only 8.5 percent of all teachers were minorities.[41]

It is certainly true that many new immigrants find living conditions in the United States an improvement over those in their native lands. It is also true that in the United States there is still a considerable measure of social freedom. For many past and prospective immigrants, the United States represents an historically powerful metaphor for what it means to be prosperous and free. It is the ideal of democracy, freedom, and social mobility that attracts a large majority of immigrants. The image of the United States has been both a rationally and an emotionally compelling force on the international stage for many decades. The pervasiveness of this image of America suggests the strength of America's international hegemony. It also suggests the power of the global communications network to shape ideology and, in some cases, to support new modes of domination, and also the capacity of American business and advertising to invade world markets and establish ideological frames of reference for measuring personal success.

We must acknowledge, however, that the real conditions of life experienced by many immigrants in the United States fall short of the ideal. In some cases the United States actually supports the regimes that oppress these people; we offer them only the "choice" between places in which to be poor.[42] The point, of course, is not to argue about which country has the worst ghettos, but rather to fight to make the principles of equality and justice a greater reality at home.

The fastest growing population in the nation today is Latino, including Mexican-Americans, Puerto Ricans, Cuban-Americans, and others. The Latino population is by and large young, and it has been hit hard by the erosion of equality in American schooling. Although the majority of Latinos enter high school with educational and career aspirations as high as any other group in our society, 40 percent of all Latino students drop out before the tenth grade. In addition, 25 percent of Latinos who enter high school are overage. Forty-five percent of Mexican-American and Puerto Rican students who enter high school never finish, compared to 17 percent of Anglo students. Latinos experience an exceptionally high rate of poverty—38.2 percent for youth under 18, compared to 17.3 percent for Anglos. The majority of Latinos (85 percent) live in metropolitan areas concentrated in California, Florida, Illinois, New York, and Texas. Thirty-five percent of Latino students are systematically tracked into vocational education programs that do not provide up-to-date training. Forty percent of Latino students are slotted into general educational programs as opposed to academic programs.[43] These are students in drastic need of a critical pedagogy, a new way of viewing schooling, that can enable them to analyze their oppression and to take steps to redress the conditions that perpetuate it.

Of every 100 children born today, 12 are born out of wedlock and 40 are born to parents who will divorce before the child is thirteen.[44] Minority children face a particularly tough road ahead of them. A report published by the Children's Defense Fund reveals that while 8 out of every 10 white children live in two-parent families, this is the case for only 4 out of every 10 black children. Thirty percent of black children under the age of three live in households headed by someone other than their parents. In addition, studies show that in only a few years 1 black child in 4 will live in a female-headed family. In other words, black children are over three and one-half times more likely than white children to live in female-headed households.[45]

Although black children in female-headed families are the poorest in the nation, with a median income of $8,648 in 1984, the problem goes far beyond the poverty problems associated with single parenthood. Black children in two-parent families are twice as likely as white children in two-parent families to live below the poverty line. In fact, almost half of all black children are poor compared to one in six white children. Black men and women at all educational levels are less likely to be employed than white men and women, and those who are employed earn less than their white counterparts. Nearly two out of every five black children are growing up in a family whose head did not complete high school, and this is twice the rate for white children. Black students at all ages are poorer readers than whites, less likely than white students to attend college, and are twice as likely to be suspended from school, to be corporally punished, or to be out of school. Six out of ten special placements of white students are in gifted and talented programs whereas only one in ten black students are in special placements in such programs. Equally alarming is the fact that black children are three times as likely to be placed in classes for the educable mentally retarded, a reality that carries with it the shame of racism.[46] Of course, the legacy of racism and inequality can be traced back to an earlier America, where official historians have often carefully overlooked dimensions of American history, especially those subjugated knowledges of marginalized and disenfranchised peoples. Some contemporary sociologists would like to blame the economic condition of blacks on teenage pregnancy, social isolation, or the impoverished aspirations of ghetto blacks who don't come into enough contact with middle-class achievers. Or else they blame the middle-class blacks who have left the ghetto for not staying there as role models for the poorer blacks. These views simply recycle the "blaming the victim" ideology by shifting the blame onto the blacks themselves and deflecting attention away from the structural causes of poverty and racism and the denial to blacks of full participation in the economic system.

Even the academy—the so-called bastion of truth-seeking, enlightenment, and tolerance—has become a setting for racist incidents that evoke images of Alabama and Arkansas in the 1950s. Incidents in the 1980s at the University of Michigan, Purdue, Northern Illinois, Columbia, and UCLA mark just the surface of a brewing racist cauldron in America. When an unauthorized Northern Illinois University magazine prints sick verse such as "Ok,/look nigger,/we are white/white is supreme/Jesus was white/God is white/All of our presidents have been white/ Thank you God,"[47] we have to wonder what the future of higher education holds. When 1,500 students engage in a black versus white brawl at the University of Massachusetts in Amherst, when fraternities try to bar black students from open parties, and when routine residence passes are checked for blacks but not for whites,[48] we need not deceive ourselves into thinking that racism is a disease that was "cured" during the civil rights movement of the 1960s. Its importunate clamor can be heard today in the ivory tower.

It appears that Jim Crow has been resurrected from the other side of the tracks. Although we are told that blacks are now "making it," it remains the case that discrimination is rampant, and many recent victims are black women. We know, for instance, that more fourteen- and fifteen-year-old black women dropped out of high school in 1981 (3 percent) than ten years earlier (1 percent), and we know also that blacks of either sex and women of any race are less likely to enroll in an academic high school curriculum than white males. Consequently, it comes as little surprise that black women are disproportionally placed in vocational programs. The percentage of black high school graduates attending college dropped 11 percent between 1975 and 1981. Both blacks and women are likely to receive less financial aid than white men, and low income women received fewer Guaranteed Student Loans than did low income men. Also, child-care expenses cannot be used in computing need, a restriction that dispropor-tionately affects women.[49]

The American commitment to equality of opportunity is violated at its very roots by the fact that local and state governments continue to pay more for one child's education than for another's. The abiding constants of American education—equality of opportunity and meritocracy—favor existing elites and place minority students in the debt column of the ledger of academic achievement. Since we finance our schools primarily through local property taxes and state revenues (with a lesser amount added by the federal government), and since some states and school districts have significantly more taxable wealth than others, the money spent per student varies significantly from district to district. Some states have tried to provide formulas to promote more state funding for poorer districts, but legislators who know they must represent positions congenial to those who vote for them frequently subordinate these efforts to other concerns designed to win support from constituents in the wealthier districts.[50] The disparities among schools *within* a district, strangely, are often just as great as those between low-income urban and rural districts and affluent suburban districts within the same state. Here also the disparity reflects the racial and economic makeup of the school population.[51]

The myth that local school boards "balance" the special interests of bureaucratic and professional influence in state education policy (accrued by political and business leaders, academic experts, and pressure groups) is shattered when we note the kind of oligarchies represented by some local boards, who wield tremendous influence over communities through the allocation of school resources and patronage. The structure and actions of local school boards in the state of Georgia, for example, suggest the barriers that local boards can raise to minority empowerment. Since desegregation was ordered in 1970, the Georgia public schools have been essentially desegregated through the reactionary policies of local school boards. Of twenty-two Georgia districts with at least 63 percent black enrollment, only two had majority black school boards. Georgia grand juries still select forty school boards, and school boards presiding over systems with more than 70 percent black students require 50 percent less in local property taxes than those with more than 70 percent white students.[52]

Lack of funding usually goes hand-in-hand with lack of school resources, competent teachers, and services. Invariably, it is the poor and minority student who is hardest hit by disparities in funding. In a report of the Board of Inquiry commissioned by the National Coalition of Advocates for Students, entitled *Barriers to Excellence: Our Children at Risk,* we discover and lament the following indicators of cultural discrimination: only about 33 percent of the estimated 2.7 million limited English proficient students aged five to fourteen receive any form of special programming responsive to their linguistic needs; in 1980, only 10 percent of Hispanic children with limited English proficiency were in bilingual programs; studies conducted in urban high schools have revealed dropout rates as high as 85 percent for Native American students and between 70 to 80 percent for Puerto Rican students; large number of textbooks used in classrooms remain culturally biased, both in their presentation of material and in their omission of material on the culture, history, or achievement of many of the national and cultural groups represented in American schools. Although nearly 25 percent of all public school teachers in the United States had students with limited English proficiency (LEP) in their classes in 1980 and 1981, only

3.2 percent of those teachers said that they were equipped to deal with these students.[53] With statistics such as these, it is hard to dispute the accusation made in the report that:

> minority children do not matter as much as non-minority children judging by the disproportionate numbers of such children who are excluded and underserved by the schools. We know, for example, that black students are placed in classes for the mildly mentally handicapped at rates more than three times those of white children. Poor children, too, are considered less important than non-poor children, if we contrast the level of financing allocated for their education with that allocated for children in more affluent districts. Non-English speaking children still face language and cultural barriers throughout America, and in many places girls still encounter lower expectations than do boys. Differential treatment of children by race, class, sex, language, and handicap subverts our nation's deepest values of fairness. Such treatment also has enormous practical consequences. In fact, the failure to educate millions of children is turning the potential for social profit into grave deficit, the cost of which American taxpayers will bear both financially and socially, in terms of increased dependency and the loss of a sense of common purpose.[54]

Sexism is ripe and spreading in America. Women, along with particular ethnic groups, continue to be discounted as relevant moral and social agents in a society priding itself on the concepts of equality and justice. Although many Americans applaud the gains made by women in school and employment opportunities over the last quarter century, the situation is not as promising as many would like to believe. Statistics reveal the following somber facts: women are less likely than men to complete four years of college; they are much less likely to continue through higher levels of education and obtain doctorates or professional degrees; at all educational levels, women have higher unemployment rates than men; women college graduates, on the average, earn less than men with an eighth-grade education; minority women earn less than any other group of workers; pregnancy is the major known cause of dropping out among school-age females; and three-fifths of women at or below the poverty line are high school dropouts.[55] Yet two-thirds of working women are widowed, divorced, or separated, have never been married, or have husbands whose annual incomes are less than $15,000—in other words, they are the sole or major source of support for themselves and their families.[56] The ''feminization of poverty'' is a growing problem in the United States, as women find themselves increasingly in low-wage work, and the substantial wage gap between men and women stubbornly refuses to close.[57] However, the very term itself tends to camouflage the fact that women throughout history have not even been given the chance to become poor because they were virtual slaves whose lives were put in the sole service of men. The domestic arena for women is still a place of unpaid work. Women have historically been ''constructed'' ideologically to complete the narcissistic wholeness of the male. Women were, and still are, considered by the dominant male culture to be redeemable only by the service they provide to their male "protectors."

Social problems in the United States weigh most heavily on minority groups, women, and the poor, but do not end there. Middle-class, suburban youth are also caught in a dilemma: they are children of the baby boom coming of age in a stagnating economy. Brought up in a televised world of self-interest and greed based on the principle that commodities buy happiness, and where schools are a full partner in the sales pitch, these young people experience a dilemma cogently expressed by Ralph Larkin:

> (Middle-class) students experience a two-fold alienation: from adult society wherein lies the power, and from each other as invidious competition and mobility undercut authenticity and understanding of each other. They are isolated as a class and as monadic individuals. Most lives are characterized by lack of depth: in their family ties, friendships, skills, and commitment to any organizations. They live at the surface, fearful yet desirous of what might happen should they "bust out" of their not quite Edenic existence . . . [they] are terrorized by their fears. Their impotence and timidity generates self-hate and despair. . . .[58]

In other words, these students do not recognize their own self-repression and suppression by the dominant society, and in our vitiated learning environments they are not provided with the requisite theoretical constructs to help them understand why they feel as badly as they do. Because teachers lack a critical pedagogy, these students are not provided with the ability to think critically, a skill that would enable them to better understand why their lives have been reduced to feelings of meaninglessness, randomness, and alienation and why the dominant culture tries to accommodate them to the paucity of their lives. Consequently the culture continues to run amuck, degrading the process of labor, encouraging volatile commodity consumption, and maintaining the market mechanism as the basis for the distribution of wealth and status, all of which work to impoverish the psychic life of our youth and contribute to the degradation of everyday life.

As educators and cultural workers, we need to recognize the various manifestations of oppression as they affect the lives of millions of North Americans. Iris Marion Young offers a detailed typology of oppression that is worth summarizing.[59] She argues, rightly in my view, that the meaning of oppression has shifted from the practice of colonial domination and conquest. That is, it can no longer be simply thought to be an evil perpetuated by others, as the exercise of tyranny by a ruling group. Young has substantially redefined the term to designate "the everyday practices of a well-intentioned liberal society" and "systemic and structural phenomena that are not necessarily the result of the intentions of a tyrant." In other words, "oppressions are systematically reproduced in major economic, political, and cultural institutions" and are part of the basic fabric of social life. In Young's view, oppression can exist even in the absence of overt discrimination, the latter term referring to an individualist concept that links discrimination to an identifiable agent. Oppression is related to "unconscious assumptions and reactions of well-meaning people in ordinary interactions, media and cultural stereotypes, and structural features of bureaucratic hierarchy and market mechanisms, in short, the normal ongoing processes of everyday life."

Oppression disempowers groups—and here Young warns us not to think of groups simply as aggregates in which group membership is linked to a simple set of attributes. Rather, group membership means that one finds oneself as a member of a group in the sense that one's identity "is defined in relation to how others identify him or her, and they do so in terms of groups that always already have specific attributes, stereotypes, and norms associated with them, in reference to which a person's identity will be formed." The oppression of a group does not mean that there is a correlating oppressor group, which is not to suggest that individual persons do not intentionally harm others.

Young explicates what she refers to as "five faces of oppression" that affect groups such as women, blacks, Chicanos, Puerto Ricans, most Spanish-speaking Americans, Native Americans, Jews, lesbians, gay men, Arabs, Asians, old people, working-class people, poor people, and physically or mentally disabled people.

Exploitation

Exploitation, notes Young, is a form of domination in which the labor of working-class groups is transferred to benefit the wealthy, reproducing and causing class division and relations of inequality. For instance, women are exploited as wage workers and also in the sphere of domestic labors; additionally, women suffer forms of gender exploitation in the workplace and within the structure of patriarchy. Race, as well as class and gender, is also a structure of oppression. Blacks and Latinos are oppressed by capitalist superexploitation due to the segmented labor market in which skilled, high-paying, and unionized jobs are reserved primarily for whites.

Marginalization

Marginalization refers to groups who constitute the growing underclass of people who suffer severe material deprivation and are confined to lives of unemployment and "expelled from useful participation in social life." Often marginalized groups are racially marked, and this includes groups both in Third World and in Western capitalist countries—"blacks or Indians in Latin America, blacks, East Indians, Eastern Europeans or North Africans in Europe." Marginalized people are often positioned by the dominant culture in relations of dependency where they are excluded from equal citizenship rights. Even if they are materially comfortable, these groups may be oppressed on the basis of their marginal status, for instance, senior citizens who suffer from feelings of uselessness, boredom, and lack of self-worth.

Powerlessness

Powerlessness deals with structures of social division, such as social status. More specifically, powerlessness "describes the lives of people who have little or no work autonomy, exercise little creativity or judgement in their work, have no technical expertise or authority, express themselves awkwardly, especially in public or bureaucratic settings, and do not command respect." Young here refers to the cultures of professionals and nonprofessionals, which, of course, are linked to the division between mental and manual labor. She specifically refers to the norms of respectability in our society and the ways in which such norms privilege "professional" dress, speech, tastes, and demeanor—and the way this privilege appears in the dynamics of racism and sexism.

Cultural Imperialism

Cultural imperialism, according to Young, refers to "the universalization of one group's experience and culture and its establishment as the norm." The dominant cultural group exercises its power by bringing other groups under the measure of its domination. Consequently, the dominant groups construct the differences of subordinate groups as lack and negation in relation to their privileging norms. For instance, "the difference of women from men, Native Americans or Africans from Europeans, Jews from Christians, homosexuals from heterosexuals, or workers from professionals becomes reconstructed as deviance and inferiority." Victims of cultural imperialism live their oppression by viewing themselves from the perspective of the way others view them: a phenomenon known as "double consciousness." Young writes:

> The dominant culture's stereotyped, marked, and inferiorized images of the group must be internalized by group members at least to the degree that they are forced to react to behaviors of others that express or are influenced by those images. . . . This consciousness is double because the oppressed subject refuses to coincide with these devalued, objectified, stereotyped visions of herself or himself. The subject desires recognition as human, capable of activity, full of hope and possibility, but receives from the dominant culture only the judgement that he or she is different, marked, or inferior.[60]

Cultural imperialism, notes Young, is the paradoxical experience of being invisible while simultaneously being positioned as different. It is the process of being defined by both dominant and subordinate cultures.

Violence

Oppression involves the fear of systematic and legitimized violence. For instance, systematic violence is directed at members of particular groups simply because members belong to those specific groups. Young notes that in U.S. society women, blacks, Asians, Arabs, gay men, and lesbians live under threats of xenophobic, random, and unprovoked attacks as do Jews, Puerto Ricans, Chicanos, and other Spanish-speaking Americans who inhabit certain regions. This form of violence is also legitimate because most white people find it a common occurrence and do little to punish the offenders. In my view, this could clearly be seen in the Rodney King beating by the Los Angeles police in 1992.

Finally, I would like to draw attention to a pressing concern of Americans both within and outside the educational system: illiteracy. In his book, *Illiterate America,* Jonathan Kozol presents us with one of the most comprehensive assessments of this crippling condition:

> Twenty-five million American adults cannot read the poison warnings on a can of pesticide, a letter from their child's teacher, or the front page of a daily paper. An additional 35 million read only at a level which is less than equal to the full survival needs of our society. Together, these 60 million people represent more than one third of the entire adult population. The largest numbers of illiterate adults are white, native-born Americans. In proportion to population, however, the figures are higher for blacks and Hispanics than for whites. Sixteen percent of white adults, 44 percent of blacks, and 56 percent of Hispanic citizens are functional or marginal illiterates. Figures for the younger generation of black adults are increasing. Forty-seven percent of all black seventeen-year olds are functionally illiterate. That figure is expected to climb by 1990.
>
> Fifteen percent of recent graduates of urban high schools read less than sixth grade level. One million teenage children between twelve and seventeen cannot read above the third grade level. Eighty-five percent of juveniles who come before the courts are functionally illiterate. Of 8 million unemployed adults, 4 to 6 million lack the skills to be retrained for high tech jobs. The United States ranks forty-ninth among 158 member nations of the U.N. in its literacy level.[61]

For U.S. citizens besieged by the relentless logic of consumerism and privatization, it is no wonder that illiteracy thrives as a means of resisting, escaping, or refusing to be part of the cultural nightmare. What is needed to meet the crisis of literacy is a critical literacy that frames reading and writing in terms of moral and political decision making. Literacy in this view is not linked to learning to read advertisements and becoming better consumers, or escaping into the pages of romance novels or spy thrillers; critical literacy links language competency to acquiring analytical skills which empower individuals to challenge the status quo.

It is difficult to perceive the full significance of the social crisis I have tried to portray in the preceding pages, for it demonstrates that history does not represent some linear progressive continuum headed towards equality and the steady enrichment and enhancement of human life; it is not a teleological unfolding of some metaphysical plan, the "essence" of which is material, spiritual, moral, or ethical progress. It is not the presence of linear reason in linear time but is, in fact, contingent upon particular regimes of truth operating in society. As a society, we are caught between an imminent sense of destruction and an inability to acknowledge it. The grim reality of the present situation is that the United States continues to be disfigured by class exploitation and sexual and racial inequality. Shadowed by the logic of nihilism, violence has become the purifying aesthetic to growing right-wing militant factions who wish to purge North America of blacks, Asians, Arabs, and Jews. Such xenophobia is but one of the consequences of a deteriorating society based on privilege and inequality, a society that has allowed a pathological and destructive structuring of social relations to occur. These relations have been heightened in recent years by the resurgence of fundamentalist evangelism and the revitalization trends of the New Right. In the words of Richard Sennet, "Lacking in America is any sense that the nation is a collectivity of difference, that the human community might indeed be enriched by the experience of the Other, of that which cannot be rendered transparent."[62]

One particularly disturbing feature of the current educational reform movement has been the appeal of the concepts of cultural literacy as advocated by E. D. Hirsch, Jr. and Allan Bloom. Bloom espouses a view of schooling in which students are required to celebrate the so-called high status knowledge of the Great Books of the Western World, while Hirsch argues that teachers are required to transmit the praiseworthy aspects of our American cultural heritage.[63] Bloom's perspective rests on the neoclassical notion that the culture somehow "contains" knowledge (as distinct from the concept that knowledge is socially constructed), and presumably high status knowledge is the only kind of knowledge esteemed enough to warrant inclusion in the curricula. Insistently denigrated in this view of what should be taught are the subjugated knowledges of economically disadvantaged groups, women, and minorities. Writers such as Hirsch argue that the cultural heritage of the United States should be taught, but in such a way as to conceal its socially derivative status and to cloak the selective interests that it serves in the mantle of the eternal principles of justice, equality, and fraternity. Bloom suggests that Americans would be better off if they jettisoned the search for equality in favor of a privileged position in Plato's Republic. The position of both writers signals the rise of a new elitism.

For some readers who remain skeptical about the extent to which oppression affects the lives of young people in this country, I'd like to share some recent statistical information with you. According to a recent publication of the Children's Defense Fund, *The State of America's Children 1991,*[64] black and Latino teenagers are twice as likely as Anglo white students to be two or more grades behind in school. Furthermore, three in ten black children and more than 50 percent of all Latino children have a parent who lacks a high school diploma. Not surprisingly, given the objective conditions of opportunity for students of color, by age twenty-two 18 percent of black youths and 43 percent of Latino youths still have not graduated from high school (compared to 14 percent of white youths). If graduation isn't as attractive to students, perhaps there is a reason. A look at employment rates can perhaps give us a clue. The unemployment rate for black high school *graduates* in 1988 was 25 percent higher than the rate for white high school *dropouts*. White high school dropouts have a better chance for success than black high school graduates.

Consider that last statement for a moment. Now consider the fact that the average black student dropout earned 60 percent less in 1980 than in 1973. This state of affairs becomes even more disturbing when we consider that homicide is now the number one cause of death among young black males. One only needs to watch the film *Boyz 'n the Hood* to get a sense of what chances are available for lower middle-class black youth in capitalist America. In a survey of 536 southside Chicago elementary school children, 26 percent had seen someone shot and 29 percent had seen a stabbing.

But what about U.S. youth—from both minority and dominant groups—who do, in fact, graduate? Only 27 percent of them can find specific information in a lengthy news article; only 3 percent can read and orally interpret distinctions between various types of employee benefits; only 5 percent can estimate the cost of an item using a grocery unit price label. Among 17-year-olds who are still in school, only half are able to compute with decimals, fractions, and percents. In fact, only 40 percent of U.S. students can solve math problems requiring at least two steps. It is no surprise that a 1988 international assessment of math achievement revealed U.S. thirteen-year-olds to be ranked last in ability to solve math problems—behind thirteen-year-olds in the United Kingdom, Spain, Ireland, Korea, and three Canadian provinces.

Of course, poverty is a major factor in determining the success of students at school. It is perhaps the greatest predictor of academic success in this country, which makes it disturbing to learn that in 1988, only 25 percent of three- and four-year-olds with family incomes of less than $10,000 a year were enrolled in a preschool program. Yet 56 percent of those with family incomes of $35,000 or more were enrolled. More than one-third of all children in families headed by someone younger than thirty are living in poverty. The Bush Administration suppressed a 1989 White House Task Force report on infant mortality which reported that 10,000 of the 40,000 infant deaths in 1988 in the U.S. could have been averted and 10,000 of those 40,000 left disabled could have been spared by applying current knowledge. Of course, the mortality rate of black infants was more than double that of white infants in 1988. By February 1990, 2000 or more cases of AIDS had been diagnosed in children younger than thirteen years of age, while it is expected that there is double that amount of HIV-infected children younger than thirteen years.

It is estimated that one in seven teens currently has a sexually transmitted disease. In the age group of fifteen to nineteen, the average gonorrhea rate in black males is about fifteen times that of their white counterparts, while the rate for black females of that age is about ten times the white rate.

Suicide—not homicide—is the second leading cause of death among young white males aged fifteen to twenty-four. Add to this the fact that 2.4 million children were abused or neglected in 1989.

Of course, the answer to this epidemic of neglect is not to blame the victims—heaping abuse on the disadvantaged in our society and blaming them for not being able to create better conditions for their children. White people often look condescendingly toward people of color who find it difficult to earn a living and provide decent conditions for their children in a white male world. In fact, a recent report in *Extra*[65] notes that white people began leaving a neighborhood when the percentage of African-Americans reaches about 8 percent—even when the African-Americans are from the same socioeconomic class. The unemployment rate for black workers in 1990 was 176 percent greater than that of white workers.

Although I think it is fair to say that people of color—especially African-Americans and Latinos—are living in a state of siege in this country, I am not suggesting that white readers paralyze themselves with self-hatred because of this state of affairs. However, I do ask that they begin to unlearn their privilege and as teachers begin to address the urgent social issues that face the country.

One recent social issue whose urgency cannot be denied nor should be ignored is the Los Angeles uprising of May 1992. The killing and looting and burning of buildings that took place during this event have received much media attention, most of it directed at the gang involvement and random violence that took place after the Rodney King verdict. When the Los Angeles police officers who were videotaped beating motorist Rodney King were initially acquitted by an all-white jury, parts of Los Angeles erupted into the worst urban rioting since the Watts rebellion in the 1960s. The media and "media analysts" largely attributed the blame to black and Latino street gangs who used the verdict to take advantage of the tension generated in the black community and eventually to exploit it through acts of arson and looting.

Yet this "analysis" largely ignored the context surrounding the uprising which deals with police racism and the plight of black and Latino people across the United States. As Mike Davis notes, the Los Angeles uprising was, in part, a result of the systematic harassment and repression of black youth for decades.[66] The media reports generally ignored the shooting of fifteen-year-old Latasha Harlin, who was shot from behind by a Korean shopkeeper after an argument over an orange juice. Latasha Harlin's head was blown off and the shopkeeper was fined $500 by a white judge and sentenced to 400 hours of community service. Just prior to this incident, a black postman was sentenced to six months in jail for shooting a dog.

As Davis points out, the Los Angeles uprising was truly multiethnic and involved African-Americans, Mexican immigrants, and Central Americans, and as many Latinos as African-Americans were killed looting by the police and National Guard. The rebellion consisted of homogeneously younger youths than in the Watts uprising and also included middle-class blacks since the L.A.P.D. policies have criminalized black youth, regardless of their socioeconomic status. This oppression by the police helped to make gang membership a more natural form of resistance. The Crips and the Bloods and the Florentia gang—the biggest Mexican gang of the East Side—are now talking about the unity of all the oppressed. But as Davis also notes, the real problem is the racism and the erosion of minimum-wage jobs through declining demand and business relocation to Mexico.

Los Angeles has been turned into a type of Third World city, but unlike a real Third World city it is unable to create squatter settlements and survival economies. Davis notes that the choice for youth now is "between blow-drying rich people's lawns or joining gangs."[67] In the face of structural unemployment and deindustrialization, gangs have become a compensatory social structure and, notes Davis, "surrogate families." It's the Mexicans, Salvadorans, and Guatemalans who are the most vulnerable to ravages of the depression, and it's not surprising that on Christmas Eve, 1992, 20,000 Latinos turned up downtown to wait all night for a blanket and a turkey. During the day, they waited in line for day labor in the slave markets (Katz and Smith, 1992).

Of course, we are not simply talking about conditions in Los Angeles. In Detroit, Malice Green was pulled from a parked car by the police. A black man, Green was savagely beaten by a white male officer in the face, chest, and stomach. Part of his scalp was torn off by a police officer wielding a flashlight like a golf club. After fourteen blows to Green's head, an officer stepped on Green's neck as he was handcuffed. Green died from blunt-force trauma to the head.

Perhaps we are seeing the beginning of what Davis has termed "an American urban Intifada."

What happens when students leave their schools as dropouts, or what Latino students refer to as being "pushed out"? Michelle Fine has written extensively on this subject and has done so with admirable erudition and sensitivity.[68] She notes that even after three decades of progressive legislation (for example, Brown I, Brown II, and Title VI), in 1985 62.5 percent of African-American students attended predominately minority schools and they were overrepresented to a very substantial degree in terms of suspension referrals, school explusions, and enrollment in special education classes. Fine also notes that 68 percent of Latino children are still enrolled in racially isolated schools. She further notes that despite Title IX, Title VII of the Civil Rights Act of 1964, and the Women's Educational Equity Act of 1974, female educational achievement in the disciplines of math, reading, social studies, and science continues to decline relative to males.

Fine has provided some important statistics to give us a better understanding of the growing gap in educational outcomes among privileged and disadvantaged groups, specifically in terms of race, class, and gender. For instance, it is currently expected that 25 percent of fifth graders will not make it to high school. Not surprisingly, social class is still the greatest predictor of who drops out and who does not. Dropouts constitute 22 percent of the lowest quartile and 8.9 percent of the highest quartile. Fine reports the following statistics on dropouts in descending order: Native Americans (22.7 percent); Latinos and Latinas (18.7 percent); African-Americans (16.8 percent); whites (12.2 percent); and Asians (4.8 percent). In urban areas, Latinas drop out more frequently than any other group (26.2 percent versus 12.6 percent Latinos, 15.7 percent white males, 15.3 percent white females, 24.4 percent African-American males, and 16.5 African-American females). Pregnancy, parenting, and marriage disrupt many young women's educational careers.

Fine reports on some of the findings dealing with attributes of schools from which the students drop out (or are pushed out). Student dropouts decrease with a rise in teacher-student ratios and they rise during times of increased teacher moves and transfer requests. A decline in student achievement follows rigid retention policies, lack of faculty interest, unfair discipline procedures, widespread truancy, teacher turnover, tracking procedures, and competency examinations.

What happens to the dropouts once they drop out? Fine provides more illuminating statistics. Those who are economically privileged and male reap the most benefits of a high school degree. For each year of education, women's returns are approximately 40 percent of men's and African-Americans' are about 63 percent of whites'. Fine further points out that high school *dropouts* living in the highest income neighborhoods of New York City have a 24.4 percent employment-to-population ratio, compared with a 30.7 percent ratio for high school *graduates* in the poorest neighborhoods. Among high school graduates aged twenty-two to thirty-four, 15 percent of the white men, 28 percent of the white women, 37 percent of the African-American men, and 62 percent of the African-American women live in poverty. In the case of both dropouts and graduates, African-American women are two to three times more likely to be poor than white women of the same age and education, and over four times more likely than white males.

In 1987, Assistant Secretary of Education Chester Finn reflected the view of many mainstream education officials when he attributed much of the dropout problem to social pathology and inherited characteristics.[69] People such as Finn like to use SAT measurements as the key instrument for judging academic success. Yet as Elaine and Harry Mensh have illustrated in their recent book, *The IQ Mythology,* IQ tests, like SAT tests, are really linked to the prior assumptions of the test-makers, and the data that generally result from these tests reinforce such assumptions.[70] The result is that such tests help to "keep academic barriers in place for those groups historically confronted by them."[71] Of course, Finn and others like him ascribe to both a "hereditarian" and "environmentalist" explanation for low IQ scores and other test results. It will sound ironic—and perhaps disturbing—to many students to learn that the current debate surrounding alleged racial intelligence differentials was given its greatest impetus by Thomas Jefferson, slaveholder and author of the Declaration of Independence. Jefferson declared that black people were mentally inferior to whites. His hereditarian position was resisted by others from the standpoint of environmentalism. This position argues that black people are not "naturally" inferior but inferior in mental skills due to their impoverished environment. The problem is that the environmentalists, who criticize biological determinism as scientific racism, still accept the general premise that race and class intelligence differentials exist. So essentially they are still keeping the claim alive that cognitive differences between blacks and whites exist. As Mensh and Mensh point out, the environmentalist position is not as antiracist and egalitarian as it is often assumed.

The real issue is that, counter to the claim made by environmentalists, mental development can take place under both favorable and unfavorable conditions. Development in cognition is not something that is passively acquired—people develop cognitively often during attempts to resist—to overcome disadvantageous circumstances.[72] Cognitive processes are also universal—but not all cultures possess the same measures of equality. The biological processing of the mind is the same in every culture—although cultures are different and there is no question that when cognitive processes are socially or culturally handicapped, then academic performance suffers.[73] But the cause of such handicapping processes does not lie in the genes or the pathological attributes of certain cultures but rather is connected to the skills being taught or not taught in the schools.[74] Who has the best chance of acquiring these ''specific'' skills and who does not? Which families provide such skills before their children enter school and why are these ''particular'' skills valued over other kinds of skills? Whose knowledge counts the most, and why? What classrooms have the kinds of resources that can be coordinated with national tests? What classrooms are best able to motivate students by teaching to the tests? How are tests used to select out certain students, to compare districts, and to classify certain groups on the base of race, class, and gender? Tests typically look for certain skills, and legitimate these and not others, and typically they demand skills that are differentially available along class and racial lines. Intelligence isn't something that should be measured—even under the best of circumstances. It is something that should be nurtured and linked to a wider project of empowerment, something that will be made clearer in the chapters that follow.

What is particularly striking in the debates over the SAT test is that few commentators have mentioned the historical context surrounding this test. The author of the SAT test, Carl Campbell Brigham, embraced the classification of races set forth in Madison Grant's book, *The Passing of the Great Race.* According to Stanley Fish, Brigham identified the Nordic as the superior race, while the others ranked, in descending order, as follows: Alpine, Mediterranean, Eastern, Near Eastern, and Negro.[75] Brigham's 1923 book, *A Study of American Intelligence,* formed the groundwork for the SAT when Brigham became director of the College Board's testing operations. Brigham was worried that integrated education would put blacks—the least mentally endowed students—in the same classes with the most superior: whites. According to Fish, Brigham worried that ''Nordic'' types would begin grave error if they married ''Negro'' types. This would only ensure the deterioration of American intelligence. Fish also tellingly notes that Brigham's racism has never been officially repudiated. However, national testing officials have maintained that his racism did not compromise his scientific ''objectivity.'' The library at the Educational Testing Service compound still bears Brigham's name.[76]

Holly Sklar provides some illuminating information that reveals the extent to which women—especially black women—are demonized by politicians, historians, and the media who use misogynist myths to perpetuate racial, gender, and class discrimination.[77] Sklar reports that most poor Americans are white and that a large number of married couples are poor. She notes that ''even if there were no nonwhite children and no single mother families, the United States would have one of the highest child poverty rates among the capitalist powers.''[78] In response to the ideological assault on single women as the cause of poverty and misery in the United States, she asks us to imagine ''labeling married-couple families as pathological breeding grounds of patriarchal domestic violence, or suggesting that women should never marry, because they are more likely to be beaten and killed by a spouse than a stranger.''[79] Sklar offers us some unsettling statistics to help make her point:

In Massachusetts during the first half of 1992, nearly three out of four women whose murderers are known were killed by husbands, boyfriends, or ex-partners. Misogynist domestic violence is so rampant that over 50,000 Massachusetts women have taken out restraining orders against former mates. Domestic violence is the leading cause of injuries to women ages 15 to 44, "more common than automobile accidents, muggings, and cancer deaths combined." It is estimated that a woman has between a one in five and a one in three chance of being physically assaulted by a partner or ex-partner during her lifetime. More than ninety women were murdered every week in 1991. In the words of an October 1992 Senate Judiciary Committee report, "Every week is a week of terror for at least 21,000 American women" of all races, regions, educational, and economic backgrounds, whose "domestic assaults, rapes and murders were reported to the police." As many as three million more domestic violence crimes may go unreported.[80]

Sklar also quotes Stephanie Coontz's profoundly disturbing pronouncement that "families whose members are police officers or who serve in the military have much higher rates of divorce, family violence, and substance abuse than do other families, but we seldom accuse them of constituting an 'underclass' with a dysfunctional culture."[81]

Sklar is absolutely correct in her account of the way in which the dominant white culture has stigmatized black communities and especially black women. Daniel Patrick Moynihan's 1965 characterization of the matriarchal black family as "a tangle of pathology"[82] is one that persists with an even greater intensity today. Black women continue to be blamed for the population explosion, a rise in juvenile delinquency, and divorce. They are labeled as "brood mares" and "welfare queens" by patriarchal white supremacists whose educational and social policies have sytematically excluded black and Latina women from opportunities granted to other groups who are not female and people-of-color. The increased institutional abuse heaped upon these women masks the growing increase in racism and income inequality. Teachers and prospective teachers need to think about some of the conditions reported by Sklar. For instance,

- Families with a net worth in the top 1 percent of families in the country now have a net worth much greater than that of families in the bottom 90 percent.
- In 1989, families with a net worth in the top 1 percent of families in the country had 37.7 percent of total net worth (assets minus debt), and the bottom 90 percent had 29.2 percent, while the bottom 95 percent had 40.7 percent.[83]

Sklar makes a provocative but entirely accurate statement in relation to these statistics. She notes that "the shrinking middle class is misled into thinking those below them on the economic ladder are pulling them down, when in reality those at the top of the ladder are pushing everyone down."[84] There is a shift toward lower-paying industries, toward a lower value of the minimum wage, and toward less unionization, especially in relation to entry-level wages for high school graduates. In fact, Sklar reports that the entry-level wage for high school graduates fell 22 percent between 1979 and 1991. And whereas entry-level wages for college graduates fell slightly between 1979 and 1991 (−0.2 percent), black college graduates lost more than 3 percent and Latino college graduates lost nearly 15 percent.[85]

We live in dangerous times, a time in which many college freshmen think it's "cool" to agree ideologically with Rush Limbaugh and to be a fan of Camille Paglia. To be fascist and brainy has never been in such fashion. Rarely are the political consequences of such allegiances thought through. This is one of tragedies of contemporary schooling.

Although we fight hard not to admit it, things are not getting much better. Walter Benjamin's "angel of history" continues to gaze through clouds of despair—not to mention a disintegrated ozone layer—at a continent whose potential is greater now than ever before for unleashing worldwide catastrophe.

In an era of falling profitability and production, where each percentage point increase in the unemployment rate brings 318 additional suicides, and a 2 percent increase in the mortality rate brings a 5 to 6 percent increase in homicides, a 5 percent rise in imprisonments, a 3 to 4 percent increase in first admissions to mental hospitals, and a 5 to 6 percent increase in infant mortality rates, consumer culture grabs at the grotesque and the decadent.[86] Images of garish and vulgar commodities litter both print and electronic media, creating an ethos of possessive and atomistic individualism, debilitating privatization, and self-seeking careerism that shunts aside the imperative to analyze existing social conditions and oppressive relations of power and privilege and to eliminate exploitation. Instead, these images reinforce a consumerist ideology characterized by the belief that the quality of everyday life is irrevocably enhanced through the continual creation of material wealth. Silicon Valley's apostles of technology and efficiency, backed by Sun Belt entrepreneurs, parade their wares as functional imperatives for modern survival, while questions of social justice and human struggle seem more and more peripheral to the commodity culture. Failing to consider how our dreams, desires, and actions have been manufactured and socially conditioned, we remain instead in the thrall of consumerist ethics. We are living collectively the American nightmare, *Death of a Salesman,* and like Willy Loman we are realizing that the exchange value of dead labor is empty hope. We seem to accept the belief that present conditions have arisen out of democratic necessity, as a prerequisite for our fetishistic quest for the best of all possible worlds. Inequality and poverty are the prices we must pay for freedom.

In reality, however, progress has become the scourge of history, an attack on human freedom, as the profound illogic of the times runs frictionless and free. Those who wish to build a society free from the din and carnage of war find it hardly comforting that many key figures in today's burgeoning New Right— including high-ranking government and military figures—harbor sweet cravings for Armageddon, use the Bible as the chronometer of history, and ascribe to a variation of "imminent rapture/holocaust" in which the "purifying violence" of nuclear war is perceived as part of God's plan. (Of course, true believers will be instantly teleported to heaven by Jesus in the sky, just before the apocalyptic showdown.)[87]

Rampant illiteracy, growing dropout rates among the poor, and a dramatic increase in classroom violence and despair exemplify the plight of today's students and teachers. As we fail to consider the possibility of practical political action or to exercise our abilities to intervene in the world, our dreams glide over the domain of ethics and continue to be manufactured in a culture of unchallenged consumer hype and moral destruction. Today more than ever before we need a pedagogical theory that is able to counter the New Right's excoriating attack on schooling, which argues that the moral vocabulary of critical pedagogy must be expunged as leftist or socialistic. The repeated assaults of reactionary ideologies, whether they are carried to us through school bashing, arms scandals, gun-running diplomacy, or television preachers hungry for corporate power, have normalized greed, the right to be racist, the logic of self-interest, a desire for private gain, and a hatred for conscientious dissent. As the dark and ambivalent wings of history beat about the stage of our present era, where hope is held hostage, where justice is lashed to the altar of capital accumulation, and where the good works of our collective citizenry have been effaced by despair, we desperately need a new vision of what education should mean.

For teachers, this means that we must begin candidly and critically to face our society's complicity in the roots and structures of inequality and injustice. It means, too, that as teachers we must face our own culpability in the reproduction of inequality in our teaching, and that we must strive to develop a pedagogy equipped to provide both intellectual and moral resistance to oppression, one that extends the concept of pedagogy beyond the mere transmission of knowledge and skills and the concept of morality beyond interpersonal relations. This is what critical pedagogy is all about.

NOTES TO PART ONE

1. I should point out that Evan Mecham, Governor of Arizona, is the same governor who feels "pickanninies" is not an offensive term and whose education advisor believes that "if (a) student wants to say the world is flat, the teacher doesn't have the right to prove otherwise." David Handelman, Lisa Hendricksson, and Lynn Hirschberg, "The Hot List," *Rolling Stone* (May 21,1987): 85.
2. This event originally came to my attention during a newscast on a Cincinnati television station; "Rambo Comes to High School," *Time* (1987, February 16): 31; the text of the officer's speech was taken from "Operation Scare-the-Pants-Off-'Em," *Harper's* 274 (April, 1987): 22–23.
3. "Born in the U.SA.," *Time* (1987, February 16): 31.
4. Ibid.
5. These ideas are expressed in Henry A. Giroux and Peter McLaren (in press), "Teacher Education and the Politics of Democratic Life: Beyond the Reagan Agenda in the Era of 'Good Times,'" in C. C. Yeakey and G. S. Johnston (Eds.), *Schools as Conduits: Educational Policymaking During the Reagan Years* (New York: Praeger Press). The metaphors belong to Giroux.

6. Tom Mirga, "Restore Family Stability, Panel Urges," *Education Week* (1986, November 19):14, 17.

7. Giroux and McLaren. "Teacher Education and the Politics of Democratic Life: Beyond the Reagan Agenda in the Era of 'Good Times.' "

8. I am referring here to reports that have played a major role in shaping educational policy at both the national and local levels. These include: The National Commission on Excellence in Education, *A Nation at Risk: The Imperative for Educational Reform* (Washington, DC: GPO, 1983); Task Force on Education for Economic Growth, Education Commission of the States, *Action for Excellence: A Comprehensive Plan to Improve Our Nation's Schools* (Denver: Education Commission of the United States, 1983); The Twentieth Century Fund Task Force on Federal Elementary and Secondary Education Policy, *Making the Grade* (New York: The Twentieth Century Fund, 1983); Carnegie Corporation, *Education and Economic Progress: Toward a National Education Policy* (New York: 1983); and Carnegie Forum of Education and the Economy, *A Nation Prepared: Teachers for the 21st Century* (Hyattsville, MD: 1986). Also considered are other recent reports on teacher education reform: The National Commission for Excellence in Teacher Education, *A Call for Change in Teacher Education* (Washington, DC: American Association of Colleges in Teacher Education, 1985); C. Emily Feistritzer, *The Making of a Teacher* (Washington, DC: National Center for Education Information, 1984); *Tomorrow's Teachers: A Report of the Holmes Group* (East Lansing, MI: Holmes Group, Inc., 1986); and Francis A. Maher and Charles H. Rathbone, "Teacher Education and Feminist Theory: Some Implications for Practice," *American Journal of Education* 101 (1986): 214–235. For an analysis of many of these reports see Catherine Cornbleth, "Ritual and Rationality in Teacher Education Reform," *Educational Researcher* 15 (4), (April, 1986): 5–14.

9. Joshua Cohen and Joel Rogers, *On Democracy: Toward a Transformation of American Society* (Middlesex, England and New York: Penguin Books, 1983), 24–27.

10. Ibid. 27–28. White men have a 1-in-131 chance of being murdered and white women a 1-in-369 chance; black women have a 1-in-104 chance and black men have a 1-in-21 chance. See Dinesh D'Souza, "Racism in the 1980s," *The World and I* (1987, March): 26.

11. Cohen and Rogers, *On Democracy,* 28, 29. In addition, twenty-six states permit underage executions. "Children Who Kill," *Newsweek* (1986, November 24): 93.

12. Michael W. Sherridan "School Dropouts in Perspective," *The Educational Forum* 51, 1 (1986, Fall): 18.

13. Spenser Rich, "Blacks on the Bottom: For an Underclass of the Poor and Alienated, Life Is Only Getting Worse," *The Washington Post National Weekend Edition* 10 (1986, February 3).

14. Jon D. Hull, "Life and Death with the Gangs," *Time* (1987, August 24): 21.

15. Judith Cummings, "White California Youth Gangs," *New York Times* (1986, January 12): 14.

16. Cohen and Rogers, *On Democracy,* 24–25, 27.

17. Ibid., 29.

18. Sherridan, "School Dropouts in Perspective," 18.

19. Cohen and Rogers, *On Democracy,* 30.

20. James P. Wright and Julie A. Lam, "Homelessness and Low Income Housing Supply," *Social Policy* 17, 4 (1987, Spring): 48–53.

21. Jane Shapiro, "The Good War: The Coalition for the Homeless Keeps on Raising the Roof," *The Village Voice* 32 (30) (1987, July 28): 21–28.

22. "Traditional Families—A Dying Breed?" *Education Week* (1986, May 14): 22.

23. Sherridan, "School Dropouts in Perspective," 19.
24. Ann Bastian, Norm Fruchter, Marilyn Gittell, Colin Greer, and Kenneth Hoskins, *Choosing Equality* (Philadelphia, PA: Temple University Press, 1986), 26.
25. See Glenna Colclough and E. M. Beck, "The American Educational Structure and the Reproduction of Social Class," *Sociological Inquiry* 56, 4 (1986): 456–476.
26. For most of the following discussion of tracking, I am indebted to Jeannie Oakes, *Keeping Track: How Schools Structure Inequality* (New Haven: Yale University Press, 1985).
27. The statistics immediately preceding are all drawn from Sherridan, "School Dropouts in Perspective," 16.
28. Russell W. Rumberger, "High School Dropouts: A Review of Issues and Evidence," *Review of Educational Research* 57, 2 (1987): 115.
29. Bastian et al. *Choosing Equality,* 26.
30. Ibid., 27.
31. Ibid., 55.
32. "Today's Numbers, Tomorrow's Nation," *Education Week* (1986, May 14): 14.
33. "The Patterns in Our Social Fabric Are Changing," *Education Week,* 16.
34. Deenan Glamser and Jim Myers, "USA Marvels at Minority's Winning Way," *USA Today* (1987, June 12–14): 1–2.
35. Yin Ling Leung, "Inter-Racial Violence: Conflicts of Class and Culture," *The Minority Trendsletter* 1, 2 (Sept.–Oct. 1987): 1–7.
36. David Brand, "The New Whiz Kids," *Time* (1987, August 31): 49.
37. *Education Week,* 16.
38. See the research presented by Samuel Bowles and Herbert Gintis, *Schooling in Capitalist America: Educational Reform and the Contradictions of Economic Reform* (New York: Basic Books, 1976).
39. *Education Week,* 16.
40. Rexford Brown, "State Responsibility for At-Risk Youth," *Metropolitan Education* 2 (1986, Fall): 5–12.
41. The National Coalition of Advocates for Students, *Barriers to Excellence: Our Children at Risk* (Boston: Author, 1985), 10.
42. This insight was offered me by Jim Giarelli, in personal correspondence.
43. The Hispanic Policy Development Project, *Make Something Happen: Hispanics and Urban High School Reform* (New York: Author, 1984), 1,10.
44. Brown, "State Responsibility for At-Risk Youth," 6.
45. Children's Defense Fund, *Black and White Children in America: Key Facts* (Washington DC: Author, 1985), 3.
46. Ibid., 7, 12, 60, 89.
47. Ezra Bowen, "Wrong Message from Academe," *Time* (1987, April 6): 57–58.
48. Ibid.
49. Elizabeth L. Ihle, *Black Women's Academic Education in the South: Modules III and IV* (Washington, DC: U.S. Department of Education and the Women's Educational Equity Act Program, 1986), 10.
50. William Proefriedt, "Education and Moral Purpose: The Dream Recovered," *Teacher's College Record* 86, 3 (1985): 399–410.
51. The National Coalition of Advocates for Students, *Barriers to Excellence,* 5.
52. Bastian et al., *Choosing Equality,* 138–139.
53. The National Coalition of Advocates for Students, *Barriers to Excellence,* 16.
54. Ibid. viii–ix.
55. Ibid. 13.

56. Kathleen Christensen, "Women and Contingent Work," *Social Policy* 17 (1987, Spring): 16.
57. Gertrude S. Goldberg and Eleanor Kremen, "The Feminization of Poverty: Only in America?" *Social Policy* 17, 4 (1987, Spring): 3–14.
58. Ralph W. Larkin, *Suburban Youth in Cultural Crisis* (New York: Oxford University Press, 1979), 210.
59. Iris Marion Young, "Five Faces of Oppression." In Thomas E. Wartenberg (Ed.), *Rethinking Power* (Albany, NY: State University of New York Press, 1992), 174–195. My summary of Young's typology also appears in Peter Mclaren and Colin Tankshear (eds.), *Politics of Liberation* (New York and London, Routledge, in press).
60. Ibid., 192.
61. Jonathan Kozol, *Illiterate America* (Garden City, NY: Anchor Press, Doubleday, 1985), 4–5.
62. Richard Sennett, "A Republic of Souls," *Harper's* (1987, July): 44.
63. See E. D. Hirsch, Jr., *Cultural Literacy: What Every American Needs to Know* (Boston: Houghton Mifflin Co., 1987). See also Allan Bloom, *The Closing of the American Mind* (New York: Simon and Schuster, 1987).
64. Children's Defense Fund, *The State of American's Children 1991* (Washington, DC: Author, 1992). All statistical information preceding the next footnote is from this report.
65. *Extra* (July/August, 1992): 11.
66. Cindi Katz and Neil Smith, "L.A. Intifada: Interview with Mike Davis," *Social Text,* 33 (1992): 19–33.
67. Ibid.
68. Michelle Fine, *Framing Dropouts: Notes on the Politics of an Urban Public High School* (Albany, NY: State University of New York Press, 1991). All statistics preceding the next footnote are from Fine's book.
69. Ibid.
70. Elaine Mensh and Harry Mensh, *The IQ Mythology: Class, Race, Gender, and Inequality* (Carbondale and Edwardsville: Southern Illinois University Press, 1991).
71. Mensh and Mensh, *The IQ Mythology,* 71.
72. Mensh and Mensh, *The IQ Mythology.*
73. Ibid.
74. Ibid.
75. Stanley Fish, "Bad Company," *Transition,* No. 56, 60–67.
76. Ibid.
77. Holly Sklar, "The Upperclass and Mothers N the Hood," *Z Magazine* 6, 3 (March, 1993): 22–31.
78. Ibid., 22.
79. Ibid., 23.
80. Ibid., 22–23.
81. Ibid., 23.
82. Ibid.
83. Ibid., 29.
84. Ibid., 23.
85. Ibid., 29.
86. Cohen and Rogers, *On Democracy,* 29.
87. Lawrence Jones and Gerald Sheppard, "On Reagan, Prophecy, and Nuclear War," *Old Westbury Review* 2 (Fall 1986): 9–22.

PART II

Cries from the Corridor: Teaching in the Suburban Ghetto

INTRODUCTION

The section that follows presents a number of incidents from my four years of teaching elementary school in one of Toronto's "inner-city" suburbs known as the Jane-Finch Corridor. I have changed the names of students, parents, and teachers and have occasionally constructed composite descriptions to further protect their identities.

Some readers may object to my shifting context from a critique of schooling and society in the United States to an inner-city school in Canada. I would argue that the disadvantaged students of whom I speak, and the teachers who work with them, face daily struggles in the classroom that do not recognize the national boundaries between the United States and Canada. The agony of this situation, in fact, is that it not only spans the border between the United States and Canada, but also occurs in a variety of settings—cities, towns, suburbs, and rural areas. The struggles of many Canadian teachers are similar to the struggles of teachers in the Bronx and Harlem, in Roxbury and Watts, and in Youngstown and Cedar Rapids. They are experiences shared by teachers across the United States. They speak to common conditions faced by teachers and students in many of our industrialized nations, and they represent a collective challenge to the teaching profession and to the youth who make up our future citizenry.

The appropriateness of incorporating my Canadian journal in this volume has been favorably gauged by reactions I have received from audiences in the United States, including inner-city teachers and graduate students (many of whom teach full-time in inner-city schools), colleagues in colleges of education, and parents from a wide variety of ethnic backgrounds. There are certainly differences between teaching in Canada and in the United States, but these are far outweighed by the similarities. The overwhelming response has been that the experiences and conditions reflected in my journal do resemble those of many teachers who work in inner-city schools in the United States. In both countries teachers are faced with overcrowded classrooms, large immigrant populations, outmoded pedagogical theories, stifling bureaucratic demands, top-down centralization of control, management by behavioral objectives, a distrust of teachers' abilities and judgment in the classroom which has led to the effective deskilling of teachers, insufficient funding and resources, tracking measures and a hidden curriculum that favor certain groups over others on the basis of race, class, and gender—the list goes on and on. Ghetto schools across the continent are similar to the one I describe. Even in the rural classrooms of the Midwest I see faces of despair—the Appalachian poor from the trailer parks and surrounding farmlands side by side with struggling blacks, Latinos, and other minorities. And here, as elsewhere, the schools are ill-equipped to meet their needs.

I would like to be clear that the purpose of reproducing my elementary classroom journal is not to illustrate what critical pedagogy is all about—that will be discussed in Parts Three, Four, and Five. The purpose of the journal is to provide you with some insights into school life as it is lived by students and teachers. These insights are presented from the perspective of a novice teacher unfamiliar with the theories discussed in later sections of this book.

This section of the book is the most problematic for me since reading it from the perspective of a critical theorist confronts me with my own ideological and pedagogical shortcomings; it places me face-to-face with my own situatedness as a young teacher in discourses that unconsciously worked against my own emancipatory intention. It is painful for me to read many of these vignettes because I recognize that I was not immune to many of the criticisms that I now lay at the feet of unjust schooling practices and the workings of a racist, sexist, and culturally imperialistic social formation. I recognize that in many of the diary entries the white, Anglo, patriarchal, and liberal humanist discourses and the missionary zeal that I now harshly criticize actually undergirded my own early teaching practices. Of course, I don't want to condemn all of my efforts, many of which did attempt to challenge (although with limited success) existing social cultural and institutional practices that worked against children of the poor and powerless. I present the reader with this diary in order to reveal my beginning experiences as a teacher. I invite the reader to analyze these experiences in light of the perspectives offered that follow my diary. I do not ask the reader to celebrate unqualifiedly my efforts or to criticize them before reading the sections that follow. It is the theoretical sections that follow the diary that I hope will provide a framework for understanding and analyzing my teaching practices.

Part of my plan in this book is to invite you to become a more critically engaged theorist after being introduced to the concepts in Parts Three, Four, and Five.

THE CORRIDOR KIDS

"Teach in an inner-city school! You're completely crazy," a friend warned me. "You'll ruin your career!"

I was taken aback. "What do you mean 'ruin my career'?"

"When you've decided you've had enough, and apply for a job in a better area, you'll be labeled an 'inner-city' teacher. Once you've been pigeon-holed as teaching mainly immigrant kids, you've had it. Be smart—get out before you get in."

But I wanted to work with inner-city kids and jobs were scarce.

The Jane-Finch Corridor is a six-square block area in the city of North York, a suburb just outside downtown Toronto, Canada. In 1970, there were twenty-one high-rise apartment buildings, and a population of 34,000. By 1975, there were fifty-nine high-rises (with four more under construction) and a population of 60,000. Thirty-eight thousand people are crammed into a two-square-mile area around the intersection of Jane Street and Finch Avenue. About 25,750 of them are nineteen years old and under. Many live in the nearly 3,000 income-assisted housing units. Twenty-two percent of the apartment buildings are government subsidized. Approximately 30 percent of the residents are black, and many are new immigrants with low-paying jobs or no jobs at all. There is a substantial West Indian population, and large numbers of Italian- and Spanish-speaking peoples.

Although the Jane-Finch Corridor is technically a suburb, it shares many demographic characteristics with the inner-city: large numbers of single-parent families, low incomes, a high juvenile delinquency rate, constant turnover in population, government-subsidized housing, high-density high-rise buildings. When we think of inner cities, we tend to visualize the ghettos of the big cities— New York, Chicago, Detroit—with their garbage-strewn streets and smashed windows, derelicts lying in doorways, and whole sections deserted in the flight to the suburbs. These same suburbs, however, frequently produce new high-rise ghettos, and behind their facades of order and containment, conditions are beginning to parallel those horrors left behind in the cities. There is crime and vandalism and racial tension. Police form "beat patrols" and special "youth squads." Shopping malls spring up like fungi at every intersection, replacing neighborhoods with sterile parking lots.

The Jane-Finch Corridor lacks the cohesive presence of established cultural forms such as local bars, clubs, and church organizations, which would give the community a collective solidarity. Given the hard economic times, ethnicity often works as a divisive force, exacerbating community conflict in the area among East Indians, West Indians, Italians, Asians, and Caucasians. Although each group bears traces of its own sociopolitical and cultural history within its ethnic sensibility, each has become part of a social order that incorporates grave disparities in wealth between oppressed groups and groups within the dominant culture. To a large extent they are lost in the tapestry of the larger society—subjugated threads, tied tightly in an historical pattern of racism and oppression.

One is immediately struck by the vast sweep of shopping malls, parking lots, fields thick with hydroelectric towers, and row upon row of housing units. Bowling alleys and movie theatres are relatively scarce, and the recreational center unofficially reserves special nights for "blacks only" and "whites only."

There is an intergenerational continuity with respect to jobs and labor, which means that many working-class students in the area are slotted through the schooling process for working-class jobs in the nearby stores, factories, or fast food outlets.

Youths drink beer, smoke dope, shoot craps long into the night; they sometimes vandalize property and break into homes.

And they come to school. . . .

1966. At seventeen, I followed world events on my parents' old RCA Victor TV. For me, as for many Canadians, the world barely existed north of the 49th parallel. It had been an interesting year: President Johnson ordered the first major bombing raids against North Vietnam; Mariner 4 transmitted the first pictures from Mars; Malcolm X was gunned down at the Audubon Ballroom in New York City; Caesar Chavez voted against Delano, California, grape growers; Queen Elizabeth made each Beatle a member of the Order of the British Empire for bringing home the megabucks from the United States and the colonies; electrical failure blacked out the Northeastern states, causing a sudden boom in the birth rate.

I rarely ventured beyond the confines of what was considered "normal" for a straight-laced kid growing up in the protective custody of the Suburban Dream. My T-shirts were so white that they rivaled Tide commercials. I had tennis shoes that squeaked. Strapped to my Austin Mini was a roof rack for the surfboard I was always talking about buying but never did.

Secretly, however, I felt entombed in a world of routine banality, guilty for thinking thoughts darker than my beige chinos. My life was drifting laterally, waiting for something to happen. Anything. The future looked predictable and grim until the day I met Zeke.

That was the summer of 1966, after which the comforting veneer on my horizon was forever scraped away. He was sitting on a street curb under a willow tree, reading a Jack Kerouac novel. Beside him were a half-empty bottle of ninety-five cent wine and a huge battery radio. Zeke sat there with a Zen asceticism, stoically ignoring the passing traffic—a placid image despite his shock of neon red hair, electrical yellow shirt, navy blue industrial overalls, bottle-green rubber hipwaders supported by fuchsia suspenders, and wine-stained moustache.

I had seen him around the school. Everybody knew about Zeke. His eccentricity was strapped on like a codpiece; incessantly he stalked and challenged our cozy conventions.

For reasons I didn't yet understand, I wanted to know him.

When he noticed my gawking at him, he shifted from the lotus position and surveyed me intently through a homemade pair of glasses—like the x-ray glasses they used to advertise on the backs of Marvel comic books. As I approached him, he removed the glasses, stood up slowly, and stretched his arms. He was extremely tall, about six-four, and slightly Neanderthal. Brilliant red hair, a broad forehead, and fierce, tufted eyebrows dominated his other features: his eyes sanguine, grey-green, strange; his skin pockmarked and leathery. Though his appearance was imbued with confidence and just the slightest trace of haughtiness, he had an aura of premature decay, as though he were someone who had lived well beyond his nineteen years—an Ancient Mariner of Suburban Sidewalks.

"Have you read Pynchon?" he asked, holding up a tattered copy of *V.*

"I don't know him," I admitted.

"How about Genet? You must read *Our Lady of the Flowers.*"

"I'm not into Catholic literature," I shrugged.

"Well," he said, breaking into a beatific grin. "I can see you're uneducated. We'll just have to do something about that."

Zeke was my first nonconformist, part scoundrel, part saint. He taught me Greek dancing in the evenings, which we practiced for hours, guzzling back ouzo to a scratchy recording of the theme from *Zorba the Greek.* In the fifties, he would have been a coffee-cup anarchist, reading his poetry in espresso bars or smoke-filled taverns, accompanied by bongos, double-drums, and a real live black person in Cuban shades playing stand-up bass.

Zeke lent me dozens of books filled with strange antics and antiheroes— *Catch 22, The Gingerman, On the Road, One Flew over the Cuckoos' Nest,* and the poetry of François Villon. I began putting aside my homework. Each day I carried to school a copy of *Finnegan's Wake,* which I propped open in the cafeteria, trying hard to appear engrossed in the pages. Zeke considered pretension a fine art. He also valued the art of conversation. Even a brief discussion with Zeke was taking a chance on having your brain wrenched. He rarely talked *with* you—more often *at* you, trying to rearrange your thinking patterns in new ways. It could be a painful—or exhilarating—experience.

Though harassed on all sides by well-furnished, split-level suburban dormitories, manicured lawns, and parks with tennis courts, Zeke's place was my Greenwich Village, North Beach, Telegraph Hill, or Left Bank.

Bored by school, Zeke still attended regularly. For him, school was a stage—a burlesque ramp where he could intellectually strut his stuff. He liked to show up his English teachers—especially when it came to drama criticism—and put everyone on with his crazy antics. He both enraged and enchanted the staff by arriving late for class one day dressed in a black velvet opera cape with pearl buttons, wing collar, and large plump cravat, clutching his latest manuscript in a tattered manila envelope. A gilded walking stick hung from the crook of his arm. His cape billowing behind him, he swept into geometry class and gallantly saluted the teachers with a click of his hobnailed boots.

I had met no one like Zeke. His off-beat brilliance and Rabelaisian worldview helped allay the anomie and restlessness of a suburban youth growing up in the electronic age, whose body and spirit had been put on hold by the morals of the industrial age. Zeke belonged to a different world. He was always excited, his voice rising, hands waving in a state of continual incandescence. Zeke educated my senses, derailing the boredom of my daily existence, stirring me from my comfortable emotional anesthesia.

I soon found it impossible to keep up with my studies. It was too easy to put down a book or put off an assignment for the excitement of Zeke's company or of entering the renegade world to which Zeke had given me access. By comparison, school often seemed like an irrelevant intrusion that obstructed rather than furthered my education.

During the sixties, Toronto's Yorkville counterculture provided me with a strange and often bizarre reality. The maze of streets graced by old brownstone homes, the artists' lofts, the rooming houses, the cafes, the head shops populated with what sociologists referred to as "alienated youth," comprised what was, in a manner of speaking, my classroom away from school. I would often observe the street life from the Penny Farthing Cafe, a volume of Kafka or Beckett under my left arm and a walking stick hung from the crook of my right.

The perennial street crowd spanned all backgrounds; their movement was based not on social class but on the ethos of a generation. Poor kids from Cabbagetown and rich kids from Rosedale dealt dope on the street corners in jeans and army fatigues; preppie girls threw away their knee socks and kilts to roam the streets in jeans, copies of *The Prophet* clutched in their hands; weekenders from Upper Canada College donned sandals, leather vests, and green felt Robin Hood caps and gamboled to Jimi Hendrix and the Doors in between algebra assignments; Kresge cashiers were transformed into beautiful and mysterious Midnight Madonnas, wrapped in shroudlike medieval gowns, silver jewelry adorning their Pre-Raphaelite hair.

I spent considerable time with a variety of colorful and creative individuals whose lives bounced paradoxically between expressive rituals of emancipation and pathological rituals of self-destruction. Drugs became a part of many lives. For many, drugs seemed to serve as a symbolic medium to penetrate the contradictions between freedom and constraint in a society nourished by the myth that progress through technology is the only objective reality. Timothy Leary, the high priest of LSD, handed me a note at a concert: DIPLOMA, it read. YOU ARE NOW FREE.

I took a room downtown with Zeke and enrolled at the University of Toronto in 1968. Zeke made our "digs" a center of Dionysian excess. I often returned from class to find the record player blaring and the room a carnival of strangers: pushers, poster-makers, poets, mystics, draft dodgers, mimes, speed freaks, junkies, aesthetes, revolutionaries, jugglers, body builders, gardeners, go-go dancers, and university professors.

At sixteen I had ruled out ever working for a large corporation. My father had just turned fifty when the new owners of the electronics firm for which he was general manager decided to let go all executives over forty-five. I watched my father try one low-paying job after another; severe bouts of asthma and emphysema finally forced him into retirement and an early death. After that, I vowed always to stay clear of the business world.

During my senior year of high school, I had become disillusioned with lessons that seemed boring and pointless. I would imagine myself standing in front of a class and teaching the most impassioned lesson possible. With the arrogance of innocence and the inspiration of Zeke, I was sure I could become the consummate teacher.

I graduated from the university in the early seventies, hung up my love beads and my beloved fatigue jacket, festooned over the years with slogans and hand-stitched doves, and enrolled in Teachers' College.

My first job was in a wealthy village outside Toronto. Although I liked the students and enjoyed teaching, I felt expendable. These students, already favored with wealth and social power, would probably get by in the world in spite of their teachers; their affluent background almost assured them success in the system. I wanted to save working-class kids. Also, I wanted to enroll in graduate school in Toronto. My wife encouraged me to look for a job in the inner city. "That's where you'll feel most needed," she said. I handed in my resignation and began job hunting.

My new principal told me he thought I'd made the right choice. He welcomed me to the ranks of inner-city teachers, leading me into his office saying. "Just call me Fred." I relaxed immediately.

In his mid-forties, he had a disarming grin and a thick shock of grey hair that looked strangely out of character. The button on his shirt read "I'm the boss." It was clear that the button was a joke. "The excellent grades I see in your Teachers' College report won't matter much here in the jungle," he began. "This is the real world." He leaned over the desk. "I only have one criterion for hiring new teachers. Every kid in this school, and I mean each one, has the right to be loved. No matter how difficult the kid is, no matter how he or she drives you batty from the very first day . . . give them all the love and affection you can. When it feels too impossible, come and see me and we'll talk. All right, Peter? Now good luck, and we'll see you in the morning."

I left his office with a good feeling. I later learned that he was somewhat of a folk legend in the city. As the "hugging principal," he had a high success rate in creating an atmosphere of trust between teachers and students.

My tour of the school was conducted by Fred's secretary, who filled me in on all the latest school gossip as she led me past various classrooms, sketching portraits of the teachers inside. Usually, the reports were favorable, but there was always at least one complaint per teacher. When she remarked, "He always sends two of his kids down to the office with a pile of stencils to be run off late in the afternoon, when I'm busiest," I considered it a warning.

Later I ventured into the staff room. Several teachers were crammed into the tiny room, dutifully cleaning up the lunch dishes. A teacher was swearing at the broken Coke machine; it had just eaten several quarters. "How do they manage to break into our staff room and screw up our Coke machine?" he complained. "I thought the caretaker locked up after we leave!" He kicked the machine several times before finally giving up.

I introduced myself.

"We heard you were coming!" answered a voice near the sink. A big, rugged-looking man came over and introduced himself as the vice-principal, Rod. I shook his hand, which was still dripping with dishwater. "I suppose you'll manage just fine," he said, as he looked me over. "You've got youth on your side at least . . . doesn't he, John?" An elderly gentleman with a friendly smile came over and gave me a pat on the shoulder. "Watch out for John," the vice-principal warned. "He's one of those health nuts!"

"Just keep yourself in shape and you'll survive, young man. Look how long I've lasted, and I've been at this game for over forty years!"

"Got any trade secrets?" I asked.

John grinned. "Sure! B-6!"

"B-6?" Suddenly, I felt stupid.

"B-6! Vitamin B-6! Good for the nerves, you know!"

I was hired to replace a teacher who couldn't handle the pressure. Her class comprised seventeen grade five students, and nineteen grade sixes, ranging in age from eleven to thirteen. This was a "regular" class, as opposed to "special" classes for kids with severe learning problems. As in most of the classes, a third of the students were black, most of them from the West Indies.

They certainly hadn't accepted the teacher I was hired to replace. On one of her last days, all thirty-six students walked into her gym class, faced the far wall with their backs toward her, and refused to move. Several of the kids spit against the wall to punctuate their protest. I wasn't told why the kids were upset, and I decided not to ask.

My classroom was in a "portable" building, about fifty feet from the main building. It resembled one of those units you see in a documentary film from World War II (prefabricated, a year old, and beginning to decay).

The inside of the portable was cold and lifeless and looked more like a funeral parlor than a classroom. An old-fashioned roller blind filtered the winter sun, shining a dead green light over the empty desks. There was only one picture on the wall: a washed out, glue-streaked poster advocating dental hygiene. The girl on the poster had freckles and a pigtail and the boy was wearing a brushcut. It could have sold as an antique at a flea-market. In comparison with the furniture in the main building, the desks and chairs of my portable looked like they had been scrounged from some storage warehouse for junked school furniture of the 1940s. Desks were hacked and gouged, while the wobbly chairs were often equipped with only three legs. The green blackboard was in such poor condition that you almost had to chisel letters onto it.

I can't recall many details from my first morning of actually working with my kids. I tried to ignore their individual differences and treat them as one giant, uniform mass. I felt that if I lumped them into a single personality, I would be less overwhelmed.

Things went reasonably well during the first part of the morning (that is, if failing to remember most of what happened is synonymous with success). I was riding much too high to pay close attention to what I was doing. But when the first recess bell sounded, I received my inner-city initiation.

There was a concussive sound of glass breaking. Every window on the north side of my portable was smashed, simultaneously. The rest of the day I remember well. I had to teach it in my woolen toque and Hudson's Bay blanket coat, while the kids murmured and laughed with nervous excitement, crouching next to the heat vents, which to their delight squeaked loudly. "Hey, this is neat!" one of the kids yelled.

CHAPTER **1**

The Frontiers of Despair

Monday, January 3

The first day I started my initial lesson on "People and Society" by asking the kids what they wanted and expected from the course. Silence.

"Okay," I continued, undismayed, "let's try it this way. How many of you are interested in what goes on in the world today—the problems, the politics, the environment, the media, the job market—that sort of thing?"

Nothing. Blank eyes.

"Well," I went on, determined, with more than a small measure of arrogance, "I'm giving you kids the chance to choose the topic for yourselves. Can you hear me over there? What will it be?! Pollution? War? More rights for kids? How about some ideas for projects you want to do?"

No cheers. No boos. Not even a yawn.

I was almost shouting now in frustration. "What is it with you kids, anyway? If you can't think for yourselves, you might as well join the army where there are plenty of orders and few decisions."

Nothing.

Great, I thought to myself. *This is going nowhere.* Maybe I'm expecting too much. Just when I thought everybody had been sworn to a conspiracy of silence, a kid wearing a Maple Leaf hockey sweater raised his hand. I felt like hugging him and called on him eagerly.

He wanted to know why I wore a beard.

Friday, January 7

I eagerly awaited picking up my mail from my personal mailbox during my first trip to the office.

Once inside the office, I saw a student lying on the bench. His knees were raised to his chest, his arms holding them tight; he looked like a pale fetus. A second glance revealed a glint of metal protruding from behind one of his ears. I looked closer. There was a heavy steel dart lodged just above his ear.

The boy responsible for throwing the dart was sitting in the vice-principal's office.

Apparently feeling no remorse, the kid remarked to a teacher who was watching. "He's just lucky I didn't hit him where I was aimin' for!" There were no abject tears.

I stuck my head through the door to get a better view. His feet up on the vice-principal's desk, and his face split by an enormous yawn, he bellowed. "Who are you, sucker? Are you new? You want a dart in your head? Hahaha . . . !"

Tuesday, January 11

The first day I was posted inside the main building on stair duty, they hit me from above. Ten or more kids spitting in unison. From the highest platform of the stairwell, the gobs of saliva picked up velocity by the time they reached my head. And if I looked up to identify the owners, my face would offer an even more tempting target. I could feel my hair growing damp as I descended.

I gathered together some of the teachers, and formed a plan. Some of us stood under stairwells at each recess, trying to inveigle the spit-kings to reappear, while other teachers crouched hidden, ready to surprise them.

We weren't able to catch them in the act. I began wearing a washable broad-rimmed hat.

Friday, January 14

Levon arrived in the class this morning after recess—a transfer from another inner-city school.

Just before lunch, he was hit on the head by a flying book. I decided he could use a Band-Aid.

"Sanjay," I called out. "Will you please take Levon to the nurse's office?"

"Sanjay couldn't find his asshole with a roadmap," Duke interjected.

"I'll take him there," Winston volunteered.

"No! I will!" Spinner blurted out.

"Let me sir, please!" Taiwo insisted.

Before long, half the class marched out of the portable.

"It didn't need no Band-Aid," Levon said when he returned with the others after only fifteen minutes.

About two hours later, he complained of an upset stomach, and asked if somebody could show him to the nurse's office.

"But half the class took you there just a few hours ago," I reminded him. "Have you forgotten where it is already?"

"Oh, ya," Levon said with a wry smile on his lips. "That was only to show me the best place to grab a quick smoke."

Tuesday, January 18

One of the more colorful characters around the school is a twelve-year-old named Buddy. Hated and feared—sometimes loved—Buddy literally runs the school, a role he plays with the virtuosity of an artist. He is a master technician when it comes to creating his own image. At a moment's notice he can become Lover, Fighter, Revenger, Champion of Freedom, King of the Sidewalks, or Defender of the Dance. Everything and everyone is a point of reference for his act.

The kids in the school accord Buddy demigod rank. When he walks down the corridor and says "Move over!" the kids move, fast! His voice is rarely loud, but it has a way of slicing through the air like cold steel.

The teachers treat Buddy with a subtle deference. Any attempt at confrontation makes them nervous. He's only twelve, but he can immobilize you with a glance, quickening the breath, causing the heart to pound.

Some of the teachers have no compunctions about treating kids roughly, if they have to. Yet Buddy could panic a whole school full of teachers. There are even warnings over the public address system when he's out of control. He is ours, and for a variety of technical reasons, we keep him in school instead of tossing him out onto the unsuspecting world. We contain him, but we are all afraid of him.

Buddy has an aggravating habit of fingering marbles, a bit like Captain Queeg in *The Caine Mutiny*. He rolls them unconsciously between his thumb and fingers like worry beads, sometimes shaking them fiercely in a loosely clenched palm as a rattlesnake-like warning that he is about to strike.

Buddy is allowed to "float." Floaters roam the halls at will, and are ignored as long as they don't leave the school building. To qualify as a floater, you have to be incorrigible, but in a soft, almost understated way. You have to conceal your violent behavior, saving it for strategic showdowns. Otherwise, the administration would send you away, to the "outside" or to another school.

Buddy spends most of the day wandering the halls with another floater called Puppy (so named because he's the youngest in his family). Buddy and Puppy spend their time window-shopping different classrooms for interesting things to do, always finding ways of breaking the monotony. They visit classrooms which have attractive girls, or they take karate lessons from the caretaker, or they catch a drag in the washroom.

Fred warned us that Buddy might appear unexpectedly in our classrooms. We were encouraged—coached—to respond in a highly positive way to any friendly gestures he might make. If you were lucky, Buddy would soon tire of you and float off somewhere else.

When you were teaching a class, it was unnerving to see Buddy pause at your doorway. He wore black boots, colorful dashikis, tight black cords. The flared bottoms of his pants had been lengthened numerous times. He was big and getting bigger. His muscular build made him a star attraction, and he seemed to walk an inch off the ground to the beat of an invisible tune. He was always in motion, often gesturing lewdly to Puppy. The first iron-clad rule when Buddy showed up was to appear to be in the middle of a boring lesson. The second rule: never turn on your record player—he tracked down music like a bloodhound—as long as there was music, he'd hang around.

When he wasn't floating, Buddy was in a special program for slow learners called a "developmental" class. Mr. Bailey, a good natured Welshman, ran it. Buddy's floating embarrassed him, and he decided to boost his reputation by trying to win Buddy back into the class for at least one day a week. Giving him more responsibility might be just the thing. Once, Mr. Bailey decided to try leaving Buddy in charge of the class while he left to run off some stencils—a last-ditch attempt by a desperate teacher to give Buddy a feeling of self-worth. It was a risky venture, and when Mr. Bailey returned the first thing he noticed was the blood on a student's swollen lip.

Once I thought that I could keep Buddy away with the raw force of purely negative emotion. Whenever I caught him standing outside my door, I would dilate my nostrils or curl my lips ever so slightly—just enough for him to pick up my hostility and leave.

But Buddy was a master of the unspoken. He talked with his eyes, or by moistening his lips, or casually mopping his brow. His favorite gesture was to yawn loudly. Today, when I dilated and curled, he walked to the front of the room and picked his rear end nonchalantly. The class howled.

He also ran a protection racket. He would walk up to a kid in a corridor and say "Hey dude, how ya doin'?" Then his lackeys would grab the kid from behind and drag him into the nearest washroom. Once inside, they would threaten to rearrange an arm, leg, or a face unless money was "donated" to Buddy the next day. In the case of small children, Buddy insisted they bring him the green pieces of paper that mommy kept in her purse.

In a month or so, Buddy's empire confiscated well over a hundred dollars. By then the police had been called in to halt the racket.

"Where do you live?" one of the cops demanded of Buddy as they hauled him away. "We'll take you home."

Buddy smiled, then slowly pursed his lips. "Take me to Nova Scotia."

Thursday, January 20

Ruth is exceptionally tall and good-looking. Her expression reminds me of a thin Elvis. She's always raising her hand to be excused. When I asked her why she had to go to the bathroom so often, she told me it was due to "personal problems."

When I asked her if she had seen a doctor about the problem, she said no, it was a "women's problem," and to "mind my own business!" I replied that doctors knew all about "women's problems," that many doctors are women.

I sent her down to see the school nurse. It appeared that Ruth was pregnant.

Monday, January 24

Duke stands out in class. He wears black boots, tight pants, and a shiny, red calypso shirt. Sometimes an old porkpie hat is balanced precariously on his black mountain of hair. If he feels like it, he'll come into class wearing a woolen beret. Sometimes he tucks the beret into the epaulet of his safari jacket and salutes the flag in mock respect. He is what his schoolmates refer to as a "classic dude."

During the first week, Duke kept silent, sometimes catnapping at his desk. Occasionally he'd shift his body around to check out the room.

Today I got fed up with his sleeping during a lesson I'd worked particularly hard to prepare. I asked the kid next to him to wake Duke up. The kid touched him on the shoulder gingerly, as if he were disarming a bomb.

Suddenly Duke shot up from his chair, shouting: "Jesus! Don't do that, man, or I'll break your ass!" He was out the door in an instant.

I didn't see him until the end of the day. He said he fell asleep on the park bench.

Wednesday, January 26

From the beginning of the year it was obvious that Barry worshipped Duke as a hero.

He admired his fighting ability—and was equally terrified of it. He toadied to Duke, fussing around him, running errands for him.

His admiration shot up as he watched Duke fight Sam. Duke hooked Sam with a left, then staggered him with a haymaker. Sam's mouth filled with blood, and he spit out bits of teeth.

Duke was a serious street-fighter, the star attraction for the school's would-be pugilists.

One day Duke turned on Barry. It was for no apparent reason, other than a lark—something to amuse Duke's other followers.

"The best way to teach you how to fight is to beat the shit out of you. Right?" Duke said, leering at Barry.

Barry cowered in terror. "Come on, Duke! Please!"

Duke walked closer to him.

"Stay back, Duke! Please! Just tell me what to do!" Barry pleaded in a plaintive, pitiful whine.

Duke drew his arm back slowly, his fist clenched. He stood inches from Barry, ready to let fly.

"*I'll* do it for you, Duke! Here, *I'll* do it!" Barry screamed. Suddenly he grabbed his metal lunchbox, raised it over his head, then brought it down hard on his skull. There was a loud *crack*. He hit himself several times, until his lunchbox was hopelessly battered and blood trickled down his forehead.

"Okay, Duke? Okay?" Barry yelled.

Delirious and in tears, he found me in my classroom, and told me what happened.

Duke remarked that he didn't even throw a punch and still did all that damage.

"He did it all to himself, man," Duke said, when I questioned him. "He's some kind of nut."

Monday, January 31

Everybody called Francine "Muscle Lady." When she flexed her eleven-year-old's biceps, eyeballs popped. Boys became jealous.

Muscle Lady wore a Superman tee shirt to school with a plastic tiger's tooth hung from a piece of thread around her neck. She always wore jeans with the legs turned up over her cowboy boots. When she walked by, you identified her by the sound of the clicking tacks she shoved into the heels of her boots.

Muscle Lady loved to fight—boys especially. But boys didn't want anything to do with her outside of having sex with somebody that tough. It was not only painful but humiliating when Muscle Lady had you pinned by the neck with her boot, then bragged to the onlookers, "Should I cut off his balls?" If the crowd gave a "thumbs down" (which it usually did), Muscle Lady had been known to grind down her heel.

The word was out: If Muscle Lady has your nuts in her sights, wear your steel hockey cup to school.

Tuesday, February 1

I was green: suffered from naivete and cultural myopia.

I obtained an 8mm movie about World War II from a United Church clergyman. I had no idea where he got it, but I jumped at using it with my class.

The film was overpowering. One section in particular, featuring Nazi war atrocities, revealed the terrible legacy of the Holocaust. All that I told the students was that the film was about war, and that it was real footage—not actors playing roles.

As they watched the film, I watched their expressions. I waited expectantly for the sequence that showed Nazis carting dead bodies toward an open grave. I had no idea what the kids were thinking. Finally, the long unusual silence shattered when a student cried out: "Stop the film!"

I felt that the film had done its work: these children, now and hereafter, would understand the horrors of war.

I switched off the projector, ready to open up a discussion on the brutality of war. But the same voice in the darkness snapped: "Turn the film backwards. Show that last part again. Did you see the arm falling off that body? Let's see it again!"

Wednesday, February 2

It was the end of another boring school day. Duke, the tough dude, sauntered through the teachers' parking lot, sipping on a Coke, and smoking. His after-school stroll often became the occasion for an impromptu gathering of his followers. Hordes of students would sometimes trail behind him, shouting "Hey, Duke!" or rhythmically chanting his name: "Duke . . . Duke . . ." Even teachers hailed him. His manner was always engaging, familiar: "Hiya pal. Whaddya say, baby?"

Everybody gathered around him, always careful not to crowd him.

"Hey, Duke!"

"Who ya punched out lately?"

"Hey Duke, whose pants you been into this week?"

Today Duke was ordered off the school property for a few days: he had cracked a kindergarten kid in the face with his fist, pushed him headfirst into the fence. Then he had stomped on his face.

When Fred phoned to explain that Duke could not return to the schoolyard, his older sister answered. She promised she'd take care of him and keep him inside, but as soon as he walked through the door, she told him to get lost.

So he decided to wander down to the bicycle paths and torment some of the kindergarten kids there. Many passed that way after school. He caught two boys who were running home and tripped them, pinching their ears. He tried to pull their pants down, taunting them in a whining voice: "Daddy's goin' to give ya a beatin'! Do what the daddy says! Be good little boys, and daddy won't beat ya no more!" Resistant students were slammed to the ground. When Duke's mother returned home from work and heard what had happened, she waited for him with her hairbrush.

The next day, the parents of the injured children reported Duke; the incident was investigated. He was suspended from school for a week, and his mother was given the name of a social agency she should contact.

When he returned to school, he was met as if he were an exiled king who had finally returned to lead his people into battle.

"Hey, Duke baby!"

"Whaddya say!"

"Hey hey, the man is back!"

Monday, February 7

My teaching methods don't seem to be going over as well as I'd hoped; a lot of the kids are resistant to my lessons. I can't believe how defiant of authority these kids are—and they're only grades five and six! When I decided to swallow a little of my pride and ask for help, I went to see Fred.

"My lessons don't seem to be capturing the kids' attention," I told him, "even though they're right out of the latest books and programs available."

Fred laced his fingers behind his head, leaning back in his chair. "Peter, you know that even the most up-to-date textbooks are still only textbooks. Mostly our texts have middle-class settings that are irrelevant to our kids. Try some role-playing. It's a good technique with our kids. They like to act out situations. Ham it up, then see what you get."

The next day I proposed the idea to my class. Tina and Sandra volunteered at once to improvise a skit.

"What do you want to do it on?" I asked, noting happily how eager they seemed.

"Let's pretend I'm the husband," Tina suggested, "and this classroom is our apartment, and Sandra is my wife."

"Okay," Sandra agreed.

"I've just got home from work, and I find out you drank my case of beer. But you were supposd to do all the housework, see? Now you gotta explain why you didn't do no housework, and why you're drunk. Ready?"

As the rest of the class watched intently, Tina walked out of the room. She closed the door behind her, then knocked loudly. Sandra answered the door wearing a scowl on her face, pretending to be drunk. Tina stepped into the room, her arms held out in greeting.

"I'm home, honey," she called, trying to embrace a resistant Sandra. "I'm so glad to come home to a clean house for a change!" She paused, looking around. "What are my clothes doing on the sofa? Your breath stinks of booze!" Tina pretended to shout, without really raising her voice. "Why are last night's dishes still piled in the sink? I oughta slap you silly."

"Why dontchya go to the track tonight?" Sandra mumbled, slurring her words. "Lemme alone. There's a good program on TV, and I don't wanna be disturbed."

"Disturb you! Why would I wanna do that?" quipped Tina. "Looks like nobody has disturbed you yet today! Why should I be different? Jus look at all those beer bottles on the floor! Get dressed and pick up this mess and fix me somethin' to eat. Go on—move it!"

"Make it yourself!" Sandra snapped.

At this point, Tina was pretending to pick up the empty bottles and throw them away. "Jus' look at this place! It's a pig sty!"

With that remark, Sandra pretended to hit Tina on the head with a beer bottle. Tina responded by fighting right back, faking slaps at Sandra and screaming, "You good-for-nothin' drunk! Why'd I marry you in the first place?"

Thursday, February 10

Kids often reveal a bizarre sense of humor—they enjoy trying to make teachers retch with sick jokes and peculiar antics. I understood all that; I'd met lots of adults at parties who enjoyed doing exactly the same things. That's why I didn't think twice about Barry's jokes. I'd heard similar ones before.

For example, Barry would stroll into the classroom and ask me: "What do ya get when you take the wings off a fly?"

Before I could reply, he'd shoot back: "A walk, stupid! Hahaha!"

He once asked me: "What goes ha-ha clunk?"

"Don't know, Barry. What?"

"A man laughing his head off! Hahahaha!"

I almost started to appreciate Barry's sense of humor until a reliable source informed me that, after school, Barry sometimes strangled cats.

Friday, February 11

Duke removed his winter coat and threw it on his desk. He was shirtless, dressed in overalls. He slumped down in his chair, munching on a sandwich.

At Teachers' College they told us to lay down the rules on the very first day and stick to them.

"There's no eating in the room, so put away the sandwich."

Duke shut his eyes, nodded his head knowingly, and said softly (but not so softly that I couldn't hear), "It figures."

But he didn't leave it at that. "I ain't had breakfast, so I'm just fillin' up early on my lunch." He studied my reaction with cool disdain.

I looked at him angrily. He went on eating.

"What do you mean?" I asked, uneasily, annoyed that he'd triggered off such a strong reaction in me. What was really bothering me was that I didn't know if he was putting me on or not. Maybe he *was* being sincere.

"Just gimme two seconds," he promised, his mouth crammed with salami. "There . . . only one bite left," he mumbled, chewing hungrily. Then he smiled: "All gone! Now what was so bad about that?"

I closed my eyes, shook my head, indicating that I wasn't to be questioned further. There was an uneasy silence.

"Listen," I said, putting an end to the awkward moment. "It's all right."

He looked at me, then nodded impertinently. "Thanks, man. You can relax now, right?"

By the end of the day an eerie, engulfing sense of panic swept over me.

"What the hell are you doing here?" That was the question a voice in my head kept repeating.

I crossed the parking lot quickly, anxious to get home. Several kids who were playing on the roof of my van jumped off as soon as I approached. For a few minutes I just sat inside, staring through the windshield at the steel-grey sky, the windswept grey high-rises towering in the distance. Everything seemed a mixture of white and black or in between—not a spot of color in the entire landscape. The moon's surface probably had more charm than this.

When I reached home I was greeted by my nine-year-old stepdaughter, Laura, her eyes blinking happily behind a pair of fluorescent cardboard glasses.

"How was school today?" I asked.

"Just great, dad!" she exclaimed. "Everybody got to make a pair of these glasses in art. The teacher bought all the material."

I nodded, then asked her, "How do the kids in your class behave?"

"Everybody does what the teacher tells them to, pretty well. Nobody even talks in class without the teacher's permission."

"Nobody even talks," I echoed blankly.

Laura groaned. "You're acting funny these days, Dad."

That evening I fell asleep at the kitchen table. Laura claims she saved me from drowning in my soup. Somehow, Jenny managed to drag me to bed.

Monday, February 14

Teaching for a year in junior high school in a wealthy neighborhood had been relatively problem free; disciplinary problems were few. My teaching style had been calm and friendly, and I rarely had reason to lose my temper. In a very short time, I realized that my present school was another matter entirely. I would have to change my approach, since the kids either ignored me completely or else went to the other extreme, continually interrupting my lessons. Soon I was shouting, trying to get my lessons heard over the din. I threatened kids with after-school work or detentions if they didn't settle down.

But I found it repulsive to act "the heavy." The kids sensed my authoritarian image was merely a tactic, and called my bluff. When a class enjoys wearing down the patience of its teacher, all that is necessary is a hint that the teacher is out of control. Then the students move in for the kill.

Since my attempts at control were backfiring, I decided to try another approach. I did a John Wayne in *The Green Berets*, pacing in front of the class and barking orders:

"Sit up straight and tall!"

"Tuck in that shirt!"

"Eyes front!"

I didn't quite make it as the hard-boiled drill instructor, berating the kids into subservience on the theory that a good soldier obeys on reflex. That method got a few laughs, but not much else.

Sometimes I tried being a tough but kindly TV detective: "Get those lessons done, kids, on accounta they're an important part of growin' up!"

"Reading will keep you off the streets, outta trouble, and outta the slammer!"

The kids sensed I was strange.

Tuesday, February 15

After the class returned from gym, I asked them what improvements they'd like to see me make in the classroom.

"You ain't gonna leave the room like that bitch had it?" Duke asked, cocking his head to one side.

"What was wrong with the room?"

"We didn't like the set-up!" he barked back. "We didn't like havin' no spare time! It was always work."

Levon stood up and walked to the back of the room, with a ruler stuck out of his open fly. "We wanna teacher with big boobs!"

Marianne, one of my West Indian girls, rose out of her chair. "We wants a black teacher!"

"A black teacher with big boobs!" Levon cut in.

"Naa!" someone else cried. "Who wants a fuzz-top for a teacher?"

"When are we gonna play floor hockey?"

"What about field trips?"

"Can we play records in class?"

For the rest of the day, I was swamped with questions. For me, the questions themselves were part of the solution. The kids were coming out of their shells, testing me out, airing some of their frustrations.

Any reasonable suggestion, I made a note of, and tried to do something about.

It was too early to know what they made of me, but I was confident that with time, they would grow to respect me.

Wednesday, February 16

Duke and Al paired off cautiously. From an upper window, I saw what looked like the entire school population in the main yard, surrounding the two fighters. The crowd was bouyant and talkative. Students jerked, twisted, strained in gleeful anticipation of the bout. I started at once for the stairs.

The shouting got louder and louder, the excitement feeding on itself, swelling with hoots and whistles.

"Kill him!"

"Break the sonofabitch's balls!"

"Punch his eyes out!"

Fever-pitch wails burst through the yard. Drops of bright red blood spattered the pavement.

Duke's foot shot out in a blur. Al coughed and gagged, dropping to his knees. "Ya goddam motherfucker!"

Smooth as a cobra, Duke took a short step forward. "Fuckin' nigger bastard!" A lightning kick to the solar plexus. The crowd screamed for more blood . . . my commands to stop were lost in the roar.

This time Al fell screaming on his side. A hard kick in the ribs as he tried to raise himself up. Another. Four kicks to the head. Al's eyes rolled up. To break up the fight, I plowed my way through the eager crowd.

Thursday, February 17

I don't like looking out the windows of my portable. The view is too bleak: an inner ring of identical bungalows, an outer perimeter of ugly high-rises. The small park near the school serves as only a partial buffer against the impersonal, almost anonymous, surroundings.

During roll call, I realized that over half my class had the same address—a large government-subsidized building nicknamed "The Jungle" by some teachers. Only one student lived in a "regular" house, and only a few lived in the public complex of townhouses.

I asked my kids what they did with their free time.

"Play in the laundromat until the super kicks us out."

"Go to the arcade at Food City."

"Ride the elevator."

"Me and Buddy," Levon offered eagerly, "watch the teenagers screw each other in the basement."

Fred once mentioned to me, "The only thing worse than being poor is being poor in the suburbs."

Friday, February 18

Nearby is a Catholic school that the kids call St. Welfare. One morning last week, Levon crawled through a hole in the fence and crept up to a window. He watched the students going through the morning's opening exercises, and when he finally showed up in *my* class, he described them in detail.

"The whole class started to pray all at once to this cross on the wall. But there were some guys at the back of the room who were playin' with hockey cards—the teacher didn't see 'em 'cause her eyes was closed. Hey, sir. Why don't them Catholic teachers pray with their eyes open?" He grinned, and scratched his head. "Anyway, sir, how come them Catholic kids get to talk to God, and we don't?"

Levon's last remark caught me a bit off guard. I quietly retreated to my desk, stalling for time.

"Well . . ." I hesitated, "we don't say prayers in class because this is a public school, and kids come here belonging to different religions. Some people have different ideas about God, and some people don't believe in God at all."

Levon looked puzzled, but he shrugged. "Who cares about talkin' to God, anyway? I heard this story from a lady in my buildin' that God was born in a barn, with a bunch of cows and donkeys, and she says He slept on some straw on the floor. Is God really on welfare?"

Monday, February 21

When I was teaching junior high, I had set foot in the principal's office only once. I had been put on the carpet because I had allowed some of my students to call me by my first name.

Fred's office, on the other hand, was a place where I spent considerably more time—but for different reasons. Fred kept his office open so teachers could use it whenever it was free.

Because Fred did most of his paperwork in the staff room, teachers could use his office for phone calls, or help themselves to the stacks of educational books and journals he stashed in a big box in the corner marked "Free." He had also replaced the standard-issue grey desk with a pine coffee table, as well as replacing his chrome and vinyl chair with a Boston rocker. One wall of his office was entirely devoted to children's art.

Teachers often went to his office simply to relax.

The vice-principal's office was right next door. Rod had the same open-door policy, but he spent more time in his office, so it wasn't as available to the teachers.

Today when I stepped inside Rod's office to use the phone, I found him sitting in his chair, calmly holding a struggling black kid.

"Would you mind watching this guy for me while I go get a coffee? I'm bushed. He went berserk in Mrs. Rogers' room. Just make sure he doesn't get out the door."

After Rod left, the kid simply smiled and quietly sat down in a chair in the corner of the office. I sat down in Rod's chair, picked up a magazine, and started skimming pages, the phone call temporarily delayed.

Without warning, I was knocked right out of my chair by a blow from behind. I looked up from the floor to see the kid standing over me waving a hockey stick!

I got to my knees, propping myself up on the arm of the chair, but before I made it to my feet the kid yanked the chair away, and I fell back on the floor.

"Vanilla trash," the kid snarled, and ran out the door.

Rod came back into his office a few minutes later to find me alone, tucking my shirt in and rubbing my sore, throbbing neck.

"Let me guess," Rod said. "You let him escape."

Tuesday, February 22

Each day the buildup in my mailbox grew. Curriculum materials, surveys, advertisements for curriculum materials, and surveys to establish an advertising policy. Subject guidelines, policy guidelines, guidelines for guidelines—it seemed endless.

At first, in my naivete, I thought everything was important and actually read it all. Somehow the educational system was nourished by all these forms and papers. However, I soon realized that I'd receive something worthwhile no more than once a week. Teachers, I learned, referred to mailbox buildup as "Administrivia."

One day, feeling particularly wretched, I simply picked up the latest pile of papers and dumped them all into the wastebasket.

"Hey," a seasoned veteran exclaimed, "you'd make a great principal."

Thursday, February 24

In spite of the fact that Ricky got on my nerves, I wouldn't call his parents for help when he got into trouble.

It was too possible that what Ricky said was true . . . that when his parents heard he had done something wrong, they strapped him on top of the dining room table and, taking turns with a belt, beat him.

Friday, February 25

Kids called Marianne "Big Mama."

She was a giant of a girl with the most beautiful braids I had ever seen. The top of her head looked like a black patch-work quilt with white stitching. Her mother had given her a button which she wore proudly. It read: "Kid for Rent (cheap)."

She became a legend one day by giving Duke an unprecedented defeat by knocking him off his feet with a swoop of her huge hand, and then sitting on his chest until he almost turned blue.

There was little sexual stereotyping in my class.

Saturday, February 26

Jenny and I decided to do some shopping at a plaza in the corridor.

Packed into the Miracle Mart, Food City, and Dominion stores were Italian mothers in black kerchiefs, West Indian families in matching dashikis, teenagers chasing each other through the aisles, and scores of young kids at the pinball machines.

As we were going out I spotted four of my students hanging out in the parking lot. Duke and Jackson were wobbling and slurring their words. Dave was sneezing violently, and Lisa was laughing, hiding her face. Duke had a smaller, frightened kid backed into a corner, cold-bloodedly trying to provoke a fight. They all looked very high on something.

"Is this what you kids do on weekends?" I asked, giving the frightened kid a chance to run away.

"We're not *kids* on the weekend," Jackson said. "On the weekend, we're the Dukes!"

Tuesday, March 1

The teachers were all crowded around a notice posted on the staff bulletin board. It was the new yard duty schedule, still smelling from duplicating fluid. Because I had been hired in midyear, my name hadn't appeared on the first list. That oversight had now, unfortunately, been corrected.

Yard duty meant the entire school population at once—more than six hundred crowded together at recess in a mass of swirling bodies.

Near the main entrance, a group of kids huddled under a blanket, trying to walk in unison. They managed to make this giant insect move only a few feet at a time before they tripped all over each other's legs. Across the yard, a group of kids stood around the drinking fountain. A tiny kindergarten kid was pushed against the metal water faucet.

I ran across the yard, but was too late. I had two girls from my class take the kid to the office to have his bleeding gums looked after. Meanwhile, kids played marbles or made bets on which way baseball cards flung against the wall would land.

A kid with a frantic look led me to the other side of the yard where I found a little six-year-old girl tied to the fence. She was being swatted across the legs by an older boy armed with a tree branch. When I grabbed the boy, he sneered defiantly, "Whatta ya doin'! Eh? She's my sister, ya know! I can do what the fuck I like with her!" and then he took off like a rocket. I untied her, and my two girls led her inside the school.

When the bell sounded, I thanked God.

Thursday, March 3

When I return home from work I usually go directly into the den and close the door. I prefer not to talk to anyone. I had halfheartedly started working on a series of children's stories that were about the real world as opposed to the world of magic and make-believe, but after about an hour that depressed me, too. My one outlet is playing a bottleneck guitar after some of the Delta blues artists who played out of the Mississippi region in the early 1920s. It gives me a tremendous emotional release.

Monday, March 7

After a few weeks of trying to teach my kids according to the Ministry guidelines and the approaches I had been taught in my teacher training, I knew that I would either have to change my entire approach or sacrifice my stomach. My health had been suffering. I continually caught colds, had dizzy spells, stomach cramps. I sometimes threw up in the staff washroom after a hard day.

I decided to enroll in a master's program in education, even if it was only part-time. For two evenings a week I would study the sociology of poverty, as well as child management.

Fred was glad that I showed concern, but he disagreed with my strategy: "You *already* know these kids are poor," he told me patiently. "You *already* know most of them come from single-parent families, and you *already* know that a great majority of them are beaten up at home. So what's a university course going to teach you?"

Wednesday, March 9

I was anxious to get some ideas about teaching from the rest of the staff, and I looked forward to our lunchtime conversations in the staff room.

The room itself was starting to look interesting. Some of the teachers were redecorating it, trying to achieve a coffeehouse atmosphere. Hieronymous Bosch prints hung on the walls, and the shell of an old radio was placed over the intercom speaker. The librarian fitted the tables with plastic checkered tablecloths, and volunteers (kids included) brought in empty wine bottles to hold candles. One teacher described it as "creating a buffer."

This afternoon I took a seat beside a teacher I hadn't seen before. She introduced herself as a supply teacher who had been working the area for a while. I was struck by how much she looked the caricature of the spinster teacher: hair in a bun, horn-rimmed glasses, worn tweed jacket. She reminded me of the middle-aged women I saw in church when I was a child. "How do you like being an inner-city teacher?" she asked.

"Things are getting easier," I replied. "I'm doing a lot of reading . . . trying to discover some new ideas. By the way, what kind of approaches do *you* use with the kids? Maybe we can exchange ideas."

She cleared her throat, looking down at her lunch, smiling. "There *is* one thing that I find helps me make it through the day," she said softly.

"Yes?"

"I never talk about the kids during lunch."

Thursday, March 10

Jabeka had a pile of letters on her desk that her mother asked her to mail, three of which were addressed to relatives in Spanish Town, Jamaica.

"Have you been back to visit since you've come to Canada?" I asked her.

"Are you kidding, Mr. McLaren?" she replied. "My father is in Jamaica and no way do I want to see him. My mother don't want to see him, no way. Ever since we came here, my dad don't bother callin' us. He never writes no letters, or calls collect on the phone—not even Christmas."

"How long have you been away from your father?"

"Five years. I got a stepdad now. He's got two kids who live with his other wife next to Food City. His wife's got a boyfriend named Mr. Jimmy who's got three kids. Mr. Jimmy buys all the best food for his own kids."

"What does your real father do in Jamaica?" I asked, trying to maintain a casual tone.

"He lives with his girlfriend. I gots two other brothers there but they don't live with my dad. They lives with my grandmother—you know, my dad's mother."

"So you never see your other brothers?"

"Last time I was in Jamaica, and then me and my mother moved away, I went to visit my grandmother and she told me to go back to where I belong."

"Where was that, Jabeka?"

"How the hell am I supposed to know? With my mother, I guess."

"So your parents split up before you came to Canada?"

"Yah. I still want to visit my dad sometimes. He likes me more than his girlfriend because when we was coming back from shopping he told his girlfriend to get off his motorcycle and he put me on the back."

"Do you have any other brothers and sisters living with you?"

"I got a younger brother and a younger sister. I don't know if they come from my real dad, but my mom says they're my brothers. My stepdad and my mom just made a baby, but it's not born yet."

"Are you glad you came to Canada, Jabeka?"

"Yah," she replied. "We never had colored TV in Spanish Town."

Monday, March 14

During recess, Spinner and Duke, opponents in ball hockey, started to argue over whether or not to allow a last-minute goal. Duke decided to settle the issue by cracking Spinner in the mouth. Spinner reeled backwards, knees buckling. Duke kicked him in the groin as he fell.

His moans were heard by the teacher on yard duty, and he was taken to the hospital with a bleeding penis.

Spinner's mother showed up at the school later that afternoon. "Show me Duke!" she demanded.

A tiny kid wearing a mass of dreadlocks said, "There!," and pointed to the open gym doors. After taking a huge drag on her cigarette, Spinner's mother suddenly bolted down the corridor after Duke.

I ran to stop her.

She caught up to Duke in time to drag him to the floor and punch him. I managed to get between them. Then I calmed Spinner's mom down. Duke hadn't been injured.

"He got what was coming to him!" she told me triumphantly.

Rod took Spinner's mother into the office, and I turned to Duke. "How're you feeling?" I asked him.

"Okay," Duke said, panting. "Okay. Nothin's busted. Shee-it! What a suck that Spinner is—sendin' his momma over to take care of his own business."

Tuesday, March 15

An announcement came over the public address system regarding a potluck luncheon for the teachers.

"Potluck, eh?" Ricky mused. "What's you bringin', sir?"

"Pot or hash?" Duke called out.

"My brother's got some dynamite Colombian at home! You want some?" Spinner volunteered.

Wednesday, March 16

The lunch bell sounded.

Children exploded from the doors and poured into the halls. Unresolved arguments that had accumulated during the morning were now settled with fists. The air was thick with screams, shouts, and well-chosen obscenities. A contingent of teachers and lunchroom supervisors waded through tiny human walls, challenging kids who refused to leave the halls. "I gotta wait for my mom!" "My teacher said I don't got to leave!" "I gotta wait for my little sister!" The excuses sounded convincing.

Kids screamed louder and louder while balls, paper airplanes, and plastic hockey pucks flew through the air.

A teacher with hair swarming over her head, her kids swarming over her classroom, ran out the door in tears. "Damn these kids! I can't take it!"

Mothers met their children in the halls to conduct them safely home. From the schoolyard could be heard do-wah medleys in sweet, piercing falsettos.

Finally weary, overtaxed teachers retreated to the staff room and quickly shut the door behind them.

Thursday, March 17

Buddy tore madly around the yard, pummeling everyone he passed on the back with a windmill series of quick blows. When the terrified kids fled, he stood in the middle of the empty corridor and threw impressive jabs at his shadow. He was celebrating new boxing gloves—initiating them, breaking them in. For Buddy, all the world was a ring.

It was my duty to tell him that gloves were not allowed in school. I figured he'd tell me where to get off. What he casually said was, "If you want me to stop, you gotta go me a few rounds first. I'll bring my brother's pair this afternoon."

At the end of the day, kids of all ages poured into my room. Buddy was the last to enter. I figured it couldn't be too bad. After all, I stood six feet and weighed 165 pounds. Buddy was a twelve-year-old kid, even if he was big for his age.

Applause accompanied his entrance. Even members of my own class cheered him; they had a right to protect themselves after school.

Buddy began wrenching his neck back and forth in an impressive limbering-up ritual. We tied on our gloves; everyone waited in suspense.

Suddenly he rushed me, almost bowling me over. I threw a jab to keep him back. Then I stood ready, and we began to box.

"You can do better than that, McLaren!"

"Come on, Buddy—move it."

"Hit 'em in the nuts."

"You're okay, man."

After the first few rounds I was tiring noticeably, while Buddy grew stronger and more confident. I wasn't trying to land solid punches, but Buddy was determined to knock me out.

I finally ended the match gracefully by saying I had to leave and get to a course. Buddy stood perspiring, in a classic boxing stance. He accepted my decision to stop the fight and walked over. "You put on a pretty good show, man," he said, not too confidentially, so everyone would hear. "Of course, I coulda decked you anytime, but I don't want you to look like a dummy in front of your kids."

Friday, March 18

In Teachers' College, budding young professionals were guaranteed at least one fool proof lesson. It would always work, no matter who the kids or what the class. In moments of desperation this lesson could turn a would-be disaster into a fantastic success. Or so the theory went.

In a moment of panic, I decided to haul out my sure-fire lesson. I wrote two sentences on a piece of paper—an opening and a closing sentence. The students were directed to fill in the story by contributing one sentence, then passing the paper to the next student.

My opening sentence was: "I wish I had more friends like the ones I met last summer." The closing sentence: "It was the most exciting vacation I ever had."

It seemed to be working. The kids were getting into it and the class quieted down, with a few giggles and knee slapping.

The finished product read:

"I wish I had more friends like the ones I met last summer. I met a girl in a bikini. She had big tits. Don't write so dirty, Duke. Shut up Tina, and let him write what he feels like. I put my hands on her big knockers and squeezed them. We necked a lot. She felt my giant cock. Change the subject. Then we went into my cottage. . . .''

Monday, March 28

"Let's have art this afternoon, Mr. McLaren!"

"Yah. We want art!"

"Well, we've got some math to do this afternoon. Perhaps after we're finished with that . . .''

"We wanna naked model . . . one with really big tits that stick out to here!"

". . . and lots of fuzzy hair down here!"

"You guys are sick! Is that all you think about?"

"Shut up Sandra! All you think about is naked boys!"

"Barry's a fag. He thinks about naked boys, too!"

"Fuck you, you stupid morons!"

"Let's keep the language clean, okay? Can we drop this naked model business and get on with the math lesson!"

"Wash out your mouth, Barry! You said fuck about a hundred times today!"

"Fuck off!"

"A hundred and one."

"Hey, sir. Barry's got the tail of a cat tied to the aerial of his bike!"

"It's a raccoon's tail! I bought it at the store!"

"Sir! Let's have floor hockey instead!"

"I hates floor hockey!"

"We don't want you girls! Hey, sir! Let the girls play skippin' or something, but let us play floor hockey!"

"There will be no playing anything until we finish our math!"

"Kids should be allowed to choose sometimes. You said so!"

"Yah! You never let us have fun—real fun!"

"Okay, okay. What does 'real fun' mean?"

"If we wanna go somewheres, the creek or somethin', then you should let us. . . .''

"Duke just wants to finger Sandra!"

"You're dead! After school you're gonna get two black eyes and you're gonna swallow your teeth, you smartass!"

"Hold it, Duke! Settle down, okay? Open your books to the math review on page 51."

"Wait a minute! I ain't gots no pencil!"

"That's because you used it to jab that little kid at recess and the teacher took it off you!"

"Get lost. . . .''

"Here, you can use my pencil."

"Thanks, sir! Hey look! I stole the teacher's pencil!"

"Can I turn on the radio during art?"

"Quietly, yes . . . quietly. But first, our math!"

"Hey Sandra, get up on the desk and take off your shirt!"

"Shaddup! Why don't you get up there and whip out your prick?"

"Question number one! You've got three minutes!"

"Hey, I need to go to the bathroom! Stop the test! If I don't go now, I'm gonna shit my pants!"

"Let's draw his shit!"

"Yah, I wanna draw his turds!"

"Anybody who doesn't finish this test gets a note to take home and get signed!"

"Sir! Can I have a note, please! I love notes!"

"Me too! I wanna note sayin' I'm bad!"

"Everybody line up for bad notes!"

"Hurry up Levon! Whip down those pants and shit on your desk! I wanna draw your stinky plops."

"Hey! Gimme back my math book!"

"Cut out the crap."

"This is boring."

Tuesday, March 29

Levon's father stumbled through the door and took a chair. He wore a faded blue tee shirt which had "Unemployed With Dignity" stenciled across the chest. After examining the room, he asked me where the washroom was.

"The boys' john is around the corner," I said.

On his way out, he turned and said, "You don't really buy beer, you know. You rent it."

On his return, I showed him a short story his son had written a week earlier. It began:

> It was so nice out, I decided to leave it out all day. I didn't feel like going to school, so I stayed home and watched the Flintstones on TV.

It ended:

> Life is like a prick. When it's hard you get fucked. When it's soft you can't beat it.

Levon's dad cracked a smile. "Takes right after his old man, don't he?"

Wednesday, March 30

I asked the class to act out what they watched on television.

Vince did a beautiful number on the evangelical TV shows by having the host of the program repeat the words "Praise the Lord!" while he made a move on one of his voluptuous guests.

Frank and Sanjay did a put-on of two cops busting a group of dissident youths for smoking pot. Then the two cops took it home for themselves.

Hamlin, a frustrated new student, made up a character he called Super Student, who went through the school socking malefactors and bumbling, bigoted, shortsighted teachers.

But in my opinion, the best was Tina's portrayal of a movie starlet. She emerged clad in a scintillating red smock, with a matching hat and scarf. She tossed aside her hat, unwound her scarf, and dropped her smock to reveal two enormous breasts, which resulted from the strategic insertion of two soccer balls under her sweater.

Tina also had another ball thrust up her back, which she described as her "spare boob—it'll start a new trend in Hollywood!"

Thursday, March 31

There was a loud knock at the door. Spinner answered it, and was almost bowled over by Mark's mother as she stormed up to my desk.

"Gimme Mark." she demanded.

Mark slumped down in his seat, peering timidly over the edge of his desk.

"Mark," I said, "you'd better go with your mother."

No sooner had Mark walked to the front of the room than his mother had him pinned to the blackboard.

"Who was it, Mark?" she ordered.

"I don't know. Lemme go." Mark pleaded.

"Not until you tell me the name of the kid that beat you up and took my twenty dollars. You stupid jerk. Why'd ya tell him you had twenty bucks on you for?"

"I don't know." Mark whined.

By now the whole class was quietly watching. Dave, another West Indian kid, asked: "Was he black?"

"No, he was goddam honkey white," Mark answered, head down.

"You goddam well pick him out of some class. Mr. McLaren, I'm taking Mark for a walk aroun' the school." She half-dragged him out of the room.

Mark found the kid in a grade six class. He still had ten dollars in his pocket. Mark's mom took the kid by the scruff of the neck, and hauled him to Fred's office.

Later, she returned Mark to class.

"I don't know what you're gonna do with this one," she said. "Sometimes he can get so stupid, he don't know whether to fart or turn blue."

Monday, April 4

Burt always seemed to know what was troubling me, even though I tried to keep my problems to myself.

He could tell if I didn't get enough sleep the night before, whether or not I was feeling rotten, or if I wasn't getting along with a particular staff member that day. Burt seemed to possess some special capacity for reading people's minds.

For example, today Burt blurted out: "Mr. McLaren's in a good mood today. That's 'cause Spinner hasn't shown up yet. Mr. McLaren can't stand the way Spinner snaps his gum when he chews. Right, Mr. McLaren?" He grinned. And continued. "You hate Spinner's buck teeth, too—dontchya, Mr. McLaren? You think they make him look like a donkey. Am I right? I'm right, ain't I, sir?" He refused to stop. "Mr. McLaren's probably prayin' right now that Spinner's sick, and not just late for class. Hey, Mr. McLaren. You got both fingers crossed?"

They were.

Tuesday, April 12

After school, over a cigarette and coffee, Fred filled me in on a bit of his background.

He had been hired here as principal after serving four years in another inner-city school in the west end. It was there that he gained his reputation as an innovative principal. Articles were written about him, and he was invited on several TV talk shows to speak about his philosophy of reaching kids through improving their self-concept.

The main reason he had put so much effort into his previous school was because his wife had died prior to the appointment, and he'd tried to lose himself in his work.

Teachers were so devoted to Fred's method that they involved themselves in group therapy sessions, and often stayed until eight or nine in the evening working out new programs for the kids. "Several marriages suffered badly," he told me. "Teachers seldom made it home to see their spouses before bedtime."

When the former principal here retired, the staff had decided they wanted a definite say in who would be chosen to succeed him. They formed a committee and approached the Board, offering a list of qualities the new principal should possess. After all, a school in the Jane-Finch Corridor had special needs, and a special person was needed to help fill them as principal.

When the staff heard that Fred was available, they called a staff meeting to decide if he would be suitable. Except for a few teachers who preferred a more authoritarian type, the majority agreed they liked Fred's philosophy.

He was hired in September, four months before he hired me.

"At our first staff meeting," he told me, "the teachers told me they wanted me to do here what I had done at my former school. I told them about my wife dying, and that was one of the reasons I had put everything I had into my work. I also explained that since that time I had remarried, and my wife was expecting a baby soon. I knew I wouldn't be able to give as much as I had previously, but I promised I'd do my best to bring a better program into the school."

Thursday, April 14

During art, Donnie drew a picture of Sharon squeezing her breasts and squirting great jets of milk into the air, and then left the drawing on Sharon's desk, waiting for her reaction.

She reddened, gritting her teeth. Crouching low, she charged and split open Donnie's cheek with a head-butt. Her eyes widened when she saw the sight of blood.

Donnie stemmed the flow with his shirt tail and retreated to his desk. I sent him down to the nurse.

"Stupid prick!" Sharon hollered. "The dummy don't even know ya gotta be pregnant before you squirt milk!"

Friday, April 15

After teaching in the area for a few months, I was aware of what the environment could do to the kids. Every so often I would see new kids with impeccable records turn into sad, battered little things. It was the particularly meek and timid child that drew my sympathy.

Such a child was Hari, a miniature bespectacled Mahatma. On his second day he walked timidly up to my desk. "Sir, some girls in the other class beat me up after school."

I knew he would have a tough time.

But Hari got the break he deserved. His father bought him a motorcycle tee shirt, black polyethylene boots, and a Leatherette jacket with lots of zippers and studs. It's a very effective disguise.

Monday, April 18

Before I started teaching, I assumed any hyperactive students would be in special classes; I had no idea there would be so many in my "ordinary" classroom.

John, a fellow teacher, told me that children in the area were particularly undernourished, and that could not be disputed. He thought they probably were suffering from allergic reactions to the food dyes in all the junk food they ate. He also warned me that the fluorescent lights installed in every classroom affected behavior, making kids jumpy, making them lose control. "Shut off those lights. Keep your blinds wide open," he advised, looking up from his latest copy of *Prevention* magazine.

I found his admonition of fluorescent lighting eccentric, to say the least, but I was desperate enough to try anything. I usually kept my venetian blinds angled downwards, to shut out the view; the slightest opening would distract the class.

Today I threw caution to the winds and opened them as far as I could. From the open windows long shafts of honey-colored sunlight fell across the children's faces, highlighting the faint cloud of chalk dust, bathing the room in a golden haze. The children's faces appeared almost angelic.

After about ten minutes of peace, Duke decided to go on "scrap patrol," dragging the wastepaper basket around the room, collecting all the paper that had fallen on the floor. Then, like a bulldozer out of control, he crashed his way through a row of desks, elbowing kids along the way. Sally tried to avoid him, only to fall backwards in her chair. Then Robbie and Sharon, ignoring all the commotion, sauntered up to the blackboard, each trying to outdo the other in a graffiti competition.

Clutching at their groins, Levon and Frank asked me if they could be excused. They ran out, giggling, to the main building, not bothering to wait for an answer.

Duke must have noticed the grimace on my face, because he bounded up to my desk with a puzzled look on his face. "Hey, sir . . . what's with you?"

I gave natural light a chance for the next few hours, but then the kids began throwing things out the open windows.

One of the teachers was delighted to bring this to Fred's attention. He suggested it would be a good idea to keep my blinds closed in the future—natural light notwithstanding.

Friday, April 22

At my previous school, I remember the boasts of the staff I overheard during lunchtime:

"One girl in my grade eight class is already working on advanced calculus."

"One of mine already has a firm grasp of quantum physics."

"I have a student who will be the next Emily Carr."

Whereas the bragging of inner-city teachers was of a different nature:

"Three kids in my class have been to court this year for vandalism."

"One of my girls was so hard to handle it took three of us, including Fred."

"Two of my students shot at each other with .22s from the balconies of their apartments, and say they'll shoot me if I hassle them."

They often painted the most dismal picture possible of their students, competing over who had the toughest kids, the worst problems; it was their red badge of courage.

Monday, April 25

Rod asked me if I'd mind taking over the lunch-hour duty; the regular supervisor was off sick. "You're pretty good with the kids," he said. With that remark, I was able to chalk up my first compliment of the year. He explained that the students were given half an hour to eat, and then were led, by me, outside to be supervised during play in the schoolyard.

The kids were already eating when I arrived. The place was in an uproar; food was spread all over: pop, Twinkies, chocolate pudding, Oreo cream wafers, brownies, hot dogs, peach pits, salami rinds, bread crumbs, potato chips, cheesies.

I took my place at the supervisor's desk, watching quietly. There was as much food trading going on as food eating. Right away one kid tried to trade me his bologna sandwich for my ham-on-a-kaiser, saying his cost twice as much.

Every so often I ducked flying baseball cards. Music blared mysteriously from a car parked across the street, the kids tapping their feet to it. And I swear every kid took his empty lunch bag, blew it up, and popped it with a bang!

A little boy wearing a sea-island shirt and wire-framed sunglasses stood up and danced "the robot" for a group of clapping girls, dreadlocks flapping.

At the half-hour mark, I told the kids it was time to go outside. Sandwich wrappings flew everywhere in the delicate stampede out the door.

Once outside, I heard screams coming from the sand pit. A big red-headed kid had tied a piece of glass to the end of a broken hockey stick and was gleefully charging a terrified pack of fleeing behinds. He held a garbage-pail lid as a shield, and wore an inverted plastic funnel as a helmet. I took the weapon from this miniature Don Quixote, which he didn't like at all.

"Gimme back my spear, you son-of-a-bitch."

"Sorry, weapons aren't allowed on school property," I said crisply.

"Hand it over or I'll break your ass, man."

I pried the glass off the end of the stick, and threw it over the fence.

"You're new here," the kid drawled, "ain't ya, turkey?"

That afternoon, as I was pulling out of the school parking lot, I glanced down at the dashboard. The eight-track stereo I kept locked in my car was missing.

Wednesday, April 27

Duke and his mom and dad had moved down to the Jane-Finch area from a mining community in northern Ontario. The only work the father managed to find lasted merely six weeks. Soon after, he packed it in and headed back up north; Duke and his mother stayed behind.

"No way I'm heading back up north," she told me today during an interview, a tremor of irritation in her voice. "There's nothing up there. The city is where you make it. Everybody knows that. I'm looking for a job as a keypunch operator. If I can get that, well it won't be easy, but maybe we'll finally move out of this dump. I don't like the gang that Duke's been hanging around with. I don't like what's happenin'."

I mentioned that Duke was settling down a little—I wanted to give her some relief. Underneath the brave exterior, she seemed worried.

"I don't like the way Duke picks on kids. I think he's reacting to the way the bigger kids pick on him. Do you really think he's getting better?"

She candidly admitted how frustrated she was, stuck in a government-subsidized building, a single parent, out of work. . . . She was feeling stagnant, dormant, even though she was in her prime years.

She found herself weeping in the elevator one day. From crying she went to drinking, gulping tranquilizers, and sometimes "running away, leaving Duke alone in the apartment all night." She felt anger against a society that didn't seem to care about her or her son. "Christ, Mr. McLaren, I don't know what I'll do."

Instead of going home directly tonight, I decided I needed to calm down. I took a stroll along the boardwalk by the lake, at the foot of my street. I thought about Duke and his mother. Then, partially restored by the sky and water, I turned toward home.

Thursday, April 28

The lunchroom, created with the intention of serving as a buffer against the hectic classroom, was not always immune to intrusions from the outside world. Just as I was digging into a plate of steaming spaghetti from the nearby Italian restaurant, a gaunt, pock-marked teenager walked into the lunchroom and sat down next to me.

"Are you Ruth's teacher? I'm Jeff—her brother."

I put my fork down. "That's me. How's Ruth been? She's missed most of the week and—"

"Don't know where the hell she is," Jeff said, taking a hand-rolled cigarette from a flat tobacco tin, lighting it.

"What do you mean?"

"Mom took off with Ruth this weekend and said she ain't coming back. My dad figures that maybe mom called you at school. He sent me here to find out."

"I haven't heard a thing." By now, I'd lost my appetite. "Are you sure she won't come back? I mean—has this sort of thing happened before?"

"Mom's always yakkin' about leavin' and takin' Ruth with her if the old man don't get a job. But she's never had the guts."

"If she notifies the school where she is," I said slowly, "the information must be kept confidential. Sorry."

"Ya? Well . . . okay." He rose to his feet and thrust his hands into his back pockets. "Because when the old man catches up with her, he'll kick her ass into tomorrow."

"And what does that mean?" I asked apprehensively.

He cocked a thin, dark eyebrow. "You'll find out."

After he left, I asked the secretary to let me know if she receives a letter from another school requesting Ruth's records.

Monday, May 2

Teachers often miss the obvious, even when it stares them in the face every day.

The school year was almost over when I noticed that, with very few exceptions, Tina was absent every Monday. I mentioned it to a parent volunteer who lived on the same block as Tina. She looked surprised: "You mean you don't know why Tina misses school on Mondays?"

"No."

"It's the same thing every Monday night," she explained. "Her mother makes her stay home to look after her baby brother during the day. That way it's easier for her mother to sleep all day long. She wants to rest up for the late night session of Bingo."

Well, that seemed like a pretty weak reason to keep a child out of school. I cornered Tina's mother during parent interviews. She was reluctant at first, but eventually she admitted the truth.

"What's one day a week, Mr. McLaren? You tell me. Tina can always make up her school work. Just keep her in the next day, after school." She kept raising and lowering her arm, drawing my attention to the fact it was in a cast. "I'm supposed to feel guilty about keepin' my daughter home one day a week? You gotta be kidding. How can I afford a baby-sitter? On a lousy Mother's Allowance check I can hardly make the rent. Come on, Mr. McLaren. What's one lousy day a week if Tina makes up for it the next day? Just a drop in the bucket. Look, I got problems. Life ain't easy. My boyfriend's one of them sadists you know."

The more she went on, the worse I felt.

"It was my birthday a few days ago. And he walks in Friday night with no present. No card, no flowers, no chocolates. And the worst part was that I kept remindin' him that my birthday was Friday.

"I started yellin' and screamin'. I called him a creep for comin' home drunk on my birthday. He never even wished me a happy birthday!"

She shook her fist angrily. "Then he tells me he's got me a birthday present. I don't believe him. So he walks up the stairs to where I'm standin', and I'm still mad at him, so he yells 'Here's your birthday present!' and throws me down the stairs!" Which explained the cast.

Tuesday, May 10

Sophie wore a limp wreath of straws, strung together from thread picked off the frayed edges of the classroom carpet. On her tee shirt was printed "Children Are People Too." Her body was bent, emaciated. She walked with her arms held protectively across her necklace, as if it were an amulet that would keep her from harm.

"I saw Sophie's dad in the elevator last night," Mark suddenly announced to the class. "He was drunk. I know, 'cause I seen lotsa drunk people before, and when he got out, he fell on the floor."

"You're lyin'!" Sophie yelled.

"Sophie's 'welfare,'" Duke taunted. "Your dad's always drunk, ain't he, Sophie?"

"He is not!" cried Sophie. "My dad's sick, that's all! He gots the flu!"

"Then how come his breath stinks?" Duke chimed in, contemptuously. "I was there, too." A flurry of giggles and sniggling passed through the class.

"He wasn't drunk." Sophie shouted, desperate. "Shut your face!"

"Okay! Okay!" I shouted. "Enough!"

Sophie was already running for the door. Duke reached out and grabbed at her straw necklace as she raced by, breaking it.

"Welfare!" he screamed, as she slammed the door.

Thursday, May 12

Over dinner, I started blaming the entire universe for the problems I was encountering at school: parents, the school system, the government, the decline of the West. I'm becoming quite a cynic. I miss the days when I was a young student radical who really believed society could be changed, poverty abolished, and everyone given an equal chance to make something worthwhile of their lives.

Was education a middle-class pablum which, upon ingestion, socialized kids into uniform amorphous lumps? It was obvious my kids couldn't fit into the system, so the most obvious solution was to make the system more accommodating to "culturally and economically disadvantaged kids."

"You're putting an educational Band-Aid over a major social wound," Jenny told me, "when what is really needed is drastic surgery."

I nodded. "But the only people who are empowered to perform the surgery are in top administrative positions, too far away from the scene."

"Become a political activist then," Jenny suggested, winking.

"Maybe I should," I laughed. "I could go out and try to abolish poverty and scream about the injustices of the system. Then they might listen enough to give me an executive position on the School Board and ask me to invent a more advanced attendance sheet!"

Friday, May 13

During "news," Dan told the class how his baby sister was run over by a car. She was running across the street to fetch an order of french fries for her mother.

He vividly described how the blood dripped onto the road from her broken nose, and the cut on her head, and the ambulance taking so long to arrive. "I saw her in the hospital today," he told us. "That's why I wasn't here this mornin'. My sister's disconscious and talks in her sleep. She talks funny—real slow and shaky like."

"Hey, man, she's drunk," Levon cracked. "What'd she drink—vodka or whiskey?"

"Maybe she was smokin' pot," Duke added.

"Hey . . . wow!" Jackson said, excited. "I gotta tell my mom. She really likes gory stories."

"Tell us about the blood."

By this time I had marched to the front of the room. "Hold it. I don't think Dan finds his sister being hit by a car that exciting."

"Yah, you guys!" Burt shouted, backing me up. "If you guys find it so neat, why don't you go play on the highway. Go up on the 401 and play in traffic."

"You guys are gross," Sandra exclaimed. "I wouldn't wanna watch somebody gettin' run over."

"News is over," I announced.

Dan walked over to his desk slowly, as if he were measuring each step. He took his seat, put his head down.

"Hey, Dan," Al said, placing his hand on Dan's shoulder. "Keep us posted, eh?"

Monday, May 16

Jabeka sidled up to Marlene's desk and solemnly stated: "You know, Marlene, I don't never wanna get married." She usually didn't initiate conversations.

"How come?" Marlene asked.

"You gotta make meals, do the washin', and do whatever the man says. You gotta do the wash on Friday night or Saturday, 'cause the laundromat's closed on Sundays."

"You don't have to do all that. You and your husband could take turns. I want to get married when I grow up."

"How come?" it was Jabeka's turn to ask.

"When you gots to pay the rent," Marlene replied smugly, "your husband can pay half."

"My mom's got to do everythin' in our house," Jabeka mused. "And she don't like it. Besides, men drinks too much. When they die, you gotta pay a lot of money for their funeral. My grandmother forgots to sign this paper so that the government would pay for my grandfather. He died because he drunk too much, so my grandmother had to pay for buryin' him—I member she was real mad. I didn't like my grandfather, he was always drunk. The only time I liked him was at Christmas, when he gave me five dollars."

"Maybe you'll marry a man who don't drinks."

"My mom says that they all drinks too much. Yesterday my mom told me she might get divorced from my dad."

Friday, May 20

The mild weather was my salvation. I took the kids outside to explore the creek at the back of the school. It was ideal for them—they could run around and shout and work off the excess aggression they had built up. When they cooled off, they eagerly started the science experiments I had planned.

Duke decided to find a crayfish and write a brief description of it as his project. Unfortunately for the crayfish, his description included a drawing of its insides, which he explored after cutting the crayfish open.

Some of the kids removed their shoes and socks and waded in the creek. That was hazardous, unless you were wearing horseshoes, because of the broken glass and cans and other garbage accumulated over the years. I had to keep a sharp eye on them, warning them away from dangerous areas.

I've started to take my kids outside for more than just science lessons. We enjoy it out there. We set up a little shelter behind some trees, and it becomes our classroom on warm afternoons. We bring our books, papers, and pencils with us. The kids use stones as paperweights on windy days to hold their papers in place. Back in class, they decorate the stones, painting them in marvelous colors.

Tuesday, May 24

Max was the school psychologist. He usually showed up on Tuesdays to assess students who had been referred to him by their teachers.

He had read my referral form for a new kid named Matthew, and wanted to see him in a classroom setting. I slipped Max into the back of the room, and the class went on as usual.

Matthew sat at his desk, tapping a book with his pen. His whole body was involved. He shook up and down in a jumping-jack motion, a strange dance in time with the pen taps. The taps were growing louder and louder. He turned and looked at Max. Then he went back to tapping his book—only this time he added some obscene gestures to his act. Matthew's mannerisms were starting to make Max look uncomfortable.

Suddenly Matthew stopped his book-tapping and took three casual steps toward the middle of the room. Then he wildly attacked his desk, pushing it into the corner and turning it completely over, spilling its guts on the floor: pens, pencils, books, binders, loose paper, magic markers I had been searching for for weeks, crayons. . . .

I rushed over to Matthew and grabbed him under the arm. Then I quickly escorted him outside, telling him to stay by the door until he cooled off.

Max agreed to test Matthew. "Once the results are in, though," he said tonelessly, "it may take him years to be placed. There are already so many kids on the waiting list. The system can't absorb them all. Maybe if Matthew's parents were better off and had some pull with the Board. . ."

On my way out the door tonight, the school secretary told me we'd received a request for Ruth's records from a small, rural school in Alberta.

Friday, May 27

Clad in a pin-stripe suit, plaid vest, and fingering the looping chain of his pocket watch, Fred entered his office, waved me a hello, and slumped down in his Boston rocker.

It was very early in the morning, but already a third of the student body had poured into the library where Dean, the librarian, had set up a special program for kids whose parents worked the early morning shift.

Fingers loosely laced behind his head, Fred kicked off both shoes in one motion, resting his stocking feet on the pine coffee table. He picked up the phone and mumbled a message to his secretary around an unlit cigar.

A tiny girl in tattered overalls and a baseball cap so large that it almost hid her face timidly knocked on the office door. Fred welcomed her in with a broad grin.

Slowly, almost reluctantly, she removed her hat, revealing a mass of wild dreadlocks that she fingered nervously.

"Who did your hair?" Fred asked, smiling approvingly.

"My auntie," she replied, giving Fred a quick, sideways glance.

"Well then, tell your auntie she did a great job, because you look terrific."

The girl's head snapped up and her eyes widened. A smile broke across her face. She rushed across the room and planted a kiss on Fred's forehead. He responded by giving her a long, extended hug.

"She comes in every morning before class," Fred winked, "just to get a hug."

The sincerity of Fred's affection for the kids was obvious. I sometimes wondered whether I was living up to his standards, being only too aware of my lack of love for certain students. Even when I tried looking at the positive side of a particular student's character—Duke's, for instance—I found it extremely difficult to let go of my hostile feelings. Only an affection that was honest and spontaneous would have any effect.

Thursday, June 2

Duke bumper-hitched a ride on my van so many times that today, as I was about to drive off for lunch, I got out and asked him to join me for a hamburger. My suggestion threw him, but after a few seconds he said, "Sure, man, as long as you're buyin'."

Around the other kids Duke was aggressive and hard, but often with me he was a completely different person. He talked about missing his dad, spoke eagerly of his plans for a newspaper route. With the money he saved up from his job, he would be able to travel to see his dad—although he admitted sadly that his dad never wrote him or his mom.

Duke and I agreed to have more excursions for hamburgers, but from now on, he says, he'll pay for his own.

Monday, June 6

"Wanna know somethin', sir?" Jabeka asked out of the blue.

"Sure. What's on your mind?"

"My stepdad went to Jamaica last night for good. He wants me to go with him, but I didn't want to. So he took my brother instead."

"Why's your stepdad leaving?"

"My mom don't like him no more. Me either. You know, when he buys us clothes they're always old, and they tear easy. When they go in the washin' machine, they shrinks."

"Is that all?"

"No, sir. When I was a little baby he changed my diapers and treated me real rough."

"Can you remember that far back, Jabeka?"

"Well, my mom told me."

"What else did she say?"

"When I was a little girl, I had a bleedin' nose and was chokin' and my stepdad just put on his coat and went to a party. And after the party he went to sleep in the park."

"Aren't you going to miss your stepdad, though?"

"No. But I'll miss my brother. My mom kicked my stepdad out for good, after last week."

"What happened last week?"

"My stepdad gave me a grown-up pill, and I started to cough. There was a pin stuck in it."

"Don't you ever want to see him again?"

"Just at Christmas, so's he can give me lots of presents. He told me he was goin' to spend lots of money on me."

Friday, June 10

There was a loud knock on the door. I opened it and was met by three grim women. The heaviest one, in a pink bathrobe with kitty fluff around the collar, carried a baseball bat.

"Where's Mr. Hartford's room?" the heavy one demanded in a raspy voice, adjusting her robe.

"Down the hall to your left," I replied. "Is there a problem?"

"One of my kids told me that Mr. Hartford roughed up my littlest one, Tony, at recess. And believe me, I'm gonna make him pay."

"I'll show you where his room is," I said nervously. "But I'm sure there must be some mistake."

We went down the hall together.

Hart was the staff heavy. He turned to face us, squaring his great shoulders. He was leaning against the wall, his massive arms folded over his Budweiser belt buckle.

"What's this about you slappin' Tony around at recess, Hartford?" the lady with the bat demanded.

"Are you his mother?"

"That's right! And I want an explanation."

"I suppose you were informed that Tony was in a fight at recess and was kicking another boy in the face when he was down? I had to grab Tony and pull him off the kid. Is that a good enough explanation?"

"I didn't hear it that way," the lady responded, looking a bit puzzled.

"There was another teacher on yard duty who can back me up. Do you want me to call her?" Hart asked.

"Forget it," the lady said. "Come on, girl." she barked. "Let's go home. Somebody's been lyin' to me, and I'll be using this bat yet."

Monday, June 13

"Sir! I gots a rotten tooth! It wiggles and this gooey stuff leaks out!"

"It's just spit. Lemme knock it out for ya!"

"I think you should see the school dentist, Levon. You'd better hurry before he leaves for the day."

"No way. That dentist is a Paki!"

"Well, you're a nigger! Haaaaa!"

"Look! I've already spoken to you about using words like that!"

"A Paki is a Paki no matter what you say!"

"I gots this big pimple under my chin!"

"I'll punch that out too! I'll give you an uppercut!"

"Go jerk off, why don't you!"

"Hey, sir. Can I whisper you a secret?"

"What is it, Dan?"

"Only if you promise not to tell Duke."

"Okay. What is it?"

"Duke and I went to this movie on the weekend . . . right?"

"Right."

"So we sits down near the back to watch the show. Then this chick sits down a few seats away . . . right?"

"Right."

"Duke sits next to her and puts this popcorn box on his lap. The box is all empty . . . right?"

"Right."

"So he takes the bottom off the box—just rips it away. Then he puts the box over his thing . . . right?"

"Go on."

"Then he says to the chick, 'Want some popcorn?' The chick says, 'Sure,' so she reaches into the box. . . ."

"Sir! Duke's tryin to break my pimple!"

"Okay, class! Settle down! You've still got your stories to finish off before recess."

"I don't feel like doin' a story!"

"Hey . . . why don't you leave sir alone. His face is grey. Can't you tell he's constipated?"

Monday, June 20

On the weekend, snipers fired rifles from the roofs of nearby high-rises. I found a bullet hole in the front door of the school.

Wednesday, June 22

I was late getting my final report cards finished and went into a mild panic. I tried to work on them during class, but it was much too noisy. I even tried to work on them during yard duty, but that, of course, was doomed to failure.

During lunch, John noticed all my report cards spread out in front of me. He said I bore a strong resemblance to a newscaster who had just thrown an epileptic seizure. So I explained.

"When the noise in my room gets too much," he told me, "I simply throw the kids a test. That usually shuts them up for at least half an hour!"

Of course! I hurried into the office, grabbed a handful of stencils, drew up a math test, and quickly ran it off on the machine.

While I worked on my report cards, the class worked steadily on their test. Until, that is, Janice shouted, "Duke threw a magazine out the window!"

I let the incident go by in favor of peace and quiet. "No talking," I said. "Keep your mind on the test!"

Next, the door was kicked open and Karen somersaulted into the room. Her mother outside bellowed, "Get into that room! Don't you try and tell *me* you're sick!"

Shortly afterwards, the recess bell sounded. I hurried over to the main building for a cigarette.

When I returned I noticed a crowd of tiny kindergarten kids gathered around a torn magazine outside my portable. I took a closer look.

On the cover was a nude and bloodied woman with mammoth breasts. She was bound by several studded leather straps, spread-eagle to a chair. Headlined over the picture was "Man Rapes Woman With Boyfriend's Bleeding Head."

"Wow," I heard one of the kids whisper.

Thursday, June 23

Now that the year was nearly over, I noticed that Duke had mellowed considerably, almost to the point where I wondered whether his toughness wasn't simply bravado all along.

It couldn't be disputed that he displayed a savagery, certainly a sadism, in several fights I witnessed. But the fighting seemed to be happening less frequently.

Last fall he had forced a kid named Lindsay to eat a piece of dog crap. Now he was acting more the benevolent despot. Since he no longer initiated fights, neither did his followers. He swore off smoking, so smoking became taboo. He took up gymnastics after school, and his gang dutifully practiced their somersaults on the gym mats.

One teacher told me she spotted Duke signing out a book from the library.

Wednesday, June 29

Rod had been asked by a Board trustee if the school could contribute some children's artwork to the Canada Day celebration at the nearby junior high school. Knowing more than a little Board politics, he agreed. Our school, he decided, would have the best display of the festival. I was to coordinate the exhibit, gathering together murals and paintings by the students which emphasized Canada as the land of opportunity, multiculturalism, solidarity, happiness, and wonderful community spirit.

Everybody showed up for the celebrations: parents, school trustees, social workers in denim overalls, red-nosed alkies, cops, glazed-eyed teenagers, senior citizens.

Buddy showed up, too. Within three minutes, my cassette tape recorder was missing. I called him over and asked if he'd like to play detective for me. He replied succinctly: "Go shovel shit, Mr. McLaren."

Then I politely asked if he'd like to reconsider playing Sherlock Holmes, only this time offering a five dollar reward. Buddy smiled. "Sure, Mr. McLaren. I'm gonna be a detective when I grows up. I'll get it back."

About five minutes later Buddy returned. The tape recorder was tucked under his arm, and there was a big grin on his face. "I caughts this son-of-a-bitch runnin' off with it to the plaza. So I runs after him, and tells him to give it back. When I caughts up to him, I says it belongs to Mr. McLaren, this real nice teacher friend of mine, so he'd better hand it over." Buddy could have easily surpassed Sherlock Holmes by simply solving only the crimes he himself committed.

I shouldn't have reinforced Buddy's theft by giving him a reward, but I needed my tape recorder for the celebrations.

Unfortunately, the festivities were canceled shortly after they began. Too many tires were being slashed in the parking lot (including the police cruisers), the lady that ran the dunking pool had her purse stolen, and one of the policemen on duty "lost" his hat!

"O Canada" blared out strangely through the cracked tape recorder speaker.

EPILOGUE

Congratulations were heaped on me by the administration—I had survived the year.

I threw a party for the kids, and they did a beautiful job of decorating the portable; it was a crepe-paper paradise. I felt it the best atmosphere to make my farewell.

The fun was cut short when Buddy floated by to check out the music. He wanted to be the disc jockey, but Muscle Lady was challenging him for the job. To avoid a confrontation, I decided to take the kids over to the gym, where a larger graduation dance was just beginning.

All the young calypsonians were there: feet were tapping and hips were swaying to the beat of West Indian reggae. Scores of kids crammed into the gym, dancing as they came through the door. A mass of swirling bodies, arms upraised in celebration describing graceful arcs, heads thrown back in blissful abandonment, they slowly gravitated toward the stage. There they were met by a multitude of other revelers, knees buckling, feet shuffling, hips rolling.

Muscle Lady whirled onto the stage amid a pulsing strobe light, lip-synching her theme song, *Vibrations,* her thin legs revealed through her translucent pants.

Buddy stood in the middle of the floor, his shiny black hair reflected by the light as sharp crisscrossed wires. He danced wildly, with a covey of onlookers applauding.

"There's my man!"

"Watch him move, ladies!"

"Hang it all out!"

"Shake those feet!"

He smiled back, obviously enjoying the spotlight.

The next day there was a staff meeting. When I heard that a grade four class was being vacated by a teacher who was transferring, I asked if I could take the class; Fred agreed.

I suppose I expected a feeling of elation or accomplishment at the end of the year, some kind of emotional ovation. I had come through a long period of fragmentation, and now I was ready for a leap toward sanity. All year it had been as if I had been homesteading on the frontiers of despair. I had changed from a relatively even-tempered and reasonably patient person into a mass of raw nerve endings and brute instinct. I had formed a shell around my emotions in an attempt to keep myself from being drawn into the deeply wounded lives of the kids.

I had been too idealistic. I wanted the classroom to be a place where the whole would contribute to the health of its parts. I wanted to show the kids how to express their conflicts without tormenting each other. I suppose in a sense I had achieved some of my aims. After all, the kids did express their feelings. But with all the role-playing, psychodrama, and class discussions, I had expected greater harmony.

For most of their lives, school for these kids had been a kind of enforced lethargy, where violence became the natural culture of the classroom. I wanted to change their perception of school, to free them from everything about learning that seems so rote and mechanical: bells keeping kids in step and on time, curriculums plotting out each separate skill to be learned, and when.

I didn't want to be just a PR man probing the fractured psyches of the kids in the name of achievement and competition; I wanted to mend some of the tears in their emotional lives. But in attempting to do so, I was becoming an emotional wreck myself. It was almost impossible to teach kids who felt like rodents in a locked cage, fed crumbs by strangers, and from which there was no escape. I had seen sporadic, impulsive, and ultimately senseless violence with very few strands of hope.

The questions I asked myself over and over were: What kind of person had I really been to the kids? How much did I really help to empower them? A public school teacher has the responsibility of helping kids negotiate with all kinds of things: language, geography, art, drama, gym, reading, film, mathematics, social skills—and making them relevant to the world outside. At the very least I should be able to help them get along with each other, or so I thought.

I debated whether or not to attend a summer course at university that might provide me with some theoretical grounding in inner-city teaching. Jenny insisted that what I really needed was a break from anything to do with teaching. So we took out a loan from the credit union and packed our bags for San Francisco. I hadn't been there since my visit in the sixties, and I looked forward to seeing that beautiful city again. The change of scenery and the chance to put my job out of my mind would be welcome.

But on the trip home I started thinking about the kids again: I couldn't put them out of my thoughts. My mind was filled with so many unanswered questions: Would the younger kids in grade four be more enthusiastic and less defiant of authority? Could I reach them before they were conditioned to be so defiant? Could school be more than just an expensive baby-sitting service? Could it alter the class structure?

My new class would be in the main building, actually the largest room in the school, the former library. When some kids had set fire to the building, the new wing was built, leaving the old library unoccupied.

A classroom would have many advantages over the portable. A delightful thought occurred: I wouldn't freeze in winter each time I had to go to the bathroom. Most of my boys, rather than trudge to the main building, preferred to urinate in the snow outside the portable. It was a fresh experience, having a gallery of yellow abstracts to gaze on. There must have been an art to it, since I definitely appreciated some more than others. Sometimes I'd walk by a row of ''angels'' that the kids had made by lying in the snow and flapping their arms and legs. All my angels had yellow eyes and yellow mouths. When I began to recognize individual artists by their style, I knew it was time to find an indoor classroom.

So now, I would have a new grade four class to teach. During our holiday I had sought spiritual refuge in books, to get ready for the following year. I also picked up some books on alternative schools and progressive teaching techniques from the local library.

At home, I searched for the grade four programs I had kept from my days at Teachers' College. I discovered I had used them to keep the refrigerator level.

CHAPTER **2**

The Invisible Epidemic

Friday, September 2

This morning I decided to get a head start on the term. I arrived at my "new" room to find chairs piled haphazardly on desks that had been pushed into a heap in the corner. The bulletin boards were still littered with debris left by the previous teacher, and old torn posters still hung on the walls.

Rather than put the desks into straight rows as I had done the previous year, I decided to arrange them in rectangular groups of six each. I dragged in a few tables from the stockroom and set up the art center near the sink. I also acquired a broken tape-recorder as an improvement for my "sound center." It complemented the record player and earphones.

My biggest challenge, I had learned, would not be in teaching the kids— my biggest challenge would not be in getting along with the other teachers—my biggest challenge would be in trying to please the caretakers!

They had insisted last year that I put my desks back into rows at the end of a day, because that way it was easier to sweep my room at night. And then, when I brought in some old furniture I had found down at the Sally Ann, they refused to help me carry it upstairs. They protested that my classroom was already a junkheap!

I found Rod in his office and asked him if I could borrow a TV for my room; there were three TV sets circulating. The one I asked for had a broken stand and was usually left idle in the stockroom. Teachers were unlikely to ask for it because it was large and heavy and a big pain to move. No one would get upset about me monopolizing *that* set! And maybe it would keep my class quiet after lunch when kids were usually at their rowdiest.

Rod helped me move the set to my room.

Tuesday, September 6

On the first day of class, I talked to the kids about the kind of program I wanted to run.

"Are we gonna to do any sports?" one student asked.

"Floor hockey?"

"I don't like floor hockey, sir," a tall kid offered, rising slightly out of his desk.

"What kind of sport do you like?" I asked, tensing.

He jerked his thumb at the lapel of his shirt. The button he wore read: "Breast Stroking Champion." "That's me!" he declared, grinning.

Friday, September 9

I had promised the kids we'd watch TV this morning. I settled on a program called "Cover to Cover" about children's books, with an artist illustrating the stories. The class sat and watched the show quietly.

As soon as the set was turned off, however, the kids became more hyperactive than ever.

I sadly reported to Rod that my TV experiment wasn't working out, and that I was going to return the set to the stockroom. One of the caretakers happened by and overheard us. "Hey McLaren! I'd be happy to lug that TV back to stockroom for you!" he volunteered, smiling.

Monday, September 12

My new location has a definite drawback—the washroom, conveniently situated just around the corner, has proven more popular than my classroom.

A steady stream of kids clutching their groins, hopping up and down, continually line up at the door waiting to be excused. Or three or four kids make a mad dash for the washroom without bothering to ask for permission. It got so bad I was forced to move my desk in front of the door to control the situation.

Then groups of kids complained about the continual noise in the classroom, and asked if they could do their seatwork in the hall. I reluctantly agreed, setting a limit of five kids at any time for my "hall group." Every five minutes or so I peeked out to check on them.

This afternoon I noticed whenever I checked that there were always some kids missing. When I asked where they were, the others simply shrugged their shoulders and exclaimed, "They're with the other freaks!"

"Other freaks?"

"Card freaks!" they shouted, and pointed to the end of the hall.

Down the hall a group of about twenty kids from different classrooms was huddled together in the stairwell tossing hockey cards against the wall. It was such a serious competition I felt a little guilty when I broke up the game and sent them all back to their classes.

Wednesday, September 14

It would drive anyone a little crazy. At least half the class wandered around the room at any given time, despite my attempts to keep them working quietly at their desks. The constant movement was threatening.

Relief happily appeared with Hartford, the gym teacher, who took my kids twice a week for half-hour sessions.

Usually I ended up chatting with a small group of kids who had forgotten their gym equipment and remained behind. It was the same group every week—a coincidence, I'm sure. I looked forward to my half-hour talks with these kids, nick-naming them "the rap pack." I dreamed of what it would be like to have a class with only six or seven students. There were kids in the group whom I could barely tolerate in a normal classroom with thirty-five students. But individually or in the small group, they were easy to talk to, sensitive, and communicative.

When the rest of the class returned from the gym, pleasant young people reverted to their former selves: distant, rowdy, agitated.

Friday, September 16

Behavioral modification was a term I was introduced to in Teachers' College. So when it came up as a topic at an "inner-city" professional development day conference, I wasn't a bit surprised.

"Behavioral mod is what you need to marshall these inner-city toughs," I was advised. One teacher described the "check system" to me, so I decided to try it out.

I stripped the bulletin boards on both sides of my room, and tacked up the names of all thirty-five of my pupils along the top. Under each name, I hammered in five nails forming a vertical straight line, spaced so that five pie plates could be punched and hung from the nails. Each pie plate stood for one day. One side of a pie plate was a happy face. The other side, a frown.

After explaining the rules to the class, I showed how I could turn over a pie plate to the frown if the child sinned. If one of my kids sinned twice, I could put a sticker on the plate. Five stickers meant the child had six checks against him or her. If a kid managed to go the entire week with only one check, he or she received a pack of gum and "free activity time." They cheered at that, of course. But if he or she managed to get zapped more than three times in any single day, then the culprit had to stay after school and do extra work from my "sad face" book.

But there was still more.

When I yelled "Carpet check!" the kids had to run over to the carpeted area and sit down. "Sound check!" meant that all the kids had to sit quietly and listen. "Desk check!" meant that all the kids should rush to their little desks. We all agreed to try it.

"Okay kids!" I began. "Carpet check!"

They all ran over each other rushing to the carpet, and knocking down a little girl in the process. Her lip started to bleed. While I made sure she was okay, I said "Sound check!" and everyone quieted down. Which was when Elvin stood up: "I don't like this game!"

"Check for Elvin!" I said at once.

Eddie, my newly chosen "check monitor," promptly took Monday's pie plate and turned it to the sad face.

"Class," I said, "the first check of the year goes to Elvin!"

I was suddenly overwhelmed with every kid demanding they get checks. Somehow, they had gotten things mixed up. I tried explaining the system all over again. Confident, I sent the kids back to their desks with a resounding "Desk check!"

After enough time had passed for the kids to finish their assignment, I called "Carpet check!" Thirty-five pairs of assorted sneakers pattered to the rug.

Wait a minute! It was only thirty-four pairs!

I heard fuming and muttering at the back of the room. T. J. was still at his desk, mumbling angrily. T. J. wasn't going to cooperate. Why should he? He was most at home in chaos, not order. The other kids would follow his lead if I didn't do something.

T. J. was staring at the ceiling, arms folded defiantly across his chest, his red woolen beret pulled over one eye. Then he started to get up. I felt a surge of confidence. Then slowly he slunk back into his chair, glaring at me. Then, he stuck out his tongue. Everyone waited for me to make my move.

"Stay at your desk!" I told him, as if I had wanted him there all along. "Open your book!"

This caught him off guard. He started to open his speller, then suddenly slammed it shut, his eyes squinting. "You sucker! You ain't getting T. J. to the rug! Not that way! You gimme some gum like everybody else is gonna get! Eh, eh? Then I'll go! But you ain't keepin' me in! I got to get right home after school 'cause I gotta go for a blood test!"

"You'll get your gum just like everybody else if you follow the rules!"

"I want a promise!" he demanded.

"Uh . . . well . . . if you've got a good reason not to stay in, I'll look into it."

Suddenly there was a room full of excuses. "I can't stay in either, sir, 'cause my mom's takin' me to Towers to get me some socks!" Betsy had to take her younger cousin right home after school. Murray had "sore tonsils," and maybe the doctor would want to "cut 'em out" after school. And so on.

I was panic-stricken. I started checking everybody: "Check T. J.! Check Winston! Check Murray! Check Betsy! Double-check Betsy!"

But Eddie, my loyal check monitor, protested louder than the others. "I can't stay in either, sir, or my dad will beat me! I have to look after my little brother."

"Check yourself, Eddie!" I groaned in despair.

The next day, I told the class we were going back to our normal routine. T. J. told everyone it was because I was too cheap to buy gum.

Tuesday, September 20

Melissa wore a plastic charm with the signs of the zodiac around her neck. It was a good-luck token for her mother, who was dying of cancer. She clutched it tightly, and sometimes shoved it under her sweater so it rested next to her skin.

The day after her mother died, Melissa ripped the pendant from her neck and threw it out the window.

Wednesday, September 21

During the first few weeks in class, Sal had a gentle manner that lulled me into complacency. There was no way this kid would ever be a problem, it was simply out of the question. On the surface, he was all friendly gestures, eagerness, and ambition.

This afternoon Sal was sitting quietly at his desk, fingers laced behind his neck, leaning back in his seat. The kid beside him called him a name—some innocuous remark, like "goofball."

He reared back with a sideways look and threw his desk against the wall. He sprang growling, seizing the kid by the neck and screaming, "Fuck right off!" Then he violently brought his chin down onto the kid's head.

Flesh tore. Blood gushed like a tiny geyser into his eyes. The kid's face twisted into a cruel mask. In the few seconds before I pulled him away, Sal sent a flurry of kicks into the ribs.

I grabbed Sal under the arms and spun him around, forcing him back to his desk. He watched me guardedly, his head lowered. Then his wild, angry face suddenly melted into an ingratiating grin.

"Lost my cool, eh sir!"

The class, which had remained silent, now sputtered and giggled. Two boys took the wounded victim downstairs, while Sal pushed his hair back from his face, grinning.

Tuesday, September 27

Professional development days are traditionally set aside to allow teachers to attend lectures, conferences, and workshops to keep up with the latest developments in education. For us, it really meant a welcome day of relief from the kids.

Most inner-city teachers I talked with found the lectures irrelevant. It was hard to wait out the boredom of the lecture so we could go out together for lunch.

The "Halfway House" restaurant at Pioneer Village was the most popular eating spot. I think the staff enjoyed the walk through Pioneer Village, an exact replica of a Canadian town in the 1800s, as much as the meal itself. It was such a stark contrast to the bleak surroundings of the Corridor.

After listening to a particularly boring lecture, Hartford whispered in my ear: "Let's skip Pioneer Village and go to the Golden Star for a beer!"

After the lecture, Hart and I rounded up Big Arnie and Mrs. Rogers, piled into Hart's station wagon, and drove off to the Golden Star.

As Hart led us to a table at the front of the tavern, Mrs. Rogers pointed to the stripper on stage, remarking, "I hope my women's consciousness-raising group doesn't find out about this!"

The stripper, a lithe blonde in her teens, had almost finished her gyrations by the time we took our seats. Hart's eyes were glued on her final gyrations as the music on the juke box slowly faded. After a bit more scrutiny he thumped his fist on the table. "I knew it. That's Cathy Huston up there."

"Cathy who?"

"Cathy Huston!" Hart said emphatically. "I'm sure of it." A look of surprise and bewilderment covered his face. "I taught Cathy in grade six."

I watched his face turn red as the stripper, her act completed, now covered herself with a black lace negligee. She made her way across the room in the direction of our table. When she got to us, she stopped and looked down at Hart, puzzled, while he sat there stone-faced. Then she smiled.

"Hiya, Hartford!"

"Hiya, Cathy," Hart managed. She then went past our table and disappeared into a room behind the bar.

We quietly finished off our beers and left.

Wednesday, October 5

Jenny mentioned last night that I seemed to be losing much of my enthusiasm so early in the term. She'd noticed that I didn't spend as much time preparing lessons, and I avoided discussing school events. I couldn't give her a ready answer. After mulling it out, I finally decided to discuss it with Fred.

I told him that I felt helpless, ineffective. My enthusiasm seemed on the wane. No longer a neophyte, I felt I should be making much more progress with the students. The signs of physical and emotional abuse that the kids brought to class from their homes and the incidents of violence I had witnessed in class all seemed to be part of the normal state of affairs, rather than isolated incidents. Isolated pockets of classroom disturbances I could handle . . . react to . . . follow up on. But it was another matter to be confronted with a situation where every day, all thirty-five pupils seemed to be out of control. How could I possibly establish a close relationship with so many students?

I thought about the books and articles I had read on disadvantaged kids. In most of them, the authors wrote about problem children in special classes, with one teacher to every ten kids. Now that seemed reasonable. But life in my class was like being machine-gunned by events so quickly that it was impossible to keep track of everything. I was feeling numbed, insensitive, apathetic.

Fred's answer was so simple, I couldn't believe it, yet it had tremendous impact on me. He told me that although I should try to reach as many of them as possible, that if I only affected a single child in my entire class, my presence would have been worthwhile. He told me to relax, and not have such high expectations.

"This is the only way you can keep your spirits up," he said. "If you're going to worry about not reaching every one of them, you won't reach any. If you tell yourself that if something positive happens with a kid, no matter how small it seems, that it's worthwhile, well then you'll do fine. You'll be in shape emotionally to help that next one who's standing in line."

Wednesday, October 12

Unless some miracle intervenes, I'll have T. J. in my class for the rest of the year. My fellow teachers admire me greatly for taking him on. Two years older than the others, by the time he'd hit grade four his records were thick with reports of classroom disruption.

T. J. is painfully thin, with the narrowest face imaginable and a shrill, bleating voice. His skin is stretched over his tiny head like a Halloween mask. He continually spews a steady stream of obscenities from thin lips that are covered with rose-colored herpes sores.

As soon as I saw him, gouging victims with pencil swipes, I feared the worst. When I asked him over to my desk for a friendly chat, he refused to move from his desk, held there by some unnatural gravity.

At ten, T. J. is the second youngest in a family of eleven. Everyone has police records, including his parents. The one exception is his six-year-old brother, Mickey.

This afternoon, while I was having lunch at T. J.'s, the police came in and arrested his second eldest brother for assault. Mickey ran after the police cruiser shouting: "You fuckin' pigs! Bastards! Bring my brother back!"

Lunch at T. J.'s is always eventful. Lining the windowsill above the sink are bowling trophies, plants in pink flamingo vases, the complete collection of Red Rose Tea china miniatures, and a toy model of an outhouse which features a plastic figurine urinating through a crescent-shaped hole in the door, a present from T. J.'s grandparents who live in a small farming community near London, Ontario.

T. J. loves to visit his grandfather. In class he tells me stories of visiting him in his stepdad's metallic green pickup truck, complete with whitewall tires. He'd show off the body work and pinstriping to Gramps, and let him feel the broadloomed dash. Gramps promised T. J. he'd buy him one of those toy dogs whose eyes burn red when the brake lights are on. T. J. wishes he could move in with his grandparents.

His mother seems interminably anxious. She directs the kitchen chaos in an orange negligee covered with black "happy face" designs, held together at the waist by a green tie belonging to her ex-husband, a security company monogram stitched on the front.

Mickey, the younger brother, shoved a pornographic wall calendar into my hands that he'd stolen from his sister's house. All of his sister's upcoming court dates had been penciled in, and they ran through to next year.

T. J.'s mother told me she had hopes that T. J. would be the black sheep of the family—the only offspring *not* to turn to crime. But her hopes were swiftly disappearing. T. J. has already been in court once for throwing gasoline at the mailboxes of a nearby high-rise and then setting them on fire. The blazes were fortunately quickly doused.

T. J.'s mother wanted me to drop by after school tomorrow to celebrate the release of her eldest son's best friend from the hospital. There was going to be lots of beer, chips, and Dolly Parton on the record player. The friend, who had been in a motorcycle accident, had been sitting behind the driver when they crashed suddenly into the rear end of a car. The driver's thigh bone popped out from its socket and shot backwards, puncturing the friend's left testicle.

T. J.'s mom commented: "In this life, you can still get by with one ball, as long as your pecker's all in one piece!"

Friday, October 14

When I went to public school, the worst you could be was the classroom informer. Squealing on somebody—anybody—was an outrage. Even among the very young, loyalty went unspoken. I was disturbed by the casual way Elvin betrayed the other kids in the class.

"Sir," Elvin began one morning, "Eddie's got two boxes of crayons in his desk instead of one. He stole one pack from your desk. I know 'cause I saw him do it."

Or, "Sir, I saw Betsy take an extra pencil from your filing cabinet. I saw her with my very own eyes."

"Hey, guess what?" one day he asked the class. "I saw sir put a box of thumbtacks in his briefcase. I bet he stole 'em for his kid!"

I borrowed a slang term used in prisons for stool pigeons: "wearing the snitch jacket." The next day I brought in one of my more beat-up jackets. The idea was to make Elvin put it on each time he finked on somebody. The kids thought it was a lark. Everybody started to snitch on their friends just to be able to put the jacket on and ham it up for the rest of the class!

I quietly took the snitch jacket home.

Monday, October 17

Big Arnie, formerly a kindergarten teacher, had been hired as the school's new compensatory teacher responsible for setting up a classroom to accommodate groups of students who found it difficult to function in regular classroom settings.

Arnie offered miniature hockey, table tennis, darts, macramé, lessons on how to use a yo-yo, and coloring Star Wars stencils. He also served as a sounding board for the kids' problems.

Teachers could choose up to five students from a class, and send them over to Arnie for half an hour at a time. Some teachers used the opportunity to go to Arnie's room as a bribe, so kids would finish their work. Other teachers admitted sending kids to Arnie that they didn't like, just to get them out of the room.

Friday, October 21

The local community center was offering soup-and-sandwich lunches for a dollar, so I went over. I met a beautiful West Indian woman named Saffron, who had a background in social work in Jamaica and was presently doing some volunteer work, counseling teenagers in our area. She started to talk about the fate of many West Indian youngsters coming into the country.

"The usual pattern is for West Indian immigrants to leave their children behind with relatives. When the parent finds a job, she—they're usually single mothers—sends for her kids. It's easy to leave kids back home temporarily, because there's always a big family, with aunts, cousins, and grandparents ready to take a child in.

"Many times, the mother marries again and starts a new family. When her children finally arrive from the Islands, they not only have to cope with a new culture, but with a new daddy."

Talking with her put the situation of one of my students into some perspective. Rhonda's brother, Leroy, had recently come from Jamaica to join her, their mom, and a new stepfather. Rhonda had joined her mother a year earlier. The transition had gone well, and Rhonda did well at school.

Her brother, on the other hand, took an instant dislike to his stepfather. Leroy was placed in Mrs. Rogers's class at school, and immediately was at odds with the other kids. During the first week, he pummeled one of his classmates after being called a "black bastard."

A few weeks later, he was caught shoplifting from the nearby plaza and charged by the police.

Monday, October 31

After we saw a slide show on West Indian culture, two of my West Indian girls asked if they could braid my hair.

Charleen, very hyperactive, and always in the throes of a high-strung dance, leaned a rickety shoulder into my back and started working on the crown of my head.

She put the comb through my hair, twisting it tightly, and winding it round and round. My hair became hopelessly entangled in the comb.

Rhonda had to get the scissors and cut the comb out.

T. J. lent me his Blue Jays cap until I got used to how ridiculous I looked.

Tuesday, November 1

When the kids asked me if they could play some music for the last half hour each day, I reluctantly agreed. They might get out of control, but it was worth the risk; music was an important part of their lives. In fact, if there was anything in the lives of the kids that could be termed "sacred," music was it. Radios, records, record players were ritual objects of worship, communication totems linking them with their gods.

More kids wanted to become rock heroes than firemen, policemen, scientists, or, perish the thought, teachers. I asked them what it felt like to listen to their favorite songs.

"Makes me feel free!"

"I feel like me!"

"I forget what's botherin' me!"

"I feel like a somebody!"

Because the kids took their music seriously and developed a tenacious loyalty to their individual favorites, fights often broke out over which records to play. Some kids were disco freaks, while others swore by rock 'n' roll. And some kids who liked radio asked for that. I agreed there could be one radio in the class, and told T. J. he could bring in one he claimed to have found in an abandoned car.

Sal argued that the class would be better off listening to his Elvis Presley collection, but T. J. plugged for his radio. I decided to let the class vote, and called a meeting to debate the issue.

Typically tough in a taut tee shirt and shades, T. J. opened the meeting by swaggering to the front of the room, hands in his pockets, clearing his throat. "Records are okay, but they got only one or two hit songs in an album. You gotta listen to all the others before you get to the hits. *Nobody* can argue about radio, 'cause radio plays *all* the hits.

"And another thing," he continued, warming up. "What happens when we go outside in the afternoon? Are we gonna plug a record player into a tree?" That brought a few laughs.

Sal hesitated before speaking, flashing an enraged look at T. J. "Okay smart-ass!" he said bitterly. "Bring in your dumb radio, but don't be surprised if it gets broke!"

"Here goes another fight," Charleen sighed.

T. J. grinned. "I got my radio right here, man!" Almost magically, he produced a tiny transistor radio, strapped to his wrist. "This is so I don't lose it!" he said to Sal, pointing to the strap.

Sal raised his fist angrily. "Who wants to listen to news? You don't get news on records!"

"News is only five minutes! And you get the hockey scores, too!"

"I hate that ole hockey!" Rhonda bellowed.

"And what about commercials?" Betsy cried.

T. J. jumped on top of his chair, waving his arm angrily. "If you don't want no radio then come and take it!" He stuck out his tongue at Sal.

I stepped in. "Class meetings are for talking things out, not fighting! I'm surprised nobody has suggested taking turns. One day bring in the radio; the next, the record player."

"Good idea!" Charleen exclaimed. "Why not let T. J. bring in his radio Mondays and Tuesdays. Sal and the other kids can bring records on Wednesdays and Thursdays!"

"What about Friday?" Betsy prompted.

"I'll bring my guitar!" Robert chimed in.

T. J. laughed, looked thoughtful, then said, "Deal!"

I rose to my feet. "Meeting adjourned!"

On the way back to my desk, T. J. suddenly turned up his radio full blast. Several kids started to dance. Soon the entire class was moving to the beat.

Friday, November 4

I joined a martial arts class to work off some frustration. I go twice a week and work out for several hours. Sometimes I even stay for an extra hour just to punch the bag.

Wednesday, November 9

Lynn was the bus driver who drove "slow learners" to the school from their homes in the outlying regions. The kids referred to her busload as "Lynn's Loonies."

Lynn was new at the job. Her first request was that the driver's area be enclosed in steel, with a shatterproof glass window directly behind her head.

When that suggestion was turned down, she asked if she could use, instead, a second-hand shark cage. She offered to install it herself if the Board would pay for it.

Lynn retired after two months.

Wednesday, November 16

John kept slipping nutrition books into my mailbox. I had resisted his attempts to sell me on the miracles of vitamins, bran, and other supplements as just food faddism. Impressed, however, by a number of scientific articles that seemed to back up John's claims, I decided to give it a chance.

I opened up a health store in the school, run solely by the students themselves. The office gave us a fifty dollar loan, with the understanding that it would be paid back at the end of the year. I stocked up on oranges, apples, bananas, papaya juice, raisins, and peanuts. The kids advertised over the public address system.

In the beginning it caught fire. I had to make emergency trips for new supplies, and we were even thinking of opening up a new line of products.

After a few weeks, the sales dropped drastically.

The proprietor of the nearby variety store felt the pinch, and was offering specials on candy to win back customers.

Thursday, November 24

Winter has arrived, so I gave my class an assignment titled "What I Like to Do in the Winter."

Stash wrote that his favorite event was snuggling into bed at night, pulling the covers tightly over his head, and farting.

Wednesday, November 30

Franko appeared to be one of my better-adjusted students. He rarely got into trouble, was well liked by the other kids, and showed a keen interest in his subjects. He seemed to be the model student.

Midway through the term, Franko was beaten up by some kids from another class, and shortly afterwards he started to become involved in more fights, sometimes with kids from other classes, sometimes with his fellow classmates. It was puzzling, unsettling—why had a seemingly nonviolent kid turned into a bully, and in such a short time!

When I talked with Franko about it, he replied proudly, "My dad tells me to do it. He's teachin' me how to street fight."

I gave his dad a call, arranging an interview after school. He arrived about four o'clock. When he took his jacket off, I was dazzled: chinos, black boots, a black shirt open to the waist with sleeves rolled up, his powerful arms covered with tattoos: fearless tigers, hearts pierced with arrows, coiled serpents. His hair was slicked back like a James Dean character, a tiny dark curl resting on his forehead.

He greeted me unsmilingly, shaking my hand firmly. "I'm Franko Senior!"

"Glad you could make it," I replied, rubbing my hand.

"Well, I figure if my son's in trouble, then I should be here, eh?"

His voice was warm and friendly. I decided to get to the point right away.

"Franko Junior's been fighting a lot, sometimes without being provoked. I've talked to him and he told me that you told him to fight. That you're teaching him how."

"I didn't know he went lookin' for fights," he said, frowning. "But if somebody's pickin' on him, that's different. I tell Franko Junior to beat the hell outta him, tell him to get the kind of reputation I had when I was a kid. Nobody wanted to tangle with me, and I'm goin' to teach Franko to do the same."

"Frankly," I said, "Franko's not simply protecting himself. He's turned into a bully."

He gritted his teeth: "Hell, if he's turned into a bully, I can fix that! I'll give him a lickin' he'll never forget!"

Tuesday, December 13

Betsy had more problems than a ten-year-old should have to cope with. An ugly red scar ran from her lips to her chin, the result of a freak accident on her bicycle. The kids called her "Flip-lip."

While Betsy was in the recovery room, the doctors had tied her into a straitjacket to prevent her from picking at the scab. Her mother felt it was the experience of the straitjacket that was at the root of her hyperactivity—one explanation for the way Betsy whirled around my classroom.

She and her family lived in a tiny brown townhouse in the middle of the neighborhood. The family included two older brothers and a German shepherd named Wolf.

Both her parents had nearly identical back problems from a near-fatal car crash they had been in several years earlier. Now they spent most of their time stretched out on their sofa or bed.

A constant, gnawing tension ate at the household. The father, now on a meager disability pension, was unable to work. The mother found it equally as difficult to cope.

One afternoon Betsy's mother appeared at my classroom door. A tall woman with short, sandy hair, she needed crutches to help her walk. While I dismissed my class for the day, she waited.

I suspected that Betsy was being beaten at home. Her mother admitted it without much prompting. "She seems to be the easiest target, since she's so active, always jumping around and getting in the way all the time."

She told me that she had been beaten occasionally by her husband. Since the car accident, the family had changed. She agreed to try and control her anger.

"Doesn't it bother you that your husband beats you, though? Wouldn't it help to work on that end of things?" I asked gently.

"Of course he beats me!" she snapped. "Wouldn't you be upset if you couldn't find work and had to sit home all day doing nothing?"

Soon something came up that gave Betsy a chance to boost her confidence: the school's talent contest. Any student could put together an act. She eagerly took a spot in the show.

She found a dilapidated banjo. For weeks she practiced, but always one simple phrase. Over and over again, she played those same three notes to a perfected monotony.

The evening of the talent show, although I was busy marshaling the kids, I gave Betsy what support I could. She had arrived an hour early, dressed in a shocking-pink outfit, her hair in tiny ringlets, her lips smeared with lipstick to hide her scar. I tried to build up her confidence, but then the sound system blew and Fred insisted I fix it. I didn't see her again until she came on stage.

She looked confident walking out to the center stage. I crossed my fingers. Using only a brittle finger, she began to play her single phrase, over and over: "Plunk-a-plunk . . . plunk-a-plunk . . . plunk-a-plunk . . ." After half a minute, the audience became fidgety. Some tried to smile to give her encouragement. Then I heard from the back what I had dreaded: shouts of "Freak!" and "Flip-lip go home!" Half-pleading, half-demanding that she make a fast exit, the audience called an end to Betsy's big night. More and more people began whistling, stomping, and complaining. She stood still, looking confused. At first she looked behind her, as if someone else on stage deserved the abuse. Finally a look of terror froze her face.

She strode off the stage dragging her banjo, fighting back tears. She stopped for a moment in the wings, looked out at the jeering audience, and stuck out a malevolent tongue.

She missed the next week of school.

Wednesday, December 14

"Mr. McLaren! T. J. punched me in the face!"

"Fuck you, Flip-lip! Quit lyin'!"

"Look at my nose, sir!"

"Did you hit her, T. J.?"

"She pinched her own face—I didn't do nothin'! She's tryin' to get me!"

"Come and see my picture on the blackboard, sir!"

"Did you use paint on the blackboard?"

"It's okay. It washes off."

"I'm not tryin' to get him into trouble! He really did hit me!"

"Will you come up and look at it now, sir?"

"In a moment."

"Is this how you do today's number work?"

"No . . . you were borrowing here. It's an addition question. What do you do in an addition question?"

"Carry!"

"Right. You carry, not borrow."

"Sir, are you comin' up to see my picture?"

"T. J. just stole my comic books from my desk!"

"You said you'd help me with my printin', sir."

"Just a minute."

"I didn't take nothin' from Frankie's desk."

"I hate printin'! Can I just draw instead?"

"Tell Sal to watch his fuckin' welfare face. I'll punch it in for him!"

"You're welfare!"

"You're mom's a nigger!"

"Okay, outside boys! We're going to have a little talk!"

"My dad used to be welfare, sir, but he ain't now. He drives a pickup truck . . . he delivers these boxes of flowers."

"When are you going to tell T. J. to gimme back my comic books!"

"I said for you guys to wait outside!"

"Garth's dad don't drive a pickup truck, sir. I never seen him drive a pickup truck, and he lives right next door to me."

"He gets the truck at work, stupid!"

"When are you gonna do somethin' about T. J., sir?"

"Who cut the cheese and didn't put out no crackers?"

"Sal did! I heard him!"

"It's Betsy!"

"Come on kids, let's drop the fart questions, okay?"

"The person that smelled it first is the one who did it!"

"Then it was Betsy!"

"You stink, Flip-lip!"

"Fuck you!"

"How do you say this word, sir?"

"Restaurant."

"Restr . . . ant?"

"Restaurant. Res . . . taur . . . ant."

"Restrant."

"Close enough."

"We havin' gym this afternoon?"

"Yes—Monday afternoon as usual."

"Can I be captain!"

"I'm suppose to be captain!"

"It's my turn!"

"Sir, come over and look at my paintin'."

"I asked to be captain first!"

"We're not having teams today, we're doing gymnastics."

"Sir, Sal cut the cheese! This time, I'm sure!"

"The next time we have teams, can I be captain?"

"My picture's dry, sir! Will you hurry up or just forget it!"

"Who said it was me that cut the cheese? Was it you T. J.? If it was, I'll bash your fuckin' head in!"

"Garth's got a *Playboy* in his desk and he's feeling up the pictures inside his desk!"

"What?"

"Ya, he put his finger up the ass of one of the naked pictures. There was this picture of a woman bending over touching her toes."

"Garth, can I see you a moment?"

"Oh, oh."

"Sucker!"

"I got my comic books back, sir. They were in T. J.'s desk, just like I said."

"They're mine! I brought them from home! Honest. My brother give them to me yesterday!"

"You asshole! You just wait until I get you outside!"

"Shut up welfare!"

"Okay, class, line up for recess."

Friday, December 16

Christmas reports are nearly due, and the only time I have to work on them is during lunch period. Since the staff room is filled with distractions, I took my folder down to the coffee shop in the local plaza and wrote while I ate.

I was about to leave when I noticed something familiar about a customer at the front counter.

Levon, hunched over a bowl, was slouching in his seat exactly as he slouched in his chair when he was in my class. His skin was grey and damp, an ugly cut hung on his forehead.

"How've you been doing?" I asked, sitting down next to him.

We shook hands. "Hi, McLaren . . . Good to see you. . . ." he said. Resting one hand on the counter, he wiped his forehead with the other. Beads of sweat reappeared at once. "Could you lend me some spare change for another bowl of soup, man?" His voice was weak. He paused frequently. I reached into my pocket. "Thanks man," he drawled. "I'll pay you back when I'm rich and famous."

Monday, December 19

Sal worked surprisingly hard, considering his well-known abhorrence of math. From time to time he glanced at me and whispered to himself. After ten minutes of concentration, his mouth tightened. "I can't do this work no more!" he howled. "I gotta get outta here! I hates my math! I won't do it no more! Nobody forces me to do nothin'!" he shrieked.

He disappeared out the door. Others followed suit.

By the end of the day, I had lost five of them.

Wednesday, December 21

Rocky is nine. He's a scruffy kid with a sincere farmlad face, big square shoulders, and extremely large hands. But his head is tiny, and he often grins.

He has the strangest habit of looking at you from an angle that should lead his sight in some other direction. All his movements seem oblique; when he approaches my desk, he never comes directly, but in zigzags. And he enters the room sideways, keeping close to the wall so that I can't make out which desk he's approaching. Then, at the last moment, he makes a dash for his own desk.

Rocky always looks perplexed. He'll raise his hand as if his life depended on it, and then withdraw it as soon as I call on him. A few moments later, he'll be standing in front of me to ask if it's time to go home. He'd sooner stare at the ceiling, scribble drawings in notebooks, anything, than read. He talks to himself out loud.

He once tricked a group of kindergarten kids into touching an icy metal fence post with their tongues. When they finally peeled themselves away, they had donated several layers of skin.

Rocky wants to join a motorcycle gang. He yearns to be an outlaw biker with full leathers, swastikas, and a club crest (his favorite was the Outlaw crest, a skull with two crossed piston rods). He likes the names bikers give themselves: Beast, Mad Dog, Chico, Pig. But the best thing about being an outlaw rider, Rocky told me, would be to have a biker funeral, to be ceremoniously carried past rows of shining bikes and be buried in his leather jacket.

I arranged an interview with Rocky's mother. She looked in her early sixties, too old to have a nine-year-old son. Halfway through our interview she told me she was actually Rocky's grandmother. He was born nine years ago to her fifteen-year-old daughter. Rocky's natural father walked out of the relationship before he was born. The daughter later married and had given birth to two more children before she and her husband filed for a divorce. His grandmother had recently informed Rocky that his older sister was really his mother, and that his nephews were really his half brothers.

The man Rocky knew as his father (really his grandfather) became an alcoholic, and had left the family only months before.

The boy was thoroughly confused. He asked why his real mother had "divorced" him when he was only a baby. He was told how his mother was really too young at the time to look after a baby, so his grandmother and grandfather raised him as if they were his parents.

The grandmother's new boyfriend was waiting outside the classroom, holding a little baby in his arms. I asked Rocky who the baby was. He told me it was a present from Children's Aid.

Thursday, December 22

I have a full beard. At the class Christmas party, I received twelve bottles of after-shave.

Monday, January 9

I had always divided the morning and afternoon into forty-minute periods, each concentrating on a different subject area. First would come spelling, perhaps, then reading, then math, etc. But now, to give the kids more flexibility and responsibility, I modified this approach. After opening the day, I put the entire day's work on the board. Then I told the kids that they had the rest of the day to cover all the topics, in any order they decided.

They had a great time charting out their timetables. Once they completed the assigned work, they were given free time. Most of them finished about half an hour before the final bell, and spent the rest of the afternoon playing.

As time went on, I kept giving the kids more and more opportunities to generate their own ideas, to choose topics they were especially interested in. It was a slow process, but the kids certainly seemed to respond better when given a chance to make some decisions for themselves.

Tuesday, January 10

I asked Sal's mother to come in for an interview. I hadn't planned on the conversation centering on her older son, Jack. "How's he been doing?" I asked, after she had indicated she was worried about him.

She lowered her head. "Not too good," she said after a pause, mumbling, "he's been in trouble." She lit a cigarette, took a slow drag. "He broke into a house with three other boys. The owner was away for the weekend and the kids heard that he kept guns."

I asked what happened.

"It wasn't my kid's idea, but he went along with it. They really messed up this guy's house—they shit on the floors, and smeared it over the walls. Then they found a little budgie bird in a cage in the kitchen and they tortured it and killed it. Just a little bird. First they cut its wings off with a pair of scissors, then poured boiling water over it, and finally killed it with a blow-torch.

"After nearly wrecking the house, the kids finally found the guns, and they brought them out of the house, wrapped in blankets. And they found bullets, too. They loaded the guns and took them over to the highway and shot them off over the cars."

A look of horror in her eyes and mine. I thought of all the people who use the highway, including myself.

"Did Jack get charged?" I asked.

"Yeah. He's got to see his parole officer, once a week."

Now I knew what Sal was referring to when he said his brother was a *big shot* in the neighborhood.

Friday, January 20

Every kid carried a comb. Combs were weapons. They were used in threatening gestures. Sometimes a wide swoop connected, leaving a light scar that became a status symbol, making me think of the sabre scars once proudly worn by Heidelberg duelists.

At first the black kids had the advantage with the five-pronged picks they used for their Afros. The white kids' standard-issue plastic combs were no match, so they all found long-handled combs to wear menacingly out of their back pockets. A long-handled comb could be used in forward lunges as well as side-swipes.

The most sophisticated comb available looked exactly like a switchblade. You pressed a button on the handle to release a jagged blade.

Wednesday, February 1

By the beginning of February the winter feels like it's dragging on forever. Both kids and teachers are despondent, lethargic. So I decided to boost my class's spirits by offering them an early Valentine's Day gift . . . I booked time at the local ice-skating rink.

A few kids nearly froze on the half-mile walk to the rink, lacking proper mitts and head-covering, and wearing worn sneakers instead of boots. But every kid managed to scrounge up a pair of skates!

While I was busy at one end of the arena, tightening some of the laces, T. J. and some friends sneaked outside to the parking lot. I saw him hacking away at a parked car with his skates, puncturing a tire and punching holes in the body.

I left my name and the school's phone number on a piece of paper and tucked it under the windshield wiper. Then I took the kids back to school. T. J. disappeared along the way.

I was shaking by the time we got back. Here I was trying to do the kids a favor, and I end up worrying about what would happen when the car's owner called!

I waited until four-thirty. There was still no call, so I decided to go home.

As I drove past the school, I glanced up at my classroom window. The kids had decorated the window with Valentine's Day messages.

I read the words "I love you, sir" on the cut-out hearts, driving down the icy road.

Thursday, February 2

John enjoyed eavesdropping at the office, and he picked up an interesting bit of information a few days ago which made me more than a bit apprehensive. One of the Board consultants would be coming in to visit my class.

"What's he like?" I asked, genuinely worried.

"Well . . ." John mumbled, scratching his chin, "he's a good man in many ways, but . . ." I looked at him doubtfully, arching my back to loosen the tight muscles. "Look," he said, running his hand through his sparse hair, "let's say he lives a little in the past . . . on the other hand, make it the Stone Age. Know what I mean?"

"What exactly *do* you mean?" I wanted to be prepared for the worst.

"Listen . . . I'm getting on in years too . . . but I've managed to keep up with the times. Let's just say the consultant was arrested in time, oh, about ten thousand years ago.

"You started out here pretty square. But now you're more like a 'guide on the side,' less like a 'sage on the stage,'" John was fond of corny sayings.

"You run a pretty flexible program. You let the kids sit where they feel the most comfortable—he wants to see them in straight rows. You make personal contracts with the kids, and assign work according to what they can handle—he wants to see the same material on everybody's desk. You're physical with your kids, you hug them and so forth—and he wants firm discipline.''

I glanced at him uneasily. "I guess he'll destroy me," I said wearily.

He shrugged. "Look . . . let me give you a suggestion." He put a fatherly arm around my shoulder, and walked me down the corridor. "Go back into your classroom and do everything *just* as you've been doing it. The *kids* like what you're doing, and *that's* the important thing . . . not that you're not still a rookie and have lots more to learn." I detected a note of hope in John's voice. "You'll do all right. Tell your kids they'll be having a visitor sometime this month, and promise to give them a reward if they're good."

"Do you really think I ought to do that? Do you think it'll work? I mean, it's bribery, isn't it?''

"I hate to see a good teacher go down the tube," John grinned, waving away my questions like so many flies.

"Any suggestions about what I could give the kids?''

John paused, thinking. "Why not buy them a giant gingerbread house, like in the fairy tales?''

Wednesday, February 8

My class had settled down somewhat. There were still fights, and kids refusing to cooperate, but most of them were getting into better working routines, sometimes teaming up with a partner to investigate items that caught their interest.

In addition to the learning centers, I had set up a drama center, consisting of a makeshift stage and a box full of old clothes.

Our science center was a tub of water filled with metric beakers of different sizes and shapes. We also had a mini-library for science, a microscope, and some slides of insects the kids had collected down by the creek.

Despite the increased response of the kids, I often wondered how much difference any of this would really make in empowering their lives.

Wednesday, February 15

This morning Rod offered to cover my class for the last half hour of the day. I wanted to get an early start downtown to hear a lecturer at the university speak on disadvantaged kids.

I drove several blocks through a heavy snowfall before realizing I'd forgotten my briefcase. I made a quick stop at the variety store down the road to buy a pen and some paper for taking notes. When I was crossing the street, I turned to see T. J. and a friend right behind me.

"Where'd you guys come from? Shouldn't you be in school, T. J.?''

"We just came from there," he boasted, "and you gave us a lift." They had bumper-hitched the entire way.

I tried to explain the danger they were courting in hitching rides that way, but they walked away laughing. I felt cautious, respectable, and old.

Monday, February 20

Bob runs a drop-in center for adolescents. He's a good friend, and I see him fairly often.

When he began working at the center, one of his first projects was to get the kids to play floor hockey. They insisted that it was impossible because they had no equipment. Bob spent the next few days teaching them how to make hockey sticks out of broom handles, pucks out of wire and cloth, and goalposts out of sticks and Javex bottles filled with sand, with string for a netting.

Wednesday, February 22

My decision to try to provide my class with more opportunities for self-direction was unpopular with a few teachers, who regarded with skepticism my attempts to experiment. They pointed to the results of a meeting we had held with some of the neighborhood parents, who preferred a more authoritarian system. In fact, several parents had complained that I was not using standard readers. Instead, I preferred to create readers out of the kids' own stories.

But, to my surprise, the biggest obstacle to creating a freer attitude in class did not come from the parents. It came from the students themselves.

All their lives they had been ordered by teachers and parents to obey rules. They asserted themselves, logically enough, by going out and breaking as many rules as they could. Removing the rules made them uncomfortable; it left them with nothing to push against.

It took months before the kids were comfortable with planning their own timetables, choosing their own topics for discussion and reports, and exploring their own questions. It also took time and effort to free myself of the odd feeling that, because I wasn't following the standard list of teacher topics, I was somehow not actually teaching. . . .

Monday, February 27

Today I talked to an administrator who has done a lot of work with inner-city kids for the Toronto Board of Education. I asked him what his perceptions were about the plight of poor kids in the suburbs.

"I've criss-crossed the entire country and see situations like the one you teach in right across the map. What makes your area a little more frightening than, say, downtown Toronto is that it's so isolated. There are a half-dozen inner-city pockets in the suburbs that are pretty spread out, and there aren't enough social services to help. From the outside the problems are so invisible, they don't get the attention they deserve. At least downtown people know the situations exist, but in the suburbs people try to forget about the problem areas."

Tuesday, March 7

Renee says her mother doesn't want her bugging her in the house. Her mother tells her to get lost.

When she gets home from school, she disappears. From late afternoon until ten o'clock at night, she spends her time reading quietly in the bathtub.

Wednesday, March 8

From the moment Charlie came into Mrs. Rogers's class he made her life miserable. At times she had to resort to pinning him on the floor and calling for help. Once during recess, Charlie tried to settle a dispute with a classmate with a heavy lead pipe. Mrs. Rogers managed to wrestle it away from him. Several times he was caught rifling coats and purses in the teachers' staff room. He and his newly won followers would come into school late, lingering in the hallway to urinate in the rows of boots outside the kindergarten classes.

Mrs. Rogers didn't give up on Charlie easily. One weekend she invited Charlie to attend church with her, planning to take him afterwards to a movie and a restaurant. He brought a friend, Tennessee. During the church service they excused themselves and went straight for the cloakroom, where they rifled the coats. They managed to steal enough money to take off for Funland, a popular arcade a few blocks away. Mrs. Rogers found them sitting in a tiny booth, watching a 25¢ strip film.

Without saying a word she drove them back to her apartment. When they arrived, she told them that she wanted to have a discussion, and asked them to wait in the living room while she went to the washroom. When she returned a few minutes later she found Charlie and Tennessee giggling together on the floor, a good portion of a bottle of her best Scotch gone.

She kept trying, but over the next few weeks she became completely fed up. After he stole eighty dollars from a secretary's purse, she had him placed on home study, which meant he had to go to court. The judge ordered him not to return to school. His education was to be provided by a home tutor. After several months of home study, Charlie's parents had him placed in Thistletown, a hospital for disturbed youths.

He'd occasionally show up in the school yard to announce to his former classmates that he was going to reform school.

"Hey Charlie!" the kids would say. "Far out!"

Friday, March 10

I constantly had to fight the conditioning I had received in my teacher training and in my first year of teaching. But more and more I was recognizing the incidental questions and conversations of the kids as a learning process. I saw that some of the most effective lessons took place spontaneously: what I often thought was disorder was, in fact, kids interacting in another form of learning.

For example, in the fall T. J. used to bring snakes in from the creek. The kids often crowded around his desk, excited, watching the snake writhe, touching its skin, exclaiming over its colors. It would take me a long time to get them back to their seats and settled down. I decided that what the kids were learning from T. J. was probably as real as any lesson I could have dreamed up.

Monday, March 13

She walked into the class with a noticeable limp, her eyes fixed on the floor. Her mouth was a black line; her eyes, which nervously scanned the class, were circled by purple streaks and red gashes; her cheeks were puffed and blue.

A student whispered to me that he had seen her running out of her high-rise building this morning pursued by her mother, who was waving a high-heeled shoe.

When I called her over to my desk, she looked up at me with an expression of guilt, as if she had done something wrong. She told me she had fallen off her bicycle.

Tuesday, March 14

One classroom activity that seemed to make the most impact on my group of grade fours involved printing out the phrase "LOVE IS . . ." in big, bold letters on a ten-foot-long sheet of paper. I tacked the paper to the inside of the classroom door. Students could volunteer their reflections on "Love is . . ."

LOVE IS . . .

A ham sandwich
Christmas presents
When my mom visits Gord in jail
McDonald's
The Ex
My parents don't fight
When I don't get it for being bad
Being allowed to smoke
Fingering your girlfriend
A honeymoon
Nobody to bug you at night
When your brother goes to dad's place
Fish and chips and vinegar
Going to see dad
Learning to drive
Seeing dad at the restaurant
Smoking grass
Looking after your little brother
Horseback riding at the Y camp
When dad comes over

Thursday, March 16

When Sal arrived in class half an hour late, I knew something was wrong. His eyes, usually clear and bright, were now red and glazed. His face looked blotchy, his hands were trembling.

"What's wrong, Sal?" I asked, giving him a hug, reassuring him I wasn't angry because he was late.

His mouth tightened. "It's . . . it's . . ." his voice quavered. "It's that dad came home last night, and . . ."

"What happened?"

Sal stared at the floor, breathing heavily, sniffling loudly. Then he blurted out, "He spent all his pay on lottery tickets, so my mom . . . she gots mad at him 'cause she needed the money to buy groceries, so I couldn't get no sleep last night 'cause they was shoutin' at each other." He raised his head and stared out the window, avoiding my eyes. "Dad was mad at me this morning, an' told me to keep out of his way or he'd bring out the extension cord."

Wednesday, March 29

T. J. arrived in class wearing a black bowling shirt with "Untouchables" stitched in gold thread on the back.

He gingerly walked to his desk and almost fell into his chair. His mouth was struggling to say something, but the words got stuck. When he managed to gain some composure, he moved from desk to desk, stammering "Hey you assholes! I'm floatin' on air!"

Most of the kids looked a little bewildered, but some of them found it uproariously funny.

"Hey T. J.!" one of the kids shouted. "Got any for me?"

"Come on over to my place after school," T. J. replied. "My mom's new boyfriend's gots lots."

It was hard to tell if T. J. was faking it. A few of the kids enjoyed acting drunk or stoned; they see it often in their environment. I tried to ignore him and continued with my work.

"What's the matter, McLaren? Don't you ever get stoned?" He began stomping around the room, hair flying, arms flailing. "Go ahead and call the principal, sucker!"

To T. J.'s surprise, I dismissed the class for recess ten minutes early. I asked if I could get him some coffee. "Sure, McLaren. Big trick, eh? Go get the principal when you go downstairs."

"T. J.," I said, "I'm going downstairs to get you a coffee. If you don't want it, I'll drink it!"

It took me only a few minutes to grab a coffee downstairs. But by the time I returned, T. J. was gone.

Friday, March 31

Betty had taught in our school for a number of years. Frustrated and bitter, she continually complained about her kids to other teachers.

During lunch, I asked Betty why she hadn't tried transferring from the school to a more middle-class setting. She assured me that the advantages, as far as she was concerned, were all with the inner city.

"In inner-city communities, parents don't really worry about what kind of program the teachers run, as long as the kid learns how to read and add. It's hard enough getting the parents to meet you for an interview!

"But when you think of it, less involvement means less pressure on you as a teacher. For one thing, you don't have to worry about too many busybody parents trying to run your class like they do in some middle-class schools. A friend of mine teaches in a pretty well-to-do neighborhood where the parents are always sticking their noses into the teachers' business: 'Why can't my Johnny do this? Why isn't my Johnny further ahead on that? Blah blah blah!'

"In this school, you don't get that kind of flack. So you put up with Johnny coming to school undernourished. You put up with his misbehaving in class. You put up with the fights at recess. For me, it's a lot better than having the community looking down your throat all the time!"

Few teachers, to be sure, felt the way Betty did. I spoke with many staff members who were proud to work in the inner city.

Monday, April 3

Today the consultant paid a visit. I had been nervous about it for weeks, and I took John's advice and promised the kids a giant gingerbread house if they behaved themselves.

A dyspeptic old crank who reminded me more of a hawk-faced prison guard, he was directed by the Board of Education to go into the classrooms of all new teachers in the area to make sure they knew how to keep the lid on.

One had to question the mentality that found succor in inspecting your cupboards, rating your blackboard script, how neatly you were dressed, how interesting your bulletin boards were and whether they had been changed recently, what kinds of seating arrangements you had and if the desks were veering off the lines marked on the floor by the edge of the tiles, and whether or not the dates in your daybook were underlined in red ink.

He sat down at the back of the room—a white-haired gentleman wearing a royal blue safari suit with a white belt, and matching white shoes. The desk was much too small for him, but he tried to squeeze in anyway. He appeared ridiculous. He tried to cross his legs, but his knees were too high. I noticed he wore diamond-patterned socks. The more foolish he appeared, the more anxious I became. This man could make or break me.

"I'll be observing you from the back of the room," he had said. "Don't be alarmed if you see me making notes." Butterflies in my stomach. "But carry on as usual," he stated matter-of-factly.

I felt like saying something to break the ice, like: "How do you feel about teaching life skills in the first grade?" But a wall of protocol stood between us. He would not break it. I didn't dare.

He stayed at the back of the room, chewing on the rims of his glasses, constantly attending to his little black book even though the lesson hadn't begun. His face alternately went blank and then animated—I had no idea what his expressions meant. I became terribly paranoid. Had something gone wrong already?

"Interesting bulletin boards," he said in a lugubrious tone, just as the kids came into the room.

What did that mean? Interesting?

I leaned back in my chair, planning ahead to myself, thinking that there shouldn't be any reason why today's lesson would be worse than any other day's. . . .

I decided that the reading lesson I had begun would have to be abandoned in favor of something where I could get away with more noise and movement. I sensed the kids were picking up on my uneasiness, and would not be able to contain themselves for long.

I decided to take the kids downstairs and play murderball—that way I wouldn't be faulted for having noisy kids. Luckily, there was a free gym period available.

He watched my control as I led the kids downstairs. I was certain he was observing how deftly I could get them into line. I imagined his breath on my neck all the way to the gym door. When I turned around at the bottom of the stairs to sneak a glance, I noticed with astonishment that he had disappeared!

All during gym period my nerves were on edge; I assumed he would pop in at any moment. The class must have wondered why I was still behaving like an armed forces sergeant with nobody there to watch. And the kids behaved beautifully. No fights, no swearing, no moaning and groaning.

When we returned to the classroom from an hour of jumping jacks, murderball, and relay racing, I was relieved to find he was gone. Apparently, he only intended to visit my room for twenty minutes.

I removed the large brown box from under my desk. Then I sat back and gleefully watched those happy kids devour the gingerbread house in less time than a school of piranha could finish off a roast beef sandwich!

Friday, April 7

Yesterday at lunch hour Fred and I played Ping-Pong. Fred prided himself on his athletic ability and, in fact, was a sensational player. I wasn't bad to begin with and, after playing so much, steadily improved.

I made a bet with Fred in front of the staff. Since I had been a bit late getting to school several times that week, I jokingly told him that if I won the game, I wouldn't have to show up till ten o'clock for a week. If he won, I'd have to arrive a half hour early for a week. Fred instantly took me on, grinning.

After a hard-fought battle, I won the game—and the bet. Of course, it was all a joke, but one teacher thought we had been serious. Today she complained to Fred privately that I was being given preferential treatment. If he didn't break the agreement between us, she'd report him to the Federation of Teachers!

Wednesday, April 12

When Laura and I stepped through the front door of her school's "Open House," I realized it was the first time I had been in any other school since I had begun working in the Jane-Finch Corridor; it was like another world. This was definitely not an "underprivileged" area.

The school was beautifully laid out—and no graffiti on the walls! The furniture looked new, and all the classrooms had wall-to-wall carpeting and tiny greenhouses off the balconies where the kids could grow plants.

I couldn't help but fantasize what my class would do to the place if they could switch schools for a day. All the fancy globe lights would be smashed, the greenhouses torn up, the carpets . . . !

I was surprised to see the sophisticated work Laura's teacher had put up on the bulletin boards. This third grade class was doing work that was more advanced academically than what my previous grade six class had been doing. I felt right out of it.

Laura's teacher told me that the only real "incident" in class had occurred when a kid took a pencil from someone's desk and broke it in half. The mother showed up after class with the kid who owned the pencil, complaining about the "permissiveness" of the teacher, since she had allowed such a "terrible" thing to happen!

I went home afterwards and opened a beer, trying to numb the culture shock.

Monday, April 17

Rhonda spent all morning in the library making a cut-and-paste picture of her stepfather. She was going to give it to him as a Father's Day gift. When she proudly showed it to the class, however, the reaction was unexpected.

"Ha!" howled T. J. "It looks like a chocolate bar with a bow tie!"

"You know what?" Sal laughed. "If you wet a nigger's lips you can stick 'em to the wall!"

The class roared. Suddenly T. J. grabbed Rhonda and tried to drag her to the fountain at the back of the room.

"Wet her lips!" Sal cried.

"Stick her to the wall!" other kids screamed.

I rushed over and grabbed T. J., pulling him away from Rhonda, ordering him outside. He took off like a shot and disappeared out the door.

"I don't want to hear the word 'nigger' again!" I told the class sternly. "It's a foul word and hurts people's feelings!"

The class laughed nervously, but they did quiet down.

For a while Rhonda sat at her desk quietly, scribbling all over the picture of her stepfather. Then she finally tore it to shreds. She took out a new blank sheet of paper and began drawing a picture of Darth Vader from *Star Wars* instead.

Tuesday, April 25

For the first time since I came to this school, most of the parents showed up for interviews. Although I had scheduled parents for only fifteen minutes each, sometimes the interviews lasted over an hour.

When they had all left, I saw Fred in the hallway and we walked down to his office for a quiet talk. I told him how depressed I was to find that over half my class came from single-parent families who lived below the poverty line.

Fred cleared his throat, leaning forward. "What we have to do in this school is to accept the child for who he or she is. We can't cloud our minds with the fact that the child comes from a single-parent family, or that the father is an alcoholic, or that the mother is rarely home.

"As teachers, we can't ignore that, but we can't let it get in our way, either. We have to try to make these kids feel like people feel like they're worth something. We can't worry ourselves about what to do with a kid who says fuck off, because that's only a symptom of how the kid feels.

"You have to ask yourself if there is any way you can get children to feel good about themselves."

"But what about the racial problem?" I asked.

"Most of the kids from this area don't feel good about themselves," he replied. "Also, they don't want anybody to feel good as long as they're feeling bad. Misery loves company. So, they pick on the blacks, they pick on you, they pick on me, they pick on the whole damn community because they feel so trapped in their own situation.

"Listen. Teachers have to understand about the prejudices they bring to their job. Somehow, they have to respect the kids' own values, and where the kid is at. We can impose our values on them, but that implies their values aren't any good. That would be destructive. We've got to develop relationships with these kids, and relationships involve feelings, not simply content or information. With poor kids, it's even harder, because you almost have to say to them that they are worthwhile human beings, that you don't care how they dress or where they come from." Fred was getting very emotional. His jaw tensed, his arms waved as he spoke, his eyes burning right through me.

"The way you reach a poor kid who's doing badly at school is not by concentrating on arithmetic, but by getting something going with him or her that tells them that you care about them as people. Forget about the curriculum, at least for the time being. Reach your kids through feelings."

Friday, April 28

I told the kids they could choose any subject they wanted for composition. Here are two I've kept.

If I Could Change Things in the World
Like no beeting childs

No punching childs

No kicking childs

No hitting childs

No burning childs

No hitting childs with brooms

No pulling childs hair

so nowne sould attak

Ther childs

When kids call other kids nigger or honkey. They are just looking for truble. And if someone calls you a nigger or a honkey it dose not mean have to start a fight. The right thing to do is to pretened that you don't hear what the person is saying. But the other day I had a fight with a girl who called me a nigger and a honkey. And I did the wrong thing. I went and started a fight. And I had a nother fight with a brown girl.

And I told her that me and her are both brown so, if I'm a honkey your a honkey too and if I'm brown your brown too.

Thursday, May 4

At the beginning of the term, Fred hired an American woman named Marsha, who had worked for a year in New York City's Bedford-Stuyvesant area, a rough urban ghetto populated mainly by blacks and Puerto Ricans. She was to replace our Special Education teacher who has resigned, on the verge of a nervous breakdown. Because she had two master's degrees in education, the staff quickly looked to her for leadership.

"Listen," Marsha confided to me, after it was obvious that the other teachers wanted her to lead workshops in class management. "I came to Toronto to get away from the problems of teaching in New York! This was the only school that had a vacancy, and that's the only reason I'm here. And from what I've seen so far, you've got some pretty serious problems. Wait about five more years, until the unemployment situation gets worse, and then you'll really be in trouble!"

Marsha was soon making great headway with her kids. We were all pleased with the support and advice she offered us. Her contract, however, was not renewed for the following year because the Immigration Department felt that a Canadian should have the job.

Marsha went back to New York. Rather than return to teaching, she found a job as a legal secretary.

Friday, May 12

Jay had greasy hair as black as shoe polish, combed in the style of an early Elvis Presley. He carried his overweight avocado-shaped body clumsily into my room late in the school year.

"I'm the new kid," he said with a nervous smile on his lips. His foot tapped impatiently on the floor while his eyes darted back and forth, up and down . . . looking at everything but focusing on nothing. Even his clothes seemed to have a mind of their own. His shirt was half tucked into his pants, his fly unzippered, and his shoes undone.

Jay was one of the most hyperactive kids I'd ever seen. For the first few days it took everything I had just to keep him at his desk. When I gave a lesson he'd just fidget around the room, constantly tapping everything and everybody with his ruler.

I decided to phone his mother. As soon as I introduced myself as Jay's teacher, she cut in. "I know . . . I know . . . he's blasting off again in class! Same thing happened in all his other schools!"

"How many other schools has he attended? I mean, he's only in grade four."

There was a brief silence at the other end of the line. "Six or seven," came the voice again. "Around six or seven other schools."

"Could you tell me why?"

"Well . . . these days you got to take each day as it comes, know what I mean? Last month I was all set to move into a house, but my boyfriend moves in with another woman. Before that I was living with a guy who started beating me up. And before that I was kicked out of my apartment because Jay started a fire in the building. Anyway, I'm not budging out of here . . . at least, not right now. My big problem now is Jay. I get so damn desperate with that kid.

"The little brat is always moving or squirming around. Try getting him into bed at night—it's like tucking in a beehive. And clumsy—like a bull in a china shop. I guess you noticed he can't even walk in a straight line. He's always stumbling into his little sister, knocking her down, and kicking her in the stomach when she tries to tell him to fu . . . to leave her alone. Every night he squirms in front of that TV and starts making all sorts of weird sounds; he thinks he's the soundtrack for the shows or something. I mean, he's always yelling and whining and screeching in the background. I get really desperate sometimes.

"He was on Ritalin 'cause the doctor said it would calm him down. But somebody told me it could screw up his sex drive when he grows up, so I stopped.

"The real problem was this neighbor I had in the building when he was first born. She's from Jamaica or one of those West Indian islands where they do all that voodoo and stuff like that. One of the tenants told me to watch out for her—she was a witch or something. I know she put a curse on him. I just know she did!"

Wednesday, May 17

Rocky's uncle, a former Black Diamond Rider in the early 1960s, and now a shoe salesman, made up a list for Rocky of all the active motorcycle gangs operating in the country.

All over the cover of his notebook he scribbled the names: Vagabonds—Satan's Choice—Para-Dice Riders—Last Chance—Outlaws Coffin Wheelers—The Wild Ones—Hell's Angels—The Henchmen—and Gatineau Popeyes.

For once, he spelled everything correctly.

Thursday, May 25

Jewel always seemed to be in a world of her own. She rarely spoke in class, but her creative writing never lacked excitement and richness of expression. Though often quiet and introspective, she always seemed to know what was going on in the outside world. Her stories dealt with adult problems: paying the rent, arguing with apartment superintendents, dealing with welfare officials, finding a decent job, making cheap but nutritious meals, picking up "hot" TVs or transistor radios, or finding ways to earn extra money.

There was a worldliness in Jewel's eyes, perhaps even a touch of smugness, and a supercilious smile rarely left her lips.

Jewel asked me to accompany her home today because some boys who had threatened to beat her up were apparently waiting for her at her building. Asking for help was out of character for Jewel; she was usually so independent. I gave her a drive right to the front door of her building.

When we discovered no suspicious looking boys waiting outside, Jewel just shrugged her shoulders and invited me inside to meet her dad.

After a long ride in an elevator that seemed to stop at every floor, we finally reached her apartment. A sign on her door read: "Cheap Housing Is a Right— Not a Luxury." Jewel quietly opened the door and led me inside. I immediately tripped over a box of kitty litter in the middle of the living room floor.

Recovering my composure, I paused and looked around. A bird cage with three loudly chirping budgies hung in a corner of the room. Dominating one wall was a large mantelpiece over a false fireplace that held a plastic, plug-in log. Covering the mantelpiece was a glass vase with plastic roses, a tarnished golf trophy, a tiny porcelain zebra, a candle in the shape of a penis and testicles, and a brown earthenware jug that had the words "Brown Jug" painted under the rim. A tattered Mickey Spillaine paperback lay on the floor beside the television. The set was tuned to the Little Rascals, but the sound was turned off. An orange vinyl couch covered in detective magazines and empty TV dinner trays stood only about a foot from the screen. On top of the set was a framed photograph of a young man in a purple tuxedo, purple shirt with black lace trim, and a peaked cap. The front of the cap bore the phrase "Do It" in big, block letters.

Jewel noticed me staring at the photograph. "That's my older brother," she said. "He just got married. He sure looks drunk, don't he?"

Beside the photograph stood a lamp with a picture of Niagara Falls painted on the plastic shade. The heat from the light bulb caused some kind of reaction in the shade which gave the appearance of moving water.

"Dad's probably out on the balcony," Jewel said, nudging my arm. "Come on."

She led me onto the balcony where a man was sitting on a lawn chair, buried in a book of detective stories. He looked to be in his mid-forties.

"Hi Dad!" Jewel exclaimed. "This is my teacher!"

I stepped across the balcony, ducking under a string of low-hanging patio lights. The man leaned back in his chair, arms dangling, his hair swept and matted up on top of his head like a greasy bird's nest. He looked up at me and extended his hand.

"Yeh. Glad to meet you. I saw you guys pull into the lot. I figured you was Jewel's teacher 'cause she said you looked like a hippie. Can I get you a brew?"

"No thanks. Beer hits me pretty hard when I'm tired, and I've had one of those days." I glanced over the balcony and saw the top of my van almost directly underneath. "Boy, you're high up here!"

He reached over, grabbed a plastic lawn chair, and dragged it beside him. "Have a seat here, but be careful. I nicknamed this chair 'The Toilet,' so don't fall through."

I noticed that the plastic braiding had been worn through at the center of the seat, so I sat perched over toward one side. Jewel's dad was grinning. He had a smile like broken glass; his front teeth were chipped and pointed, almost geometrical.

"I didn't know you was comin'," he said, removing his book from his lap and placing it gingerly on the floor. "Jewel always wanted me to meet you." He turned his head, blinking at me.

"Well, Jewel's a fine girl and doing well in my class. I brought her home today because she said there were some boys waiting around here to beat her up. I didn't see anyone when we came in."

"Damn kids around here!" he said. "Some of them are okay when you get to know them, but a lot of them are just punks." He spoke with a strange mixture of intensity and detachment, and kept patting his hand through his hair to smooth it back behind his ears, but the oily brown strands kept falling forward again. "There are always the rotten apples," he said, his mouth fixed in a stiff smile.

I glanced down from the balcony again. The sun was beginning to bathe the parking lot in an eerie, sulphur-colored light. A gang of kids got into a rust-splotched car. The car screeched away, leaving a cloud of blue smoke that lingered in the lot long after the car had disappeared.

"Damn kids!" Jewel's dad remarked bitterly. "Ain't they ever heard of noise pollution?" He took a pipe out of his vest pocket and clenched it, unlit, between his teeth. He sucked hard several times. "I feel sorry for all the riff raff you gotta teach in your class. If I were a teacher today, I'd carry a gun."

Jewel, who was sitting quietly in the corner, jumped up. "Daddy. Would you want Mr. McLaren to shoot me?"

Her father swung around in his chair. "Not you sweetheart. Just the punks." He turned around slowly and faced me again. There was a sad expression in his eyes. "I sometimes wonder what's happenin' in the world. I don't want Jewel mixed up with a lot of these kids. I was just readin' a story about two thirteen-year-old hit men charged with the killin' of a numbers racketeer in New York. It's a true story. Some crook gave the kids a loaded 20-gauge shotgun. And I just read that a coupla teenagers set a wino on fire for kicks. The mother of one of the kids is mad because her son is going to jail for killin' a bum. And here, in this country, this teenage girl threw herself off a balcony—only a mile or so from here. This guy finds the body, drags it behind the buildin', and rapes it like a piece of cold meat. I think the guy was from South America. They sent him back home." He paused. "Tell me Mr. McLaren, do you believe in castrating rapists? I do."

I stared at the floor. My head was swimming. I didn't know what to say. "Life is hard. Nobody has to tell you that. We live in troubled times. I don't know what's happening in the world. I'm just as confused being a teacher as you are as a parent. Somehow we've got to carry on—teachers and parents—and not give up and even work together." I was just mouthing the words, feeling an obligation to say something.

Jewel's dad sucked again on his unlit pipe. His jaw began to tighten and his aquiline nose gave his expression a certain regal quality. "Jewel likes you. At first I wanted her to have a woman teacher 'cause her mother walked out on us last year. Maybe now I should feel lucky she has you. You know, I just pray I can go through life without anythin' happening to Jewel. I mean . . . I mean I really worry about her. She's all I got and I'm all she's got. If anything ever happens to her I think I'll throw in the towel for keeps."

Monday, May 29

I told Marta that she couldn't go to the library before I dismissed the other kids; she had to wait her turn. She grabbed the stapler out of my desk, and before I could stop her, she had pumped three staples into her thumb.

Wednesday, May 31

It was a professional development day at Laura's school today, so I decided to bring her along with me to work. Even though she was a year younger than my students, she was looking forward to meeting them and seeing my classroom.

When I pulled into the parking lot, T. J. and Sal ran up to my van. "Who's that?" they asked.

"I'd like you to meet my daughter, Laura."

"I didn't know you had a kid," T. J. laughed. "Hiya, Laura. I'm the leader of the class, and I own all the kids in the room. They do what I tell them to."

Laura smiled as we made our way through the crowd of kids toward my room, Sal and T. J. following close behind.

"Hey, Laura," T. J. snickered. "You gotta nice ass."

"Easy does it, T. J.," I cautioned, "I want her to have a nice day."

Once inside, Laura took a seat next to my desk. The kids poured into the room, giggling and pointing at her. She just stared at the floor, feeling very embarrassed. Halfway through the morning art lesson, Betsy began shifting uneasily in her chair. Then she started to groan softly, smoothing her hands down her legs. "Oh, sir," she whispered, licking her lips slowly and sensuously, "you really turn me on." Her hands started to cup her underdeveloped breasts. "I wish I had X-ray glasses on so I could see your balls."

My face grew red. "Step outside the room, Betsy."

Laura continued staring at the floor. I picked up a yardstick, gripped it tightly, and started tapping the back of my chair.

Suddenly T. J. stood up. "Hey sir, can I go outside with Betsy?"

"Stay where you are!"

"But you got her mad!"

"She deserves to feel mad."

"Why're ya hasslin' her, just 'cause she's got the hots for you?"

"Okay, T. J. Change the subject. Everybody take out your math notebooks—we're going to have a little drill."

When the recess bell rang, I took Laura over to the main building, where the caretaker played Ping-Pong with her for the rest of the morning. During the afternoon she helped the librarian arrange books.

On our trip home she noticed something in her coat pocket—a crude drawing that depicted me having sex with a voluptuous woman.

After that, Laura never wanted to come back to the school.

Friday, June 2

T. J. enjoyed staying in the room at recess to fiddle with parts from a car engine that I had brought in for the class. When I wasn't on yard duty, I'd often join him. Despite the unpleasantness with Laura, I tried initiating conversations with him, with the idea that he needed somebody to talk to about his troubles, an adult who would actually listen.

When we talked, T. J. would doodle in his notebook. We started off slowly, so I wouldn't scare him off. At first, he doodled pictures of racing cars. He designed a special car that appeared in many of his drawings: the "Death Machine," as he called it. Later on, he drew other things . . . whatever came into his mind. Sometimes, when he was feeling burnt around the edges because of events at home, he'd illustrate some unpleasant episode centering around his family.

I showed his pictures to a friend of mine who was a trained art therapist. He told me that whoever drew those pictures was a very sick boy . . . possibly with alarming tendencies. But an art therapist can never know for sure until he interviews the child over a period of time.

Since it was almost impossible to talk to T. J.'s mother at her house, I tried to convince her to come to see me after school. I told her I wanted to try and improve their communication with each other.

"We're *communicating* just fine!" she told me over the phone. "He gets my message! When I tell him to do something, he does it, or else! And he knows what the 'or else' means!"

She also said that she didn't believe in all that "psychology bullshit." "If *I've* never had it, and *I've* made it this far, why can't T. J.?"

Thursday, June 8

Teresa hated going home after school. She asked me if she could stay after class not because she liked school; she wanted to avoid the gang of boys who waited outside for their "collection."

The gang demanded different things from different kids. Willy was told to bring coins; Tracy, comic books; and Teresa was to steal gum from the variety store at the plaza. Punishment for not coming through with the goods was a beating. No matter how carefully the teachers tried to prevent it, we simply couldn't be everywhere at once.

So Teresa's mother went to the store each week and bought bags full of gum for the gang members. She didn't want her daughter to be forced to steal.

Saturday, June 10

I decided to bring groups of kids home to my tiny bungalow in the Beaches district. We could walk down to the lake and explore the beach, stroll along the boardwalk, or skip stones in the water. Over four Saturdays, I planned to entertain the entire class.

Jenny spent hours dreaming up games and activities, and even more time overspending our budget, gathering an assortment of food that included oyster soup, lasagne, quiche lorraine, and shrimp.

This afternoon at the beach the kids ran around happily. They gathered odd bits of glass and stone, played games of tag and British bulldog, and sunbathed near the water. Some kids danced to blaring transistor radios, while others postured for my movie camera, much to the delight of the people strolling along the boardwalk.

The day went beautifully . . . until we decided to try having a campfire. Immediately, Sal and T. J. started fighting over who would light the fire. T. J. angrily threw a rock at Sal. I watched helplessly as the rock sped through the air and narrowly missed his head. He collapsed in a half-faint. First I made sure he was okay, then I calmed T. J. down. No one was physically hurt.

Later, I found the large rock T. J. had thrown. When I picked it up, I could barely manage to heave it any distance. His anger must have generated a great burst of strength. I could understand why he won so many fights.

Dinner was a big success.

At the end of the day, Jenny made her farewells to the kids.

"Did you kids have a good time?" she asked brightly, as they were getting into the van for the trip home.

One kid said, "Well, it was all right, I guess. . . ."

Another chimed in, "We shoulda gone to Ontario Place!"

"Na," T. J. jeered. "Who needs this, anyway? I have more fun at my place, just hangin' around."

Monday, June 12

Today I bumped into Brian, a boy I had taught in the middle-class school of my first year. I was sure he had been destined for good things—a textbook paradigm of a writer-to-be. At thirteen he was composing prolific verse which was incredibly sensitive and insightful for a boy his age.

He now loomed before me, over six feet tall, wearing a checked peaked cap, fatigue jacket over a goose-down vest, and worn Kodiak boots. His face, formerly soft and placid, had grown tight and severe. He looked as hard as a clenched fist.

"Hey McLaren, how you doin'?" he asked huskily, taking my hand in a vise grip and shaking it vigorously. "Are you still teachin'?"

"I sure am," I replied. "Tell me, how's that wonderful writing of yours coming along?"

A profound sigh. "I gave that shit up last year. I got a girlfriend now, though. She likes to dance so I'm into dancin' now."

I smiled. "How's your schoolwork coming along? Still at the top of the class?"

Brian's face twitched slightly and he nervously began playing with the peak of his cap. "I quit school last year," he said defiantly. "I'm over sixteen."

"Oh."

"Ya . . . well . . . I'm learning to lay foundations for cottages now. So if you ever want to build a cottage, you know who to call. But I've nearly decided to move down here. Damn mosquitoes up north this time of year are big enough to fuck hens!"

"Not exactly a poetic metaphor," I chuckled.

Brian smiled widely, revealing two missing front teeth, partly camouflaged by a flimsy moustache. "If I'm still up there this winter, why don't you gimme a holler and come up for a ride on my cat?"

"Your cat?"

"Ya—you know—Arctic Cat. I'm really heavy into snowmmobiles."

He scribbled his address and phone number down on a piece of paper and pushed it into my hand. "See you later, sir. Don't do anythin' I wouldn't do and if ya do, name it after me."

Thursday, June 15

I was interrupted in class by a cry of "Sir! Sir! Your shoe!" Since it was raining heavily outside, my first thought was that my shoes were muddy, and I had trekked dirt into the classroom.

But when I looked down at my crossed legs, I was astonished to see one of my pupils, new to the school, vigorously licking the underside of my shoe.

I jerked my foot away. When I turned the shoe over, I saw a large patch on the sole had been licked clean.

Tuesday, June 20

At the end of the school year, I took the kids to the Metro Zoo. They seemed excited by the idea.

At first things went well, but problems arose almost as soon as the tour guide opened her mouth: "Now, boys and girls, let's find out as much as we can about these strange and wonderful creatures, shall we?" she minced, smiling sweetly.

"Do you mean T. J.?" Betsy quipped.

At once, the tour guide became angry. She tried to draw the kids' attention to the tapir and its snout, but the kids rapidly drowned her out with cries of: "What's a snout?," "Who cares?," and "I wanna see the gorillas!"

The tour guide's lines were well rehearsed, with a slogan-like rigidity my kids understandably couldn't handle: "This is a peacock, look at its pretty tail!" or "Look at all the wrinkles on the elephant . . . doesn't it remind you of your grandfather?" I didn't have the heart to tell her most of the kids probably weren't interested.

The kids soon found her an annoyance, and wanted her to get lost. I decided I'd better take them around on my own.

To placate the zoo's security staff, who were beginning to give us rueful looks, I marshaled the kids into a semblance of order, and started out for the hippos.

The Metro Zoo's plan for keeping the animals separated from the human visitors involves a series of dry moats instead of the usual pens and steel cages, though in some places there were fiberglass shields. It was possible to leap across the moats, if you were crazy enough to want to. Naturally, that's just what some of my kids wanted to do. It didn't seem to matter if the animals were hippos, rhinos, or giraffes. The kids wanted to shake hands—though I noticed they didn't try anything with the lions.

At the pink flamingo exhibit, T. J. thought it would be hilarious to see if he could throw a stone and snap the bird's spindly leg. "Its leg is so skinny I could break it with my little finger," he boasted.

At the gorilla exhibit, he pointed to one of the West Indian kids, remarking: "Hey, Winston! There's your mom and dad! Jump in, and let 'em wipe your ass!"

Next to the gorillas and Egyptian fruit bats (which, to the kids' delight, defecated upside down), the kids thought the best part of the trip was McDonald's restaurant.

Friday, June 30

I threw a class party, and it went very well. Afterwards, Muscle Lady dropped by to wish me happy summer holidays. Her tee shirt read: "Four out of five dentists recommend oral sex." I asked her how my former students were doing. "Same as always," was the reply. "We ain't changed a bit."

On my way out I met a visiting teacher from the nearby junior high. "You taught Buddy in grade six, didn't you?" he asked.

"Not officially, but I spent a great deal of time with him. How did he make out this year?"

"He's a real behavior problem. But last week he ran into some problems outside the school, too."

"Problems?"

"Yeh," the teacher continued, "he was rushed to York-Finch Hospital on the weekend."

"No kidding. What for?"

"He got stuck to a dog—sexually, if you know what I mean. It took the intern in the emergency ward to get them apart."

Buddy had always been curious about the world.

EPILOGUE

During the last week of school, I asked Fred to reserve a position in the primary grades for me, just in case somebody decided to resign or transfer during the summer. He told me there was a vacancy in grades two–three; I could have it if I wanted it. Well, I told him I was still searching for my right grade level and was happy to take the offer.

Fred was glad to have a male teacher in the lower grades. He felt that kids should be exposed to male teachers as early as possible. Many of the children at the school, he felt, needed male teachers because they didn't have any permanent father figures at home.

Teachers make a ritual of getting together at the end of the year to discuss who would be getting this year's kids next year. Sometimes a big fuss was made when a teacher knew he was getting a student who was a real problem. Teachers trying to avoid having a certain child placed in their classroom might say their program "wasn't appropriate," or that their classroom wasn't designed to "accommodate excess motion." Staff members would even trade certain students for others; it was a marketplace, a slave auction.

T. J.'s little brother, Mickey, ended up on my list; Mickey's grade two teacher thought I was the right person for him. She had observed my program, liked what I was doing, and decided that a more tolerant atmosphere would be the best thing for him. At first, I didn't mind. But then I began to feel apprehensive. I remembered what I had just gone through with T. J., and every day Mickey was getting to be more like him.

I also remembered that first time I saw him—when I had gone to T. J.'s for lunch and saw Mickey running and swearing after a police cruiser carting one of his brothers to jail.

I was a little resentful about always being given the hard cases. Male teachers were usually given the wildest and most truculent students because males were better able to physically defend themselves. I didn't mind taking my share of hard cases, but I felt that some teachers sent me certain students to relieve other teachers who were their friends. It was a con game using the children as dice, and like any other con, it stank.

Still, in the end, I took Mickey.

"What kind of a plan do you have for him?" Rod asked when he'd heard that I'd finally agreed to take on a student no one else wanted.

"What Fred always prescribes. Tender loving care," I replied, somewhat sanctimoniously.

I had learned to be a better teacher and had made it through another year, doing my best to care for the kids. I knew I couldn't become one of the gang because kids have their own friends and certainly don't want their teacher to be one. I felt they were starting to respect me more because they knew I cared about them, and at the same time they knew I had reasonable expectations of them.

Now that I had a permanent teaching certificate, my future work seemed set. But could I remain happy as a teacher for the rest of my life? I was having misgivings about surviving emotionally for the next twenty or thirty years. I wasn't the type to become an administrator and had no intention of becoming a vice-principal, something many other teachers seem to long for and so many of them get trapped by. My mortgage payments looming every month tamped down my growing feelings of frustration. But I promised myself that once I felt that I wasn't offering a hundred percent to my class, I'd pack it in.

Jenny and I had been planning all spring to celebrate my new status with a trip to Cape Cod, and two days into the holidays we packed our van and left.

I saw T. J. toward the end of the summer vacation when I went back to the school to prepare my classroom for September. As I drove into the school parking lot, I noticed a wry-necked figure hunched over a skateboard. He was crouching on the curb, trying to fasten together the broken laces of his Kodiak boots. I smiled at him, but he didn't smile back.

"I came back to visit," he said dryly, balancing on the tip of his skateboard with admirable skill.

"Visit?"

"Didn't ya know? We got kicked out." He spoke quietly. "Ontario Housing kicked us out . . . we didn't have the bread."

"Where are you living now?"

"In the zoo, a couple of blocks over."

"How do you like it there?"

"It's the pits. The cops there are real turkeys. I got charged with assault, man. Can you believe it! This cop said I punched this kid out, but I didn't, so I clobbered the cop over the head with a stick. He tried to put the cuffs on me, but I didn't let him" He started riding his skateboard in little circles. "Can I still come and see you?"

"Of course, you're welcome any time."

"See you," he said, waving goodbye. "I gotta look up a few kids—got some unfinished business."

CHAPTER 3

"The Suburbs Was Supposed to Be a Nice Place..."

Tuesday, September 5

It was a great convenience keeping the same room. I was spared the job of moving all my paraphernalia; even the bulletin boards could remain the same. During the summer the caretaker had replaced all the desks and chairs with smaller versions to accommodate the younger students.

As they began hurrying through the door, I was amazed at how tiny they were. I felt like a giant shambling among a room full of elves.

"He's the first man teacher I ever had," I overheard one kid say. "If he's like my stepdad, I'm gettin' outta here."

Friday, September 8

"Does anybody know what the hardest part of the body is?" I asked the class during a science lesson.

"The head." "Feet." "My chin." "Knees." "Back." "A fist."

Finally a kid called out: "Teeth."

"Right you are," I exclaimed. "Now, does anybody know what teeth are made out of?"

"Stones." "Cement." "Bones." "Shells." "Plastic."

"It's called enamel," I told them, "and it's the hardest substance in the body."

At which Mickey shot up his hand at once, yelling, "If it's the hardest part of the body, then how come I broke a guy's front teeth with my fist?"

Monday, September 11

I decided to work on Fred's philosophy of improving the child's self-image—a difficult undertaking sometimes, trying to show concern for a child who is driving you crazy. But the method had worked fairly well for me with T. J., and I was confident that Fred's approach would be even more effective with the younger kids; they would be less hardened and would find it a little easier to accept a teacher as someone who actually cared about them.

I looked forward to giving students the support they needed, while not having to endure the resistance exhibited by the older students.

At first, I organized programs for the kids in role-playing and psychodrama, as well as other activities geared to improve their self-image. Later on, I abandoned the idea of working with the class as a whole.

Smaller groups proved more effective. Some of the students responded by calling me ''daddy,'' and a few of them asked me if I'd marry their mothers. But, as usual, there just wasn't enough time in the day to give each child the care and attention he or she deserved.

Tuesday, September 19

Samantha and Priscilla were talking at my desk.

''I'm glad I'm black, aren't you?'' Samantha asked her friend.

''Yah,'' Priscilla replied. ''Black is beautiful. My mom keeps tellin' me that, over and over.''

''We're brown now cause we're small. But when we gets older, we'll turn dark black.''

''Yah. I wish sir was black, don't you? Mr. McLaren, will you be black?''

''How am I supposed to do that?'' I asked.

''My mom says that if you're brown, you can go to the hospital and they make you white. If you're white, you can come out black. You gots to have a operation, though.''

''If you're a girl and wanna be a boy,'' Samantha added, ''you can get the doctor to make you a boy.''

''I don't wanna be no boy,'' Priscilla protested.

''Me neither! My mother had a sister friend, you know, who don't want to be black. So she had a operation and came out white.''

Thursday, September 21

Mickey worshipped his older brother, T. J. He acted as part sidekick, part slave, following T. J. wherever he went, scurrying down the halls ahead of T. J. just to open doors for him.

At the beginning of the term, T. J. dropped by my room to voice his approval of Mickey's being in my classroom. ''Keep him outta trouble,'' he warned me, grinning.

"I'll do my best, T. J."

"If he gets outta hand, just call on me, man. I'll come down and smack him silly."

Friday, September 22

I went for a walk to the nearby variety store after school. It had been raining and the streets were glistening wet. I made my way past rows of identical bungalows with square hedges and bedraggled petunias. There were lots of dogs, including several fierce Dobermans on chain leashes sitting in the front yards.

The variety store was located in a tiny plaza, comprising a milk store, variety store, fish-and-chips shop, and a women's hairdressing salon. Scribbled over a long-faded sign was the warning: "Keep Out! Property of the Dukes!" Crowds of kids filled the streets and sidewalks, which were littered with refuse.

To prevent break-ins the variety store was covered by a protective wire mesh. One kid was trying to scale it like a human fly, but his feet were too big to gain a secure footing and he soon gave up. Outside the store several boys stood spitting into rain puddles which filled the holes in the sidewalk. Two teenagers in overalls slumped against the wall, uncorked a bottle of cheap wine, and took several quick swallows. The empty bottle was tossed down a mud slope to the street below, where it smashed into pieces and woke up a toddler sleeping nearby, who started to cry. Children sat on the slope, watching the street and drawing figures in the dirt with their bare toes, while two laughing kids somersaulted down, somehow managing to stop themselves before they tumbled into the traffic.

I saw two girls from my class sitting on the curb across the street, smoking. One waved her hand while the other frowned and flicked her cigarette in my direction.

I bought some pipe tobacco in the store and watched the store manager threaten some kids with a sawed-off broom handle. Then I headed back to the school, wondering what I would teach the following day.

Monday, September 25

Victor had a problem. He was always pulling his pants down in front of other kids—and he was encouraging them to do the same. His mother would beat him for it, to no avail.

Once, in class, Victor swaggered up to Mickey, unzipped his fly, and stuck a glue bottle inside. Then while Mickey stood there startled, just staring at him, Victor wiggled the glue bottle up and down, chanting: "Mickey's got a sticky cock! Mickey's got a sticky cock!"

Mickey slugged him.

Victor did it again and, before I could intervene, Mickey hit him again.

This week Victor's mother enrolled him in a clinic.

Thursday, September 28

Anna and Suzanne asked if they could clean the classroom up during recess.

"We promise to make it look great, sir!"

"Wait till you see it, sir!"

When I returned after recess, I found that the desks were covered with fresh Magic Marker swipes and obscene graffiti. "Moosecock" was scribbled across the map. The ribbon on my typewriter was in shreds in the sink and inky blue water was spilled all over the floor.

Kids complained that their lunches were missing and one girl couldn't find her glasses. I noticed the window facing the street was open and looked outside to see books, papers, lunch pails, and glasses scattered on the ground.

Thursday, October 5

Tracy now wears a brace.

Late one afternoon, she tried to imitate Evel Knievel's jump over the Snake Canyon, her version a make-shift wooden ramp in back of the local Miracle Mart. She had even less luck than Evel: she broke her back.

Her elaborate brace thrilled and inspired the other kids when she returned to class. They'd seen reruns of "The Bionic Woman" on TV, and decided to find out if Tracy was bionic too. They left tacks on her chair to see if she felt pain; they poked her in the legs with pencils to see if she would short-circuit. And not a few asked her to jump up to the school roof with her bionic legs to retrieve their lost balls.

Wednesday, October 11

Charlotte taught perceptually handicapped students. She wanted to integrate her kids occasionally into a regular class setting for part of the day, and asked if we could combine our two classes. I enthusiastically agreed.

She owned a giant Great Pyrenees dog, Pip, which she brought to school each day. Usually that's an impossibility, since there are always students who suffer allergies. But so far there hasn't been a single complaint. Everybody loves Pip.

One of Charlotte's kids—Bruce—took a special liking to Pip. He soon became obsessive about sitting next to the dog, developing a wild possessiveness that scared the rest of the class away. Bruce is a big kid. One day he attacked several of his classmates because they fed Pip some scraps from their lunch boxes.

Charlotte got in touch with Bruce's father. His parents were separated and the father had custody of Bruce, while the mother kept his two brothers. Bruce had wanted to take his own dog with him when he left. But his father had moved into a building where dogs weren't allowed, so the dog remained at his mother's house.

Once Bruce left, his two brothers stoned the dog to death.

Friday, October 13

Today Mickey turned to me, smiling, and said, "Watch this, Mr. McLaren!"

Then he hit himself against his forehead with the steel edge of his ruler: three sharp blows. Deep red welts rose over his eyes. He continued to smile.

Tuesday, October 17

Samantha was staring at me, full of anger.

"Something wrong?" I asked her, walking up to her desk.

She put her hands on her hips, hissing: "Your face looks sickly pale today. You need a suntan!"

I frowned. "Do I look pale? I feel fine!"

"She means you're a whitey!" Sue snapped, also angry.

"Samantha's mad at you today!" Priscilla, sitting on the other side, barked.

"Is that true?" I asked. "Are you mad at me Samantha? If you are, let's talk about it."

Snorting at my suggestion, Samantha instead got up and walked slowly to the reading center, her face full of exasperation and suspicion, Sue and Priscilla following. The three girls had grown up together in Jamaica and were fast friends.

I followed them over. "Samantha, are you going to tell me what's bothering you?"

There was a profound hurt in her eyes. "Why do white people always fire black people from their jobs?" She used a tone of voice I'd never heard her use before.

Her question caught me by surprise. "What do you mean?"

"My dad got fired from his work yesterday. He told me whitey likes to fire black people. Is that true?"

"Well," I said, swallowing hard, "sometimes there is prejudice, but—"

"Last year we had a black teacher! Now she's gone!" Sue spat out. "We got lots of black kids in this school. How come we don't have more black teachers? How come Mrs. Jones was fired and not some white teacher?"

"Yah," Priscilla chimed in. "And how come the people who do all the firing's always white?"

I explained that the Board had fired all teachers who had the least experience, because of budget cutbacks. "Honest, Samantha, Mrs. Jones wasn't fired because she was black." But my voice lacked conviction.

A pause.

Samantha's brow raised in a curious puzzled expression. "I told my dad *you* don't lie, sir. So I guess I believes you. But you know what my dad said?" Her eyes softened and her mouth relaxed.

"What?"

"He said if you don't lie, you must be the only honkey that don't." She grinned.

I laughed and the girls laughed.

Friday, October 20

Mickey picked his nose and ate the snot. When I was a kid, one of my best friends was an avid snot-eater.

Sometimes several nose-pickers would have "snot wars," and often their assignments reflected the results of these battles in the form of little green boogies caked to the paper. Snot wars were not popular, but they did exist.

Snot competition was more commonplace, although it was not the sort of thing you would see every day. Kids would compete for the longest piece of snot, dangling their glistening finds on the ends of a raised fingertip.

Monday, October 23

A rummy lived in the park behind the school. The kids first spotted him picking through junk and putting choice items in a duffel bag he kept beneath the sewer pipe he called home. They were fascinated with his wizened old face festooned with coarse, scarlet patches. His lank, black hair was long and greasy.

Some kids claimed Rummy exposed himself to small kids who came across his hideaway. Then again, Rummy was accused of everything from mutilation to murder. I got a lot of mileage out of Rummy in the kids' creative writing assignments.

If a kid lost something on the way to school, Rummy had it. If there was a family fight, Rummy caused it. If a kid was mysteriously absent from class, Rummy had captured him on the way to school and was in the process of devouring him raw. The kids had found someone to blame for all the problems in their universe.

Now that Rummy has moved out, they continue to use him as a long-distance scapegoat.

Friday, October 27

"My dad's gettin' a new van," Jessie proudly told the class.

"Great," I prompted. "What kind?"

"I don't know, sir. But you know what, sir? It's gonna have a bar, and a bed, and lots of pictures of girls, naked girls, with big tits stickin' out and tips on them like bottle caps, Mr. McLaren! From magazines! Me and my brother gots a bunch we ripped out for the walls," he smirked wickedly, "and we gots to get some more for the ceilin'!"

I felt myself beginning to blush. Teachers aren't supposed to blush; we're always supposed to be in control. So I cleared my throat and tried to nip this in the bud. "What's your brother and a seven-year-old kid like you going to do with a van like that? And those naked girls. What do your mom and dad think?"

"Well, I can't drive yet. But my mom and dad says my brother can use it to screw his girlfriend in, but they has to have it for campin' in the summer."

Monday, October 30

Megan is a quiet, almost invisible child. She always stands alone at recess, almost motionless, except for fondling her lank hair. She hardly ever speaks, never gets into trouble, always completes her assignments, never interrupts a lesson or shows up late for class. I like her, but usually I hardly know she is there.

This afternoon the secretary left a message for me to call Mrs. Llewellyn. Who was Mrs. Llewellyn? When I returned the call, Mrs. Llewellyn turned out to be Megan's mother, and she was angry: "Now listen Mr. McLaren! I'm getting ready these psychiatrist papers on Megan! Tell me this! Does she daydream in class?"

"Megan? What's wrong?"

"How do I know! I just know I'm fed up with her! Fed up! I've got a nitwit for a daughter!"

I was able to calm Mrs. Llewellyn down and promised to have a closer look at Megan. Apparently she never talks at home, either, and spends most of her time alone in her room.

Thursday, November 2

When Gracie threw a heavy glue bottle at Pasquale, I called her mother in for an interview.

Gracie's dark-rimmed brown eyes, spiked lashes, and her long platinum-dyed hair presented a bizarre image. Only eight years old, she carried herself like a Vogue fashion model.

Gracie's mother wore an enormous cleavage and a blonde, lacquered bouffant hairdo with black roots. Her first question was: "Has Gracie been acting different lately?"

I mentioned the glue bottle incident.

This was her explanation: A while ago, Gracie and her mother returned home from Food City to find her dad in bed "shakin' the sheets" with a woman neighbor. He had been drinking steadily since his release from jail a month earlier, and was finding it extremely difficult to find a job.

When Gracie's mother cried out, he casually walked across the room and split her nose with an ashtray. Gracie ran out of the room. Her mother told me the scar from the incident was carefully hidden under a layer of makeup, and she pointed to her nose.

Gracie's dad moved out. He ended up living two floors below, with the other woman. Gracie would periodically bump into him in the elevator. To avoid him, she used the stairs—even though she lived on the twelfth floor.

What chagrined Gracie's mother the most was that all the neighbors told her that her husband was a fool, that she was so much better looking.

"Can you imagine how I feel? Like a bloody fool. This woman comes in and does a number with my man—right under my friggin' nose at that! He decides for hamburger when he could be getting a steak! Fine! Let him starve himself to death!"

Gracie had thrown the heavy glue pot at Pasquale because Pasquale's mother was the woman Gracie's dad had the affair with.

Friday, November 3

Faith was so hungry one day she brought a bottle of Kraft Thousand Island dressing to class and drank over half of it. Then somebody grabbed it away at recess.

Faith's mother showed up at the school today to ask me if I thought Faith had any acting potential. According to Faith's mother, there was money to be made in children's commercials.

Wednesday, November 8

Substitute teachers often claimed to be sick when asked to fill in at our school. And who could blame them? (One substitute lasted only fifteen minutes in my classroom.)

As everyone knows, a substitute teacher is fair game. And Mr. Cummings was new. He arrived early and eager.

Later that morning, I heard somebody screaming. I looked into a classroom and could hardly believe my eyes. Standing in the center of the room, dressed in bright green leotards and carrying a crossbow, was Mr. Cummings! A sheepskin vest and Alpine hat completed the outfit.

The costume was part of Mr. Cummings's innovative teaching. He was trying to tell the class the story of William Tell. He thought the kids would be bowled over by his colorful outfit. Instead, the kids were laughing and shrieking "Fairy boy," and "Fag," and mincing about in front of him.

I watched as he slipped his pants on over the leotards. Then he put math questions on the board.

He advised the office that he would not be available in future.

Monday, November 13

Cecelia, a beautiful West Indian child in my class, has sickle-cell anemia. The disease keeps her absent for weeks at a time. Her eyes are yellowed by the daily destruction of her blood cells.

She bears her pain stoically. When she is pushed, shoved, or knocked over in gym, she never complains. I often find her alone at her desk, crying silently.

Thursday, November 16

A parent stormed into school. "Those kids!" he complained. "They live like pigs! They ain't got no respect for the human race!"

He warned me that I should be on guard at all times, explaining that seemingly loyal dogs sometimes turn on their masters for no apparent reason. "And blacks! They contaminate everything they touch! Don't let them breathe in your face!"

If the kids' families had problems he didn't want to hear about it. "Let those people booze away their lives with no jobs . . . just because they're too lazy to take the jobs you see advertised. Just look at the want ads! There are plenty of jobs! And besides, the wine they're soppin' up each day was paid for by me! That's right—by me!"

He barely stopped to take a breath.

"You should see all the money the government takes off my check each week so them winos can buy their bottles of brain rot! Their lives are paid for by the sweat of the workingman's brow! Damn foreigners come into this country and take away our jobs. Went into their garage and let the air out of their tires. That's so he'll learn not to park so close to the sidewalk.

"And I own a gun. Bought it last Saturday when somebody broke the latch on my gate and made off with the barbecue. Don't ever want to have to use it, mind you. But just let one of them jungle bunnies cross over onto my property, we'll see what happens!"

Friday, November 17

Although I was experiencing considerably more success with the kids, I was beginning to feel uncertain as to how effectively their needs were being met.

Most of the kids in my class faced hardships I'd never had to imagine coping with. Education should give every kid a chance to succeed. And I feared the prejudice and hostility of the society would make life rougher for them.

I was lucky; I was white and middle-class; I owned my home in the fashionable Beaches; I'd gone to university; I held a place in society.

The more I brooded about it, the more antisocial and withdrawn I became. I stopped eating in the lunch room, preferring instead to eat alone in the nearby Italian restaurant. I wondered what else I could do to earn a living besides teach.

Monday, November 20

Priscilla brought a picture of her newborn sister, Olivia, to school.

"How d'ya like her?" she asked Samantha.

"Looks like she's gonna turn out white, just like your mom!" Samantha exclaimed.

"But she might grow darker later, like my dad."

"If it turns out white, I'll give you my Barbie doll jumpsuit. If it gets dark by the end of the year, you gimme your Barbie halter top!"

"Deal!"

Tuesday, November 21

Dale had a mother whose wan face came alive when she remembered her life as a little girl on a farm: "Those were the best days of my life."

We were talking after class. Dale was aimlessly kicking a scrap of paper the caretaker had missed on his four o'clock round. I had asked his mother to come in because I wanted to know more about Dale's home life.

"I wish we were still living on a farm," she continued. "That's what I regret most—not raising Dale in the country." Suddenly she was brushing away tears from her cheeks. Dale looked embarrassed and left the room. "I want something out of life for Dale, but I just don't know how I can do it. He's still upset about his father leaving, and he just won't seem to settle down. I'm out working and I don't really have time for him when I get home. You don't know what factory work is like. It sucks all the energy out of you, so I don't have that much left over for him."

Dale reappeared and sat in a chair near the window. His mother started talking again, but soon broke down.

"Look," I said, doing my best to reassure her any way I could, "I'll try to keep Dale out of trouble in school. Don't worry."

When they left, Dale shot me his first smile of the term. Somebody's fist had punched out one of his teeth.

Wednesday, November 22

Mickey wasn't doing his assignment; he complained his arm was sore. When I asked him what was wrong with it, he replied, "It has bad germs in it."

"Okay, Mickey," I said. "Roll up your sleeve so I can see where the 'bad germs' are."

He could barely pull his sleeve past his elbow. With my help, we inched the sleeve up higher, revealing a running sore that looked like a face.

Mickey explained: "I asked T. J. to give me a tattoo like all the other kids. I wanted a 'screamin' skull.'" His brother had carved a skull into Mickey's arm, using a pin and some ink he had leaked out of a pen.

Mickey was too embarrassed to go to the school nurse. I had to insist.

Monday, December 4

A friend of mine introduced me to a teacher from British Columbia who was in Toronto for a speaking engagement. She worked with disadvantaged kids herself, and was starting up a new magazine to deal with teaching and capitalism. Before she left, we made arrangements to meet over a drink. She was a stunningly beautiful woman of about thirty, with something very compelling about the way she spoke.

At a nearby "working-class" tavern she told me over a beer that most curriculum materials presently used in classrooms condition working-class readers to have negative self-images, to believe in the inevitability of their lot in life, to perceive their predicament in an isolated way, and to regard the possibility of change in the class structure as futile, or at least merely wishful thinking. She maintained that as my kids grew up, they would become more and more aware of how much their social class places them outside of the "mainstream of society."

Over another round of beer she talked about class differences. "Your kids are too young for you to make them socially active. But already you can see what's happening to them as a result of their poverty. It must upset you, as a teacher, to feel so helpless."

Protesting that things weren't that hopeless, I outlined some of the units I was using in class to promote self-concept, understanding, and harmony. But I had to admit they weren't working very effectively.

"You're still working within the capitalist ideology!" she remarked, grabbing my arm in a friendly gesture, almost knocking over her draft in the process. "You're romanticizing the idea that people share a fundamental humanity that occurs through a common understanding. But, under the capitalist system, this basic humanity is perverted because the class structure of our society denies working-class kids equal opportunities. You're merely accommodating inequality."

I had to remind her that I was teaching seven- and eight-year-olds, and that nothing I could do in one year, even if I agreed with her philosophy, would dramatically change their lives.

"Kids who grow up feeling hopeless," she said, her voice rising, "become self-effacing and self-deprecating. If you can't reach your class because they're too young, then get your parents together! Organize them!"

I couldn't help but agree that there was a lot of truth in what she was saying. The real problem *was* the class system. In this kind of society, they had a right to be deviant.

Monday, December 11

I didn't notice Mickey leave. I sent some of the kids to find out where he had vanished to. They had one hell of a time finding him.

Finally, they noticed a pair of tiny brown shoes under the cubicle doors in the boy's washroom. When they opened the door, they found Mickey asleep on the toilet.

Wednesday, December 13

Charlotte's group of ten perceptually handicapped kids wanted to repay me for taking them on a field trip to the waterfront. She suggested to them that an interesting way to say thanks would be to make me up a nice hot lunch.

Mad Sid became the most excited. Mad Sid earned his name by jumping out of a second story window—and surviving without a scratch. Charlotte always had to keep one eye on him.

She took her kids down to the staff room kitchen. The idea was to surprise me with a spaghetti lunch, the recipe contributed by Mad Sid's mother.

Chester the Hypo (chondriac) was especially eager to help make the sauce. Like Mad Sid, he could be difficult in class. He complained daily that he had everything from an upset stomach to a brain tumor. He complained to Charlotte that Sid's mother probably put something poisonous in the recipe, warning her to watch out for suspicious-looking material.

There was a critical element in the recipe they didn't know about: I had a meeting with a parent during my lunch hour. I was, in fact, particularly eager to get that interview over with. Brad's mother always spieled out her woes for what felt like hours.

When I arrived, she was sitting on the staff room sofa looking as theatrical as ever. In her mid-forties, she was a platinum blonde (this time) and her eyebrows were plucked into thin half-circles.

"Sit over here, please, Mr. McLaren," she began at once. "I've a lot to talk about. Now, about Brad—"

Charlotte's kids had sneaked into the kitchen while I began my conversation with Brad's mother. On a signal from Charlotte, they formed a line, and with Sid in the lead holding the pot of steaming spaghetti, they marched into the staff room.

"All right!" Mad Sid ordered. "Right face!"

Everyone swung around.

"Ready, troops? Let's go!"

They marched up between us. Mad Sid was wearing army fatigues and a plastic German army helmet. Chester wore a pink 1950s sports jacket that came down to his knees and a pair of Charlotte's black leotards, which he claimed were giving him a rash. A kid named Sweeney was carrying the cutlery in a straw basket suspended from his mouth. He peered out at everybody through a pair of moss-green diving goggles. Candy, who was carrying up the rear, sported a black velvet opera cape and shook a noisy tambourine. I pretended to be embarrassed by this procession, but Charlotte knew I enjoyed every minute of it!

Brad's mother became upset. She rose to her feet, dramatically threw her coat around her shoulders, and paused at the door to tell me, "I'll be in touch with you when you aren't playing zookeeper!"

Monday, December 18

A few weeks ago, I decided to try a new strategy for stopping fights. Whenever two kids started to throw punches, I gathered the entire class around the combatants, and we all hummed the old "look sharp" Gillette Friday Night Fight theme. It was so silly, the fighters started to laugh. I broke up a lot of fights in class that way.

Rod told me that he was going to submit the idea to HAID (Humane Alternatives in Discipline), an organization of teachers and parents who opposed corporal punishment.

Wednesday, December 20

Yesterday, when Fred saw me wearing overalls stained with paint from the previous evening's art therapy course, and carrying some of the latest school journals under my arm, he laughed. "If you don't slow down and lay off a bit, you're going to steal my act!"

Some of the staff members, however, were raising more than merely curious eyebrows at my apparent headlong plunge into Fred's philosophy. As long as

I confined my activities to my classroom, they didn't object, but when I let my class work in the hall or staff room, they felt threatened. The few teachers on staff who didn't really approve of Fred's approach felt he was filling the staff with "hippies"—me, for example—and at the staff meeting, with both Fred and Rod absent, they decided it was the opportune moment to nail me. They took me totally by surprise.

"I hear music coming from your class a lot, Peter. What kind of courses are you teaching?" one of them asked.

"Young kids need to be controlled. I'm going to get some of your hellions next year, and I don't want them running wild all over *my* class," another contributed.

"And why are you letting your kids work out in the halls?" one teacher demanded in a peremptory tone, rising out of her chair.

I was startled, unable to react to all this hostility.

John tried to come to my rescue. "Are they disturbing your kids?" he asked one of the irate teachers.

"Well . . . not exactly . . . but some of us have seen Peter's kids making his breakfast in the staff room! And they were unsupervised."

I found myself rising slowly out of my chair. "There were some grade six kids supervising the cooking," I said, trying to remain calm. "They weren't making my breakfast; they happened to be making their own breakfasts, because they didn't get a breakfast that morning or a dinner the previous night!" My voice was rising, but I couldn't hold back. "And if you're worried about the school budget, you can rest easy. The money for the eggs and oatmeal came out of my pocket!"

I called Fred later to tell him I'd had it.

"Peter, I want you at the school for as long as I'm here. And if you alter your program one iota, I'll fire you!" he reassured me.

Charlotte and Liz, buddies of mine, admitted they were too shocked at the staff meeting to say anything. To give me a lift, they treated me to a spaghetti lunch at the best Italian restaurant in the Corridor, and presented me with a gift. "It's to help you get over yesterday's staff meeting," Charlotte said.

It was a book on biofeedback.

Friday, December 22

I enjoyed celebrating Christmas with the kids. The class spent hours decorating the room with Christmas posters I was given or had bought. A plastic tree was donated by a previous staff member, and we decorated it with crepe paper, tinsel, popcorn, and cotton batting.

I played some Christmas carols on my guitar, not very well, I'm afraid, since I usually prefer to play Mississippi Delta blues.

The kids had shown up with presents for me: socks, wallets, bottles of wine, chocolates, beer mugs; well over half the class brought something for me. I had stressed that presents didn't matter, but I could see Mickey was upset because he didn't have anything for me. When he saw all the other kids giving me gifts, he ran out of the room.

About fifteen minutes later, he returned with a plastic bag. "This is a Christmas present for you" he said, handing me the bag, head lowered.

"Thanks, Mickey," I replied, cordially. He walked over to his desk and stood there, sort of squirming. "Why don't you come over here while I open it?" I suggested.

He took a few steps, then stopped.

I reached into the bag and pulled out a tattered copy of *National Geographic*. I immediately recognized it as one of the many I kept in the stockroom.

"Thanks, Mickey!" I exclaimed. "Just what I need for my collection."

"I . . . I," he stuttered. "I bought it at the store yesterday. Cost me five bucks."

"How did you know it was my favorite magazine?"

"'Cause it's got naked people inside."

The class laughed, and we all went on with the Christmas festivities.

Samantha, slouched despondently in her chair, refused to join in. All the kids were eating pizza and playing their favorite tunes on the record player, but she ignored them. Every so often she would look at someone with a sideways glance, but most of the time she stared glumly ahead.

"What's wrong, Samantha?" I asked, coming over when I had the chance. "Why aren't you joining the party?"

She looked up at me, her eyes dark and surly. "My head's playin' funny tricks again."

"Tricks?"

"It's that person in my head." Her voice was choked with anger. "Somebody's inside and won't leave!" She whirled around in her seat, contemptuously swept her hand through her dreadlocks, and rose out of the chair. Then she began trembling. "The voice keeps telling me about the end of the world, so there won't be no more Christmas, or summer, or winter, or nothin'!" Normally, she was not this disturbed.

"Look, Samantha, why on earth are you thinking of such awful things? This is Christmastime."

"My dad told me the world was gonna end soon, and Jesus was gonna come back." She fidgeted nervously.

"Try to think of something nice," I tried reassuringly. "I'm sure if Jesus did come back, he'd be okay. You wouldn't get hurt."

"On Saturday, this voice told me to gets rid of my sister friend, so I don't play with her no more. I like my best friend, but this voice inside me told me she's bad." Her tone was so bitter.

"What do you think the voice is?"

Her eyes dilated slightly. "It's the devil."

"Why do you think that?"

"My dad says the devil is strong and can go inside people's heads, and makes them think bad thoughts." Then she started to cry.

I put my arms around her. "Are you sure it's the devil and not just your imagination?" I was at a loss as to how to handle this.

"I . . . I don't know." She wiped away the tears. "I think so. Can you make the voices go away?"

"Well, I don't know, but I'll have a talk with your dad this evening. Anyway," I continued, "I'm sure that God is stronger than the devil. So don't you worry so much."

I called her dad tonight and told him the story. At my suggestion, he agreed to play down the devil and accent the more positive aspects of his beliefs.

Friday, December 29

An old friend of mine named Phil, who teaches in an inner-city school in Winnipeg, visited Jenny and me during the Christmas holidays. I brought out a bottle of Phil's favorite gin, and we talked late into the evening. Phil, as usual, was not at a loss for words, and he wasted no time in leading the discussion.

"So many kids in this country are emotionally starved," he told me. "Most of the kids I see pass through my door seem so wholly defeated and demoralized by life. They're filled with fear, suspicion, anger, hatred, you name it. Schools have to make these kids feel that they're human beings and worth something.

"I end up doing what you're doing, Peter; I end up functioning both as teacher and therapist. As a teacher, I try to inculcate a love of learning and impart knowledge and skills, and unfold some creative capacities. But as a therapist, I have to reduce so much excessive anxiety in these kids and try to dissolve so many emotional blocks that I'm becoming an emotional wreck myself!"

"Aren't we, as teachers, partially responsible for causing some of the problems?" I asked. "I mean . . . we support a system of education that's obviously failing the kids. What can we do when we're given thirty-five kids to teach in a crowded classroom who have already developed a mistrust and hatred for the world?"

Phil was always ready with an answer. "We've got to get the support of the community; we have to make them realize that their children aren't getting a fair shake. And listen, that includes all of them; they've got just as many problems as your immigrant kids. People are too ready to believe the poor are all welfare cheaters, or lazy, or that they keep having illegitimate children to get more mother's allowance checks. Somehow we've got to bridge that gap between the world of the ghetto and the middle-class pablum game of school."

We talked about the growing violence in the schools.

He shrugged his shoulders and breathed deeply. "Like jails and looney bins, schools isolate students from the real problems in society. I often wonder whether schools aren't just simply glorified baby-sitting institutions. . . . Look at it this way. We don't really need more manpower, and schools just delay the time the kids have to get out there and find jobs.

"Students are frustrated and feel like they don't belong. We expose them to aggressive models of success and then scream 'achieve! achieve!' until they turn off. And when they fail in school, they feel like failures in life. Look at what they're exposed to: TV, radio, newspapers, magazines, movies, ads. Then we drop these overstimulated kids into the slowest-moving institution in our society—our schools.

"Time for another drink. Am I pouring or are you?"

Monday, January 8

Dean, the school librarian, quit his job. He told me he simply couldn't take the kids any more—the noise level was unbearable. His new job is out in Moose Jaw, Saskatchewan, teaching at a private school.

A number of staff applied for Dean's job, and by secret ballot Helen, a special education teacher, was elected. I owe much of my sanity to her reorganization of the library.

Helen realized that, for inner-city kids, libraries were often boring places, and a library had to be a place for more than simply reading books. She set about changing the library from a place of passive silence to a center of creative activity.

Working late into the evenings, she set up over twenty activity areas where kids could work with sand, water, or blocks. They could also make their own newspapers, play with hockey cards, research just about any topic, make comics, tape stories, act out their own dramas on a makeshift stage, even play with the variety of puppets Helen had created. She arranged a schedule enabling a teacher to send a maximum of ten kids at a time each day. The kids loved the library more than anything else, with the possible exception of Big Arnie's room.

It was a relief to have ten fewer students for half an hour. But more important, the kids learned a lot there (whether they realized it or not); it was obvious from their projects and completed assignments.

Friday, January 12

Suzanne was dropped off at my door late this morning by her father. He wore a green snowmobile suit and a black cap with "Davey Boy" stitched in yellow across the brim, and he reeked of booze. "Suzanne hurt her leg this morning. Here," he grumbled, thrusting her toward me.

She hobbled up to my desk, eyes sunken into reddened sockets. Her father muttered goodbye through a half-smile of blackened teeth.

"That cocksucker!" Suzanne cried when he was gone. "He cracked me right across my leg with a stick just 'cause I wouldn't let him take my babysittin' money! Now he'll just go and buy another bottle!"

Tuesday, January 16

Mickey spent half the art period modeling his clay into a hot dog. When he finished, he walked to the front of the class and proudly showed it to me. Then he pretended to eat it, smacking his lips.

"That's too big for a hot dog!" Marta complained.

"My mom's got a plastic thing at home that looks like Mickey's hot dog," Diana chimed in. "Hers got bumps on it, and a battery inside to make it shake."

Wednesday, January 31

Well, all right. I do have a tendency to rattle on during a lesson. But this time, I had barely started when I noticed that Samantha looked bored. She was sitting at her desk, in deep thought. Her head moved from side to side as if she were struggling against an insistent voice inside her. I could see the muscles along her jaws tense as she seemed to forcibly stop herself from speaking.

As I went on with the lesson, I kept an eye on her.

She looked down, nervously tapping on her desk. Then her hands suddenly jerked back and she shot to her feet, with both eyes bulging. When she had everyone's startled attention, she began to sing in a sweet, melodic voice:

> "As I was walkin' down the lane, shh shh
> I met a pretty girl in Spain, shh shh
> When she leaned against the wall, shh shh
> I gives her my balls and all, shh shh
> Wouldn't momma be surprised, shh shh
> To see her belly-button rise, shh shh
> Won't momma be sad, shh shh
> When she finds dad's mad, shh shh
> Mommy on the bottom
> Daddy on the top
> Baby in the middle
> Saying give it all you got!"

Tuesday, February 6

Angie's mother, looking very worried, came in this afternoon and told me that a child had been molested in the elevator of her apartment building. (Half my class lived in that building.) From tomorrow on, she would pick up Angie and her sisters from school every afternoon and escort them home to make sure nothing happened to them. "I'm going to do this every day, every week, every month of the year, for as long as my kids go to school," she told me, her voice filled with worry and anger. "If Angie has any work to finish after school, you'll just have to send it home with her."

She expected Angie to meet her in the school lobby at three-fifteen every afternoon.

Friday, February 9

Tasha, a grade six student from Mrs. Rogers's class, enjoyed staying after school to help me clean up my room. Mrs. Rogers was delighted that Tasha had taken a liking to me—she needed a male figure at this point in her life. Her father had recently walked out.

Always pale, with sad red eyes, Tasha shuffled listlessly around my room each afternoon, picking up scrap paper and depositing it in the wastepaper basket.

Nearly every day she wore the same powder-blue denim dress, worn thin at the elbows.

Somewhere Tasha acquired a whisk broom, which she briskly used on the carpet. Down on her knees to brush chalk, she was very much the figure of Cinderella. After gathering all the debris into the wastepaper basket, she would carry it awkwardly down the stairs and empty it in the caretaker's office.

As soon as she finished, she would go to the art center I had set up at the back of the room. She always chose to play with modeling clay, shaping it into a figure resembling a man wearing a hat, carrying a suitcase. When I asked her who the figure was, she said only that it was "a traitor." After completing the figure, she would then viciously tear it apart.

She seemed to get a strange kind of comfort from the time she spent with me, but after a few weeks, Tasha no longer showed up to help with my room. Some of the other kids, I heard, had been teasing her about having a crush on me.

Monday, February 12

I met Priscilla's mother in the shopping mall at lunchtime. "Are you Mr. McLaren?" she said, her eyes wide and sparkling. "I'm Priscilla's mother."

"How are you?"

"I'm feelin' a lot better these days. The ladies in my buildin' finally got together this week and we had a meetin' in the basement." Her eyes roved over my face, a steaming hot dog clenched in her fist. "Well . . . a lot of us are getting fed up with nothin' happenin' around here. We decided to take things into our own hands, so we're trying to set up some kind of day care for our kids. I mean, we have to do *something*!" She paused to watch a group of teenagers with large blaring transistors wander by, looking at clothing displays in the store windows.

"That sounds great. Do you think you'll be able to do it?" I asked.

"We can if we try. I was glad to see everybody really tryin' to help each other."

I wished her good luck and she shook my hand.

"Good luck to you, too," she said. "You know, you've got half the kids from my building in your class!"

Tuesday, February 20

A conversation I had with Marta's mother about her first night in the city, in the Jane-Finch area, sticks in my mind:

"We had just moved into the city from Tillsonburg," she began. "You know, a farming community. Well, it was our first real overnight in the new townhouse, and all of us were tickled to death, if you know what I mean.

"The furniture didn't arrive and we had to sleep right on the floor, but I told the kids to pretend it was just like camping in a brick tent.

"In the morning my husband, George, heard this knock on the door. When he opened it, he saw this bottle on the porch with a piece of burning rag crackling and sticking out of the top . . . one of those Molotov cocktails you see in the war movies. George just gives it a big kick, and the bottle goes flying onto the sidewalk. The rag pops out and lands away from all that spilled gasoline, so nothing burned. Later, I found out that the next-door neighbor put it there."

"Did you talk to your neighbor about it?"

"Oh yes, we're good friends now. You see, the bomb was really for the former tenants. They had this child that kept the neighbor up all night. It had colic or something."

Monday, February 26

I had been getting depressed again. From the moment I woke up, I dreaded the thought of going to school. I found myself puttering around the house each morning: doing dishes, reading a book, finding any excuse not to leave until the very last minute. Usually I arrived at the school only moments before the bell.

Fred began to mention that I was "cutting my arrivals pretty close," so I decided to make a concerted effort to arrive early. Perhaps I could work out some material before the kids arrived: I could prepare the room, or have the work already on the blackboard. Maybe more advance preparation would get me in a better frame of mind.

So I set my alarm for six-thirty, and if I rushed breakfast and traffic wasn't a problem, I could make it to the school before eight.

Every morning a depressed-looking kid, wearing a rumpled brown jacket and a Super Fly cap, would be standing in the same spot in the teachers' parking lot. Sometimes he whistled loudly, sometimes he hummed.

After the first few days, I decided he was trying to attract my attention. Usually I just gave him a wave or a smile. Now I began to invite him to come inside with me. He timidly introduced himself as Ralph.

He showed his appreciation by eagerly dashing around my room, tidying my cupboards, scrubbing graffiti off desktops, placing a freshly run-off mimeo sheet at each desk. After about half an hour of helping out, he'd curl up on my desk, tired and hungry.

He apologized for tiring out so fast. To combat hunger pangs he always carries a small brown envelope filled with jello powder, taking huge mouthfuls when he needs a lift.

Thursday, March 1

I was startled when Rod commented on the way I was dressing for work: bottle-green railroad overalls, Birkenstock sandals, lumberjack shirt. "You look just like the kids!" he explained, trying an engaging smile. "Maybe that's why they like you so much; they can't tell you apart from their classmates. When you first started teaching here, you were much straighter."

I was glad that the administration had a flexible dress code for the staff. I first began switching my dress pants and sports jackets to casual clothes for practical reasons: my good clothes always got covered in paint or torn when I tried to break up fights. One of my favorite jackets had to be thrown out when I found Magic Marker swipes all over the back.

I decided I could relate to the kids better if I didn't distance myself from them by wearing expensive clothes. I knew I was on the right track when a kid remarked, nodding at my attire: "You dress just like my dad does when he goes on shift."

Several teachers who are very fashion conscious objected to the "deterioration" in teacher image. They made a formal protest to Fred and Rod, requesting that teachers be forbidden to wear jeans, except for field trips or extracurricular sports. When the administration refused to make any such rule, the protesting teachers grew more upset. They're muttering about transferring to other schools, not wishing to be associated with a school full of "beatniks."

Tuesday, March 6

My gas tank was dry when I tried to start my van this afternoon. Empty container in hand, I headed off toward the nearest gas station.

My route took me through the housing project that some of my kids called "the zoo." Kids were everywhere. A few of them were climbing a TV antenna that ran up the side of a townhouse. Another group piled into a shopping cart that was pushed into the street. Passing cars swerved to a shrieking halt, narrowly missing running children. "Ya fuckin' kids! Get off the fuckin' streets!" a driver yelled.

A group of teenagers slumped on the sidewalk, waving a can in the air. One of them shouted: "Hey mister! You gonna get high on all that gas?" I grinned and kept walking.

A kid of about ten grabbed a screaming toddler by the hair and dragged him into a nearby townhouse. "Get in the goddam house before I fry your balls off on the stove!" The door slammed.

Monday, April 2

Ros handed me a shiny, cracked snapshot of her hometown in Nicaragua. The photo showed her grandmother standing outside of a cinderblock house, smiling.

Standing next to the house was a church that looked as if it were made from corrugated aluminium. Pointing to the church, Ros exclaimed: "God rests there on his trips 'round the world!"

Next to the church stood her father, wearing a moss-green military uniform and holding a submachine gun. "He shoots the people who robs the stores."

Standing next to him was a hollow-cheeked woman. "That's my mother. My sister just died—she was only three and she made my mother cry and cry."

I looked at the photo for a long time.

"All the kids tease me 'cause I talk funny," Ros finally said. "I wanna go back home."

Thursday, April 12

Teachers can order special marking stamps from a supply catalogue or retailer. Usually the stamps bear standard captions: "Excellent," "Good work," "Do over," "Neater please," and so forth. A little cartoon figure accompanies each caption. Priscilla stole one of my stamps inscribed with an angel holding up a scroll which read "You can do better."

She was found in the girl's washroom, stamping sheet after sheet of toilet paper.

Tuesday, April 17

This morning there was a violent windstorm. Kids on their way to school were literally blown across the streets, cars were forced over to the curb; garbage littered the sidewalks. Naturally, few kids showed up for school, only ten in my class. Most of them wanted a free day in the library to work on projects of their own choice, and I gave them my permission. Only Colin wanted to stay in the classroom. Characteristically quiet and sullen, he was now unusually talkative. He began to tell me stories. He told me that on weekends he took a plane to either the White House or Elvis Presley's gravesite . . . depending on how he felt. He spoke very seriously.

With the wind howling outside, he talked about his sleepwalking. His mother would find him out in the hall in the middle of the night, pounding his fists against the wall. He told me about how he almost murdered a little girl.

"I get this funny feelin' inside of me," he said slowly. "It's like somebody else comes inside my body. When I get this feelin', I feel like I want to kill somebody. One night I saw this little girl down by the creek, and I almost killed her with my penknife. I would've killed her, too, if her brother hadn't come along. My mom and dad went to court with me, afterwards."

I didn't know what to think.

"Sometimes I dream of blood," Colin continued. "I love blood and guts and things like that. I dream sometimes about kissin' blood. That's why I like fightin'—all that blood! Once my dad cut his finger with a carving knife at dinner. He didn't want blood to drip all over the carpet, so I sucked his finger for him." The wind rattled the windows.

Thursday, April 19

Yesterday, I met with a group of about twenty teachers and principals from fourteen different schools in the city. We were trying to form a committee to investigate ways to help schools further meet the needs of working-class and immigrant children from poor families. Over hot pizza in a public school about a mile outside of the Corridor, we talked about some of our concerns.

We talked about the problems immigrant children have to cope with when adjusting to schools in the area: language or dialect barriers; conflicting traditions and customs; culture shock; parental expectations and personal goals; heavy workloads both in school and at home; academic upgrading; family conflicts. The children were often called names, misunderstood, made to feel inferior.

A grade five teacher told us that recently she was phoned late at night by a parent of one of her students. The parent was a single mother. Alone in her townhouse with her daughter at the time, she became panic-stricken as two adolescent boys tried to break down her door with a crowbar to get at her daughter. The parent demanded that the teacher "do something about it."

Another teacher spoke of two children in her class that were locked outside by their parents in the middle of winter, as punishment.

One teacher told the group in a husky voice, trembling with emotion, that she couldn't bear to see one child bring a lunch, day after day, consisting of only pieces of dried toast.

As the afternoon progressed, we all shared scores of classroom horror stories.

"There are lots more of us," one teacher told me, "who are afraid to speak out against the conditions in our schools because we're afraid of getting our knuckles rapped by the administration!"

Friday, April 20

Like so many other teachers, I joked about quitting after a hard day with the kids. Only now I was beginning to take the idea more seriously. I had been accepted as a graduate student in education, and two years of full-time study was compulsory. That would also mean two full years without earning a regular salary. But it would give me the chance to do some research, and perhaps work to make changes outside the system.

Wednesday, April 25

T. J. knocked on my door to give me a warning. "Sir!" he explained. "There's a fire engine parked out the front! A fire drill!" Unannounced fire drills occurred sporadically. Fire marshals and a truck would always show up just before a drill, so we could always prepare for them.

I turned to the kids and quickly reviewed fire-drill procedures: no talking, no shoving, no sliding down banisters. Also, the last person to leave shuts the door.

The fire bell began to ring. I swung open the door and came face-to-face with one of the fire marshals. Mickey suddenly broke out of line and shouted: "Lance called me a cocksucker! I'm gonna give him a punch!"

The fire marshal looked more embarrassed than I was.

"We'll settle it later, Mickey!" I yelled, urging the kids out the door and down the stairs.

"But sir!" Mickey insisted. He wasn't about to give up, especially in front of a fire marshal. "He called me a cocksucker!"

By now most of the kids had made their way downstairs on their own. A few hung around to watch the scene, as Mickey suddenly grabbed Lance and pounded his head on the floor screaming, "Goddam welfare prick!" I grabbed them both, one under each arm, and carried them down the stairs and out into the yard. The rest of the kids followed.

Once outside, Mickey kicked the wall angrily. "We didn't have to come outside. You tricked us! Look . . . there's no fire!"

The fire marshal gave me a rueful glance, tipped his hat to me, and murmured, "Nice place you got here," and walked quickly to his car.

Thursday, April 26

A senior administrator on the Board paid a visit to my classroom. Every few years he makes his rounds, visiting all the elementary schools in his jurisdiction to pay his respects. He walked into my room smiling. "Glad to see you!" he said heartily. "Fine group of kids you got here!" I smiled and shook hands.

"Like your set-up here," he continued. "Room sure is colorful." He was short and on the plump side, and he fingered a cufflink nervously. "Nice bunch of kids!"

The kids laughed and applauded themselves. "Who's the turkey?" one of them stage-whispered.

Mr. Brooks cleared his throat. "Hear you're doing a good job," he said. I nodded, and he smiled and walked out.

Mickey watched him go, then pulled urgently at my sleeve. "I've seen guys like that at my house. They come to see my brothers. He's your parole officer, ain't he!"

Friday, April 27

Georgette and Wendy picked up some dolls at the activity center. Georgette chose a G.I. Joe, and Wendy picked up a Farrah Fawcett doll.

"Let's pretend we're married," Georgette said.

"Okay," Wendy agreed, "let's start!"

Georgette took G.I. Joe's arm and promptly slapped the Farrah doll across the face with it, shouting: "That's what you get for talkin' to me like that!"

Monday, April 30

On the weekend I went to a neighborhood party held in a posh house near the lakefront. I'm not much of a party-goer, but I was feeling weary and depressed.

After downing a stiff martini, I heard a voice behind me say, "I hear you're a teacher."

I turned and discovered a woman who was staring at me rather intensely. "You *are* a teacher, aren't you?" she asked, ingenuously brightening up her smile.

I wasn't in the mood for niceties. I removed my plastic union card from my wallet and presented it to her. "I think I'm a teacher," I said sarcastically. "At least . . . I think that's what it says on my card."

"I've always wanted to be a teacher," she continued, with a pretentious, almost commercial civility. "I just love little kids. Youth is so much fun and so exciting . . . teaching must be so rewarding. Tell me, what are your pupils like?"

I paused for a long time. "Well," I said, "let me see. I have shy kids . . . aggressive kids . . . kids that need prodding . . . kids that balk if pushed . . . kids susceptible to colds . . . kids that never get sick . . . kids who aren't interested in playing music . . . kids who will bang out a tune on anything . . . black kids, white kids, mulatto kids, Spanish kids, Italian kids, West Indian kids, WASP kids,

Catholic kids, kids from South America, kids from Nova Scotia . . . kids that had polio . . . kids that have sickle-cell anemia . . . kids that have cold sores and hangnails . . . one kid who had a nervous breakdown at seven . . . kids who have scars from beatings . . . kids whose parents never discipline them . . . kids who wear tattered clothes . . . kids who wear the latest fashions . . . kids who love me . . . kids who think I screw the teacher down the hall . . . kids that frown all the time . . . kids that never stop smiling. . . .''

I stopped. The woman stared at me as if I were crazy. I probably was crazy. After a few moments of silence the woman reached over and touched my arm and sensuously planted a fuchsia-colored kiss on the nape of my neck. "I'm curious," she said, stroking my arm. "Do you really screw the teacher down the hall?''

Tuesday, May 1

I was surprised when the mayor's secretary phoned me today and asked me to participate in a special session at City Hall involving a council that had been set up to help relieve the tension in the Jane-Finch Corridor.

Speaking through a stiff headcold, I told the council, using my experiences as ammunition, that schools must do more to meet the needs of poor children. I said it was a moral concern. Blank expressions nodded in unison.

Thursday, May 3

Upset with his son's progress report, Mr. Corelli called me at the school and requested an interview. Because he worked the late afternoon shift at a glass and paint factory, he was unable to come to the school during regular hours. I told him I'd be glad to drop by his place on Sunday afternoon.

I knocked on the door of the tiny brick townhouse shortly after twelve. A thin, wiry man in a sleeveless white tee shirt answered the door.

"I'm Frank's dad," he said, motioning me inside, offering me the lazy-boy armchair that dominated the tiny living room. I found myself facing about a dozen bowling trophies crowded together on top of a rusty filing cabinet. Portraits of John and Robert Kennedy, painted on black felt, hung above the window.

"As you can see, we're beer drinkers here!" and he pointed to the hall. I saw it was completely papered in Labatt's "50" beer bottle labels. "My wife did that," he proclaimed proudly. "Took her six months. If you can find even a speck of space between the labels, I'll give you a twelve-pack free!"

He brought me a beer, slumped down in the sofa, and groaned. "Frank ain't been doin' so good in school . . . has he?" he finally asked.

"No . . . not exactly," I replied, pushing back on the arms of the lazy-boy, trying to get comfortable.

"Do you think Frank's gonna pass?"

"I don't believe in failing pupils."

"But is he tryin'?" he snapped.

"I think it takes Frank a lot to get himself motivated," I hedged, uncertain of exactly what to say.

"Look," Mr. Corelli said matter-of-factly, as he smoothed back the black tufts of his thinning hair, "tomorrow I think I'll show up in your class and give him a few belts."

I was shocked. "You mean in front of the class?"

"I give him lickin's at home, but it doesn't do any good," he replied, shaking his head. "Maybe in front of his friends—"

"That's out of the question! You can't teach a kid anything through violence or humiliating punishment. I can't stop you from punishing your son at home, Mr. Corelli, but I would never allow him to be hit at school. Not under any circumstances." I was trying to control my anger.

"Well then," he said calmly, "*you* give it to him in front of the kids, if you don't want me to."

My face felt hot, and I laughed nervously. "No way, Mr. Corelli! Let's talk about the problem first, and maybe we can come up with some solution."

Head tilted, a somber expression on his face, Mr. Corelli then fired questions at me in swift progression, ranging from the "too lenient" disciplinary approach of most teachers to the high cost of school taxes. Eventually he got around to what was really bothering him.

"It's hard coping with Frank alone. Ever since his mother walked out on me it's been hell. She went out to the variety store one day and never came back. I know Frank blames me, 'cause we used to fight so much."

I placed Frank in an individualized program consisting mostly of arts and craft–oriented activities, and tried not to pressure him on his academic subjects, at the same time searching for a strategy.

I had previously put Frank in a special reading series, but he went through the readers perfunctorily. Then I remembered his dad mentioning Frank's comic book collection, and I asked him to bring some in. We went over the comic books together, and soon Frank's working vocabulary improved.

Monday, May 7

From a distance I could see Lambchops, a grade six student, standing at the end of the hall. He hitched up his pants, lifted his shoulders, and snapped his fingers. Responding to his signal, three kids suddenly ran out of the washroom and pounced on a kid whom Lambchops had seen walking by. "Kick his fuckin' head in," one of them cried.

The kids took off like a shot when they saw me coming. The victim was left to nurse a split lip and a few bruises.

"It was only a joke," the kid whined when I questioned him. His eyes searched mine, sad and pleading. "Don't do anything, please! They'll get me on the way home."

Friday, May 11

Orantes, nine, swaggered over to my desk. "You got any hair on your chest?" It wasn't the kind of question I expected to be asked. "Sir," Orantes continued, "you ain't got no hair on your chest. My daddy gots lots of hair on his."

"You're wrong, Orantes. I do happen to have some hair on my chest," I replied, with a mixture of embarrassment and pride. "Most men do. But I'm sure your dad has more than anybody else."

"Lemme see then!" was the immediate shouted response. I had been trapped, outfoxed. "Lemme see! Undo your shirt and lemme have a look!"

I tried to gracefully ease myself out by saying, "Take my word for it, Orantes. Your dad has lots of hair on his chest. I don't have very much. Your dad wins!"

"You gots more hair on your head," he continued, undaunted, "but my dad gots more on his chest. He looks like a hairy monster."

"I'm sure your dad looks much more like a monster than I do, Orantes. And I really don't have any hair on my chest, either. I was just kidding."

"Show me then," he demanded at once. I had been suckered right in. "Show me right now! Prove you ain't got no hair!"

I gave up. I opened my shirt a little and pulled down the neckline of my tee shirt, revealing a few blond tufts. "See! I've just got a few—not like your dad. Okay?"

But Orantes had more up his sleeve. "My dad's gots a cock this big!" he went on, holding his hand a good two feet apart.

Monday, May 14

Fred warned me he wouldn't be around next September. He was taking a year's sabbatical to study in England. He thought he'd probably be placed in a new school on his return. It was Board policy to move a principal to a new school every five years. He offered me a job on his new staff if I ever wanted to join him.

"Would you like to be principal of a nice middle-class school?" I asked.

"Not really. And even if I did, the Board would stick me in another inner-city school anyway. Once you've been successful as an inner-city school principal, they always place you in another one. That's their idea of a reward."

Wednesday, May 16

It was one of the first warm days after the long winter. After class I decided to soak up some sun on a park bench near the school. The air smelled fresh and the sun felt good on my face. I lit my pipe and started marking a batch of exercise books I had brought along.

Shortly afterwards I was approached by three black kids—two boys and a girl—about ten years old. They wore identical shiny nylon jackets, tight-fitting jeans, and orange fluorescent sneakers. I didn't recognize them as students from the school.

As soon as the girl caught my eyes she flashed a wide smile and started snapping her fingers. The two boys also joined in, finger-snapping and slowly rocking back and forth. Weaving gracefully in my direction, they stopped only a few feet from where I was sitting and began a rhythmic cooing. Then the girl began to strut and sashay, moving faster, her companions following. I put down my book and drew heavily on my pipe, swaddled by the soft beauty of their voices, and mesmerized by the fluid movements of their bodies that shifted effortlessly from one intricate pattern to another.

Suddenly the girl's arms shot up and the voices and dancing stopped. They stood there motionless, hands on their hips. After a few seconds, blissful smiles drooped into frowns. I reached into my pocket, pulled out some change, and handed it to the girl—a small price for the pleasure they had given to me. Wide smiles blossomed once again. Then they turned and headed back toward the street.

Thursday, May 17

I stayed at the school late last night, setting up a reading clinic in my class. At one end of the room I equipped a large rectangular table with a record player and a dozen headphones. In the other corner I set up a language master and two filmstrip projectors so the kids could watch cartoon strips of classic fairy tales.

My pièce de résistance was an eight-track cassette machine complete with tapes of children's stories. I recorded the stories myself, and my voice was still hoarse from reading aloud into the microphone.

Whenever I stayed late at the school, I usually spent the night at my parents' house, just a couple of miles outside the Corridor.

That night I woke up about four o'clock in the morning, and couldn't get back to sleep. Rather than toss and turn, I decided to go for a drive. Almost instinctively, I headed back to the Corridor. I parked my van in the school lot and sat on the street curb across from the school.

For a long time, I just sat staring at the school in the predawn light, thinking of all the events that had gone on behind those drab, brown walls. From the outside, the building looked just like any other school; it was hard to imagine all the lost and troubled souls that passed through those doors each day.

One by one, people emerged bleary-eyed from the nearby buildings, clutching lunch pails or brown bags, heading toward the bus stops. A drizzle of rain began to fall.

I sat in the rain watching the Italian laborers in heavy shirts and trousers of thick fabric, West Indian workers in woolen caps, some carrying transistor radios the size of small suitcases. One black woman lifted her skirt and whirled in a little dance. Another woman in a colorful print shawl looked up into the sky, inviting the rain to cool her face.

The whole area looked so bleak, so sterile, yet strangely at peace. The grey high-rises seemed aloof, almost stoic in the soft mist that was forming. I listened to the steady rumble of trucks down the nearby industrial streets, birds chirping on the telephone wires, the screech of the garbage trucks pulling up to the backs of the buildings. Everything seemed so integral, even purposeful. But I knew that behind the faceless concrete facades, families were awakening to a new day of troubles . . . hustling to survive . . . or just giving in to despair.

I needed a wake-up coffee before the school day began. I headed over to the local plaza.

Friday, May 18

This morning John decided I should purify my blood. He sent a strange drink up to my class, which he claimed would do the trick. Made of vinegar, water, and honey, and perhaps several other unidentified ingredients, it emitted a putrid stench.

Phil watched me taste it, and then remarked: "Jeez, sir, you're just like my dad. He needs his shot in the mornin', too!"

Sunday, May 20

On Sunday, I went down to the boardwalk for a stroll along the lake. As I strolled along, hands in my pockets, head down, the planks in the boardwalk seemed like measured steps in an uphill climb to sanity. I was mentally calculating my fitness for another year in the classroom. Was I up to it? The thought of teaching for another year made me feel that I was trapped in a dungeon, losing all count of time. The warden might be a nice guy and the food palatable, but I was suffocating. I had to get out. I'd put in my time.

I decided to quit. I took a deep breath and started for home.

Jenny was sitting in the living room. When I told her she looked at me intently. "I know. I sensed it."

"Well? How do you feel about it?"

"I feel you'll be an old man by the time you're thirty-five if you keep on the way you're going. You know I'm behind you . . . and the kids will still be there."

Tuesday, May 22

I couldn't sleep last night; my mind was flooded with doubts. Did it really make any difference, my being there? Am I copping out, running away? And so on and so on . . . .

I loathed to tell Fred; I felt I was betraying him. When I finally got up the nerve, he took it well, understanding my position.

"Sure, Peter, I'll sign your leave of absence papers, only because I know you'll change your mind."

Wednesday, May 23

After lunch, Mickey told me he had tried to take a bite out of his townhouse. He showed me a chipped tooth and bleeding gums to prove it.

Friday, May 25

Duke, my wild and unruly former student, liked to return periodically for a talk. He had quit school after junior high. When he was in my class, he often wore a button: "Sure I raise hell. So what?"

Out in the parking lot, he showed me the new paint job on his motorcycle. Like always, he wore faded jeans, a wrinkled tee shirt, and a leather jacket. A fat friend was kneeling beside Duke's bike, checking the engine. Painted on the deep-blue gas tank was a picture of the earth and a distant star, with a bright beam of white light shooting from the star toward the earth. The words "The King Is Coming" were stenciled in gold letters over the picture. Running down the back fender were the fluorescent-green words "Bikers for the Lord."

"Remember when I got Lindsay to eat that dog shit, after shoving a Kleenex full o' snot in his mouth?"

"Do I!"

"Well," he said, leaning against his bike, "I didn't really mean it. I don't do things like that no more. I've changed."

Wednesday, May 30

I visited the group home where Barry lives. It had been two years since he left my class, and I decided to see how he was doing.

A teenage girl, both of whose arms were wrapped in gauze from fingertips to armpits, opened the door for me. She was bandaged to prevent her from hurting herself: she bit spoon-sized chunks from her arms with her own teeth. One side of her head was a mass of black scabs, with a few remaining tufts of hair sticking out. Barry, she told me, was out on a camping trip.

Friday, June 1

One of Mickey's older brothers had just been released from jail, and Mickey was excited about it. All day long, he drew pictures of the event. One picture showed his brother being led away from jail by a giant creature.

"What's that thing with your brother?" I asked.

"Don't you know who *that* is?" Jessie asked, a puzzled grin breaking across his face as he leaned across to Mickey's desk.

"Not really. Who is it, Mickey?"

"It's the Amazing Hulk! *He saved my brother!* Didn't you know that? He sprang Tommy from jail!"

Monday, June 4

Last March, Fred invited several art therapists to speak to the staff on the benefits of spontaneous art for inner-city children. A recently published research paper, demonstrating that kids who had difficulty talking about their anxieties often had remarkable success drawing pictures of what was troubling them, caught his interest.

After listening to the art therapists describe their program, the staff agreed to hire one for a probationary period, with an option for extending the program if it was successful.

We were each asked to submit the name of one student who might benefit. Although I felt I had many kids who could be helped by the program, I decided to put Mickey's name on the list.

Each week Anthony, his therapist, would withdraw Mickey from class and take him down to a corner of the student lunch room. Under his expert guidance, Mickey was encouraged to express himself with crayons, paint, and clay. He responded by painting pictures of army tanks in battle and, later, of his house and family.

Anthony also encouraged him to talk about his paintings. After the first month, Mickey was able to open up to him and talk freely, and soon a good relationship grew between them.

While following Mickey's progress through weekly meetings with Anthony, I began to know the therapist as a person, and was impressed. He explained that art therapy had its theoretical roots in the psychoanalytic work of Sigmund Freud, utilizing his theories of the anal, oral, and genital personalities. As he analyzed Mickey's drawings within this framework, I became fascinated.

"Mickey didn't even have to draw a thing before I knew he was a combination of oral and anal personality development," Anthony told me the first time we spoke about Mickey.

"Really?"

"Because the first thing he said to me was 'Eat shit!'"

But the staff eventually decided that not enough kids were receiving help; teachers could send only one student per class. And although we all agreed the therapy was beneficial, some teachers wondered whether more kids would be helped if the money was spent instead on school supplies. So the art therapy program died. The option was not picked up; there was simply not enough support for it.

When Mickey had to say goodbye to Anthony, he became extremely upset. Anthony was one person he'd become attached to. Now his behavior began to revert, and it was as if nothing had happened at all.

Wednesday, June 6

Suzanne stormed into the staff room while I was eating lunch—"I just went home for lunch and the super in my buildin' kicked us out! He changed the lock on our door so's we can't get back in! I couldn't even get my sweater!"

I offered her some of my lunch and she sat down beside me. "Why did your super kick you out?" I asked.

"He says my mom's a welfare bum and can't pay the rent. But mom's already paid! She just got a new job! And he threw out my baby sister and her babysitter and says we're good-for-nothin' niggers! My mom's gonna go to court 'cause she's real mad and she don't even know where we're gonna stay tonight."

I thought only for a moment. "Tell your mom you can stay with me." She smiled and threw her arms around my neck.

After speaking to her mom, Suzanne told me they would be staying with a neighbor on another floor in their building, but she thanked me for the offer.

For the next two days her mother went to court, trying to settle the problem. She got her apartment back, but because of the days she took off to appear in court, she lost her new job.

Thursday, June 7

At nine o'clock, I assembled the kids on the carpet. "Well, boys and girls, does anybody have any news?" I asked, as I did first thing every morning.

Two kids immediately leaped up, as if the law of gravity had been temporarily suspended. Esther Anne was one of them. I was surprised she volunteered; she seldom spoke, even when asked. For her to volunteer news was quite an event.

"Me first! Me first!" Georgette howled suddenly. She jumped up, waving her arms wildly. "Me first! I'm before Esther Anne! You promised!"

She was right. "I'll be right with you, Esther Anne, but I already promised Georgette that she could be the first today to give the news."

I was impatient as Georgette described her sister's birthday party. Esther Anne was on my mind, and I was eager to hear what news she had to report.

When Georgette finished, I turned to Esther Anne. She stared at me for a moment, her burning eyes darting from my face to the floor. "I changed my mind," she said at last. "I ain't got no news today."

I was disappointed, but tried to be positive. "Okay, Esther Anne. Maybe you'll have some news tomorrow...."

At the end of the day, she came up to me as I was packing up. "Sir, do you want to know what my news was?"

"Why, I sure do," I answered, eager to draw her out of her shell.

"Well..." she began, slowly, "my mom, she burned me with a cigarette yesterday."

"Where?"

"Right here... and here... and here," she replied, pointing to her neck, hand, and forearm.

Friday, June 8

Carmen and Sasha were delightful. In other schools they might have been labeled "slow learners" or "behavior problems," but I thought they were great. At the end of a long day, it was always a joy when they volunteered to stay after class and help me tidy up.

This afternoon, while they were helping me clean out the cupboard, I casually remarked that kids today don't seem to really try to get along with each other.

"How you expect them to get along with other folks," replied Sasha, "when they don't even like the person that they are?"

Monday, June 11

During the last weeks of school, I took the kids to the park almost daily. I brought a cassette machine along with some vintage tapes of blues artists. Listening to the blues has always had a peaceful effect on me, and I hoped they could relax to some of the songs.

I put the machine under a tree and turned it on. A half dozen kids started tapping their feet almost immediately as Bessie Smith, Charlie Patton, Blind Lemon

Jefferson, and Billie Holiday sang haunting parables about the tragicomic underbelly of urban life.

Kids who weren't interested in the music ran across the park to the baseball diamond or else made for the swings. I lay down on the park bench and watched a sky full of dark clouds move slowly overhead, as if they were slowed in passing by the beauty of the music. A brisk gust of wind scattered paper and debris; the leaves flicked and eddied about the bench.

Mickey inched up to me and nudged my arm. "The music sounds real good," he said. "But it's sad."

Birds fluttered in the tops of nearby trees. A group of kids, groaning, puffing, and wet with sweat, tried to grab onto a large overhanging branch on one of the large trees. Finally, after many failed attempts, Lance dragged over a trash can and tipped it upside down. The kids propped the can against the tree and used it to boost themselves up.

Samantha sat down in the dirt in front of me. She stared for a few minutes across the field, her eyes scanning the rows of high-rise apartments that loomed on the outer edges of the park. They resembled giant gravestones under the low, menacing sky.

"You wanna know somethin', sir," she said wistfully, still staring into the distance. "We used to live right downtown in this rotten place called Regent's Park. Then my mom said, 'We're gonna move to the suburbs.' Now that we're here we gots more people callin' us names and beatin' us up more than before. I thought the suburbs was supposed to be a nice place. Now I wanna go back downtown."

I put my arm around her shoulder and watched a tiny figure making its way from the school yard across the field to the park. As the figure grew closer I realized it was Priscilla, who had been absent during the morning. She ran the last few yards up to my bench, a sweet smile wrinkling her face.

"I'm the best kid in the class now, sir!" she announced triumphantly.

"No you're not!" Samantha snapped and impulsively kissed me on the cheek. "I am!"

Priscilla placed her hands on her hips and looked up at the sky. "I gots baptized last night—so there! Hallelulia and praise the Lord!"

"Congratulations, Priscilla," I said.

"I went to a healin' meetin, too," she continued, a tumult of emotions. "This man touched people on the head and the Holy Spirit knocked them out. There was this fat lady there, and the man with the Spirit touched her and turned her skinny. I saw it! Her shoes was so big they didn't fit her no more! Then the man cured my brother's sickle-cell blood. Praise the Lord!"

"I don't believe you!" Mickey broke in viciously. "You're a liar!"

"Shut your face!" Priscilla snapped back.

Vinnie came running up to the bench, arms pumping and face sweat-streaked. He sat down heavily beside Priscilla, trying clumsily to fasten his sneakers.

"God praise you Vinnie!" cried Priscilla.

Vinnie looked stunned. "What?"

"I gots the spirit, Vinnie!" she cried, grinning widely.

Vinnie stopped struggling with his shoelaces and sat still. "There's no such thing as spirits!" he declared. "The guy in our buildin' everybody says is a boogey man, he's jus' an ole drunk."

Priscilla was annoyed. "I'm not talkin' about boogey men. I mean God's spirit. I gots religion!"

Mickey scowled and muttered, "You're crazy!" and ran across to the tree where kids were starting to climb down. Then he pulled away the trash can just as Pasquale was about to descend. Pasquale dropped from the tree onto the ground, landing with a loud thud—and a curse. Priscilla watched the event with growing disdain. "You needs the spirit!" she shouted. Mickey raised his fist in a mock salute. "Up yours!"

Tuesday, June 12

Usually, if you have to hide out, the bathroom is the place to do it. At least you're assured privacy in the toilet, if nowhere else. And that was why I began hiding out in the staff washroom during recess, trying to get the peace and quiet I needed to finish off some paperwork.

During recess this afternoon I was sitting on the throne marking papers, when I heard the door to the washroom open. I froze.

A pair of red sneakers appeared suddenly under the door of my hideaway cubicle. Just as suddenly the sneakers disappeared, only to be replaced by a pair of knees, then two hands, and then Mickey's head thrust under the door, grinning up at me.

"Havin' a nice shit, sir?"

Wednesday, June 13

Mickey's teenage sister showed up at my door, Mickey standing behind her, crying. He had been beaten on the way to school, she explained, and had returned home in tears. So she decided to walk him to school.

As soon as Mickey entered the room, he started screaming. "T. J.'s going to kill fuckin' Leroy," he shouted. "He's gonna punch him out for beatin' me up!" He wailed, blinking away tears, and flailing his arms as if at an invisible adversary.

I drew him close to me, and it was the only time he didn't push me away. While I wiped the tears from his eyes, I began rubbing his back slowly, rhythmically. His tight little face began to relax as I stroked his damp forehead soothingly and told him to take a deep breath. He sighed, and slowly the frenzy melted away. His shoulders loosened, then he crawled up on my lap and fell asleep.

Oddly enough, my kids just went on quietly with their work, and no one disturbed us.

Thursday, June 14

I took the class to Ontario Place as an end-of-the-year outing. Most of the kids had never been there, although they had heard stories about the excellent playground and the giant water slide. Because of the budget cuts I wasn't able to reserve a school bus, so we had to travel by public transportation. Several parent volunteers came along to help me with the kids.

Except for a scuffle between Mickey and Vinnie over who was going to sit at the very back of the bus, the kids were reasonably well behaved. The bus let us off at Exhibition Stadium, and we walked the rest of the way to Ontario Place, a short stroll.

Once inside, the children ran off everywhere and it took about half an hour to round them up.

We saw a short film about Ontario that was playing at Cinesphere, a theater with a giant, curved screen. At the beginning of the film the Premier of Ontario, William Davis, also known as 'Smiling Bill,' appeared on the screen, mouthing homilies about the greatness of the province.

"Hey . . . lookit him!" Mickey blurted. "It's Al Capone!"

"Yahoo," Vinnie exclaimed, "a real gangster!"

"He ain't no hood!" Samantha cried. "He's a millionaire. Lookit his clothes!"

"So what if he's rich!" Priscilla bellowed, "who wants to get dressed up like that all the time!"

I hushed the kids, explaining to them that other people were trying to watch the film, and that they had to behave if they wanted to go to the playground.

"He's bribin' us again," Mickey laughed. But they did settle down for the remainder of the film.

After the film the kids complained that they were hungry, so we ate lunch by the water, outside the entrance to the theater. Vinnie started throwing rocks at the swans and was joined by several other kids. I moved the class to the middle of an open area.

After lunch we marched over to the adventure playground, full of activities designed for children: rope forts, climbers of every shape and description, teeter-totters, pulley rides, tunnels, and slides. Most of the kids wanted to go on the water slide, but couldn't afford the two dollar charge.

"Everywhere kids go they gotta pay money for the most fun thing!" Priscilla complained. She kicked the fence outside the water slide, and watched the kids who could afford it laugh deliriously as they sailed down the giant curving slide, landing in various positions in the pool below. Most of the other kids forgot about the slide and amused themselves with other things. But Priscilla stood staring at the water slide for a long time.

After several hours of horsing around, we left. Samantha threw up all over my lap on the bus ride home, much to my wife's disgust when I arrived at my front door.

Friday, June 15

When I found out the local junior high was putting on a year-end variety show, I decided to go. Maybe I'd see some of my old kids.

Sure enough, several showed up. The first performer, in fact, was none other than Buddy. Even though he hadn't officially been one of my students, he was still one of the family—sort of.

Buddy was part of a dancing troupe, which did a beautifully choreographed disco set to the background of a Thelma Huston song. He was dressed in patchwork quilt knickers, striped suspenders, and platinum-colored satin shirt, his former mountain of Afro hair now neatly dreadlocked. The name of his group was "Fight the Power!"

The performance ended with some teenage girls reading an essay called "The Black Manifesto," aimed at getting the black community organized in fighting racism.

After the show, Buddy and I had a friendly chat. It's funny how much affection I had for this character who gave me so many rough moments. He told me he didn't hang out anymore with his old friends; most of his buddies were older. He was seriously taking up boxing. "And if I ever get to be Champ, I'll mention your name to the TV guys."

Tuesday, June 19

"This world is dumb! A man on the TV said a piece of a spaceship is gonna fall on our heads!"

"Hey, gimme back my pencil!"

"Yes, Vinnie, I agree. The world really does seem dumb sometimes."

"It's my pencil! I found it on the floor!"

"Sir! Wasn't Elvis the best?"

"He was pretty good. I liked him."

"See! I told you! White people are the best singers!"

"Hey, I didn't say white people were the best singers."

"There are good black singers as well as white singers."

"Liar! You just said Elvis was the best!"

"Brown people can sing good, too!"

"My aunt put my little cousin in the dryer last night. He lost five dollars at the store so my aunt put him in the dryer and he went 'round and 'round."

"Is that true, Mickey?"

"Wipe your nose Georgette! It's full of snot!"

"Welfare face!"

"It's true! I saw it!"

"Don't eat it! Mr. McLaren! Georgette's licking off her snot!"

"You looks just like my dad, sir. Exceptin' my dad's black."

"My friend said I look like Elvis."

"I look like Debbie Boone then!"

"Yuck! I hates Debbie Boone! She's gots pimples."

"You . . . you light up my life . . ."

"Shut up your stupid singin'!"

"You gots an awful voice, Samantha."

"My mom threw a wooden spoon at me this mornin'."

"What happened?"

"It missed. That's all."

"I was at the creek last night, Mr. McLaren. I saw these teenagers with their pants down."

"Wait a minute. Mickey wants to tell me about his cousin and Vinnie wants to tell me about his mother."

"I don't wanna talk no more about my mother."

"Take your finger out of your zipper!"

"Awww! I thought it was his cock stickin' out!"

"Mr. McLaren! Georgette's nose is all green again from snot. There's a little green worm comin' out of her nose!"

"You . . . you light up my life . . . light up my life . . . ."

"Shaddup! You sound welfare!"

"My mom told me I look just like Harry Belafonte."

"He's an old man, stupid. I seen him on a record. My mom says he's an Oreo cookie—black on the outside and white in the middle."

"What does that mean?"

"I dunno. He tastes good."

"I gots a new mom. She's deaf."

"She's a mental!"

"No she ain't! She just can't hear."

"You ain't nothin' but a hound dog . . . ."

"Shaddup! You ain't no good either!"

"Is the sky really gonna fall, Mr. McLaren?"

"Probably the bits from the space station will land in the ocean."

"I hope it lands on Vinnie's balls."

Wednesday, June 20

On our daily walk to the park, everything was going smoothly until little Carlos, a moment before happy and cheerful, suddenly fell to the ground, weeping uncontrollably.

"I miss my mom! My *real* mom!" he cried out to me.

"Your real mom? Where is she?" I asked, as I picked him up in my arms to comfort him.

"She's in New Brunswick," he whimpered. "My dad's sendin' me on the train to see her in July and they're gettin' a divorce!"

I tried to cheer him up by saying, "Why, that's only a few weeks away; all you have to do is wait awhile."

But he continued to sob. "But my dad's getting divorced now from my other mom so that means I'm gonna have three moms!"

I had no idea what to say, trying to sort out which mom he meant when, as suddenly as he began to cry, he jumped up, wiped away his tears, and headed over to a bunch of kids playing soccer.

Thursday, June 21

Guy taught English to new Canadians who could barely understand a word of what was being said to them. He was a valuable resource. Every day he withdrew three or four kids from each class, and in unique ways taught them to speak

English: he took them to supermarkets and had them read the food labels; he showed them places like the Kensington Market and other ethnic communities that radiated different atmospheres.

I didn't really get to know Guy until recently, when we had a chat in the staff room. He had just finished a frustrating interview with the father of one of his students and looked exhausted.

"I finally met the father of one of my kids . . . finally," he began. "For the last two months, Wally has been telling me, 'My daddy's gone away! My daddy's gone away again!' I didn't know if he was a traveling salesman, or what.

"Well, his dad just showed up, and we had a long talk. It turns out he's a mercenary, he hires himself out to fight in wars all over the world. He just came back from a campaign in Arabia, where he said it had been 'particularly gory'— that's all he'd tell me, just that it was a 'private war.' Now he's decided to take an interest in his kid. I told him that Wally missed him when he was away, and he just looked at me and said, 'What can I do? It's my job.'"

Guy and I compared notes and found we had much in common; our teaching philosophies were very similar. He was a bit worried that Fred hadn't come around to see what he was doing—he didn't know whether that meant Fred thought he was doing a good job, or whether he simply wasn't interested. "The only time he's ever come into my room," Guy remarked, "was to get a light for his cigar."

I explained that it was Fred's philosophy not to go into a teacher's room until the end of the semester, unless he was invited.

Guy had been hired on a short-term basis in January, so he was on the teachers' surplus list. Although he had ten years' experience teaching with the Toronto Board, he had been with North York only for a short while, and the Board does not consider work done for other Boards to count when compiling the seniority list.

He received his pink slip and has decided to go into the travel agent business.

Last night I ran into an old acquaintance at a shopping mall, who told me that Zeke had killed himself in a Paris rooming house. Over the years, I had realized just how important his friendship had been to me. Zeke symbolized an era; he had always thought that somehow life's rules didn't apply to him. Now he was permanently exempt from playing the game. I can still see him dancing on a hilltop, shaking his fists at the sky. The least I can do is remember him at his best.

Friday, June 22

As I was walking through the parking lot at lunch I met Duke on his "Bikers for the Lord" motorcycle. His tee shirt read, "A message to all you virgins: Thanks for nothin'!" Straddling the back of the seat was a young girl about twelve, on the back of her windbreaker a fluorescent slogan: "Save a Mouse—Eat a Pussy."

"This is Mary Lynn," Duke announced. "I'm workin' on savin' her soul."

I smiled and shook her hand.

Duke cleared his throat and reached into his pocket: "This note's from my mom. She heard you was leavin' the school. Whatever she says goes for me, too."

Then Duke and his girlfriend put on their helmets and raised their fists in a salute. "You're one of the decent ones!" Duke yelled, revving up the engine. "So long, sir!" he cried, pulling one last dramatic "wheelie" and waving goodbye. It reminded me of a scene from the old Lone Ranger television series when the Lone Ranger reared on his white horse and waved into the camera.

I opened the note.

"When Duke told me you were leaving teaching to go back to school, I felt I had to write you a note. I hope you will always work with children in some way. I would like every child to have at least one teacher like you. You make learning fun, but still learning. Thanks for all you've done for Duke."

It was rare for a parent to say thank you. Not that they weren't often grateful, but many found it difficult to communicate their feelings openly.

I put the note in my wallet and headed off toward the restaurant, the smoke from Duke's bike still lingering in the parking lot.

Monday, June 25

There was only one day of school left before the summer holidays. I earlier had sent home a note with each kid, reminding the parents not to forget to send some cookies or cakes or other treats for our party.

Kim arrived this morning looking depressed. "My mom won't give me nothin' to bring," she said, wiping away tears. "She says she's savin' all our money to move out of this crappy neighborhood."

Liz invited my class to her room to share some of the fun of the final party of the year. She put a disco album on, and started dancing with the kids. "Let's *really* give them something to talk about," she said to me, grinning. She stuck out her hip my way, and for the next few songs we did "the bump." Our hips bounced and we twirled around and around, much to the delight of the kids.

To our surprise, there were no lewd remarks or obscene gestures. Some of the kids had tears in their eyes; others couldn't wait to get out the door.

Tuesday, June 26

On the last day of school, Samantha left a note on my desk.

Dear Sir. I have something to tell you. I want to tell you that I love you I not only love you because you are my teacher. I love you and I'm respecte. I love you like a father not just because you teacher. But I wich that I had the hart to tell you I love you other than write this letter.

Yours truly

From Samantha

Summer Vacation

Priscilla's mother phoned me during the summer to tell me about the growing number of mothers in the community who were organizing themselves to create some kind of recreational program and get a day-care center going. "We're really pickin' up steam. We've felt hopeless for so long it feels good to be gettin' somewhere. Maybe we can hang in here for a while longer, and thanks for taking such an interest in Priscilla."

Driving down Yonge Street one hot August day, I heard a familiar voice shouting at me from the curb.

"Sir! Sir!" T. J. was standing on the street corner waving his arms. "Hey, sir! Gimme a lift!"

I pulled my van over and he hopped in. He asked me to take him to the nearest subway station, pulling a package of cigarettes from his shirt pocket and offering me one.

"Export A's the strongest you can get," he grinned. "It's a real man's brand."

I sighed. "No thanks, T. J. I'm smoking a pipe these days."

"Well, if you need some hash, I can get you the best stuff on the street."

I gave him a friendly scowl and he winked, taking a drag.

"You're such a square, man," he laughed.

When I asked him how his mother was, his face suddenly became serious. "I'm not livin' at home," he said. "I'm in a group home now. There's me, four other guys, and two girls. Me and one other guy fuck one of the girls. The other girl is a hose bag—nobody'd ever fuck her. The counselors there give us spendin' money, and I usually buy cigarettes and skin mags."

"Still the same T. J.," I said. "How're your parents?"

"Still separated," he said. "Last time I was at my mother's my dad called up and told her she was a fuckin' whore, so I went over to my dad's place and he was so drunk he could hardly stand up. So I beat the shit out of him. I took off my boots and hammered him good. The first shot hit him in the throat with the steel toe—he went right down and didn't get up. I gave him a few more shots in the head and left."

I stopped the van outside the subway.

"Anyway, sir," T. J. concluded, "you don't want to hear all that shit." He squeezed my arm and jumped out of the van. I called out to him, but he disappeared down the subway entrance.

At the end of August, I took a last walk through the Corridor.

Boisterous, ragged kids ran pell-mell through the dark warrens of the tenements. A fat, ruddy-nosed man leaned over a balcony and cried, "Get your butts outta here!" Women wearing black shawls and carrying shopping bags waited anxiously at the bus stop.

I walked past "St. Welfare" and recalled a conversation I once had with one of the Catholic teachers. She quoted a few lines from the Trappist monk and writer Thomas Merton: "We refuse to love our neighbors, and excuse ourselves on the premise that society's laws will take care of everything, or that a revolution will solve all our problems."

I finally reached the school and looked in through a front window. The room was clean, waiting for the new year. I glanced up at the window. Bits of tape were still stuck to the glass, tape that had held the February Valentines. For a moment I thought I saw a student's face pressed against the glass, but it must have been my imagination. . . .

During quiet walks along the beach on the long, summer nights I remembered good times and bad, and silently made my farewell to my kids.

AFTERWORD

> *. . . When You Wish Upon a Star*
> *It Makes a Difference*
> *Who You Are . . .*

In too many instances where the politics of education is played, it's the children who lose out—especially the children of the poor. Economically disadvantaged children are being groomed by society at an early age to fail, doomed to perpetuate a vicious and endless cycle of poverty created by a culture obsessed with success and wealth.

When I first began teaching, I ascribed to certain myths and assumptions about education. I believe many educators and parents today still cling tenaciously to these myths. We have learned to believe the formal goal of our education system, that it is the "great equalizer" of our society, that it will assist disadvantaged students to bridge the chasm of opportunity that divides them from children from more affluent backgrounds. Unfortunately, this type of platitude hides more than it reveals. I believe this notion of equality to be false. In fact, I would reverse the argument by saying that it's the latent function of the educational system to maintain the status quo, including existing social inequalities.

We claim to live in a meritocracy where social salvation is supposedly achieved through scholastic merit: every student will, more or less, reap the academic rewards of his or her own initiative, regardless of sex, religion, or family background. That all sounds fine on the surface, but in reality it's simply hollow rhetoric. Research has shown that one of the greatest predictors of academic success is socioeconomic status. In other words, although we profess to believe in equal opportunity for rich and poor alike, the fact remains that an individual's social class and race at birth have a greater influence on social class later in life than do any other factors—including intelligence and merit. Put simply, each child appears to get as many chances for success in school as his or her family has dollars and privileged social status.

The race of each generation through our classrooms usually enhances the success of those with the most "favored" environment. I liken this race to one in which the disadvantaged students line up and "get set" at the starting line, while the more affluent students wait for the whistle at the other end of the track a few feet from the finish line.

As someone raised to believe in the virtues of equality, I find this fact of life particularly disturbing. The root cause of this inequality can be traced directly to the disproportional access to wealth in a society where, despite lip service, the poor are often ostracized to states of unworthiness and inferiority. I found this time and again in my teaching experiences. I could have written a "safer" book by emphasizing the more positive aspects of my teaching career. But that would have ignored the real issue.

Democracies like ours exhort equal opportunity but often ignore ways in which our schools operate unconsciously and unknowingly to guarantee that there will be no real equality. Despite intentions to the contrary, schools reproduce and perpetuate the inequalities and injustices of society-at-large. Children from affluent backgrounds generally get ahead. Yet the chances that disadvantaged students will finish high school—let alone attend university—are staggering. There are, of course, exceptions to the rule, and by focusing on the exceptions we are able to take some of the sting from our guilt.

It would be a mistake to think of the reproduction of social inequality in the schools as an educational conspiracy: In my angrier moments I styled education officials as belligerent despots huddled in smoky back rooms, sporting diamond derrick stickpins in their "old boy" ties; they munched on Davidoff cigars, poured through their Tory blue file folders, and plotted ways to keep poor students out of the universities. Although I don't deny that these officials sometimes exhibit spectacularly cramped forms of imagination—if not, at times, a facile ambivalence toward their vocations (especially when it comes to addressing the needs of disadvantaged students)—I don't believe that they're *consciously* trying to reduce the competition for their sons at Harvard.

My perspective now is not to point an inquisitorial finger at any specific group of persons, but is directed toward the ideologies, structures, and myths that help reproduce our present culture.

While it is probably true that schools cannot *remake* society, they must find better ways of making themselves vital places for all students—places where students can be empowered to gain a sense of control over their destinies rather than feel trapped by their social status.

Though many poor parents continue to struggle with dignity to better their lives and their children's lives, they themselves are victims of society's myths about them: that the poor deserve their lot in life because they're lazy . . . because they don't care if their children succeed . . . because their children carry a scanty pack of intellectual baggage with them when they enter school. This is absurd. Yet we continue to perpetuate these myths and to blame the victims for *society's* collective irresponsibility.

The incidents of violence and brutality in this book are undeniably part of the working-class experience. (I suspect there are subtler, but equally as debilitating, forms of violence in middle-class communities.) But before we judge too quickly the casualties of societal oppression, we would do well to examine the inhumane conditions in which the poor are permitted to become entrapped. We need only to witness the growth of "instant cities" springing up in the suburbs— high-density apartment living with few, if any, social or recreational services—to realize the extent of our "benign" neglect. Family violence cannot be considered solely as individual action outside the context of social forces that position the poor within asymmetrical relations of power.

The school system is mostly geared to the interests, skills, and attitudes of the middle-class child. Though I also argue that the system is failing to educate middle-class students, it is the children of poverty who really suffer, being streamed into courses that prepare them for a life of temporary, dead-end, underpaid, undignified, and menial jobs. And it isn't only the minimum-wage employers, greedy developers, and other sharks who benefit from this poverty. We *all*, to some degree, are dependent on poverty for our own security.

A prevalent educational preoccupation of ours is to concentrate on the failure of society to socialize the "deviant" or "underachiever" to be homogeneous, amorphous, passive, docile, compliant—willing to embrace the time-clock world and mind- and body-deadening norms of the assembly line: the ethos of the shop floor; or the boring routines of fast food restaurants: the new factories for youth.

Educators especially must resist the misperception that regards immigrant students and students from low-income backgrounds as "deficient," "pathological," or "undersocialized dopes."

Such a condescending and patronizing attitude can only reinforce a vicious myth that too often becomes a self-fulfilling prophecy in the classroom. We must begin to acknowledge the fact that underachievement in disadvantaged students is not individual or personalized failure as much as a product of economic and social life as we know it.

The present failure of inner-city education is not in the genes or the attitudes of the poor, but in the failure of society to change the economic and social structures that regulate their lives. Rather than blaming the victims—the students and their parents—for problems in our inner-city schools, it is important that we take into account our tolerance of the existence of grinding poverty, frightened and condescending teachers, self-serving politicians, irrelevant curricula, the spirit-breaking quality of many current administrative and teaching practices, lack of community participation in the educational process, and the reluctance of educational officials to meet the special needs of inner-city students.

The Corridor kids I worked with had enormous potential to learn and enjoy learning. But in order to build a more positive view of the abilities of my students, I had to struggle to unlearn a great many of my middle-class prejudices. During my teaching career, I began to realize I couldn't talk about culturally deprived students, but rather *culturally depriving schools.* Certainly these kids didn't have easy lives. But the majority of them possessed the intelligence and will to adapt— and learn—despite their often forbidding surroundings.

As soon as I became less outraged by what my students said and did, as soon as I stopped expecting T. J. and Duke and the rest of them to become upright, middle-class, productive, consuming citizens, then I had a chance to understand them. Actually, I had rejected the validity of some of these values myself. Yet, I found myself asking my students to mirror back to me images of the world I had been reluctant to embrace.

I finally accepted the fact that my students needed to be taught on their own terms first, and then taught to critically transcend those terms in the interest of empowering themselves and others. The traditional middle class images of success were not open to them, images which they, in turn, were able to resist. In the classroom, they had become, understandably, street-wise cynical about the social candy of academic rewards such as good grades on term papers or tests. I began to be effective with these students when I dignified their own experiences as worthy of inquiry.

What teachers and parents are summoned to do—and this is part of the purpose of this book—is to confront the structures of oppression, and the myths legitimating injustices toward disadvantaged students in the name of equality and democracy. Immediate actions are obvious: Improved social planning, smaller classes, breakfast programs for those who need them, respect by teachers for the values and abilities of the disadvantaged student, striving to eliminate poverty rather than altering the attitudes of the impoverished working class, adequate daycare facilities for working parents, more specialized teachers, more teachers from a wide variety of ethnic backgrounds, more preschool programs, improvements in the welfare system as well as tax reforms that will truly benefit the needy as opposed to *appear* to benefit the needy.

But governments—national, state, or local—rarely have ears for the "cries from the corridor."

The battle to save our children will never be won as long as we sit back comfortably and let history take its course instead of actively taking part in *creating history.*

In Memoriam—Jim Montgomerie ("Fred") 1930–1985
He was an ethical rebel, an educational outlaw. He was visionary, a seeker, driven by a desire to remake schools. No one involved with the fate of our children fought with such determination against the fettering of the human spirit and imagination than this man.

His name was Montgomerie. Many Canadians prefer to remember him as "the hugging principal."

I shall attempt in a short space to sketch out the measure of Jim's spirit and vision, knowing that no words can do justice to the history of his personal accomplishments.

Jim's death from cancer in April came suddenly and stunned those of us who knew him as tenacious and unstoppable. His vibrant personality, his unmatched and unbounded wit, and his keen and discerning intellect provided a combination so formidable that it earned Jim a national reputation as one of education's finest leaders. Although his humanitarian efforts as vice-president of the Canadian Association for the Mentally Retarded, immediate past president of the Ontario Association for the Mentally Retarded, and fund-raising chairperson of the Cash for Life lottery have been well documented and duly acclaimed, it was Jim's pioneering style as an inner-city school principal that made him a legend in his own time. Jim's philosophy of "loving each and every child" and his self-concept approach to teaching stirred considerable controversy in the days before the Hall-Dennis Report. And, in these days of conservative assaults on social equality and public schooling, Jim's symbol of the rocking chair (which he used to replace the standard executive chair used by most principals) becomes all the more significant.

The road to winning acceptance for his humanistic approach to teaching was often rough, but invariably rewarding.

"I was lucky," Jim once told me, "I landed in a school (Flemington) where the staff was willing to take risks along with me. It was an incredible experience. For many of us, it was the most rewarding time of our lives."

As a teacher who served under Jim at Driftwood School in North York's Jane-Finch Corridor, I remember the way he was able to instill in the staff a respect for all students. They were tumultuous times back in the seventies, but the caring and trust that developed among us as a staff will never be forgotten.

Jim would be sent to a different school and in his remarkable way would turn things around; then he would be sent to another school that was experiencing problems and he would turn things around again. Though other, less gifted, individuals may wish to take credit for North York's attempts at inner-city reform, it was undeniably Jim's pioneering efforts that laid the groundwork and made it easier for others to do their jobs. Regrettably, nobody could ever quite fill Jim's shoes.

A gifted teacher, Jim was unwilling to disengage love from the teaching of practical skills or abstract ideas. For Jim, teaching was fundamentally a moral craft. Jim's way of doing things became a powerful metaphor for the consummate teaching act. Jim's entire life embodied and gave substance to the meaning of the word *love*. Many of us stood in awe of Jim's extraordinary capacity to love and care for others. Undoubtedly, this had to do with the love and strength Jim gathered from his family.

Had Jim been more compromising in his beliefs, had he been more willing to go against what his conscience told him was in the best interest of students, his career would no doubt have been less turbulent politically. But for Jim the interest and well-being of his staff and students always came before personal gain.

Jim's enigmatic and often unpredictable methods of reaching out to students sometimes threatened more conservative-minded educators. Yet even those who found Jim's values a challenge to their own could not deny the positive impact Jim made on teachers, students, and administrators alike.

Jim understood how, through the mediations of class, capital, and relations of power and privilege, schools served to disempower the children of the dispossessed and disenfranchised. Much of his time was spent in finding ways to encourage fellow administrators and teachers to give up their antiquated pedagogy in the face of a changing society so that school sites could be remade into laboratories of freedom. Jim was very knowledgeable in the realm of theorizing, but his mission could hardly be defined in the abstract; Jim was fundamentally a "hands-on" administrator—a "doer."

Although Jim's methods were humanistic, he rarely hid his disdain for educational leaders who were committed only to the reproduction of the moribund and for a system which, if left unchecked, could easily become burdened by a philistinism and unimaginative pedagogy. Jim understood better than most that schooling was not a value-free enterprise and that could often become antagonistic to the true meaning and purpose of democracy.

For many of us involved with schooling and social change, Jim's philosophy of education was—and remains—a catalyst for much of our work. Had Jim been able to write with the same verve and creative lucidity that he brought to the articulating of his ideas through conversation, he would have become an international figure. And I make bold to say that his name would appear alongside better known educators.

Since some critics and colleagues questioned the accuracy of my book [*Cries from the Corridor*], I was particularly grateful to Jim when he was quoted in the *Toronto Star* as saying: "Everything in that book is true." He told reporter David Vienneau: "I'll vouch for all the things that happened. . . . It has to be seen as a cry from disadvantaged kids by a person who had the insight to put down what he saw." Naturally the North York Board was not pleased that he defended a book which generally condemned its policies and practices in inner-city schools. Jim knew he would take flak for this and he did.

Several months before his death, Jim visited Brock University in St. Catharines, where a student committee had arranged for him to address the College of Education's student teachers. I was in the audience as a new professor of education and recall vividly the impact he made on the student body. His address was not just a call to humanize the classroom; it was a challenge to fight against racism and discrimination, and was a challenge to meet the needs of those who are less fortunate.

After his speech, it became evident to me that Jim was in considerable physical discomfort. Although he never once mentioned being sick, I could tell by the look in his eyes and his shortness of breath that something was wrong. Others would probably have canceled the engagement. But that wasn't Jim's style. In the following weeks, a number of students made a point of telling me that they felt Jim's talk was beyond a doubt the single most important event of the college year. I could not agree with them more.

During our last conversation together, Jim told me not to forget about his retirement party later in the year. When I told him that I could never imagine him as retired, he proceeded to tell me how he planned to study to become a lawyer so that he could represent the mentally handicapped. Jim was accepted by Osgoode Hall law school.

Jim died beloved and revered by many. Some will remember him as a maverick administrator who was able to work within the system while attempting to reform it. Others will remember him best as a gifted communicator and humanist who spent his life trying to educate others to become more active in living out their moral and democratic ideals of creating a just society where the needs of the disadvantaged and disaffected would be met. Still others will remember Jim as a dedicated husband, father, son, and brother.

Jim exemplified, in his own life, the possibilities that exist for us to realize our humanitarian goals. Although Jim did not exemplify the practice of critical pedagogy (to be discussed throughout the remainder of the book), he still was able to weave new meanings into the tapestry of contemporary schooling without losing sight of the overall pattern of social justice. Jim has bequeathed to us, through his own example, a new model for teaching and leadership. Jim's life provides an incentive for us all.[1]

NOTE

1. Reprinted with minor alterations from the Ontario Public School Men's Teachers Federation, *News,* June 1, 1985, now defunct.

PART III

Critical Pedagogy:
An Overview

CRITICAL PEDAGOGY AND THE EGALITARIAN DREAM

In the following section, you will be introduced to the tradition of critical educational theory, or *critical pedagogy*. My purpose in culling perspectives from a variety of critical theorists extends beyond providing an explanation for the harmful effects schooling has had on minority students and the poor. Rather, I urge you to connect these theoretical perspectives to the journal entries in Part Two, and more importantly, to your own experiences in the schools. I am asking *you* to mediate among the theory presented in the following sections, my journalistic documentation of my experiences as an inner-city teacher, and your own personal history which, if it is not already rich in teaching experiences, is most certainly rich in the experiences of being a student. This book can then provide a dialectical tension among theory, practice, and experience—a tension necessary for critical learning.

I want to make clear from the outset that my own elementary school teaching experiences are not offered as evidence that in some way "proves" the theories that follow. This book is not meant to be read either as an empirical study or as a devout acolyte's conversion journal to the critical tradition. A concern with the validity and verifiability of theory is beyond the scope of this book; those wishing for empirical studies are encouraged to consult my book, *Schooling as a Ritual Performance,*[1] or the numerous others books within the critical educational tradition listed at the back of this volume. I do hope that my journal accounts add some flesh and blood to what are essentially abstract theoretical formulations. But my decision to include the journal is more than a cry for texture. Rather, I hope to illustrate the contradictions embodied in the teaching process itself and to chart out the tension between the perspectives held by the beginning teacher, who is trying to find a larger purpose in the day-to-day *practice* of teaching, and the social theorist, who presumably has a better *theoretical* grasp of what should be done and who is calling for practitioners to appropriate critical theory into their own work.

Why should you believe the theories presented throughout these pages if they are not all clearly illustrated by my own teaching experiences? Conservative critics could easily offer my journal accounts as evidence that schools are in need of stricter discipline, more rules, regulations, and enforcement procedures, tougher standards for evaluating students and teachers, and a return to the basics. Liberal critics might argue for more funds and specialized programs. But all this is just the point. The literature on schooling abounds with both conservative and liberal perspectives.

In this book, you are given access to a *different kind* of analysis. The challenge of critical pedagogy does not reside solely in the logical consistency or the empirical verification of its theories; rather, it resides in the moral choice put before us as teachers and citizens, a choice that American philosopher John Dewey suggested is the distinction between education as a function of society and society as a function of education. We need to examine that choice: do we want our schools to create a passive, risk-free citizenry, or a politicized citizenry capable of fighting for various forms of public life and informed by a concern for equality and social justice?

CHAPTER 4

The Emergence of Critical Pedagogy

In the context of that choice, a radical theory of education has emerged in the last twenty years. Broadly defined as "the new sociology of education" or a "critical theory of education," critical pedagogy examines schools both in their historical context and as part of the existing social and political fabric that characterizes the dominant society. Critical pedagogy poses a variety of important counterlogics to the positivistic, ahistorical, and depoliticized analysis employed by both liberal and conservative critics of schooling—an analysis all too readily visible in the training programs in our colleges of education. Fundamentally concerned with the centrality of politics and power in our understanding of how schools work, critical theorists have produced work centering on the political economy of schooling, the state and education, the representation of texts, and the construction of student subjectivity.

Critical educational theory owes a profound debt to its European progenitors. A number of critical educational theorists, Henry Giroux, for example, continue to draw inspiration from the work of the Frankfurt School of critical theory, which had its beginnings before World War II in Germany's Institut für Sozialforschung (Institute for Social Research). The membership of this group, who wrote brilliant and ethically illuminating works of Freudo-Marxist analysis, included such figures as Max Horkheimer, Theodor W. Adorno, Walter Benjamin, Leo Lowenthal, Erich Fromm, and Herbert Marcuse. During the war, a number of Institute members fled to the United States as a result of persecution by Nazis because they were Leftist and Jewish. After the war they reestablished the Institute in Frankfurt. Members of the second generation of critical theorists, such as Jurgen Habermas, have since moved from the Institute to carry on elsewhere the work initiated by the founding members. In the United States, the Frankfurt School of critical theory is currently making new inroads into social research and influencing numerous disciplines such as literary criticism, anthropology, sociology, and educational theory.

Critical pedagogy has begun to provide a radical theory and analysis of schooling, while annexing new advances in social theory and developing new categories of inquiry and new methodologies. Critical pedagogy does not, however, constitute a homogeneous set of ideas. It is more accurate to say that critical theorists are united in their *objectives:* to empower the powerless and transform existing social inequalities and injustices. The movement constitutes only a small minority within the academic community and public school teaching as a whole, but it presents a growing and challenging presence in both arenas.[2]

FOUNDATIONAL PRINCIPLES

Critical pedagogy resonates with the sensibility of the Hebrew symbol of *tikkun,* which means "to heal, repair, and transform the world, all the rest is commentary." It provides historical, cultural, political, and ethical direction for those in education who still dare to hope. Irrevocably committed to the side of the oppressed, critical pedagogy is as revolutionary as the earlier views of the authors of the Declaration of Independence: since history is fundamentally open to change, liberation is an authentic goal, and a radically different world can be brought into being.

Politics

A major task of critical pedagogy has been to disclose and challenge the role that schools play in our political and cultural life. Especially within the last decade, critical educational theorists have come to view schooling as a resolutely political and cultural enterprise. Recent advances in the sociology of knowledge, cultural and symbolic anthropology, cultural Marxism, and semiotics have led these theorists to see schools not only as instructional sites, but also as cultural arenas where a heterogeneity of ideological and social forms often collide in an unremitting struggle for dominance. Within this context, critical theorists generally analyze schools in a twofold way: as sorting mechanisms in which select groups of students are favored on the basis of race, class, and gender; and as agencies for self and social empowerment.

Critical educational theorists argue that teachers must understand the role that schooling plays in joining knowledge and power, in order to use that role for the development of critical and active citizens. The traditional view of classroom instruction and learning as a neutral process antiseptically removed from the concepts of power, politics, history, and context can no longer be credibly endorsed. In fact, critical researchers have given primacy to the social, the cultural, the political, and the economic, in order to better understand the workings of contemporary schooling.

Culture

Critical theorists see schooling as a form of *cultural politics;* schooling always represents an introduction to, preparation for, and legitimation of particular forms of social life. It is always implicated in relations of power, social practices, and the favoring of forms of knowledge that support a specific vision of past, present, and future. In general, critical theorists maintain that schools have always functioned in ways that rationalize the knowledge industry into class-divided tiers; that reproduce inequality, racism, and sexism; and that fragment democratic social relations through an emphasis on competitiveness and cultural ethnocentrism.

Although critical pedagogy is indebted to a wide variety of European intellectual traditions, it also draws upon a uniquely American tradition extending from the mainstream progressive movement of John Dewey, William H. Kilpatrick, and others, through the more radical efforts of the social reconstructionists of the 1920s such as George Counts and the work of Dwayne Huebner, Theodore Brameld, and James McDonald. In Roger Simon's terms, *pedagogy* must be distinguished from *teaching*.

> "Pedagogy" [refers] to the integration in practice of particular curriculum content and design, classroom strategies and techniques, and evaluation, purpose, and methods. All of these aspects of educational practice come together in the realities of what happens in classrooms. Together they organize a view of how a teacher's work within an institutional context specifies a particular version of what knowledge is of most worth, what it means to know something, and how we might construct representations of ourselves, others, and our physical and social environment. In other words, talk about pedagogy is simultaneously talk about the details of what students and others might do together and the cultural politics such practices support. In this perspective, we cannot talk about teaching practices without talking about politics.[3]

Economics

Unfortunately, in their discussion of "critical thinking" the neoconservatives and liberals have neutralized the term *critical* by repeated and imprecise usage, removing its political and cultural dimensions and laundering its analytic potency to mean "thinking skills." In their terms, teaching is reduced to helping students acquire higher levels of cognitive skills. Little attention is paid to the purpose to which these skills are to be put. The moral vision that grounds such a view encourages students to succeed in the tough competitive world of existing social forms.

By defining academic success almost exclusively in terms of creating compliant, productive, and patriotic workers, the new conservative agenda for a "resurgent America" dodges any concern for nurturing critical and committed citizens. Instead, students are viewed as the prospective vanguard of America's economic revival. Critical educational theorists have responded to the New Right by arguing that the increasing adoption of management-type pedagogies and accountability schemes to meet the logic of market demands has resulted in policy proposals that actively promote the deskilling of teachers. This is most evident in the proliferation of state-mandated curricula claiming to be "teacher-proofed," which effectively reduce the role of the teacher to that of a semiskilled, low-paid clerk. The neoconservative agenda has, in effect, brought the advancement of democracy in our schools to a state of arrest. Neoconservatives reject the view that schools should be sites for social transformation and emancipation, places where students are educated not only to be critical thinkers, but also to view the world as a place where their actions might make a difference.

Critical pedagogy is founded on the conviction that schooling for self and social empowerment is *ethically prior* to a mastery of technical skills, which are primarily tied to the logic of the marketplace (although it should be stressed that skill development certainly plays an important role). Concern over education's moral dimension has provoked critical scholars to undertake a socially critical reconstruction of what it means to "be schooled." They stress that any genuine pedagogical practice demands a commitment to social transformation in solidarity with subordinated and marginalized groups. This necessarily entails a preferential option for the poor and the elimination of those conditions that promote human suffering. Such theorists are critical of the emphasis that liberal democracy places on individualism and autonomy from the needs of others.

According to critical educational theorists, analyses of schooling undertaken by liberal and conservative critics necessarily favor the interests of the dominant culture. The liberal perspective especially has been reappropriated by the very logic it purports to criticize. By contrast, the *critical* perspective allows us to scrutinize schooling more insistently in terms of race, class, power, and gender.

Americans traditionally have assumed that schools function as a mechanism for the development of democratic and egalitarian social order. Critical educational theorists argue otherwise; they suggest that schools do *not* provide opportunities in the broad Western humanist tradition for self and social empowerment and in fact often work against those opportunities. Critical pedagogy also challenges the assumption that schools function as major sites of social and economic mobility. Theorists like Michael Apple argue that American schooling has defaulted on its promise of egalitarian reform and does not, in fact, provide opportunities for large numbers of students to become empowered as critical, active citizens. Rather, they argue, the economic returns from schooling are far greater for the affluent than for the disadvantaged.

In their attempts to explode the popular belief that schools are fundamentally democratic institutions, critical scholars have begun to unravel the ways in which school curricula, knowledge, and policy depend on the corporate marketplace and the fortunes of the economy. Their goal is to unmask the inequality of competing self-interests within the social order that prohibits equal opportunity from being realized. They warn against being deluded as educators into thinking that either conservatives or liberals occupy a truly progressive platform. In their view, no decisions can be made on the basis of transparent and disinterested standards of value, and no educational practices—whether they center on the issue of excellence, evaluation, or accountability—are ever innocent of the social, economic, and institutional contexts in which schooling takes place. Rather, they suggest that schooling must always be analyzed as a cultural and historical process, in which select groups are positioned within asymmetrical relations of power on the basis of specific race, class, and gender groupings. In other words, critical scholars refuse the task capitalism assigns them as intellectuals, teachers, and social theorists, to passively service the existing ideological and institutional arrangements of the public schools. These scholars believe that the schools serve the interests of the wealthy and powerful, while simultaneously disconfirming the values and abilities of those students who are most disempowered in our society already: minorities, the poor, and the female. In short, educators within the critical tradition argue that mainstream schooling supports an inherently unjust bias, resulting in the transmission and reproduction of the dominant status quo culture.

Central to their attempt to reform public education is a rejection of the emphasis on scientific predictability and measurement which has been tacitly lodged in models of curriculum planning and in other theoretical approaches to educational practice. Critical theorists challenge the often uncontested relationship between school and society, unmasking mainstream pedagogy's claim that it purveys equal opportunity and provides access to egalitarian democracy and critical thinking. Critical scholars reject the claim that schooling constitutes an apolitical and value-neutral process. In fact, to argue that schools are meritocratic institutions is a conceptual tautology: successful learners are those whom schools reward. If you happen to be successful, it must be because of your individual merit. Missing from this logic is a recognition that students from white, affluent backgrounds are privileged over other groups, not on the basis of merit but because of the advantage that comes with having money and increased social status. Critical pedagogy attempts to provide teachers and researchers with a better means of understanding the role that schools actually play within a race-, class-, and gender-divided society, and in this effort, theorists have generated categories or concepts for questioning student experiences, texts, teacher ideologies, and aspects of school policy that conservative and liberal analyses too often leave unexplored. In effect, critical pedagogy has sharply defined the political dimensions of schooling, arguing that schools operate mainly to reproduce the values and privileges of existing elites. Critical pedagogy commits itself to forms of learning and action undertaken in solidarity with subordinated and marginalized groups. In addition to questioning what is taken for granted about schooling, critical theorists are dedicated to the emancipatory imperatives of *self-empowerment* and *social transformation.*

Critical pedagogists would like to pry theory away from the academics and incorporate it in educational practice. They throw down the gauntlet to those conservative and corporate multiculturalists, who wish schools simply to teach students about America's great cultural heritage.[4] They aim at providing teachers with critical categories, or concepts, that will enable them to analyze schools as places that produce and transmit those social practices that reflect the ideological and material imperatives of the dominant culture.

Critical educators argue that we have responsibility not only for how we act individually in society, but also for the system in which we participate. Critical theorists put forward what might be labeled pedagogical surrealism: They attempt to make the strange familiar and the familiar strange. They set out to ''relativize'' schools as normalizing agencies—i.e., as agencies that essentially legitimate existing social relations and practices, rendering them normal and natural—by dismantling and rearranging the artificial rules and codes that make up classroom reality. Unlike the humanist who begins with the different and renders it comprehensible, the critical education theorist attacks the familiar, perturbing commonplace perspectives.[5] Critical theorists attempt to go beyond the conventional question of *what* schooling means by raising instead the more important question of *how* schooling has come to mean what it has. The result is that schools—often seen as socializing agencies that help society produce intelligent, responsible, committed, and skilled citizens—turn out to be strange and disturbing institutions that not only *teach* subjects but also *produce* unreflective human subjects who, in their day-to-day activities, play out the ideologies of the dominant culture.

Critical educational theorists argue that Marxism has not been taken seriously in this country as a means of social-historical analysis; Marxist theorists and those who work within traditions of radical social thought indebted to Marxism often are subject to knee-jerk "marxophobia." Though many if not most critical educational theorists work outside the orthodox Marxian tradition and do not consider capitalism an irrevocable evil, they do insist that its pattern of exploitation has produced an economic rationality that infuses current thinking on social and educational issues and continues to contribute to massive social problems such as racism, sexism, and classism. In order to ensure that all individuals have a voice in the surplus value their labor generates, critical educators argue that those responsible for our current brand of capitalism must be held morally accountable. A new economic ethic is needed that will help guide and eventually reshape economic policy in the interests of *everyone,* one with the vision and power to counter the dehumanizing effects of modern supply-side capitalism.

Critical educators question the very basis of school funding. Why, they ask, are schools funded on the basis of property taxes, which ensures that the children of the wealthy and privileged will inherit better schools in terms of resources, teacher salaries, clean buildings, etc.? Why don't state governments and the federal government assume responsibility for full educational funding? After all, the federal government assumes responsibility for operations such as Desert Storm. Critical educators oppose deregulation and opening school success to the logic of the marketplace, supposedly through the new "choice" schemes and voucher plans. Letting the market "equalize" education through vouchers will only exacerbate the disparity of chances between rich and poor students—inner-city schools will collapse. "Choice" means that the poor are "free" to become poorer while the rich are given the "choice" of becoming richer. Choice means Jim Crow education for the 1990s. Choice schemes need to improve the conditions of low-performing schools or else state funding will shrink due to declining enrollments, and students and teachers will transfer to other schools.

Theories of Interest and Experience

Critical educational theorists such as Henry Giroux argue that curriculum must be understood in terms of a *theory of interest* and a *theory of experience.* By theory of interest, Giroux means that curriculum reflects the interests that surround it: the particular visions of past and present that they represent, the social relations they affirm or discard. By theory of experience, Giroux means that curriculum is an historically constructed narrative that produces and organizes student experiences in the context of social forms, such as language usage, organization of knowledge into high- and low-status categories, and the affirmation of particular kinds of teaching strategies. Curriculum represents not only a configuration of particular interests and experiences, however; it also forms a battleground where different versions of authority, history, the present, and the future struggle to prevail. Critical theorists want to provide for educational theorists in general a public language that not only confirms the voices of teachers and of subordinate groups in the student population, but also links the purpose of schooling to a transformative vision of the future.

Beyond agreeing that schools reproduce inequality and injustice, contemporary critical theorists differ in many points of analysis. Recent work in the critical tradition can generally be divided into two categories: *theoretically based works* such as my own and those by Henry Giroux, Stanley Aronowitz, Bill Pinar, and Michael Apple; and *critical ethnographies and case studies* of schools, such as those by Paul Willis, Kathleen Weiler, Barry Kanpol, myself, and others, which have begun to make the categories of gender, race, and class problematic.

Critical pedagogy deals with numerous themes, many of which are situated in distinct fields of research and criticism. Some of these relatively new fields include feminist pedagogy, critical constructivism, and multicultural education. In addition, postmodern social theory has been taken up by some educational critics. Cultural studies is another area that in recent years has also generated a burgeoning interest among some critical educators. Transdisciplinary scholarship is growing among educational theorists and is likely to continue. For instance, some of the recent work of Lankshear and McLaren[6] has drawn upon postmodern social theory to advance the analysis of literacy. Patti Lather's[7] work combines postmodern social theory and feminist theory. Critical literacy and media literacy are important new directions that are making serious inroads in school reform efforts, especially in urban areas. Disciplinary boundaries are beginning to blur, and in my estimation this makes for more innovative and important research within the critical tradition. More will be said about these fields throughout the volume.

There are many different strands to critical pedagogy: the libertarian, the radical, and the liberationist, all with points of difference and fusion. In addition to discussing my own theoretical work, this book draws primarily on radical perspectives exemplified in the works of such theorists as Paulo Freire and Henry Giroux, who make an important distinction between *schooling* and *education*. The former is primarily a mode of social control; the latter has the potential to transform society, with the learner functioning as an active subject committed to self and social empowerment.

CHAPTER 5

Critical Pedagogy: A Look at the Major Concepts

In practice, critical pedagogy is as diverse as its many adherents, yet common themes and constructs run through many of their writings. I have talked about the general characteristics of critical pedagogy in the previous chapters. In the chapters that follow, I will outline in more detail the major categories within this tradition. A category is simply a concept, question, issue, hypothesis, or idea that is central to critical theory. These categories are intended to provide a theoretical framework within which you may reread my journal entries and perhaps better understand the theories generated by critical educational research. The categories are useful for the purposes of clarification and illustration, although some critical theorists will undoubtedly argue that additional concepts should have been included, or that some concepts have not been given the emphasis they deserve.

THE IMPORTANCE OF THEORY

Before we discuss individual categories, we need to examine how those categories are explored. Critical theorists begin with the premise that *men and women are essentially unfree and inhabit a world rife with contradictions and asymmetries of power and privilege.* The critical educator endorses theories that are, first and foremost, *dialectical*; that is, theories which recognize the problems of society as more than simply isolated events of individuals of deficiencies in the social structure. Rather, these problems are part of the *interactive context* between individual and society. The individual, a social actor, both creates and is created by the social universe of which he/she is a part. Neither the individual nor society is given priority in analysis; the two are inextricably interwoven, so that reference to one must by implication mean reference to the other. Dialectical theory attempts to tease out the histories and relations of accepted meanings and appearances, tracing interactions from the context to the part, from the system inward to the event. In this way, critical theory helps us focus *simultaneously on both sides of a social contradiction.*[8]

Wilfred Carr and Stephen Kemmis describe dialectical thinking as follows:

> Dialectical thinking involves searching out . . . contradictions (like the contradiction of the inadvertent oppression of less able students by a system which aspires to help all students to attain their "full potential"), but it is not really as wooden or mechanical as the formula of thesis-antithesis-synthesis. On the contrary, it is an open and questioning form of thinking which demands reflection back and forth between elements like *part* and *whole, knowledge* and *action, process* and *product, subject* and *object, being* and *becoming, rhetoric* and *reality,* or *structure* and *function.* In the process, *contradictions* may be discovered (as, for example, in a political *structure* which aspires to give decision-making power to all, but actually *functions* to deprive some access to the information with which they could influence crucial decisions about their lives). As contradictions are revealed, new constructive thinking and new constructive action are required to transcend the contradictory state of affairs. The complementarity of the elements is dynamic: it is a kind of a tension, not a static confrontation between the two poles. In the dialectical approach, the elements are regarded as mutually constitutive, not separate and distinct. Contradiction can thus be distinguished from paradox: to speak of a contradiction is to imply that a new resolution can be achieved, while to speak of a paradox is to suggest that two incompatible ideas remain inertly opposed to one another.[9] (Italics original)

The dialectical nature of critical theory enables the educational researcher to see the school not simply as an arena of indoctrination or socialization or a site of instruction, but also as a cultural terrain that promotes student empowerment and self-transformation. My own research into parochial education, for instance, showed that the school functions *simultaneously* as a means of empowering students around issues of social justice and as a means of sustaining, legitimizing, and reproducing dominant class interests directed at creating obedient, docile, and low-paid future workers.[10]

A dialectical understanding of schooling permits us to see schools as sites of *both* domination and liberation; this runs counter to the overdeterministic orthodox Marxist view of schooling, which claims that schools simply reproduce class relations and passively indoctrinate students into becoming greedy young capitalists. This dialectical understanding of schooling also brushes against the grain of mainstream educational theory, which conceives of schools as mainly providing students with the skills and attitudes necessary for becoming patriotic, industrious, and responsible citizens.

Critical educators argue that any worthwhile theory of schooling *must be partisan.* That is, it must be fundamentally tied to a struggle for a qualitatively better life for all through the construction of a society based on nonexploitative relations and social justice. The critical educator doesn't believe that there are two sides to every question, with both sides needing equal attention. For the critical educator, there are *many* sides to a problem, and often these sides are linked to certain class, race, and gender interests.

Let's turn for a moment to an example of critical theorizing as it is brought to bear on a fundamental teaching practice: writing classroom objectives. In this example, I will draw on Henry Giroux's important distinction between *micro* and *macro* objectives.[11]

The common use of behavioral objectives by teachers reflects a search for certainty and technical control of knowledge and behavior. Teachers often emphasize classroom management procedures, efficiency, and "how-to-do" techniques that ultimately ignore an important question: "Why is this knowledge being taught in the first place?" Giroux recasts classroom objectives into the categories of macro and micro.

Macro objectives are designed to enable students to make connections between the methods, content, and structure of a course and its significance within the larger social reality. This dialectical approach to classroom objectives allows students to acquire a broad frame of reference or worldview; in other words, it helps them acquire a political perspective. Students can then make the hidden curriculum explicit and develop a critical political consciousness.

Micro objectives represent the course content and are characterized by their narrowness of purpose and their content-bound path of inquiry. Giroux tells us that the importance of the relationship between macro and micro objectives arises out of *having students uncover the connections between course objectives and the norms, values, and structural relationships of the wider society.* For instance, the micro objectives of teaching about the Vietnam war might be to learn the dates of specific battles, the details of specific Congressional debates surrounding the war, and the reasons given by the White House for fighting the war. The micro objectives are concerned with the organization, classification, mastery, and manipulation of data. This is what Giroux calls *productive knowledge*. Macro objectives, on the other hand, center on the relationship between means and ends, between specific events and their wider social and political implications. A lesson on the Vietnam war or more recently the invasion of Grenada and the Desert Storm assault on Iraq, for instance, might raise the following macro questions: What is the relationship between these invasions as rescue missions in the interests of U.S. citizens and the larger logic of imperialism? During the Vietnam era, what was the relationship between the American economy and the arms industry? Whose interests did the war serve best? Who benefited most from the war? What were the class relationships between those who fought and those who stayed home in the university?

Developing macro objectives fosters a dialectical mode of inquiry; the process constitutes a sociopolitical application of knowledge, what Giroux calls *directive knowledge*. Critical theorists seek a kind of knowledge that will help students recognize the *social function of particular forms of knowledge*. The purpose of dialectical educational theory, then, is to provide students with a model that

Sexism

permits them to examine the underlying political, social, and economic foundations of the larger society.

CRITICAL PEDAGOGY AND THE SOCIAL CONSTRUCTION OF KNOWLEDGE

Critical educational theorists view school knowledge as historically and socially
rooted and interest bound. Knowledge acquired in school—or anywhere, for that
matter—is never neutral or objective but is ordered and structured in particular
ways; its emphases and exclusions partake of a silent logic. Knowledge is a *social
construction* deeply rooted in a nexus of power relations. When critical theorists
claim that knowledge is socially constructed, they mean that it is the product
of agreement or consent between individuals who live out particular social
relations (e.g., of class, race, and gender) and who live in particular junctures
in time. To claim that knowledge is socially constructed usually means that the
world we live in is constructed symbolically by the mind through social interaction
with others and is heavily dependent on culture, context, custom, and historical
specificity. There is no ideal, autonomous, pristine, or aboriginal world to which
our social constructions necessarily correspond; there is always a referential field
in which symbols are situated. And this particular referential field (e.g., language,
culture, place, time) will influence how symbols generate meaning. There is no
pure subjective insight. We do not stand *before* the social world; we live *in the
midst* of it. As we seek the meaning of events we seek the meaning of the social.
We can now raise certain questions with respect to the social construction of
knowledge, such as: Why do women and minorities often view social issues
differently than white males? Why are teachers more likely to value the opinions
of a middle-class white male student, for instance, than those of a black female?

Assumption of racist and sexist attitudes

Critical pedagogy asks how and why knowledge gets constructed the way
it does, and how and why some constructions of reality are legitimated and
celebrated by the dominant culture while others clearly are not. Critical pedagogy
asks how our everyday commonsense understandings—our social constructions
or "subjectivities"—get produced and lived out. In other words, what are the
social functions of knowledge? The crucial factor here is that some forms of
knowledge have more power and legitimacy than others. For instance, in many
schools in the United States, science and math curricula are favored over the liberal
arts. This can be ·explained by the link between the needs of big business to
compete in world markets and the imperatives of the new reform movement to
bring "excellence" back to the schools. Certain types of knowledge legitimate
certain gender, class, and racial interests. Whose interests does this knowledge
serve? Who gets excluded as a result? Who is marginalized?

Let's put this in the form of further questions: What is the relationship
between social class and knowledge taught in school? Why do we value scientific
knowledge over informal knowledge? Why do we have teachers using "standard
English"? Why is the public still unlikely to vote for a woman or a black for
president? How does school knowledge reinforce stereotypes about women,

minorities, and disadvantaged peoples? What accounts for some knowledge having high status (as in the great works of philosophers or scientists) while the practical knowledge of ordinary people or marginalized or subjugated groups is often discredited and devalued? Why do we learn about the "great men" in history and spend less time learning about the contributions of women and minorities and the struggles of people in lower economic classes? Why don't we learn more about the American labor movement? How and why are certain types of knowledge used to reinforce dominant ideologies, which in turn serve to mask unjust power relations among certain groups in society?

Forms of Knowledge

Critical pedagogy follows a distinction regarding forms of knowledge posited by the German social theorist Jurgen Habermas.[12] Let's examine this concept in the context of classroom teaching. Mainstream educators who work primarily within liberal and conservative educational ideologies emphasize *technical knowledge* (similar to Giroux's *productive knowledge*): Knowledge is that which can be measured and quantified. Technical knowledge is based on the natural sciences, uses hypothetico-deductive or empirical analytical methods, and is evaluated by, among other things, intelligence quotients, reading scores, and SAT results, all of which are used by educators to sort, regulate, and control students.

A second type, *practical knowledge,* aims to enlighten individuals so they can shape their daily actions in the world. Practical knowledge is generally acquired through *describing and analyzing social situations historically or developmentally,* and is geared toward helping individuals understand social events that are ongoing and situational. The liberal educational researcher who undertakes fieldwork in a school in order to evaluate student behavior and interaction acquires practical knowledge, for instance. This type of knowledge is not usually generated numerically or by submitting data to some kind of statistical instrument.

The critical educator, however, is most interested in what Habermas calls *emancipatory knowledge* (similar to Giroux's *directive knowledge*), which attempts to reconcile and transcend the opposition between technical and practical knowledge. Emancipatory knowledge helps us understand how social relationships are distorted and manipulated by relations of power and privilege. It also aims at creating the conditions under which irrationality, domination, and oppression can be overcome and transformed through deliberative, collective action. In short, it creates the foundation for social justice, equality, and empowerment.

Class

Class refers to the *economic, social, and political relationships that govern life in a given social order.* Class relationships reflect the constraints and limitations individuals and groups experience in the areas of income level, occupation, place of residence, and other indicators of status and social rank. Relations of class are those associated with surplus labor, who produces it, and who is a recipient of it. Surplus labor is that labor undertaken by workers beyond that which is necessary.

Class relations also deal with the social distribution of power and its structural allocation. Today there are greater distinctions within the working classes and it is now possible to talk about the new *underclasses* within the American social structure consisting of black, Hispanic, and Asian class fractions, together with the white aged, the unemployed and underemployed, large sections of women, the handicapped, and other marginalized economic groups.

Culture

The concept of *culture,* varied though it may be, is essential to any understanding of critical pedagogy. I use the term "culture" here to signify *the particular ways in which a social group lives out and makes sense of its "given" circumstances and conditions of life.* In addition to defining culture as *a set of practices, ideologies, and values from which different groups draw to make sense of the world,* we need to recognize how cultural questions help us understand who has power and how it is reproduced and manifested in the social relations that link schooling to the wider social order. The ability of individuals to express their culture is related to the power which certain groups are able to wield in the social order. The expression of values and beliefs by individuals who share certain historical experiences is determined by their collective power in society.[13]

The link between culture and power has been extensively analyzed in critical social theory over the past fifteen years. It is therefore possible to offer three insights from that literature which particularly illuminate the political logic that underlies various cultural/power relations. First, culture is intimately connected with the structure of social relations within class, gender, and age formations that produce forms of oppression and dependency. Second, culture is analyzed not simply as a way of life, but as a form of production through which different groups in either their dominant or subordinate social relations define and realize their aspirations through unequal relations of power. Third, culture is viewed as a field of struggle in which the production, legitimation, and circulation of particular forms of knowledge and experience are central areas of conflict. What is important here is that each of these insights raises fundamental questions about the ways in which inequalities are maintained and challenged in the spheres of school culture and the wider society.[14]

Dominant Culture, Subordinate Culture, and Subculture

Three central categories related to the concept of culture—dominant culture, subordinate culture, subculture—have been much discussed in recent critical scholarship. Culture can be readily broken down into "dominant" and "subordinate" parent cultures. *Dominant culture* refers to social practices and representations that *affirm the central values, interests, and concerns of the social class in control of the material and symbolic wealth of society.* Groups who live out social relations in subordination to the dominant culture are part of the *subordinate culture.* Group *subcultures* may be described as subsets of the two parent cultures (dominant and subordinate). Individuals who form subcultures often use distinct symbols and social practices to help foster an identity outside that of the dominant culture. As an example, we need only refer to punk sub-culture, with its distinct musical tastes, fetishistic costumery, spiked hair, and its attempt to disconfirm the dominant rules of propriety fostered by the main-stream media, schools, religions, and culture industry. For the most part, working-class subcultures exist in a subordinate structural position in society, and many of their members engage in oppositional acts against the dominant middle-class culture. It is important to remember, however, that people don't inhabit cultures or social classes but *live out class or cultural relations,* some of which may be dominant and some of which may be subordinate.[15]

Subcultures are involved in contesting the cultural "space" or openings in the dominant culture. The dominant culture is never able to secure total control over subordinate cultural groups. Whether we choose to examine British sub-cultural groups (i.e., working-class youth, teddy boys, skinheads, punks, rude boys, Rastafarians) or American groups (i.e., motorcycle clubs such as Hell's Angels, ethnic street gangs, or middle-class suburban gangs), subcultures are more often *negotiated* than truly *oppositional.* As John Muncie points out, this is because they operate primarily in the arena of leisure that is exceedingly vulnerable to commercial and ideological incorporation.[16] Subcultures do offer a symbolic critique of the social order and are frequently organized around relations of class, gender, style, and race. Despite the often ferocious exploitation of the subcultural resistance of various youth subcultures by bourgeois institutions (school, work-place, justice system, consumer industries), subcultures are usually able to keep alive the struggle over how meanings are produced, defined, and legitimated; consequently, they do represent various degrees of struggle against lived subjuga-tion. Many subcultural movements reflect a crisis within dominant society, rather than a unified mobilization against it. For instance, the hippie movement in the 1960s represented, in part, an exercise of petit bourgeois socialism by middle-class radicals who were nurtured both by idealist principles and by a search for spiritual and life-style comfort. This often served to draw critical attention away from the structural inequalities of capitalist society. As Muncie argues, subcultures constitute "a crisis within dominant culture rather than a conspiracy against dominant culture."[17] The youth counterculture of the sixties served as the ideo-logical loam that fertilized my pedagogy in Part Two. I had learned the rudiments of a middle-class radicalism that was preoccupied with the politics of expressive life and avoided examining in a minded and a critical manner the structural inequalities within the social order.

Cultural Forms

Cultural forms are those symbols and social practices that express culture, such as those found in music, dress, food, religion, dance, and education, which have developed from the efforts of groups to shape their lives out of their surrounding material and political environment. Television, video, and films are regarded as cultural forms. Schooling is also a cultural form. Baseball is a cultural form.

Cultural forms don't exist apart from sets of structural underpinnings which are related to the means of economic production, the mobilization of desire, the construction of social values, asymmetries of power/knowledge, configurations of ideologies, and relations of class, race, and gender.

Hegemony

The dominant culture is able to exercise domination over subordinate classes or groups through a process known as *hegemony*[18]. Hegemony refers to the maintenance of domination not by the sheer exercise of force *but primarily through consensual social practices, social forms, and social structures produced in specific sites such as the church, the state, the school, the mass media, the political system, and the family.* By *social practices,* I refer to what people say and do. Of course, social practices may be accomplished through words, gestures, personally appropriated signs and rituals, or a combination of these. *Social forms* refer to the principles that provide and give legitimacy to specific social practices. For example, the state legislature is one social form that gives legitimacy to the social practice of teaching. The term *social structures* can be defined as those constraints that limit individual life and appear to be beyond the individual's control, having their sources in the power relations that govern society. We can, therefore, talk about the "class structure" or the "economic structure" of our society.

Hegemony is a struggle in which the powerful win the consent of those who are oppressed, with the oppressed unknowingly participating in their own oppression. Hegemony was at work in my own practices as an elementary school teacher. Because I did not teach my students to question the prevailing values, attitudes, and social practices of the dominant society in a sustained critical manner, my classroom preserved the hegemony of the dominant culture. Such hegemony was contested when the students began to question my authority by resisting and disrupting my lessons. The dominant class secures hegemony—the consent of the dominated—by supplying the symbols, representations, and practices of social life in such a way that the basis of social authority and the unequal relations of power and privilege remain hidden. By perpetrating the myth of individual achievement and entrepreneurship in the media, the schools, the church, and the family, for instance, dominant culture ensures that subordinated groups who fail at school or who don't make it into the world of the "rich and famous" will view such failure in terms of personal inadequacy or the "luck of the draw." The oppressed blame themselves for school failure—a failure that can certainly be additionally attributed to the structuring effects of the economy and the class-based division of labor.[19]

Hegemony is a cultural encasement of meanings, a prison-house of language and ideas, that is "freely" entered into by both dominators and dominated. As Todd Gitlin puts it,

> Both rulers and ruled derive psychological and material rewards in the course of confirming and reconfirming their inequality. The hegemonic sense of the world seeps into popular "common sense" and gets reproduced there; it may even appear to be generated *by* that common sense.[20]

Hegemony refers to the moral and intellectual leadership of a dominant class over a subordinate class achieved not through coercion (i.e., threat of imprisonment or torture) or the willful construction of rules and regulations (as in a dictatorship or fascist regime), but rather through the general winning of consent of the subordinate class to the authority of the dominant class. The dominant class need not impose force for the manufacture of hegemony since the subordinate class actively subscribes to many of the values and objectives of the dominant class without being aware of the source of those values or the interests which inform them.

Hegemony is not a process of active domination as much as an active structuring of the culture and experiences of the subordinate class by the dominant class. The dominant culture is able to "frame" the ways in which subordinate groups live and respond to their own cultural system and lived experiences; in other words, the dominant culture is able to manufacture dreams and desires for both dominant and subordinate groups by supplying "terms of reference" (i.e., images, visions, stories, ideals) against which all individuals are expected to live their lives. The dominant culture tries to "fix" the meaning of signs, symbols, and representations to provide a "common" worldview, disguising relations of power and privilege through the organs of mass media and state apparatus such as schools, government institutions, and state bureaucracies. Individuals are provided with "subject positions," which condition them to react to ideas and opinions in prescribed ways. For instance, most individuals in the United States, when addressed as "Americans," are generally positioned as subjects by the dominant discourse. To be an "American" carries a certain set of ideological baggage. Americans generally think of themselves as lovers of freedom, defenders of individual rights, guardians of world peace, etc.; rarely do Americans see themselves as contradictory social agents. They rarely view their country as lagging behind other industrial economies in the world in providing security for its citizens in such areas as health care, family allowance, and housing subsidy programs. As citizens of the wealthiest country in the world, Americans generally do not question why their government cannot afford to be more generous to its citizens. Most Americans would be aghast at hearing a description of their country as a "terrorist regime" exercising covert acts of war against Middle Eastern countries such as Iraq. The prevailing image of America that the schools, the entertainment industry, and government agencies have promulgated is a benevolent one in which the interests of the dominant classes supposedly represent the interests of all groups. It is an image in which the values and beliefs of the dominant class appear so correct that to reject them would be unnatural, a violation of common sense.

Within the hegemonic process, established meanings are often laundered of contradiction, contestation, and ambiguity. Resistance does occur, however, most often in the domain of popular culture. In this case, popular culture becomes an arena of negotiation in which dominant, subordinate, and oppositional groups affirm and struggle over cultural representations and meanings. The dominant culture is rarely successful on all counts. People *do* resist. Alternative groups do manage to find different values and meanings to regulate their lives. Oppositional groups do attempt to challenge the prevailing culture's mode of structuring and codifying representations and meanings. Prevailing social practices are, in fact, resisted. Schools and other social and cultural sites are rarely in the thrall of the hegemonic process since there we will also find struggle and confrontation. This is why schools can be characterized as terrains of transactions, exchange, and struggle between subordinate groups and the dominant ideology. There is a relative autonomy within school sites that allows for forms of resistance to emerge and to break the cohesiveness of hegemony. Teachers battle over what books to use, over what disciplinary practices to use, and over the aims and objectives of particular courses and programs.

One current example of the battle for hegemony can be seen in the challenge by Christian fundamentalists to public schooling. Fundamentalist critics have instigated a debate over dominant pedagogical practices that ranges all the way from textbooks to how, in science classes, teachers may account for the origins of humankind. The important point to remember, however, is that hegemony is always in operation; certain ideas, values, and social practices generally prevail over others.

Not all prevailing values are oppressive. Critical educators, too, would like to secure hegemony for their own ideas. The challenge for teachers is to recognize and attempt to transform those undemocratic and oppressive features of hegemonic control that often structure everyday classroom existence in ways not readily apparent. These oppressive features are rarely challenged since the dominant ideology is so all inclusive that individuals are taught to view it as natural, commonsensical, and inviolable. For instance, subordinate groups who subscribe to an ideology that could be described as right wing are often the very groups hurt most by the twelve years of Republican government they elected. Yet the Republican party has been able to market itself as no-nonsense, get-tough, anti-Communist, and hyper-patriotic—features that have always appealed to subordinate groups whose cultural practices may include listening to country and western music, following the televangelist programs and crusades, or cheering the pugilistic exploits of the Terminator. Those who seek to chart out the ways in which the affluent are favored over subordinate groups are dismissed as wimpish liberals. Who needs to use force when ideational hegemony works this well? As Gore Vidal has observed about the United States: "The genius of our system is that ordinary people go out and vote against their interests. The way our ruling class keeps out of sight is one of the greatest stunts in the political history of any country."[21]

Ideology

Hegemony could not do its work without the support of ideology. Ideology permeates all of social life and does not simply refer to the political ideologies of communism, socialism, anarchism, rationalism, or existentialism. Ideology refers to *the production and representation of ideas, values, and beliefs and the manner in which they are expressed and lived out by both individuals and groups.*[22] Simply put, ideology refers to the production of sense and meaning. It can be described as a way of viewing the world, a complex of ideas, various types of social practices, rituals, and representations *that we tend to accept as natural and as common sense.* It is the result of the intersection of meaning and power in the social world. Customs, rituals, beliefs, and values often produce within individuals distorted conceptions of their place in the sociocultural order and thereby serve to reconcile them to that place and to disguise the inequitable relations of power and privilege; this is sometimes referred to as "ideological hegemony."

Stuart Hall and James Donald define ideology as "the frameworks of thought which are used in society to explain, figure out, make sense of or give meaning to the social and political world. . . . Without these frameworks, we could not make sense of the world at all. But with them, our perceptions are inevitably structured in a particular direction by the very concepts we are using."[23] Ideology includes both positive and negative functions at any given moment: The *positive function* of ideology is to "provide the concepts, categories, images, and ideas by means of which people make sense of their social and political world, form projects, come to a certain consciousness of their place in the world, and act in it;" the *negative function* of ideology "refers to the fact that all such perspectives are inevitably selective. Thus a perspective positively organizes the 'facts of the case' in *this* and makes sense because it inevitably excludes *that* way of putting things."[24]

In order to fully understand the negative function of ideology, the concept must be linked to a theory of domination. *Domination* occurs when relations of power established at the institutional level are systematically asymmetrical; that is, when they are unequal, therefore privileging some groups over others. According to John Thompson, ideology as a negative function works through four different modes: legitimation, dissimulation, fragmentation, and reification. *Legitimation* occurs when a system of domination is sustained by being represented as legitimate or as eminently just and worthy of respect. For instance, by legitimizing the school system as just and meritocratic, as giving everyone the same opportunity for success, the dominant culture hides the truth of the hidden curriculum—the fact that those whom schooling helps most are those who come from the most affluent families. *Dissimulation* results when relations of domination are concealed, denied, or obscured in various ways. For instance, the practice of institutionalized tracking in schools purports to help better meet the needs of groups of students with varying academic ability. However, describing tracking in this way helps to cloak its socially reproductive function: that of sorting students according to their social class location. *Fragmentation* occurs when relations of domination are sustained by the production of meanings in a way which fragments groups so that they are placed in opposition to one another. For instance, when conservative educational critics explain the declining standards in American education as a result of trying to accommodate low-income minority students, this sometimes results in a backlash against immigrant students by other subordinate groups. This "divide and rule" tactic prevents oppressed groups from working together to secure collectively their rights. *Reification* occurs when transitory historical states of affairs are presented as permanent, natural, and commonsensical—as if they exist outside of time.[25] This has occurred to a certain extent with the current call for a national curriculum based on acquiring information about the "great books" so as to have a greater access to the dominant culture. These works are revered as high-status knowledge since purportedly the force of history has heralded them as such and placed them on book lists in respected cultural institutions such as universities. Here literacy becomes a weapon that can be used against those groups who are "culturally illiterate," whose social class, race, or gender renders their own experiences and stories as too unimportant to be worthy of investigation. That is, as a pedagogical tool, a stress on the great books often deflects attention away from the personal experiences of students and the political nature of everyday life. Teaching the great books is also a way of inculcating certain values and sets of behaviors in social groups, thereby solidifying the existing social hierarchy. The most difficult task in analyzing these negative functions of ideology is to unmask those ideological properties which insinuate themselves within reality as their fundamental components. Ideological functions which barricade themselves within the realm of common sense often manage to disguise the grounds of their operations.

At this point it should be clear that ideology represents a vocabulary of standardization and a grammar of design sanctioned and sustained by particular social practices. All ideas and systems of thought organize a rendition of reality according to their own metaphors, narratives, and rhetoric. There is no "deep structure," totalizing logic, or grand theory pristine in form and innocent in effects which is altogether uncontaminated by interest, value, or judgment—in short, by *ideology.* There is no privileged sanctuary separate from culture and politics where we can be free to distinguish truth from opinion, fact from value, or image from interpretation. There is no "objective" environment that is not stamped with social presence.

If we all can agree that as individuals, we inherit a preexisting sign community, and acknowledge that all ideas, values, and meanings have social roots and perform social functions, then understanding ideology becomes a matter of investigating *which* concepts, values, and meanings *obscure* our understanding of the social world and our place within the networks of power/knowledge relations, and which concepts, values, and meanings *clarify* such an understanding. In other words, why do certain ideological formations cause us to misrecognize our complicity in establishing or maintaining asymmetrical relations of power and privilege within the sociocultural order?

The *dominant ideology* refers to patterns of beliefs and values shared by the majority of individuals. The majority of Americans—rich and poor alike—share the belief that capitalism is a better system than democratic socialism, for instance, or that men are generally more capable of holding positions of authority than women, or that women should be more passive and housebound. Here, we must recognize that the economic system requires the ideology of consumer capitalism to naturalize it, rendering it commonsensical. The ideology of patriarchy also is necessary to keep the nature of the economy safe and secured within the prevailing hegemony. We have been "fed" these dominant ideologies for decades through the mass media, the schools, and family socialization.

Oppositional ideologies do exist, however, which attempt to challenge the dominant ideologies and shatter existing stereotypes. On some occasions, the dominant culture is able to manipulate alternative and oppositional ideologies in such a way that hegemony can be more effectively secured. For instance, "The Cosby Show" on commercial television carries a message that a social avenue now exists in America for blacks to be successful doctors and lawyers. This positive view of blacks, however, masks the fact that most blacks in the United States exist in a subordinate position to the dominant white culture with respect to power and privilege. The dominant culture secures hegemony by transmitting and legitimating ideologies like that in "The Cosby Show," which reflect and shape popular resistance to stereotypes, but which in reality do little to challenge the real basis of power of the ruling dominant groups.

The dominant ideology often encourages oppositional ideologies and tolerates those that challenge their own rationale, since by absorbing these contradictory values, they are more often than not able to domesticate the conflicting and contradictory values. This is because the hegemonic hold of the social system is so strong, it can generally withstand dissension and actually come to neutralize it by permitting token opposition. During my teaching days in the suburban ghetto, school dances in the gym often celebrated the values, meanings, and pleasure of life on the street—some of which could be considered oppositional—but were tolerated by the administration because they helped defuse tension in the school. They afforded the students some symbolic space for a limited amount of time; yet they redressed nothing concrete in terms of the lived subordination of the students and their families on a day-to-day basis.

The main question for teachers attempting to become aware of the ideologies that inform their own teaching is: How have certain pedagogical practices become so habitual or natural in school settings that teachers accept them as normal, unproblematic, and expected? How often, for instance, do teachers question school practices such as tracking, ability grouping, competitive grading, teacher-centered pedagogical approaches, and the use of rewards and punishments as control devices? The point here is to understand that these practices are not carved in stone, but are, in reality, socially constructed. How, then, is the distilled wisdom of traditional educational theorizing ideologically structured? What constitutes the origins and legitimacy of the pedagogical practices within this tradition? To what extent do such pedagogical practices serve to empower the student, and to what extent do they work as forms of social control that support, stabilize, and legitimate the role of the teacher as a moral gatekeeper of the state? What are the functions and effects of the systematic imposition of ideological perspectives on classroom teaching practices?

In my classroom journal, what characterized the ideological basis of my own teaching practices? How did "being schooled" both enable and contain the subjectivities of the students? I am using the word *subjectivity* here to mean forms of knowledge that are both conscious and unconscious and which express our identity as human agents. Subjectivity relates to everyday knowledge in its socially constructed and historically produced forms. Following this, we can ask: How do the dominant ideological practices of teachers help to structure the subjectivities of students? What are the possible consequences of this, for good and for ill?

Prejudice

or positive

Prejudice is the negative prejudgment of individuals and groups on the basis of unrecognized, unsound, and inadequate evidence. Because these negative attitudes occur so frequently, they take on a commonsense or ideological character that is often used to justify acts of discrimination.

CRITICAL PEDAGOGY AND THE POWER/KNOWLEDGE RELATION

Critical pedagogy is fundamentally concerned with understanding the relationship between power and knowledge. The dominant curriculum separates knowledge from the issue of power and treats it in an unabashedly technical manner; knowledge is seen in overwhelmingly instrumental terms as something to be mastered. That knowledge is always an ideological construction linked to particular interests and social relations generally receives little consideration in education programs.

The work of the French philosopher Michel Foucault is crucial in understanding the socially constructed nature of truth and its inscription in knowledge/power relations. Foucault's concept of "power/knowledge" extends the notion of power beyond its conventional use by philosophers and social theorists who, like American John Dewey, have understood power as "the sum of conditions available for bringing the desirable end into existence."[26] For Foucault, power comes from everywhere, from above and from below; it is "always already there" and is inextricably implicated in the micro-relations of domination and resistance.

Discourse

Power relations are inscribed in what Foucault refers to as *discourse* or a family of concepts. Discourses are made up of discursive practices that he describes as

> a body of anonymous, historical rules, always determined in the time and space that have defined a given period, and for a given social, economic, geographical, or linguistic area, the conditions of operation of the enunciative function.[27]

Discursive practices, then, *refer to the rules by which discourses are formed, rules that govern what can be said and what must remain unsaid, and who can speak with authority and who must listen.* Social and political institutions, such as schools and penal institutions, are governed by discursive practices.

> Discursive practices are not purely and simply ways of producing discourse. They are embodied in technical processes, in institutions, in patterns for general behavior, in forms of transmission and diffusion, and pedagogical forms which, at once, impose and maintain them.[28]

For education, discourse can be defined as a "regulated system of statements" that establish differences between fields and theories of teacher education; it is "not simply words but is embodied in the practice of institutions, patterns of behavior, and in forms of pedagogy."[29]

From this perspective, we can consider *dominant* discourses (those produced by the dominant culture) as "regimes of truth," as general economies of power/knowledge, or as multiple forms of constraint. In a classroom setting, dominant educational discourses determine what books we may use, what classroom approaches we should employ (mastery learning, Socratic method, etc.), and what values and beliefs we should transmit to our students.

For instance, neoconservative discourses on language in the classroom would view working-class speech as undersocialized or deprived. Liberal discourse would view such speech as merely different. Similarly, to be culturally literate within a conservative discourse is to acquire basic information on American culture (dates of battles, passages of the Constitution, etc.). Conservative discourse focuses mostly on the works of "great men." A liberal discourse on cultural literacy includes knowledge generated from the perspective of women and minorities. A *critical* discourse focuses on the interests and assumptions that inform the generation of knowledge itself. A critical discourse is also self-critical and deconstructs dominant discourses the moment they are ready to achieve hegemony. A critical discourse can, for instance, explain how high-status knowledge (the great works of the Western world) can be used to teach concepts that reinforce the status quo. Discourses and discursive practices influence how we live our lives as conscious thinking subjects. They shape our subjectivities (our ways of understanding in relation to the world) because it is only in language and through discourse that social reality can be given meaning. Not all discourses are given the same weight, as some will account for and justify the appropriateness of the status quo and others will provide a context for resisting social and institutional practices.[30]

This follows our earlier discussion that knowledge (truth) is socially constructed, culturally mediated, and historically situated. Cleo Cherryholmes asserts that dominant discourses determine what counts as true, important, and relevant. Discourses are what gets spoken and are generated and governed by rules and power.[31] Truth cannot be spoken in the absence of power relations, and each relation necessarily speaks its own truth. Foucault removes truth from the realm of the absolute; truth is understood only as changes in the determination of what can count as true.

> Truth is a thing of this world: it is produced only by virtue of multiple forms of constraint. And it induces regular effects of power. Each society has its regime of truth, its "general politics" of truth: that is, the types of discourse which it accepts and makes function as true; the mechanisms and instances which enable one to distinguish true and false statements, the means by which each is sanctioned; the techniques and procedures accorded value in the acquisition of truth; the status of those who are charged with saying what counts as true.[32]

In Foucault's view, truth (educational truth, scientific truth, religious truth, legal truth, or whatever) must not be understood as a set of "discovered laws" that exist outside power/knowledge relations and which somehow correspond with the "real." We cannot "know" truth except through its "effects." Truth is not *relative* (in the sense of "truths" proclaimed by various individuals and societies are all equal in their effects) but is *relational* (statements considered "true" are dependent upon history, cultural context, and relations of power operative in a given society, discipline, institution, etc.). The crucial question here is that if truth is *relational* and not *absolute,* what criteria can we use to guide our actions in the world? Critical educators argue that *praxis* (informed actions) must be guided by *phronesis* (the disposition to act truly and rightly). This means, in critical terms, that actions and knowledge must be directed at eliminating pain, oppression, and inequality, and at promoting justice and freedom.

Lawrence Grossberg speaks to the critical perspective on truth and theory when he argues:

> The truth of a theory can only be defined by its ability to intervene into, to give us a different and perhaps better ability to come to grips with, the relations that constitute its context. If neither history nor texts speak its own truth, truth has to be won; and it is, consequently, inseparable from relations of power.[33]

An understanding of the power/knowledge relationship raises important issues regarding what kinds of theories educators should work with and what knowledge they can provide in order to empower students. *Empowerment* means not only helping students to understand and engage the world around them, but also enabling them to exercise the kind of courage needed to change the social order where necessary. Teachers need to recognize that *power relations correspond to forms of school knowledge that distort understanding and produce what is commonly accepted as "truth."* Critical educators argue that knowledge should be analyzed on the basis of whether it is oppressive and exploitative, and not on the basis of whether it is "true." For example, what kind of knowledge do we construct about women and minority groups in school texts? Do the texts we use in class promote stereotypical views that reinforce racist, sexist, and patriarchal attitudes? How do we treat the knowledge that working-class students bring to class discussions and schoolwork? Do we unwittingly devalue such knowledge and thereby disconfirm the voices of these students?

Knowledge should be examined not only for the ways in which it might misrepresent or mediate social reality, but also for the ways in which it actually reflects the daily struggle of people's lives. We must understand that knowledge not only distorts reality, but also provides grounds for understanding the actual conditions that inform everyday life. Teachers, then, should examine knowledge both for the way it misrepresents or marginalizes particular views of the world and for the way it provides a deeper understanding of how the student's world is actually constructed. Knowledge acquired in classrooms should help students participate in vital issues that affect their experience on a daily level rather than simply enshrine the values of business pragmatism. School knowledge should have a more emancipatory goal than churning out workers (human capital) and helping schools become the citadel of corporate ideology.[34] School knowledge should help create the conditions productive for student self-determination in the larger society.

CRITICAL PEDAGOGY AND THE CURRICULUM

From the perspective of critical educational theorists, the curriculum represents much more than a program of study, a classroom text, or a course syllabus. Rather, it represents the *introduction to a particular form of life; it serves in part to prepare students for dominant or subordinate positions in the existing society.*[35] The curriculum favors certain forms of knowledge over others and affirms the dreams, desires, and values of select groups of students over other groups, often discriminatorily on the basis of race, class, and gender. In general, critical educational theorists are concerned with how descriptions, discussions, and representations in textbooks, curriculum materials, course content, and social relations embodied in classroom practices benefit dominant groups and exclude subordinate ones. In this regard, they often refer to the *hidden curriculum.*

The Hidden Curriculum

The *hidden curriculum* refers to *the unintended outcomes of the schooling process.* Critical educators recognize that schools shape students both through standardized learning situations, and through other agendas, including rules of conduct, classroom organization, and the informal pedagogical procedures used by teachers with specific groups of students.[36] The hidden curriculum also includes teaching and learning styles that are emphasized in the classroom, the messages that get transmitted to the student by the total physical and instructional environment, governance structures, teacher expectations, and grading procedures.

The hidden curriculum deals with the tacit ways in which knowledge and behavior get constructed, outside the usual course materials and formally scheduled lessons. It is a part of the bureaucratic and managerial "press" of the school—the combined forces by which students are induced to comply with dominant ideologies and social practices related to authority, behavior, and morality. Does the principal expel school offenders or just verbally upbraid them? Is the ethos of the office inviting or hostile? Do the administration and teachers show respect for each other and for the students on a regular basis? Answers to these questions help define the hidden curriculum, which refers, then, to the *non-subject-related* sets of behaviors produced in students.

Often, the hidden curriculum displaces the professed educational ideals and goals of the classroom teacher or school. We know, for example, that teachers unconsciously give more intellectual attention, praise, and academic help to boys than to girls. A study reported in *Psychology Today* suggests that stereotypes of garrulous and gossipy women are so strong that when groups of administrators and teachers are shown films of classroom discussion and asked who is talking more, the teachers overwhelmingly choose the girls. In reality, however, the boys in the film outtalk the girls at a ratio of three to one. The same study also suggests that teachers behave differently depending on whether boys or girls respond during classroom discussions. When boys call out comments without raising their hands, for instance, teachers generally accept their answers; girls, however, are reprimanded for the same behavior. The hidden message is "Boys should be academically aggressive while girls should remain composed and passive." In addition, teachers are twice as likely to give male students detailed instructions on how to do things for themselves; with female students, however, teachers are more likely to do the task for them instead. Not surprisingly, the boys are being taught independence and the girls dependency.[37]

Classroom sexism as a function of the hidden curriculum results in the unwitting and unintended granting of power and privilege to men over women and accounts for many of the following outcomes:

- Although girls start school ahead of boys in reading and basic computation, by the time they graduate from high school, boys have higher SAT scores in both areas.
- By high school, some girls are less committed to careers, although their grades and achievement-test scores may be as good as boys. Many girls' interests turn to marriage or stereotypically female jobs. Some women may feel that men disapprove of women using their intelligence.
- Girls are less likely to take math and science courses and to participate in special or gifted programs in these subjects, even if they have a talent for them. They are also more likely to believe that they are incapable of pursuing math and science in college and to avoid the subjects.
- Girls are more likely to attribute failure to internal factors, such as ability, rather than to external factors, such as luck.

The sexist communication game is played at work, as well as at school. As reported in numerous studies, it goes like this:

- Men speak more often and frequently interrupt women.
- Listeners recall more from male speakers than from female speakers, even when both use a similar speaking style and cover identical content.
- Women participate less actively in conversation. They do more smiling and gazing; they're more often the passive bystanders in professional and social conversations among peers.
- Women often transform declarative statements into tentative comments. This is accomplished by using qualifiers ("kind of" or "I guess") and by adding tag questions ("This is a good movie, isn't it?"). These tentative patterns weaken impact and signal a lack of power and influence.[38]

Of course, most teachers try hard not to be sexist. The hidden curriculum continues to operate, however, despite what the overt curriculum prescribes. The hidden curriculum can be effectively compared to what Australian educator Doug White calls the *multinational curriculum.* For White,

> The multinational curriculum is the curriculum of disembodied universals, of the mind as an information-processing machine, of concepts and skills without moral and social judgment but with enormous manipulative power. That curriculum proposed the elevation of abstract skills over particular content, of universal cognitive principles over the actual conditions of life.[39]

White reminds us that no curriculum, policy, or program is ideologically or politically innocent, and that the concept of the curriculum is inextricably related to issues of social class, culture, gender, and power. This is, of course, not the way curriculum is traditionally understood and discussed in teacher education. The hidden curriculum, then, refers to learning outcomes not openly acknowledged to learners. But we must remember that not all values, attitudes, or patterns of behavior that are by-products of the hidden curriculum in educational settings are necessarily bad. The point is to identify the structural and political assumptions upon which the hidden curriculum rests and to attempt to change the institutional arrangements of the classroom so as to offset the most undemocratic and oppressive outcomes.

Curriculum as a Form of Cultural Politics

Critical educational theorists view curriculum as a form of *cultural politics,* that is, as a part of the sociocultural dimension of the schooling process. The term cultural politics permits the educational theorist to highlight the political consequences of interaction between teachers and students who come from dominant and subordinate cultures. To view the curriculum as a form of cultural politics *assumes that the social, cultural, political, and economic dimensions are the primary categories for understanding contemporary schooling.*[40]

School life is understood not as a unitary, monolithic, and ironclad system of rules and regulations, but as a cultural terrain characterized by varying degrees of accommodation, contestation, and resistance. Furthermore, school life is understood as a plurality of conflicting languages and struggles, a place where classroom and street-corner cultures collide and where teachers, students, and school administrators often differ as to how school experiences and practices are to be defined and understood.

This curriculum perspective creates conditions for the student's self-empowerment as an active political and moral subject. I am using the term *empowerment* to refer to the process through which students learn to critically appropriate knowledge existing outside their immediate experience in order to broaden their understanding of themselves, the world, and the possibilities for transforming the taken-for-granted assumptions about the way we live. Stanley

Aronowitz has described one aspect of empowerment as "the process of appreciating and loving oneself;"[41] empowerment is gained from knowledge and social relations that dignify one's own history, language, and cultural traditions. But empowerment means more than self-confirmation. It also refers to the process by which students learn to question and selectively appropriate those aspects of the dominant culture that will provide them with the basis for defining and transforming, rather than merely serving, the wider social order.

Basing a curriculum on cultural politics consists of linking critical social theory to a set of stipulated practices through which teachers can dismantle and critically examine dominant educational and cultural traditions. Many of these traditions have fallen prey to an *instrumental rationality* (a way of looking at the world in which "ends" are subordinated to questions of "means" and in which "facts" are separated from questions of "value") that either limits or ignores democratic ideals and principles. Critical theorists want particularly to develop a language of critique and demystification that can be used to analyze those latent interests and ideologies that work to socialize students in a manner compatible with the dominant culture. Of equal concern, however, is the creation of alternative teaching practices capable of empowering students both inside and outside of schools.

SOCIAL REPRODUCTION: A CRITICAL PERSPECTIVE

Over the decades, critical educational theorists have tried to fathom how schools are implicated in the process of *social reproduction*. In other words, they have attempted to explore how schools *perpetuate or reproduce the social relationships and attitudes needed to sustain the existing dominant economic and class relations of the larger society.*[42] Social reproduction refers to the intergenerational reproduction of social class (i.e., working-class students become working-class adults; middle-class students become middle-class adults). Schools reproduce the structures of social life through the colonization (socialization) of student subjectivities and by establishing social practices characteristic of the wider society.

Critical educators ask: How do schools help transmit the status and class positions of the wider society? The answers, of course, vary enormously. Some of the major mechanisms of social reproduction include the allocation of students into private versus public schools, the socioeconomic composition of school communities, and the placement of students into curriculum tracks within schools.[43] A group of social reproduction theorists, known as *correspondence theorists* have attempted to show how schools reflect wider social inequalities. In a famous study by Bowles and Gintis[44], the authors argue in deterministic terms that there is a *relatively simple correspondence between schooling, class, family, and social inequalities.* Bowles and Gintis maintain that children of parents with upper socioeconomic standing most often achieve upper socioeconomic status while children of lower socioeconomic parents acquire a correspondingly low socioeconomic standing. However, schooling structures are not always successful in ensuring privilege for the students' advantaged class positions. The correspondence theorists *could not explain why some children cross over from the status of their parents.* Social reproduction, as it turns out, is more than simply a case of economic and class position; it also involves social, cultural, and linguistic factors.

This brings into the debate the *conflict* or *resistance theorists,* such as Henry Giroux and Paul Willis, who pay significantly more attention to the *partial autonomy* of the school culture and to the role of conflict and contradiction within the reproductive process itself.[45] *Theories of resistance* generally draw upon an understanding of the complexities of culture to define the relationship between schools and the dominant society. Resistance theorists challenge the school's ostensible role as a democratic institution that functions to improve the social position of all students—including, if not especially, those groups that are subordinated to the system. Resistance theorists question the processes by which the school system reflects and sustains the logic of capital as well as dominant social practices and structures that are found in a class-, race-, and gender-divided society.

One of the major contributions to resistance theory has been the discovery by British researcher Paul Willis that working-class students who engage in classroom episodes of resistance often implicate themselves even further in their own domination.[46] Willis's group of working-class schoolboys, known as "the lads," resisted the class-based oppression of the school by rejecting mental labor in favor of more "masculine" manual labor (which reflected the shop floor culture of their family members). In so doing, they ironically displaced the school's potential to help them escape the shop floor once they graduated. Willis's work presents a considerable advance in understanding social and cultural reproduction in the context of student resistance. Social reproduction certainly exceeds mobility for each class, and we know that a substantial amount of class mobility is unlikely in most school settings. The work of the resistance theorists has helped us understand how domination works, even though students continually reject the ideology that is helping to oppress them. Sometimes this resistance only helps secure to an even greater degree the eventual fate of these students.

How, then, can we characterize student resistance? Students resist instruction for many reasons. As Giroux reminds us, not all acts of student misbehavior are acts of resistance. In fact, such "resistance" may simply be repressive moments (sexist, racist) inscribed by the dominant culture.[47] I have argued that the major drama of resistance in schools is an effort on the part of students to bring their street-corner culture into the classroom. Students reject the culture of classroom learning because, for the most part, it is delibidinalized (eros-denying) and is infused with a cultural capital to which subordinate groups have little legitimate access. Resistance to school instruction represents a resolve on the part of students not to be dissimulated in the face of oppression; it is a fight against the erasure of their street-corner identities. To resist means to fight against the monitoring of passion and desire. It is, furthermore, a struggle against the capitalist symbolization of the flesh. By this I mean that students resist turning themselves into worker commodities in which their potential is evaluated only as future members of the labor force. At the same time, however, the images of success manufactured by the dominant culture seem out of reach for most of them.

Students resist the "dead time" of school, where interpersonal relationships are reduced to the imperatives of market ideology. Resistance, in other words, is a rejection of their reformulation as docile objects where spontaneity is replaced by efficiency and productivity, in compliance with the needs of the corporate marketplace. Accordingly, students' very bodies become sites of struggle, and resistance a way of gaining power, celebrating pleasure, and fighting oppression in the lived historicity of the moment.

What, then, are the "regimes of truth" that organize school time, subject matter, pedagogical practice, school values, and personal truth? How does the culture of the school organize the body and monitor passion through its elaborate system of surveillance? How are forms of social control inscripted into the flesh? How are students' subjectivities and social identities produced discursively by institutionalized power, and how is this institutional power at the same time produced by the legitimization of discourses that treat students as if they were merely repositories of lust and passion (the degenerative animal instincts)? How is reason privileged over passion so that it can be used to quell the "crude mob mentality" of students? What is the range of identities available within a system of education designed to produce, regulate, and distribute character, govern gesture, dictate values, and police desire? To what extent does an adherence to the norms of the school mean that students will have to give up the dignity and status maintained through psychosocial adaptations to life on the street? To what extent does compliance with the rituals and norms of school mean that students have to forfeit their identity as members of an ethnic group? These are all questions that theorists within the critical tradition have attempted to answer. And the answers are as various as they are important.

Some versions of student resistance are undoubtedly romantic: The teachers are villains, and the students are antiheroes. I am not interested in teacher-bashing, nor in resurrecting the resistant student as the new James Dean or Marlon Brando. I much prefer the image of Giroux's resisting intellectual, someone who questions prevailing norms and established regimes of truth in the manner of a Rosa Luxemburg or a Jean-Paul Sartre.[48]

I would like to stress an important point. Our culture in general (and that includes schools, the media, and our social institutions) has helped educate students to acquire a veritable passion for ignorance. The French psychoanalyst Jacques Lacan suggests that ignorance is not a passive state but rather an active excluding from consciousness. The passion for ignorance that has infected our culture demands a complex explanation, but part of it can be attributed, as Lacan suggests, to a *refusal to acknowledge that our subjectivities have been constructed out of the information and social practices that surround us.*[49] Ignorance, as part of the very structure of knowledge, can teach us something. But we lack the critical constructs with which to recover that knowledge *which we choose not to know.* Unable to find meaningful knowledge "out there" in the world of prepackaged commodities, students resort to random violence or an intellectual purple haze where anything more challenging than the late night news is met with retreat or despair; and of course, it is the dominant culture that benefits most from this epidemic of conceptual anesthesia. The fewer critical intellectuals around to challenge its ideals, the better.

What do all these theories of resistance mean for the classroom teacher? Do we disregard resistance? Do we try to ignore it? Do we always take the student's side?

The answers to these questions are not easy. But let me sketch out the bare bones of a possible answer. First of all, schooling should be a process of understanding how subjectivities are produced. It should be a process of examining how we have been constructed out of the prevailing ideas, values, and worldviews of the dominant culture. The point to remember is that if we have been made, then we can be "unmade" and "made over." What are some alternative models with which we can begin to repattern ourselves and our social order? Teachers need to encourage students to be self-reflexive about these questions and to provide students with a conceptual framework to begin to answer them. Teaching and learning should be a process of *inquiry,* of critique; it should also be a process of *constructing,* of building a social imagination that works within a language of hope. If teaching is cast in the form of what Henry Giroux refers to as a "language of possibility," then a greater potential exists for making learning relevant, critical, and transformative. Knowledge is relevant only when it begins with the experiences students bring with them from the surrounding culture; it is critical only when these experiences are shown to sometimes be problematic (i.e., racist, sexist); and it is transformative only when students begin to use the knowledge to help empower others, including individuals in the surrounding community. Knowledge then becomes linked to social reform. An understanding of the language of the self can help us better negotiate with the world. It can also help us begin to forge the basis of *social transformation*: the building of a better world, the altering of the very ground upon which we live and work.

Teachers can do no better than to create agendas of possibility in their classrooms. Not every student will want to take part, but many will. Teachers may have personal problems—and so may students—that will limit the range of classroom discourses. Some teachers may simply be unwilling to function as critical educators. Critical pedagogy does not guarantee that resistance will not take place. But it does provide teachers with the foundations for understanding resistance, so that whatever pedagogy is developed can be sensitive to sociocultural conditions that construct resistance, lessening the chance that students will be blamed as the sole, originating source of resistance. No emancipatory pedagogy will ever be built out of theories of behavior which view students as lazy, defiant, lacking in ambition, or genetically inferior. A much more penetrating solution is to try to understand the structures of mediation in the sociocultural world that form student resistance. In other words, what is the larger picture? We must remove the concept of student resistance from the preserve of the behaviorist or the depth psychologist and insert it instead into the terrain of social theory.

Cultural Capital

Resistance theorists such as Henry Giroux focus on *cultural reproduction* as a function of class-based differences in *cultural capital.* The concept of *cultural capital,* made popular by French sociologist Pierre Bourdieu, refers to the general cultural background, knowledge, disposition, and skills that are passed on from one generation to another. Cultural capital represents *ways of talking, acting, and socializing, as well as language practices, values, and styles of dress and behavior.* Cultural capital can exist in the embodied state, as long-lasting dispositions of the mind and body; in the objectified state, as cultural artifacts such as pictures, books, diplomas, and other material objects; and in the institutionalized state, which confers original properties on the cultural capital which it guarantees. For instance, to many teachers, the cultural traits exhibited by students—e.g., tardiness, sincerity, honesty, thrift, industriousness, politeness, or a certain way of dressing, speaking, and gesturing—appear as natural qualities emerging from an individual's "inner essence." However, such traits are to a great extent culturally inscribed and are often linked to the social class standing of individuals who exhibit them. Social capital refers to the collectively owned economic and cultural capital of a group.[50] Taking linguistic competency as just one example of cultural capital, theorists such as Basil Bernstein contend that class membership and family socialization generate distinctive speech patterns. Working-class students learn "restricted" linguistic codes while middle-class children use "elaborated" codes. This means that the speech of working-class and middle-class children is generated by underlying regulative principles that govern their choice and combination of words and sentence structures. These, according to Bernstein, have been learned primarily in the course of family socialization.[51] Critical theorists argue that schools generally affirm and reward students who exhibit the elaborately coded "middle-class" speech while disconfirming and devaluing students who use restricted "working-class" coded speech.

Students from the dominant culture inherit substantially different cultural capital than do economically disadvantaged students, and schools generally value and reward those who exhibit that dominant cultural capital (which is also usually exhibited by the teacher). Schools systematically *devalue* the cultural capital of students who occupy subordinate class positions. Cultural capital is reflective of material capital and replaces it as a form of symbolic currency that enters into the exchange system of the school. Cultural capital is therefore symbolic of the social structure's economic force and becomes in itself a productive force in the reproduction of social relations under capitalism. Academic performance represents, therefore, not individual competence or the lack of ability on the part of disadvantaged students but *the school's depreciation of their cultural capital.* The end result is that the school's academic credentials remain indissolubly linked to an unjust system of trading in cultural capital which is eventually transformed into *economic* capital, as working-class students become less likely to get high-paying jobs.

When I worked with students in my suburban ghetto classroom, those whose cultural capital most closely resembled my own were the students with whom I initially felt most comfortable, spent the most instructional time, and most often encouraged to work in an independent manner. I could relate more readily and positively—at least at the beginning—to those students whose manners, values, and competencies resembled my own. Teachers—including myself—easily spotted Buddy, T. J., and Duke as members of the economically disadvantaged underclass, and this often worked against them, especially with teachers who registered such students as intellectually or socially deficient. Intellectual and social deficiencies had little, if anything, to do with their behavior. Class-specific character traits and social practices did.

QUESTIONS FOR DISCUSSION

1. If teachers unwittingly participate in what critical educational theorists call social reproduction, what would you as a teacher do to overcome the worst dimensions of this process?
2. As teachers or prospective teachers, what can we do to make the hidden curriculum less hidden and less harmful?
3. If teaching and learning are forms of cultural politics, what are the ways in which we unconsciously silence or exclude different student voices in our classrooms, such as the voices of minority and economically disadvantaged students? How do we speak in the name of emancipation without showing scorn for those who are caught in the grip of domination or ignorance, regardless of their class positions? Discuss using examples from Part Two's classroom journal.
4. How does our approach to curriculum help shape student attitudes and perceptions about the nature of the world? Is the world made problematic? Is it open to questioning and analysis? Do you see the social structure as unchanging and inviolable or, as open to new possibilities for emancipatory change? How can we develop an education discourse that integrates the language of power and purpose with the language of intimacy, friendship, and caring?
5. Should teachers attempt to change a student's cultural capital to be more like the teacher's? How can teachers give legitimacy to the cultural capital of disadvantaged or minority students? Should they still provide them with an opportunity to ''act middle class'' for the purposes of strengthening their chances for job placement? Can you relate these issues to your own teaching experiences or experiences as a student?
6. Should teachers be answerable for the larger social consequences of their collective individual acts? Should a consistent failure of teachers to act on the obligations incurred at the social level—i.e., to redress social injustice, racism, and sexism—be legitimate ground for challenging their personal actions in the classroom? What are the moral variants against which we shall construct ourselves as social agents of change?
7. If educational hegemony means the incorporation of students and teachers into relations of consumption and consumerist ethics, what kind of pedagogy can we develop to challenge the ability of the dominant culture to win our consent in these matters?
8. How would you evaluate my role as a beginning teacher? What would you have done differently if you were in my place, and why?

This last question raises the sensitive issue of how well-intentioned teachers willingly or unwillingly create classroom environments that mirror the social division of labor in the workplace. The implicit messages transmitted by teachers about work, authority, and social rules are essential to the functioning of society and the reproduction of the social division of labor and economic privileges enjoyed by dominant social groups. For instance, can you see how teachers in my school exercised forms of symbolic violence (cultural domination) through their imposition of white, Anglo-Saxon perspectives, thereby devaluing the experiences of minority and disadvantaged students? In what ways did my colleagues and I inculcate the cultural capital (i.e., the linguistic and cultural competencies that one inherits by virtue of the social class into which one is born) of the dominant class and thereby (unconsciously or otherwise) disconfirm and delegitimate the voices of students who did not happen to share our cultural capital? All of this raises yet another issue: that is, in what ways does the moral leadership of teachers and administrators help the dominant class secure hegemony over subordinate groups?

Some readers may be offended at the suggestion that teachers frequently function as unwitting pawns in class and cultural domination. Schools, of course, are much more than instruments of the dominant culture in its ideological struggle, its "war of positions," so to speak, against the proletariat. I certainly do not view my role as an elementary school teacher as entirely oppressive. In fact, I believe much good came out of my classroom teaching.

Just as teachers are not total oppressors, it is equally true that students don't sit passively and absorb the culture of the classroom without some resistance. We need to relate such resistance to the symbolic domination characteristic of dominant pedagogical practices and to see student resistance not as a measure of wanton destructiveness (although some resistance is undeniably of this nature) or learned helplessness but as a form of moral and political indignation. Many students resist what the school has to offer, including the subtextual contours of instruction—what we have termed the "hidden curriculum"—in order to survive with a measure of dignity the vagaries of class and cultural servitude. In what ways, then, do schools serve as contradictory sites which both empower students and oppress them? Is this contradiction inevitable, or is it a process that needs to be seriously examined?

There are many more issues to be raised. I have provided the above questions simply as a starting point to help you unravel some of the implications that the critical perspective has to offer for rethinking schooling in the light of transforming society. To raise more questions here would be to undercut the purpose of this book. It remains for *you* to raise other issues, for it is with you that the real struggle for human freedom begins.

NOTES TO PART THREE

1. Peter McLaren, *Schooling as a Ritual Performance: Towards a Political Economy of Educational Symbols and Gestures* (London and New York: Routledge and Kegan Paul, 1986).

2. Stanley Aronowitz and Henry A. Giroux, *Education Under Siege: The Conservative, Liberal, and Radical Debate Over Schooling* (South Hadley, MA: Bergin and Garvey Publishers, Inc., 1985), 69–114. See for a review and critical analysis of this literature.
3. Roger Simon, "Empowerment as a Pedagogy of Possibility," *Language Arts* 64, 4 (1987, April): 370.
4. William J. Bennett, *What Works: Research about Teaching and Learning.* (Washington, DC: The United States Department of Education, 1986). Also, Henry Giroux and Peter McLaren, "Teacher Education and the Politics of Democratic Life: Beyond the Reagan Agenda in the Era of 'Good Times'," in C. C. Yeakey and G. S. Johnston (Eds.), *Schools as Conduits: Educational Policymaking during the Reagan Years* (New York: Praeger Press, in press).
5. James Clifford, "On Ethnographic Surrealism," *Comparative Studies in Society and History* 23, 4 (1981): 539–564.
6. Colin Lankshear and Peter McLaren (Eds.), *Critical Literacy* (Albany, NY: SUNY Press, 1993).
7. Patti Lather, *Getting Smart: Feminist Research and Pedagogy with/in the Postmodern* (New York and London: Routledge, 1991).
8. The sources for this section are as follows: Bertell Ollman, "The Meaning of Dialectics," *Monthly Review* (1986, November): 42–55; Wilfrid Carr and Stephen Kemmis, *Becoming Critical: Knowing Through Action Research* (Victoria: Deakin University, 1983); Stephen Kemmis and Lindsay Fitzclarence, *Curriculum Theorizing: Beyond Reproduction Theory* (Victoria: Deakin Univeristy, 1986); Henry A. Giroux, *Ideology, Culture, and the Process of Schooling* (Philadelphia: Temple University Press and London: Falmer Press, Ltd., 1981); Ernst Bloch, "The Dialectical Method," *Man and World* 16 (1983): 281–313.
9. Carr and Kemmis, *Becoming Critical,* 36–37.
10. McLaren, *Schooling as a Ritual Performance.*
11. This discussion of micro and macro objectives is taken from Henry A. Giroux, "Overcoming Behavioral and Humanistic Objectives," *The Education Forum* (1979, May): 409–419. Also, Henry A. Giroux, *Teachers as Intellectuals: Towards a Critical Pedagogy of Practical Learning* (South Hadley, MA: Bergin and Garvey, 1988).
12. See Jurgen Habermas, *Knowledge and Human Interests,* trans. J. J. Shapiro (London: Heinemann, 1972); see also Jurgen Habermas, *Theory and Practice,* trans. J. Viertel, (London: Heinemann, 1974). As cited in Kemmis and Fitzclarence, *Curriculum Theorizing,* 70–72.
13. For a fuller discussion of culture, see Enid Lee, *Letters to Marcia: A Teacher's Guide to Anti-Racist Teaching.* (Toronto: Cross Cultural Communication Centre, 1985).
14. Henry A. Giroux and Peter McLaren, "Teacher Education and the Politics of Engagement: The Case for Democratic Schooling," *Harvard Educational Review* 56 (1986): 3, 232–233. Developed from Giroux's previous work.
15. For this discussion of culture, I am indebted to Raymond A. Calluori, "The Kids are Alright: New Wave Subcultural Theory," *Social Text* 4, 3 (1985): 43–53; Mike Brake, *The Sociology of Youth Culture and Youth Subculture* (London: Routledge and Kegan Paul, 1980); Graham Murdock, "Mass Communication and the Construction of Meaning," in N. Armstead (Ed.), *Reconstructing Social Psychology* (Harmondsworth: Penguin, 1974); Dick Hebidge, *Subculture: The Meaning of Style* (London and New York: Methuen, 1979); Ian Connell, D. J. Ashenden, S. Kessler, and G. W. Dowsett, *Making the Difference: Schooling, Families, and Social Division* (Sydney, Australia: George Allen and Unwin, 1982). Also, Stuart Hall and Tony Jefferson, *Resistance Through Rituals: Youth Subcultures in Post-War Britain* (London: Hutchinson and the Centre for Contemporary Cultural Studies, University of Birmingham, 1980).

16. John Muncie, "Pop Culture, Pop Music, and Post-War Youth Subcultures," *Popular Culture,* Block 5, Units 18 and 19/20, The Open University Press (1981): 31–62.

17. Muncie, "Pop Culture," 76.

18. The section on hegemony draws on the following sources: Giroux, *Ideology, Culture, and the Process of Schooling,* 22–26; *Popular Culture* (1981), a second level course at The Open University, Milton Keynes, England, published by The Open University Press and distributed in the United States by Taylor and Francis (Philadelphia, PA). Several booklets in this series were instrumental in developing the sections on ideology and hegemony: Geoffrey Bourne, "Meaning, Image, and Ideology," *Form and Meaning 1,* The Open University Press, Block 4, Units 13 and 15, 37–65; see also Tony Bennett, "Popular Culture: Defining Our Terms," *Popular Culture: Themes and Issues I,* Block 1, Units 1 and 2, 77–87; Tony Bennett, "Popular Culture: History and Theory," *Popular Culture: Themes and Issues II,* Block 1, Unit 3, 29–32. Another important source is a booklet for a third level course at The Open University: *The Politics of Cultural Production,* The Open University Press, 1981. Relevant sections include: Geoff Whitty, "Ideology, Politics, and Curriculum," 7–52; David Davies, "Popular Culture, Class, and Schooling," 53–108. See also P. J. Hills, *A Dictionary of Education* (London: Routledge and Kegan Paul, 1982), 166–167; and Raymond Williams, *Keywords: A Vocabulary of Culture and Society* (London: Fontana, 1983), 144–146.

19. William Ryan, *Blaming the Victim* (New York: Vintage Books, 1976).

20. Todd Gitlin, *The Whole World Is Watching: Mass Media in the Making and Unmaking of the New Left* (Berkeley and London: University of California Press, 1980), 253–254.

21. Gore Vidal, *Monthly Review* 19 (1986, October), as cited in Allen Fenichel "Alternative Economic Policies," *The Ecumenist* 25, 4 (1987, May–June): 49.

22. For this section on ideology, I am indebted to Henry A. Giroux, *Theory and Resistance in Education: Pedagogy for the Opposition* (South Hadley, MA: Bergin and Garvey, 1983), 143. See also Stanley Aronowitz and Henry A. Giroux, *Education Under Siege* (South Hadley, MA: Bergin and Garvey, 1985); Douglas Kellner, "Ideology, Marxism, and Advanced Capitalism," *Socialist Review* 8, 6 (1978): 38; Gibson Winter, *Liberating Creation: Foundations of Religious Social Ethics* (New York: Crossroad, 1981), 97. See also: Geoff Whitty, "Ideology, Politics, and Curriculum," 7–52, and David Davies, "Popular Culture, Class, and Schooling," 53–108; Williams, *Keywords,* 153–157; Tony Bennett, "Popular Culture: Defining Our Terms," 77–87; and Geoffrey Bourne, "Meaning, Image, and Ideology," 37–53.

23. James Donald and Stuart Hall, "Introduction," in S. Donald and S. Hall (Eds.), *Politics and Ideology* (Milton Keynes: Philadelphia, The Open University Press, 1986), ix–x.

24. Donald and Hall, *Politics and Ideology,* x.

25. John Thompson, "Language and Ideology," *The Sociological Review* 35, 3 (1987, August): 516–536.

26. John Dewey, in J. Ratner (Ed.), *Intelligence in the Modern World: John Dewey's Philosophy* (New York: The Modern Library, 1939), 784. See also Michel Foucault, *Power/Knowledge,* in C. Gordon (Ed.) (L. Marshall, J. Mepham, and K. Spoer, Trans.), *Selected Interviews and Other Writings 1972–77* (New York: Pantheon, 1980), 187.

27. Michel Foucault, *The Archaeology of Knowledge* (New York: Harper Colophon Books, 1972), 117.

28. Foucault, *Power/Knowledge,* 200.

29. Richard Smith and Anna Zantiotis, "Teacher Education, Cultural Politics, and the Avant-Garde," in H. Giroux and P. McLaren (Eds.), *Critical Pedagogy, the State, and Cultural Struggle* (Albany, NY: SUNY Press, 1989), 123.

30. See Chris Weedon, *Feminist Practice and Post-Structuralist Theory* (Oxford: Basil-Blackwell, 1987).

31. Cleo Cherryholmes, *Power and Criticism: Post-Structural Investigations in Education* (New York: Teachers College Press, 1988).

32. Foucault, *Power/Knowledge,* 131.

33. Lawrence Grossberg, "History, Politics, and Postmodernism: Stuart Hall and Cultural Studies," *Journal of Communication Inquiry* 10, 2 (1987): 73.

34. For more about the relationship of power and knowledge, see Kathy Borman and Joel Spring, *Schools in Central Cities* (New York: Longman, 1984); Henry Giroux, "Public Education and the Discourse of Possibility: Rethinking the New Conservative and Left Educational Theory," *News for Teachers of Political Science* 44 (1985, Winter): 13–15. The term *particular from of life* belongs to Henry Giroux.

35. See Doug White, "After the Divided Curriculum," *The Victorian Teacher* 7 (1983, March); Giroux and McLaren, "Teacher Education and the Politics of Engagement," 228.

36. See the wide range of articles in H. Giroux and D. Purple (Eds.), *The Hidden Curriculum and Moral Education: Deception or Discovery?* (Berkeley, CA: McCutchen Publishing Corp., 1983).

37. Myra Sadkev and David Sadkev, "Sexism in the Schoolroom of the 80's," *Psychology Today* (1985, March): 55–57.

38. Sadkev and Sadkev, "Sexism in the Schoolroom," 56–57. Also, the 1980 *Nova* television program, *The Pinks and the Blues* (WGBH, Boston), summarized by Anthony Wilden. "In the Penal Colony: The Body as the Discourse of the Other," *Semiotica,* 54, 1/2 (1985): 73–76.

39. White, "After the Divided Curriculum," 6–9.

40. Giroux and McLaren, "Teacher Education and the Politics of Engagement," 228–229.

41. Stanley Aronowitz, "Schooling, Popular Culture, and Post-Industrial Society: Peter McLaren Interviews Stanley Aronowitz," *Orbit* (1986): 17, 18.

42. See Kemmis and Fitzclarence, *Curriculum Theorizing,* 88–89. Also, H. A. Giroux, *Ideology, Culture, and the Process of Schooling.*

43. Glenna Colclough and E. M. Beck, "The American Educational Structure and the Reproduction of Social Class," *Social Inquiry* 56, 4 (1986, Fall): 456–476.

44. Samuel Bowles and Herbert Gintis, *Schooling in Capitalist America* (New York: Basic Books, 1976); see also Kemmis and Fitzclarence, *Curriculum Theorizing,* 90; and Colclough and Beck, "The American Educational Structure," 456–476.

45. See, for instance, Peter McLaren, "The Ritual Dimensions of Resistance: Clowning and Symbolic Inversion," *Boston University Journal of Education* 167, 2 (1985): 84–97, and Giroux, *Theory and Resistance.*

46. Paul Willis, *Learning to Labour: How Working Class Kids Get Working Class Jobs* (Westmead, England: Gower, 1977).

47. Giroux, *Theory and Resistance,* 103.

48. Aronowitz and Giroux, *Education under Siege.*

49. Jacques Lacan, "Seminar XX," *Encore* (Paris: Editions du Seuil, 1975): 100. As cited in Constance Penley, "Teaching in Your Sleep: Feminism and Psychoanalysis," in C. Nelson (Ed.), *Theory in the Classroom* (Chicago: University of Illinois Press, 1986), 135.

50. Pierre Bourdieu, "Forms of Capital," in John G. Richardson (Ed.), *Handbook of Theory and Research for the Sociology of Education* (New York: Greenwood Press, 1986), 241–258. See also Henry A. Giroux, "Rethinking the Language of Schooling," *Language Arts* 61, 1 (1984, January): 36, and Henry A. Giroux, *Ideology, Culture, and the Process of Schooling,* 77.

51. Paul Atkinson, *Language, Structure, and Reproduction: An Introduction to the Sociology of Basil Bernstein* (London: Methuen, 1986).

PART **IV**

Analysis

I want now to explore in more detail the process of schooling. You are familiar now with the social problems that beset both schools and society (Part One), have some sense of the day-to-day challenges and demands of inner-city teaching (Part Two), and have been introduced to some basic theoretical concepts with which to analyze the process of schooling (Part Three). Again, I ask you to draw upon your own experiences and the journal transcription in Part Two to understand this new material. Some of you may have begun to formulate an analysis of schooling in the inner city. Here, then, are some further critical perspectives on why disadvantaged students often don't "make it" in school. A number of the concepts presented in this part draw both from the more recent work of Henry Giroux and from a number of projects we have undertaken over the last few years with respect to critical teaching and school practices.

CHAPTER 6

Race, Class, and Gender: Why Students Fail

THE BLACK UNDERCLASS: RACIAL STRATIFICATION AND THE POLITICS OF CULTURE

The development of an underclass in American society can be linked not only to economic stratification but also to racial stratification. Economically disadvantaged whites and many ethnic minority groups undeniably make up such an underclass, but I limit myself here to a discussion of subordinated and marginalized blacks. A number of theorists within the critical tradition argue that it is virtually impossible to understand the classroom behavior and performance of economically disadvantaged and minority students without understanding their history as oppressed groups, their cultural frames of reference, and their everyday social practices. Despite his tendencies toward functionalism, John Ogbu argues convincingly that dominant and subordinate groups occupy caste-like strata in our society. Ogbu maintains that the subordinate positioning of black students in the larger society constitutes a *folk system* that embodies

> the attitudes, knowledge, and competencies transmitted to and acquired by black children as they grow up and form a part of what the children bring to school pertaining to schools, schooling, and white people who control the schools.[1]

Ogbu maintains that in the face of past and present job ceilings and technocratic barriers, blacks have evolved folk theories of "making it" which do not necessarily emphasize strong academic pursuit. Personal survival strategies undertaken by black students foster a particular *cultural capital* that is seldom congruent with mainstream or dominant practices associated with success. The disillusionment among black youth about "making it" through education results, in part, from observing both their parents' situation and that of other adults in their communities. It is not hard to imagine the deep distrust between blacks and public schools and blacks and white authorities, which Ogbu claims is communicated to children from a very early age by parents, relatives, and neighbors.

As a result of their subordinate position, blacks have formed an identity system that is perceived and experienced not merely as different from but *in opposition* to the social identity of their white dominators. Of course this is true to some degree for all members of the underclass, and not just blacks. Ogbu claims that within the black community itself, there are informal and formal sanctions against blacks who step into what their peers and the black community in general regard as the "white cultural frame of reference." School learning in white-controlled institutions often is equated with abandoning the imperatives, values, and collective solidarity of black culture.

> Specifically, blacks and similar minorities (e.g., American Indians) believe that in order for a minority person to succeed in school academically, he or she must learn to think and act white. Furthermore, in order to think and act white enough to be rewarded by whites or white institutions like the schools, a minority person must give up his or her own minority-group attitudes, ways of thinking, and behaving, and, of course, must give up or lose his or her own minority identity. That is, striving for academic success is a subtractive process: the individual black student following school standard practices that lead to academic success is perceived as adopting a white cultural frame of reference . . . as "acting white" with the inevitable outcome of losing his or her black identity, abandoning black people and black causes, and joining the enemy, namely, white people.[2]

Ogbu draws attention to no less than seventeen behavioral categories that constitute for black students what it means to "act white." These include speaking standard English, working hard in school to get good grades, being on time, and so on. *Resistance* among black students cannot, therefore, be attributed solely to their subordinate socioeconomic status; it also stems from *racial stratification,* which cuts directly across class boundaries. Ogbu points out that problems of school "dropouts" and "suicide" plague not only high school students but also college students and blacks who have "made it" in traditionally white positions within the corporate economy. Certainly Ogbu's analysis can be applied to many of the black students I worked with in my inner-city classroom.

Despite my own attempts at establishing a strong relationship with the students, I nevertheless remained at some level one of "them"—the "other." As a white, middle-class teacher, I was always confronting my own position in the dominant culture which, in relation to my minority and disadvantaged students, constituted a fundamental part of the problem. To what extent did I, due to my inability to name racism and link it to its originating source in the social structure, become for them a symbol of the age-old history of domination and legacy of exploitation that had planted seeds of bitter resentment in generations of black families? To what extent did I unconsciously collude with formations—both discursive and institutional—that reproduced white, patriarchal, Anglo supremacy?

What about other minorities and disenfranchised white students? I would argue that each group needs to be understood separately, within its own cultural, class, race, and gendered frames of reference. A study I did on Azorean students who had immigrated to Toronto and were attending an inner-city high school there explored the contradictory notion that many of these students held toward doing schoolwork. Portuguese parents frequently encouraged their children to drop out of school at sixteen to help out their families economically, often in the family business. Consequently, doing homework and being successful in school constituted for many of them an attempt to escape the social conditions of the family and an insult to those relatives who accepted the conditions. As members of the working class, Portuguese parents had come to realize that a diploma from high school would not necessarily give their children a chance for more than a blue-collar job. Though many Portuguese parents held high aspirations for their children to succeed and pushed them to do well in school, their own struggles as semiskilled laborers and unemployed workers served as a tacit message to their children not to depend on school as a way out of their poverty.[3] Success in school for working-class students usually means making it through the vocational level tracks, and this success does not necessarily guarantee that they will secure a good job, or that adult life will be any less harsh or conflictual.

RESISTANCE AND THE REPRODUCTION OF CLASS RELATIONS

We were introduced to the topic of resistance in Part Three under the category of "social reproduction." Let's take a closer look now at Paul Willis's work and the concept of resistance.

Paul Willis's *Learning to Labor,* a classic analysis of a group of twelve non-academic working-class English boys through their last two years of school and their first six months of work, considerably alters the view held by many orthodox Marxist educators that schools function mechanically to reproduce social class divisions in the larger society.[4] Willis's study explains why many working-class students reject the possibility of high-status careers, apparently committing themselves willfully to a life of boring, drudging, generalized labor jobs. According to Willis, the "lived sense of difference" of these students in their everyday class-based culture expresses a *realistic* understanding of their future options in the labor force, an understanding acquired from their families, peers, and the values encoded into working-class life in general.

Moreover, the lads see the career counseling offered by the school as a hostile act of class imposition. Through such an imposition, the school creates an oppositional culture, and the lads actually appropriate working-class values for the purpose of actively *resisting* the bourgeois values of the school. In their resistance and in their often brash yet innovative flouting of conventional classroom maxims, the lads consider the "mental labor" of schoolwork an essentially "weak" and passive ploy to control their free time. Manual work, on the other hand, is masculine, independent, and active. Yet by rejecting mental labor so vehemently—especially at a time when their life chances are at stake—the lads freely implicate themselves in their own domination by foreclosing alternative career options. They unwittingly secure their own subservient positions in the division of labor. Resistance, then, is a process in which the working-class student further solidifies his or her position in the lowest tier of the class system, helping to confirm the view established by critical theorists that a nation's educational system is subservient to its economic system.[5]

In general terms, resistance is part of the process of hegemony, which works through the ideology-shaping characteristics of the school. Schools help structure the ideological field in which students participate by establishing and certifying the limits placed on competing definitions of reality. In light of Willis's observations, we can now see that *social reproduction* occurs with both the willing compliance and the active refusal of its own victims—a striking example of how *hegemony* is maintained by the dominant class at the *cultural level* through the very resistance of students to the oppressive logic and practices of schooling.

In summary, Willis's study illustrates how schools serve as more than simple sorting stations that unproblematically reproduce the labor stratification and occupational differentiation that exists in the wider society. Students are not merely passive victims. They actively contest the hegemony of the dominant culture through *resistance.* They act in opposition to the process of social reproduction but, as a result of these very acts of opposition, they sadly foreclose the few options available to them to break out of their lived class subordination. In other words, they fail to take advantage of the school's potential to give them at least a slight edge in the job market over their peers who choose to drop out.

I would argue that Buddy, T. J., Duke, and the others in my own experience are actively participating in securing their domination by resisting what school has to offer them. But we cannot unqualifiedly condemn such resistance in view of the students' subordinate social position. Their "failure" in school cannot be interpreted as resulting simply from individual deficiencies; it must be understood as part of a play of differences between radically disparate *cultural fields.* For example, the students were actively contesting the unconscious efforts of teachers—including me—who valued their own middle-class *cultural capital* over that of the students. The teaching encounter in this instance served to disconfirm, delegitimate, and at times erase the cultural meanings and social relations valued by the students. My students were experiencing the material constraints of economic and racial stratification and were living the painful contradictions between *street-corner culture* and *student culture.* Knowledge acquired by T. J., Buddy, Duke, and others in their street-corner world was qualitatively different from knowledge acquired in the school. In the streets, knowledge was "felt," whereas classroom knowledge was objectified and often sullied by an inflated rationalism, including a stress on deductive reasoning. In the street, students made more use of bodily engagement, organic symbols, and intuition. Students struggled daily to reconcile the disjunction between the lived meaning of the streets and the subject-centered approach to learning in the classroom. School placed an inordinate emphasis on knowledge *about* (a stress on precision, procedure, and logic); on the street, emphasis was on knowledge *of* (the stress on description, ambiguity, and equivocation). Robert Everhart has commented that during classroom resistance students acquire a *regenerative knowledge* by which they are able to assert at least some creative control over the process of knowledge production.[6] It is a knowledge formed out of *interpretive* (open to question) rather than *assumed* (taken for granted) experiences and within a shared sense of community. This may be contrasted with the *reified* (presenting concepts and facts as concrete *things*) knowledge of the classroom which is often treated by teachers as unproblematic and which places students in the role of passive recipients.

For many economically disadvantaged students, success in school means a type of forced cultural suicide, and in the case of minority youth, racial suicide. During her study of a group of South Bronx students, Michelle Fine discovered that those who remained in school, when compared to dropouts, *were significantly more depressed, less politically aware, less likely to be more assertive in the classroom if they were undergraded, and more conformist.* According to Fine, "A moderate level of depression, an absence of political awareness, the presence of self blame, low assertiveness, and high conformity may tragically have constituted evidence of the 'good' urban student."[7]

At what price do we ask our students to conform to our version of "the good student"? For some, the price we exact is obviously too much to bear. That's when dropping out becomes not so much an option as an urgent and necessary act of survival. On the other hand, we have to recognize that students rarely "drop out" by reflective choice. More realistically, they are "pushed" out. In other words, they are placed in a double-bind situation. If they remain in school and desire to be successful, they are forced to forfeit their own cultural capital, street-corner knowledge, and dignity. They are made to compete at a decided disadvantage. Without a critical pedagogy, they lack the analytical skills both to analyze their location within the social order and to alter the conditions of their oppression. Yet if they leave school, they face a future in which they can carve out some self-esteem in the streets, but come up against a social order decidedly antagonistic to their aspirations for material success. Mainstream schooling offers disadvantaged students little choice but to negotiate a life for themselves somewhere among the psychologist's office, the compensatory program set up to remediate their deficiencies, and the streets where they will eventually be dumped. If the economic climate is good, perhaps they will end up in low-skilled, low-paying jobs.

BEIN' TOUGH: BEIN' FEMALE

The disadvantaged female population represents one of the largest segments of any stratified society.[8] It remains the unfortunate case, however, that educational researchers have generally been shortsighted about female culture, as if only males inhabit subordinate groups. The female in contemporary school culture is often overlooked—fenced off from the mainstream of sociological writing on youth—which may be explained in part by the predominance of males in the field of classroom study. However, promising work has recently emerged on disaffected female youth.

The diary entries presented in Part Two tend to overturn the stereotypes of the thrifty, industrious, docile, and well-mannered schoolgirl. For the purposes of analysis, however, we must situate the behavior of these girls within the context of class, race, and gender and the way in which these distinctions are treated in the public school. The female underclass does not exist in a social vacuum; it is not independent of the multiplicity of relations that constitute the larger society. Disadvantaged females not only constitute an economically subordinate group; they are also oppressed by the very fact that they are females.

The West Indian female students in my class had a particularly difficult time. Not only did they suffer the sting of racism on a day-to-day basis, they often had to adjust to stepparents and a separation from supportive kin that had existed in their homeland. Common-law marriages were frequent, and grew out of a history of poverty in their homelands (which necessitated the father working away from home) and the social relations of slavery (which prized maternity). Great stress at home was placed on domestic labor. Parents usually had high aspirations for their children, and many joined grass roots organizations that offered support in the struggle against racism and exploitation.

The rituals and slang of Muscle Lady, Ruth, Jabeka, and others are largely symbolic responses to basic societal constraints and structural inequalities; they are reactions on the part of an oppressed group. The social lives of these girls have been developed as a distinctive subcultural style—a "lived sense of difference" from their middle-class teachers and peers, as "us" against "them."

Schooling transmits and reinforces those ideologies that reflect the prevailing values and ethos of a male-dominated, hierarchical, middle-class social structure. Conflict broke out in my classroom when the girls deliberately resisted the role expectations and concomitant patriarchal codes that the schools tried to impose on them. Much of their abrasive behavior was a direct rejection of middle-class propriety. Although a number of teachers in my school attempted to provide more flexible classroom procedures, most of the girls remained in passionate opposition to the intentions of the school as a vehicle for upward mobility—for eventually attaining monetary benefits and improved social status through the Protestant ethic of hard work and good deportment. Sympathetic teachers could not dissolve their ingrained hostility to institutionalized forms of domination and authority. *To Sir with Love* is, after all, a Hollywood fantasy. According to many of the girls, school failed to make a difference in the lives of their parents. Who could say that the educational system would be any kinder to them? The girls fatalistically accepted their position in society as members of a subordinate class and gender grouping.

Many incidents of violence, sexism, and racism in the classroom are in reality reactions to economic and cultural dislocation and to what is perceived as the oppressive experience of schooling. As Paul Willis points out in *Learning to Labor,* the resistance of British working-class boys to the dominant ideology of the school ultimately supports the modes of oppression it attacks. Physical labor and masculinity are celebrated; mental labor is defined and rejected as effeminate and therefore socially inferior. Such adulation of masculinity is fueled by a deep-rooted sexism. Subordinate roles are adopted more easily when they are enhanced by the appeal of regressive machismo. Patriarchy serves less as a relic of the social past, as some historians maintain, than as an Archimedian fulcrum for capitalism.[9]

The girls in my class were primarily concerned with popularity and physical attractiveness—areas of interest that far superseded academic aspirations. Girls were constantly experimenting with makeup and improvising clothing styles. Subcultural dress codes (tight-fitting denims, taut tee shirts covered with sexual slogans, bright red nail polish, Afros, dreadlocks, Kodiak boots) established by the disaffected denizens were not only symbolic challenges to the conservative sartorial codes of teachers and more affluent peers, but a way of fostering group identity and solidarity.

One way in which girls combat class-bound and oppressive features of school is to assert their "femaleness," to replace the officially sanctioned code of neatness, diligence, application, femininity, passivity, and so on, with one that is more womanly, even sexual, in nature.[10] It is significant that dress and makeup for the girls in my classrooms constituted a direct rebellion against the authorized ideological codes of the school. It was fundamentally a reaction against the policing of the body and the moral regulation experienced in school; the girls' dress constituted a struggle for social power within a male-dominated culture and an oppressive economic system. The manifestly masculine, but tight-fitting "sexy" look was a refusal by the girls to be positioned as feminine subjects, as agents of patriarchal hegemony. The girls were rejecting the patriarchy inscribed in stereotypical feminine clothes: the neat blouses, the print skirts, the "wholesome girl" look. The girls then became "resisting subjects," exerting control in the cultural process of constructing meaning and social identity. They were transgressing the codes governing "good girlishness." Such acts of sartorial resistance inverted consensually validated norms of appearance, symbolically violating the magazine-stand iconographies of women's publications—especially the back-to-school issues of *Seventeen*.

Just as male resistance in the schools often serves to more firmly cement the boys in their low-caste status, female resistance often means rejecting the culture of the classroom only to be positioned in a culture in which girls are viewed as sex objects. The Corridor girls started to "go" with boys as early as age twelve. If in the process of "making out" they responded to the boys' advances too readily or indiscriminately, however, they were labeled as "sluts." Such names, employed viciously and randomly, were also bestowed on girls who were physically unappealing. Girls often found themselves in the double bind of losing their group status if they engaged in "too much" sexual activity, or of being rejected as "cold" if they engaged in too little. The boys' status, however, was fundamentally enhanced by similar incidents of increased sexual engagement. This double standard has existed historically, of course, and feminists have consistently and rightly attacked it.

The girls in the Corridor often rejected marriage as a desirable option for the future. At the same time, however, some felt that marriage would be preferable to working in a meaningless job. Marriage at least provided the status of "wife"—undoubtedly worth more than having no status at all. For many, however, marriage appeared as a trap from which they saw few avenues of escape.

I witnessed numerous daily incidents in which girls clashed physically and violently with boys or with other girls. In fact, some of the girls were among the school's most menacing and gifted pugilists.

It was important for the girls to assert very early their capacity to defend themselves physically. For girls, as well as for boys, "bein' tough" was a way to win respect and a coterie of followers.

Many of the girls had home lives that were turbulent and difficult. A large percentage lived in single-parent families with a number of brothers and sisters. Some parents were frequently out of work or on the dole. Even if they were fortunate enough to be working, many held menial, dead-end jobs in which their pride was constantly perforated. Girls with younger siblings took on parental roles very early, especially when mothers or fathers were working. Consequently, a number of girls would routinely miss part of the school day in order to look after brothers and sisters. Others were latchkey children who went home after school to an empty apartment. Parents who held menial jobs could rarely afford a babysitter, and day-care facilities were either inadequate or nonexistent. For both boys and girls, the most stinging insult was to be stamped as "welfare," a symbolic defilement.

Family violence frequently erupted as a result of the pressures of daily life. The theme of violence in the home often came up in discussions with girls and their parents. You may recall in Part Two an interview with the mother of one of my students:

> "Doesn't it bother you that your husband beats you, though? Wouldn't it help to work on that end of things?" I asked gently.
> "Of course he beats me!" she snapped. "Wouldn't you be upset if you couldn't find work and had to sit at home all day doing nothing?"

Although the girls found life full of antagonistic relationships and domestic dilemmas, home represented, at the very least, a place where commonsense knowledge and practice were appreciated and where a lack of mastery over middle-class discourse and rhetoric did not make the girls feel "deficient" or "deprived." My work with female students in inner-city classrooms confirmed many of the findings of critical educational theorists who describe the latent function or "hidden curriculum" of schooling as an attempt to reproduce the values, attitudes, and behaviors necessary to maintain our society's present class-based division of labor and male-dominated gender relations.

Although many of the Jane-Finch girls suffered the indignities of poverty, racism, sexism, physical abuse, and, in some cases, the culture shock of recent immigration, they managed to create and maintain a distinct subcultural resistance to the consensually validated norms of the school—norms which attempted to make girls into passive, pliable, docile, tidy, neat, and diligent workers. In order to resist this conventional version of femininity, designed to nurture their "domestic instincts,'' the girls developed attributes that were drawn from working-class culture in general: toughness, aggressive sexuality, distrust of authority, rebellious-ness. The girls then resisted the contradictory myth that schools function as agencies of equality, that educational institutions possess the power to help disadvantaged students bridge the chasm of opportunity that separates them from their more affluent peers.

Because the school system is structured tacitly to reinforce and reward middle-class values, attitudes, and behavior (and thereby penalize the "deprived" by omission), educators and the public alike often assume that the failure of the schools to educate disadvantaged girls is really the failure of the girls themselves. The girls fail because they are perceived to be mindless, shiftless, worthless, pathological, burdened by dubious hereditary traits, or the products of deviant home backgrounds. We blame the victim rather than looking for ways in which the class and educational systems militate against the success of those who are economically powerless and who are disadvantaged by gender and race.

So pervading and intransigent is this myth of equal educational opportunity that many working-class girls come to believe that their school failure is their own fault, that they must be "stupid or something." In their day-to-day behavior, the Jane-Finch girls resisted what they unconsciously felt to be an oppressive situation; yet paradoxically, because school did not provide the rhetoric with which to articulate the experience of this oppression, they blamed themselves.

The liberal ideology that promises success to anyone who is prepared to work and sacrifice prevented the girls from understanding how they were being fed into a preordained future by the patriarchal, economic, and cultural forces of consumer capitalism. Paralyzed by the belief that they lacked the intelligence of the more affluent girls, many of the working-class girls gave up. (Naturally, there were some exceptions. But since bookish intelligence was equated with middle-class status, most girls soon abandoned any attempts to please teachers or achieve academic excellence. Instead their attention was soon diverted to the enhancement of their subcultural status.) For the most part, their class/cultural identity became defined for them by dirt-stained high-rises, unemployment, sexism, the strip-plaza splendor, and the general failure of educators and poli-ticians to redress their plight. This led to strong emotional bonding, as networks of "girlfriends" were created collectively to resist the world of the dominant class. Many of the girls had a sense that the cards were stacked against them from the very beginning. After all, did not the legacy left by our ancestors emphasize the superiority of one class of people over another? And one sex over another? And what more natural reaction to this predicament than to jettison the official ideology of the school through rituals of resistance?

When we embrace the derisory ideology that conceives of disadvantaged girls as undersocialized, as "unfinished products" on the conveyor belt of social success, we place a veneer on the basic class structure and gender bias of society and obscure the ways in which the structure of the system determines to a great extent which class and gender will be successful and which will fail. In this way, the educational system ensures the hereditary transmission of the status

sexism

by appearing neutral, by concealing its social function of reproducing class relations by constructing technologies of gender, by perpetuating the myth of equality of opportunity based on scholastic merit.

Until the educational system from kindergarten to high school reevaluates the working-class culture of femininity, schools will continue to underwrite the restricted and inferior role of women and function as sorting and processing stations through which girls are prepared for a lifetime of routine labor or dependency on men: the spirit-breaking and mind-deadening norms of the factory floor or the oppressive limbo of domestic labor, either paid or for husbands for whom they also function as baby machines. Until schools are recognized as sites of class and gender conflict, they will remain boot camps for bureaucracy; they will continue to emphasize the need for passive rule compliance, cooperation, and meager skill development in order to prepare disadvantaged students to accept unquestioningly the sexist and exploitative aspects of the world of domestic and manual labor. Educators must begin to question the class and value assumptions informing our dominant forms of pedagogy and the gender discrimination inherent in present-day schooling and social life.

In reading through my elementary school diary, it is painfully evident that at that time I was not able to confront my own sexism or sufficiently contest my own inscription in the discourses and practices of white supremacist patriarchy. Critical educators need to confront their own limitations in order to surpass them and eventually transform their pedagogies into a praxis of liberation.

PSYCHOLOGIZING STUDENT FAILURE

If we understand that the active refusal of blacks, other minorities, and working-class whites, male and female, to adopt or appropriate the *cultural capital* of the dominant culture (often translated by teachers as doing homework, being punctual, speaking politely, working quietly, not distracting your neighbor, showing deference to authority, etc.) is in fact a class-, culture-, or race-specific form of resistance, then we can understand that school failure is more than just *individual deficiencies* on the part of students.

The *deficit model of student failure* rests on the propensity of teachers to "psychologize" that failure. "Psychologizing" student failure amounts to blaming it on an individual trait or series of traits (e.g., lack of motivation or low self-concept). This is what William Ryan refers to in his famous phrase "blaming the victim."[11] This attitude is particularly frightening because teachers often are unaware of their complicity in its debilitating effects. Psychologizing school failure is a part of the hidden curriculum that relieves teachers from the need to engage in pedagogical self-scrutiny or in any serious critique of their personal roles within the school, and the school's role within the wider society. In effect, psychologizing school failure indicts the student while simultaneously protecting the social environment from sustained criticism.

Teachers must be aware of how *school failure is structurally located and culturally mediated,* so they can work both inside and outside of schools in the struggle for social and economic justice. Teachers must engage unyieldingly in their attempt to empower students both as individuals and as potential agents of social change by establishing a critical pedagogy that students can use in the classroom and in the streets.

When middle-class students and working-class students are matched for intelligence and ability, the differences in academic achievement are the result of what Boudon calls *secondary effects.*[12] These secondary effects are related to the differences in students' cultural capital and the social practices lived out within various cultural fields of experience. Working-class students operate within differ- ent "decision-fields" (i.e., family, workplace, peer culture) that involve specific class, gender, and race relations.[13]

Understanding school failure as the secondary effect of cultural capital and class- and gender-specific social practices runs directly counter to the prevailing neoconservative social logic, which attributes school failure to individual deficien- cies on the part of a lazy, apathetic, and intellectually inferior underclass of students or to uncaring or selfish parents. This kind of logic works as a form of purity rite, a social mechanism that protects the educational system by projecting the myth of minority inferiority onto those who in some way are perceived to threaten or jeopardize the system. Within the dominant class, many believe that in order to accommodate "inferior races" the schools must lower standards, an act which is disastrous for society as a whole. Eventually the myth of the inferiority of minorities and working-class groups becomes part of the social heredity of the dominant culture. Such a perspective, which carries with it the shame of racism, prevails in many mainstream theories of schooling.

Schools, by their nature, are caught in a paradox of being both agents of the state which must promote a hegemony and conformism, while at the same time preserving + nurturing the students' individual identity.

CHAPTER 7

New and Old Myths in Education

TECHNOLOGIZING LEARNING

Many mainstream approaches to curriculum development and implementation currently offered to classroom teachers are politically laundered and culturally sterile programs of learning in which students are taught to think componentially—in fragments isolated from the flow of everyday experience.[14] Students develop a mechanistic cognitive style within classrooms that appears at times to conform to Henry Ford's rust-proofed assembly lines. The file keepers, accountability-mongers, and "knowledge specialists" at both state and local levels have instructed teachers to segment behavior, measure fluid social activity in terms of "inputs" and "outputs," and reduce human beings to computer printouts. They inscribe the terrain of our crisis-ridden classrooms with the logic of domination through an insistence that teachers take the experiences, values, and cultural capital of working-class and minority students *less seriously than they do those of the dominant culture.* This situation often unknowingly helps to perpetuate the reproduction of social and cultural inequality. As teachers, we are encouraged to be good "systems people," to create synthetic environments for our students. We dish out knowledge like fast food; burger specials arrive limp and overcooked from the Insight Kitchens of IBM and Xerox.

Today, technocratic consciousness is looked upon as the new educational mechanism for generating classroom health. Teachers often give technocratic theories the benefit of the doubt and exhibit at times an incredulous penchant for following instructions and deferring to the "experts." Some of the new curriculum technologies have even been "teacher-proofed," which only contributes further to the devaluing and deskilling of teachers by removing them from the decision-making process. As teachers, we need collectively to demythologize the infallibility of educational programmers and so-called experts, who often do nothing more than zealously impose their epistemological assumptions on unassuming teachers under the guise of efficiency and procedural smoothness. What we are left with is an emphasis on *practical* and *technical* forms of knowledge as opposed to *productive* or *transformative* knowledge.

A particularly serious problem with the technocratic mentality is its appearance of objectivity and value-neutrality. What its adherents don't tell you is that a hidden political agenda oftentimes informs new policy and program directives.

Our classrooms need theory, but not the life-obstructing theories that are embedded in a technocratic worldview. We need theories that provoke teachers to question the value assumptions that underlie their technocratic cultural terrain and throw open to scrutiny the classroom practices and social relations that future teachers are forced to acquire during the course of their teacher education.

NEOCONSERVATISM AND THE MYTH OF DEMOCRATIC SCHOOLING

Rarely discussed—or even considered—in proposed solutions to the plight of students in our nation's schools are the many invidious myths that underlie current approaches to urban education. By myths, I refer to the resurgent "truths" of conservative educational thinking that were temporarily buried in the sixties but began stirring their bones again in the educational compost during the seventies and continue to be embraced in the nineties.[15] One of the most dangerous of these is the myth of *equal opportunity,* which maintains that the educational system is the glorious equalizer of our free society. Success can be achieved by intelligence, hard work, and creativity. Like many myths, this one forms part of our everyday perception, even though it has been continually proven untrue.

Believers in this myth suggest that inequality results from our established form of "meritocracy," which provides students who are more capable—who try harder and have more innate intelligence—with their rightful rewards and excludes those who are less able. Some neoconservatives even claim that biology is at the root of class division, and that minority and working-class students are at the greatest disadvantage due to their unfortunately deficient gene pool. In other words, culturally and economically disadvantaged students have *inherited* a lower intellectual aptitude. It is only natural and desirable, then, that our society rewards the brightest and most able students differentially. This "intellectual impediments model" stresses that different racial and class groups are endowed with different intellectual capacities, which regrettably inhibit the success in school of minority and economically disadvantaged students.

Neoconservatives choose to ignore or misinterpret recent research which indicates that one of the greatest determinants of academic success is parental income. Referring to this cruel reality as the "Frankenstein and Einstein" syndrome, Paul Olson, a critical educational theorist, points out that parental background makes a greater difference to school achievement than measured IQ.[16] The myth of equal opportunity therefore masks an ugly truth: the educational system is really a loaded social lottery, in which each student gets as many chances as his or her parents have dollars.

Neoconservatives argue that the desire for parity is in reality a "cult of envy." They equate the liberal vision of equality for all with their perception of Chinese society: zombie-like, conformist, and emotionally malleable. What a dull world equality would bring. But no one argues that individual differences don't exist. The real issue is that *the education system gives those who begin with certain advantages* (the right economic status and thus the right values, the right speech patterns, the right mannerisms, the right behavior) *a better chance to retain those advantages all through school, and ensures that minority and economically disadvantaged students will remain at the bottom rung of the meritocratic ladder.*

Neoconservatives will tell you that not everybody can be president of General Motors. What you can read between the lines translates somewhat differently: Why waste good taxpayers' money on the lesser breeds? They're hardly going to lead this country, except maybe at the head of the welfare rolls. This view completely ignores Noam Chomsky's argument that "success is also correlated with traits much less sanguine than intelligence: manipulativeness, greed, dishonesty, a disregard for others, and so on."[17]

Neoconservatives predict a resurgence of the individual. Horatio Alger, we are told, will be resurrected from the cultural woodwork where he has lurked for decades. In this atmosphere, the perennial failure of the ghetto student can often be blamed on a lack of motivation and will to succeed. Though most mainstream educational pundits fortunately don't ascribe to the myth of genetic inferiority or lack of natural ability, they do continue to rationalize the failure of lower-class, minority, and immigrant students by blaming their home environments.

This is the myth of *cultural deprivation,* which interprets social and educational problems in terms of student failure to "fit" into the social milieu. As a result, economically disadvantaged and minority students are labeled "deviant," "pathological," or "impulse-ridden" when they don't behave in the ways expected by middle-class teachers. Of course, this theory cannot account for why "deficiencies" are consistently grouped along class lines. Schools foster programs to correct these problems, to build up the skills and attitudes of ghetto children, to make up for their so-called cultural deficits and motivate their lazy, apathetic souls— rather than consider structural changes in the wider society, changes in school policy, negative teacher feeling, or curriculum implementation that might be exacerbating the problems in the first place. This again amounts to blaming students for their own miseducation.

Please don't let me be misunderstood: a student's self-image and a teacher's attitude in school do play important roles to be certain, but they are not as likely to alter the ghetto student's class position as they are to affect where he or she ultimately resides within a particular class grouping. Those within the critical tradition know that the majority of parents among the working poor do hold reasonably high expectations for their children. Nevertheless these parents have a *realistic expectation* of how schools work for their own children, as distinct from how they work for more privileged children.

As Feinberg and Soltis point out, some advocates of the "cultural impediments model" claim that since achievement is largely the function of class culture, and since it is believed that little can be done to alter behavior that is rooted in class culture, compensatory school programs will have a negligible effect on school achievement.[18] These same advocates claim that schools may even make matters appreciably worse in trying to change the social standing of the working poor, since by catering to the poor, educators water down the entire curriculum and relax academic standards for everyone. These theorists argue that inequality is the natural outgrowth of urban development, an attitude that effectively undercuts the imperatives for equality of opportunity and equality of outcome.

Once educational programs have been shrouded in these myths, they need not be abandoned when they fail. Failed programs can—and are—used by the dominant culture as evidence to support the myth-based definitions of academic failure: that failure lies in the genes, character traits, or home lives of the students themselves. Even good programs can fail because the clientele is unreachable, hence unteachable. Failure, therefore, simply proves the assumptions on which the policy was based.

Life chances are *socially conditioned* to a greater extent than they are determined by individual effort. Yet we live in a culture that stresses the merits of possessive individualism, the autonomous ego, and individual entrepreneurship. In this prevailing view, social conflicts are reduced to individual, subjective concerns rather than problems having to do with social and material inequality and collective greed and privilege.

CHAPTER **8**

Teachers and Students

THE PRIMACY OF STUDENT EXPERIENCE

The pedagogy that I propose *takes the problems and needs of the students themselves as its starting point.*[19] On the one hand, a pedagogy based on student experience encourages us to analyze the dominant forms of knowledge that shape student experiences; on the other hand, it attempts to provide students with the means to examine their own particular experiences and subordinate knowledge forms. We must help students analyze their own experiences so as to illuminate the processes by which those experiences were produced, legitimated, or disconfirmed. R. W. Connell and his associates in Australia provide a cogent direction for this curricular approach in their formulation of the kinds of knowledge that should be taught to empower working-class students.

> Working-class kids get access to formal knowledge via learning which begins with their own experience and the circumstances which shape it, but does not stop there. This approach neither accepts the existing organization of academic knowledge nor simply inverts it. It draws on existing school knowledge and on what working-class people already know, and organizes this selection of information around problems such as economic survival and collective action, handling the disruption of households by unemployment, responding to the impact of new technology, managing problems of personal identity and association, understanding how schools work and why.[20]

Any emancipatory curriculum must emphasize student experience, which is intimately related to identity formation. Critical educators need to learn how to understand, affirm, and analyze such experience. This means not only understanding the cultural and social forms through which students learn to define themselves, but also understanding how to use that student experience in ways that neither unqualifiedly endorse nor delegitimate it. As Giroux has often pointed out, knowledge must be made meaningful to students before it can be made critical. School knowledge never speaks for itself; it is constantly filtered through the ideological and cultural experiences that students bring to the classroom. To ignore the ideological dimensions of student experience is to deny the ground upon which students learn, speak, and imagine.

Students cannot learn "usefully" unless teachers develop an understanding of the various ways in which student perceptions and identities are constituted. Teachers need to understand how experiences produced in the various domains of everyday life produce in turn the different voices students employ to give meaning to their worlds and, consequently, to their existence in the larger society. Of course, not all student experiences should be unqualifiedly affirmed, since some of them undoubtedly will draw from an uncritical categorization and social construction of the world (racist and sexist stereotyping, for example). Teachers must understand that student experience arises from multiple discourses and subjectivities, some of which must be questioned more critically than others. It is crucial, therefore, that educators address the question of how the social world is experienced, mediated, and produced by students. Failure in this will not only prevent teachers from tapping into the drives, emotions, and interests that give students their own unique voice, but will also make it difficult to provide the momentum for learning itself.

Unfortunately, most approaches to teaching and learning treat knowledge as an isolated product of meaning and abjectly deny the knowledge and social forms out of which students give relevance to their lives and experiences. Lusted is worth repeating on this issue:

> Knowledge is produced in the process of interaction, between writer and reader at the moment of reading, and between teacher and learner at the moment of classroom engagement. . . . To think of fields or bodies of knowledge as if they are the property of academics and teachers is wrong. It denies an equality in the relations at moments of interaction and falsely privileges one side of the exchange, and what that side "knows" over the other. Moreover, for critical cultural producers to hold this view of knowledge carries its own pedagogy, an autocratic and elite pedagogy. It's not just that it denies the value of what the learners know, which it does, but that it misrecognizes the conditions necessary for the kind of learning—critical, engaged, personal, social—called for by the knowledge itself.[21]

Teachers often fall into the trap of defining success solely through the *ideological correctness* of what they teach. Giroux offers the example of a middle-class female teacher who is horrified by the blatant sexism exhibited by her male students. Predictably, the teacher presents her students with a variety of feminist tracts, films, and other curricular materials. Instead of responding with interest and gratitude for this political enlightenment, however, the students demonstrate only scorn and resistance. The teacher is baffled; the students' sexism appears only further entrenched. As Giroux points out, the teacher "falsely assumes the self-evident nature" of the correctness of her position; she has refused to allow the students to "tell their own stories, to present and then question the experience they bring into play." She has also denied her students an opportunity to question sexism as a problematic experience; she is, in other words, simply telling them once again what to think—as middle-class/institutional authority so often does.[22]

Sharon Welch argues that the most important concern in teaching is *to support the process of theorizing and not the mere exposure to correct ideas.* Yet she points out the inherent trap in teaching theory: that theory can function as a form of social control. Teachers often, for instance, greet student ideas with the smug reminder that those ideas are not new, that they have been formulated many times previously, often with greater sophistication. Teachers also often teach theory only in its final form, rather than moving through the complex process of engendering ideas. Welch encourages teachers to use the elementary-level technique of "reinventing the wheel"—students are given the problems that encourage them to create the formula for solving the area of a rectangle, the volume of a box, etc. By creating the formulas themselves, students are able to understand the mathematical theory more thoroughly, and gain confidence as thinkers.[23]

In my own situation as an inner-city teacher, I was unequipped to examine many of the ideological assumptions that informed my own pedagogy. My "authoritative discourse" was immune to its own hidden biases and prejudices. When I was too caught up with my role as teacher, I failed to learn more from my students. There is often a defensiveness surrounding the practice of letting students tell their own stories. Teachers must be careful not to silence students unwittingly through hidden biases lodged in their own pedagogical practices.

Certainly students should on occasion be encouraged to listen rather than speak, especially if their voices tend to dominate and control others. But teachers *should never tell students that their stories don't count.* Michelle Fine provides an excellent example of one teacher who unwittingly silences a student during an attempt to establish a lively debate on an issue relevant to the lives of her students:

> In early Spring, a social studies teacher structured an in-class debate on Bernard Goetz—New York City's "subway vigilante." She invited "those students who agree with Goetz to sit on one side of the room, and those who think he was wrong to sit on the other side." To the large residual group who remained mid-room the teacher remarked, "Don't be lazy. You have to make a decision. Like at work, you can't be passive." A few wandered over to the "pro-Goetz" side. About six remained in the center. Somewhat angry, the teacher continued: "OK, first we'll hear the pro-Goetz side and then the anti-Goetz side. Those of you who have no opinions, who haven't even thought about the issue, you won't get to talk unless we have time." Deirdre, a black senior, bright and always quick to raise contradictions otherwise obscured, advocated the legitimacy of the middle group. "It's not that I have no opinions. I don't

like Goetz shootin' up people who look like my brother, but I don't like feelin' unsafe in the projects or in my neighborhood either. I got lots of opinions. I ain't bein' quiet cause I can't decide if he's right or wrong. I'm talking.'' Deirdre's comment legitimized for herself and others the right to hold complex, perhaps even contradictory positions on a complex situation. Such legitimacy was rarely granted by faculty—with clear and important exceptions including activist faculty and para-professionals who lived in central Harlem with the kids, and understood and respected much about their lives.[24]

The social studies teacher in Fine's anecdote has unreflectively favored her own ideological position and consequently undermined Deidre's refusal to simplify what she considers a complex issue. Teachers frequently unintentionally devalue student experience despite the best political and ethical intentions. As a consequence, any sense of equality in the exchange between teacher and students is lost. In other words, a teacher's own pedagogy can be unintentionally elitist and autocratic.

THE PRIMACY OF VOICE

In the welter of accountability schemes, management pedagogies, and rationalized curricula now flooding the schools, there is an ominous silence regarding how teachers and students produce and reconstruct meaning in everyday life. In the attempts to rationalize and streamline classroom pedagogy, the New Right is promoting curriculum approaches that remove both the teacher and the student from the center of action. The categories that students themselves use to make sense of the world, to understand why they act in a particular way, or why they resist in the face of dominating practices, appear superfluous to the champions of the new high-tech accountability schemes.

I would argue with Henry Giroux that a critical and affirming pedagogy has to be constructed around the stories that people tell, the ways in which students and teachers author meaning, and the possibilities that underlie the experiences that shape their voices. It is around the concept of *voice* that a theory of both teaching and learning can take place, one that points to new forms of social relations and to new and challenging ways of confronting everyday life.[25]

Giroux's concept of *voice* refers to the multifaceted and interlocking set of meanings through which students and teachers actively engage in dialogue with one another. *Voice* is an important pedagogical concept because it alerts teachers to the fact that all discourse is situated historically and mediated culturally and derives part of its meaning from interaction with others. Although the term *voice* may refer to an internalized, private discourse, such a discourse cannot be understood without situating it in a universe of shared meanings, that is, in the symbols, narratives, and social practices of the community or culture in which the dialogue is taking place. The term *voice* refers to the cultural grammar and background knowledge that individuals use to interpret and articulate experience.

Individual voice must be understood within its cultural and historical speci-ficity. How students, teachers, and others define themselves and name experience is a central pedagogical concern because it helps educators understand how class-room meaning is produced, legitimated, or delegitimated. This is not merely a technical concern but more importantly a moral and political consideration that must provide the basis for any critical pedagogy, especially a pedagogy that is attentive to the dialectic of power and meaning. In many cases, schools do not allow students from disadvantaged or subordinate groups to affirm their own individual and collective voices, yet teachers rarely understand how this happens.

A *student's voice* is not a reflection of the world as much as it is a *constitutive force that both mediates and shapes reality within historically constructed practices and relationships of power.* Each individual voice is shaped by its owner's particular cultural history and prior experience. Voice, then, suggests the means that students have at their disposal to make themselves "heard" and to define themselves as active participants in the world. Exhibiting an individual "voice" means, to cite Bakhtin, "retelling a text in one's own words."[26]

The dominant school culture generally represents the privileged voices of the white middle and upper classes. In order for teachers to demystify and make the dominant school culture an object of political analysis, they need to question those voices that emerge from *different* ideological spheres or settings, such as the school voice and the teacher voice.

Each of these voices works simultaneously to produce specific pedagogical experiences within different configurations of power. Teachers must analyze the interests that these different voices represent less as oppositional in the sense that they work to counter and disable each other than as an interplay of dominant and subordinate practices that shape each other in an ongoing struggle over power, meaning, and authorship.

To "learn the discourse of *school voice,*" teachers must analyze the directives, imperatives, and rules that shape particular configurations of time, space, and curricula within the institutional and political settings of schools. The concept of school voice, for example, helps to illuminate particular ideologies that struc-ture how classrooms are arranged, what content is taught, and what general social practices teachers are required to follow. More often than not, school voice repre-sents what Bakhtin refers to as "authoritative discourse"—that which permits little or no flexibility within the context that frames it.

Teacher voice reflects the values, ideologies, and structuring principles that teachers use to understand and mediate the histories, cultures, and subjectivities of their students. For instance, teachers often use the voice of "common sense" to frame their classroom instruction and daily pedagogical activities. As in the case of school voice, teacher voice partakes of an authoritative discourse that frequently silences the voices of the students. On the one hand, the *oppressive power* of a teacher's authoritative voice can be seen in instances of what Bourdieu refers to as *symbolic violence.*[27] Symbolic violence is exercised when, for instance, a teacher draws his or her values narrowly in order to challenge and disconfirm the experiences and beliefs of students from subordinate groups. On the other hand, the *emancipatory power* of a teacher's authoritative voice is exercised when a student's voice is allowed to assert itself so as to be both confirmed and analyzed, in terms of the particular values and ideologies that it represents. In the latter instance, the teacher voice can provide a critical context within which students can understand the various social forces and configurations of power that have helped give shape to their own voices. Students who exhibit the values and everyday practices of subordinate groups can learn to free themselves from the authoritative hold of middle-class discourse as a means to self-empowerment, without rejecting either their own working-class discourse or, for that matter, middle-class discourse.

It is often through the mediation of teacher voice that the very nature of the schooling process is either sustained or challenged. The power of teacher voice to shape schooling according to the logic of emancipatory interests is inextricably related not only to a high degree of self-understanding, but also to the possibility for teachers to join together in a collective voice as part of a social movement dedicated to restructuring the ideological and material conditions both within and outside of schooling. Thus, we must understand the concept of teacher voice in terms of its own values, as well as in relation to the ways it functions to shape and mediate school and student voices.

Giroux's work on the concept of voice acknowledges the political and pedagogical processes at work in the construction of forms of authorship within different institutional and social spheres. Moreover, it represents an attack on the unjust practices that are actively at work in the wider society. But most important, such a pedagogy begins with the assumption that the stories that schools, teachers, and students construct can form the basis for a variety of approaches to teaching and learning in which hope and power play integral roles.

BEYOND CONVERSATIONS WITH THE "OTHER"

The journal entries presented in Part Two, which I wrote during my first four and a half years as an elementary teacher, illustrate the debilitating way in which poverty entraps groups of individuals. My preoccupation at that time with the more disturbing characteristics of resistance among disadvantaged and minority students illustrates my own entrapment in bourgeois culture. I both admired and loathed the students' visceral rebellion.

Unfortunately, at the time I wrote my journal I had little access to theoretical constructs that would help me make sense of what was occurring in my classroom. My inability to criticize my own ideological shortcomings undoubtedly foreclosed opportunities for empowering my students and raised the danger of demoting their experiences to a lesser status than my own.

My views toward my students sometimes lapsed into a form of liberal pity that is incompatible with the critical frame of reference I now use to examine schooling. Throughout my days in the classroom, I had unknowingly ascribed to the pedagogical mainstay of many liberal teachers: I felt sympathy and compassion for my students while employing a pedagogy geared to "compensate" for the deficiencies of society's young victims. Because mine was the "stronger and superior culture,'' I felt I could penetrate and give shape, meaning, and hope to the mystery of the deprived. My pedagogy was bourgeois populism spiced with a liberal dose of humanism; it rendered me ineffective in educating community members about how power relations in society work under a dominant regime of truth. This was an index of how far I had succumbed to the power and pervasiveness of the dominant culture.

We need to ask what injustices may be perpetrated in the name of liberal pedagogy. The ability to articulate and change the real relationships of power and privilege was not part of my pedagogical repertoire; consequently, such relationships remained camouflaged in my language of moral outrage.

As I tried to help my students succeed in their schooling by teaching them relevant social and educational skills, I was culpable at another level: I was a teacher employed by an oppressive and inequitable system. I failed to minimize my individual complicity in institutional oppression, and liberal humanism in no way exonerated me. I failed to recognize that my pedagogy was rooted in the very reality I was attempting to challenge. The liability remains, and with it the imperative to do more than lessen the harshness of the world for our students. We must try to provide them with the ability to overcome oppression and transform the world. The interests of the dominant class were implicit in the very teaching practices I used—practices readily handed to teachers and student teachers which are steeped in the ideology of domination. I refer here to the institution of tracking, the stress on individualism, the employment of the ''cultural deficit'' model of pedagogy, and the prevalence of teacher-centered learning, to name just a few. I was unable to see that my liberal theories of education were in fact ideologically loaded. The fateful irony of combating the oppressors with their own weapons instituted for me a crisis of legitimation and accountability with respect to my own teaching.

Were I to do it all over again, I would construct my curriculum around the celebration, validation, and critical questioning of the symbolic and expressive forms within the specific cultural practices of the students' street-corner milieu. I would follow with concerted attempts to understand and appreciate the meanings invested in students' opposition to the dominant culture. I would make a conscientious effort to link symbolic resistance to the goal of empowerment, and I would treat curriculum as a form of cultural politics. In addition, I would attempt to make active alliances with popular constituencies outside the classroom—the workers', women's, and peace movements, among others.

A critical pedagogy situates itself in the intersection of language, culture, and history—the nexus in which the students' subjectivities are formed, contested, and played out. The struggle is one that involves *their history, their language,* and *their culture* and the pedagogical implications are such that students are given access to a critical discourse or are conditioned to accept the familiar as the inevitable. Worse still, they are denied a voice with which to be present in the world; they are made invisible to history and rendered powerless to shape it.

Philip Corrigan has developed a three-part form of analysis and action that I appropriate here to suggest an approach to critical pedagogy.[28] First, encourage students to develop a *pedagogical negativism*—to doubt everything, and to try to identify those forms of power and control that operate in their own social lives. Second, assist students in *making a judgment* about these forms of power and control. What can be used to promote empowerment, and what must be discarded? Finally, help students *affirm* their judgments. Return to history to help them find a language which registers or *names* the dominant forms of power and control that deny the knowledge of subjugated groups.

To achieve these steps, I suggest a special kind of classroom approach that Michelle Fine calls *naming*.[29] Naming is simply identifying and defining those social and economic relationships that most clearly affect students' lives, particularly the inequitable distribution of power and resources. During my own teaching days, naming those social inequities that contribute to insidious social class, racial, ethnic, and gender divisions in the wider society might have provided an initial step in permitting students to analyze their own situations. Macro objectives for my classroom that linked knowledge to wider social arrangements might have provided directive knowledge useful in students' daily lives. Such objectives would have encouraged students to draw on their own cultural histories and neighborhood experiences to discuss *how they saw and experienced oppression and social injustice.* I could have asked Duke, Buddy, and T. J., for instance, to interview members of the community, beginning with their parents, and to develop an oral history of the area. We could have documented grievances, discussed reasons why people in the area were suffering, and analyzed their oppression. We might then have raised these issues with local agencies, providing at least a beginning step in linking self-empowerment and social change.

I might also have invited students to understand youth protest in its various forms through music and culture. We might have compared the cultures of various local gangs with those of more publicized gangs, like the Bloods and Crips of Los Angeles. A comparison of well-studied British groups—skinheads, punks, Rastas, rude boys, mods, rockers, teddy boys—with the local manifestations of protest in the Jane-Finch youth subculture might have taught students to be more critical about their own culture and the dominant culture that subordinates them. I might then have given my students the opportunity to move beyond self-criticism to self and social transformation: I might have asked how we can struggle to become active agents of social change.

Unfortunately, in most schools the act of *naming*—of identifying and defining the oppressive social and cultural facts of life—is deemed "dangerous conversation." It runs counter to the politically laundered beliefs about equality and meritocracy that dominate public schooling. *Not naming,* however, constitutes an active refusal to create reflective citizens; it is quite simply a means of silencing students.

Michelle Fine argues that not naming leads to exceptionally damaging outcomes, particularly for low-income and minority students. "To not name is to systematically alienate, cut off from home, from heritage and from lived experience and ultimately severs these students from their educational process."[30] Fine goes on to describe how an administrative policy of not naming can, for instance, restrict information provided to potential dropouts concerning the severe economic and social consequences of dropping out of high school. When students are discharged from school in New York State, crucial conditions are *not named,* thereby denying students what amounts to informed consent.

> [Discharged students] are guaranteed an exit interview, which, in most cases, involved an attendance officer who asked students what they planned to do, and then requested a meeting with parent/guardian to sign official documents. The officer handed the students a list of GED/outreach programs. The student left, often eager to find work, get a GED, go to a private business school, or join the military. Informed conversations about the consequences of the students' decision are not legally mandated. As they left, these adolescents *did not learn*:
>
> - that over 50% of black high school dropouts suffer unemployment in cities like New York City (U.S. Commission on Civil Rights, 1982);
> - that 48% of New Yorkers who sit for the Graduate Equivalency Diploma test fail (New York State Department of Education, 1985);
> - that private trade schools, including cosmetology, beautician and business schools have been charged with unethical recruitment practices, exploitation of students, earning more from students who drop out than those who stay, not providing promised jobs, and having, on average, a 70% dropout rate;
> - that the military, during 'peacetime' refuses to accept females with no high school degree, and only reluctantly accepts males, who suffer an extreme less than honorable discharge rate within 6 months of enlistment.[31]

My own teaching experiences were rife with the politics of not naming. Although I did encourage students to tell their own stories, the most that I could accomplish was a liberal version of moral outrage at the injustices of the system, followed by a sympathetic embrace or reassuring pat on the shoulder that told the students I identified with their plight. Let me stress that the pedagogical position I am advocating does not prohibit students or teachers from acquiring a sense of outrage, or students and teachers from developing a sympathetic, affectionate, confidence-building relationship with each other; rather, it emphasizes that *such sentiments and relationships need to be pursued within a pedagogical context in which the issue of self and social transformation is taken seriously.*

My teaching would have been more effective if I had been able to engage in a critical analysis of those aspects of everyday life that resonated with and affirmed the dreams, desires, and histories of the students. I suggest, with Henry Giroux and Paulo Freire, that we must take the *experiences* and *voices* of students themselves as a starting point. We must *confirm and legitimate the knowledges and experiences through which students give meaning to their everyday lives.* Such experiences, however, must not be unqualifiedly endorsed. We must be attentive to their *contradictory nature* and establish grounds whereby these experiences can be questioned and analyzed in both their strengths and their weaknesses. For instance, some of Duke's expressive values might have been confirmed by celebrating his love of music, his sense of humor, his personal style, and his street wisdom. Duke is undeniably wise (as opposed to academically "smart"), in that he recognizes the subtle ways in which the system works to disempower himself, his peers, and his family. But he lacks a language in which to further ground his insights into the dominant ideology. Duke's way of resisting the "authoritative discourse" of the school is steeped in racist and sexist behavior that needs to be named, understood, and eventually transformed through the process of understanding that Freire calls *conscientization.* (See Part Three discussion on Paulo Freire.)

Although Freire's approach empowers students through language, language *is not a tool to express an already made self. Rather, as Giroux notes, language is one of the means whereby we give form and shape to the development of a more critical self.* Freire's approach to learning is based on genuine dialogue between students and teachers, who work as partners in a united quest for "critical consciousness" leading to a humane transformation of, rather than a passive accommodation to one's world.

This partnership approach is directly opposed to most mainstream learning, which Freire refers to as "banking education." In the banking approach, the teacher "deposits" information into an "empty account" (the student) who "receives, memorizes, and repeats." Students are passive objects of the teacher's knowledge. Freire's "problem-solving" approach turns students into active and critical subjects who work collaboratively to construct historically—and politically—sensitive analyses of existing social practices in order to transform them.

Giroux adds that critical pedagogy must develop out of *a politics of difference* and a sense of community not rooted simply in a celebration of plurality. In other words, tolerance of differences is not enough. *Students, despite their differences, must become unified in a common struggle to overcome the conditions that perpetuate their own suffering and the suffering of others. Critical pedagogy must be undertaken within a language of public life, emancipatory community, and individual and social commitment.*[32] In other words, this critical approach to teaching is based on a social imagination rooted in history and intent on a resurrection of the "dangerous memory" and "subjugated knowledges" of oppressed groups such as women and minorities. The task of such an imagination is to build a world in which power relations are contested actively and suffering is finally overcome.

Giroux's work involves assisting students in analyzing their own theoretical and political positions. This means teachers must attempt to understand the often contradictory nature of subjectivity, and the reasons why students adopt some ideological positions over others both within and outside schools.

To do this, teachers must uncover the hidden ideological interests that underlie their own pedagogical practices and their ability to both teach and learn with others. Teachers and students must engage each other as agents of different/similar cultures. For Giroux, this suggests being critically attentive not only to the teacher's relationship to the established apparatus of power, but also to the fears, resistance, and skepticism that students from subordinate groups bring with them to the classroom.

The critical pedagogy suggested here is one in which students are continually asked to examine the various codes—that is, the beliefs, the values, and the assumptions—that they use to make sense out of their world. They are also encouraged to examine how they "codify" events themselves, not only in the classroom but outside the school as well. One way to implement this is to ask students to write a number of short papers in which they not only consider various ways of making sense of an issue or event, but also reflect upon their own previous writings in order to rethink past perspectives and to modify or reshape positions. For instance, I ask my undergraduate students to examine what traits and characteristics in the opposite sex they consider appealing and attractive. This leads to a discussion of how ideals of masculinity and femininity are constructed and then to an examination of sexual stereotyping and how gender distinctions are manufactured through various cultural forms (i.e., magazine advertisements, television commercials, soap operas, music videos). We then view a video, Tony Wilden and Rhonda Hammer's "Chorus Line: Women in Production," which graphically illustrates the militarism, sexism, racism, and symbolic violence so prevalent in Hollywood depictions of female chorus lines from the 1930s to the present.[33] Finally, I ask students to reconsider their initial ideals of masculinity and femininity and account for any changes in their personal views. Students are thus encouraged to sort through the contradictions of their own experiences; they are given the chance to raise a fundamental question put forward by Giroux: "What is it this society has made of me that I no longer want to be?" In short, students are asked to look at their everyday, taken-for-granted experiences (the ideologies of everyday life), as possible sources of learning.

In his masterful work, *The Grain of the Voice,* Roland Barthes warns teachers against assuming a voice of power—a voice that can smother student talk by assigning the teacher's meanings (his or her "authoritative text") to the texts students have read or the ideas in which they are presently engaging.[34] Barthes suggests that teachers should employ the strategy of *disappropriation;* that is, they should deliberately cast off authority as speaker so that students can claim some authority of their own. In this way, the teacher is no longer a hegemonic overlord, a representative of the dominant culture who tells students whether their interpretations of events are valid—in short, who tells them *who they are.* Instead the teacher actively assumes a *counterhegemonic* role; the teacher actively contests existing relations of power and privilege. The overall purpose of the critical educator is to reveal to students the forces behind their own interpretations, to call into question the ideological nature of their experiences, and to help students discover the interconnections between the community, culture, and the larger social context: in short, to engage in the dialectic of self and society.

NEW DIRECTIONS

Since the publication of the first edition of *Life in Schools,* educators, parents, administrators, and community workers have frequently asked me for the names of educators and social theorists who offer perspectives similar to those expressed in my book. I will attempt in this section to identify other writers and researchers in the field of critical education. In doing so, however, I would like to emphasize that although critical pedagogy has sometimes been referred to (jokingly, I hope) as a ''cult'' coming out of Miami University of Ohio, until its primary exponents left for other universities, it is, in reality, a movement that professes no gurus or ''master interpreters.'' It should be stressed that there is no one critical pedagogy but rather various strands of critical pedagogies, feminist pedagogies, postcolonial pedagogies, and postmodern pedagogies that sometimes are described by using the umbrella term *critical pedagogy.*

Educators often ask me to identify and further locate the work that I do in their attempt to link it to a discipline with which they are more familiar. I think this is a fair request. Most often I identify myself as a critical social theorist whose work is concentrated in the area of curriculum and cultural studies and, more recently, in multiculturalism. Though my work spans the disciplines of philosophy, social theory, anthropology, semiotics, sociology, curriculum theory, and literary criticism, it is usually focused in the area of curriculum, policy analysis, and classroom practice.

Life in Schools and *Schooling as Ritual Performance* are two current books I've written that most directly examine classroom school and community contexts. Like the work of other critical social theorists, a large number of my writings are generally but not exclusively more engaged with theoretical and ethical debates in the field and are not always written with the classroom practitioner as the primary audience (although this has not precluded classroom practitioners from either reading or responding to this work). Although educational activists have seen or might see this ''other'' work as ''elitist,'' and dismiss it as such, I think that they are wrong to do so. There are many battles to be fought both at the level of theoretical debate and classroom and institutional practices. As educators, we need to broaden our grasp of different languages and our ability to explain schooling and its relationship to wider social, cultural, and economic practices, and to expand the horizon of our reform efforts. Of course, those of us in the academy need to remember why we first got into education—for the students. Yet by the same token, it would be unfair of classroom practitioners and activists to think that their struggles are more ''authentic'' than those of educators who work to reconceptualize the politics of education at the level of philosophical or theoretical debate. Look at all the important work in literacy that has been accomplished by teachers worldwide as a result of Paulo Freire's landmark text, *Pedagogy of the Oppressed,* hardly a text one could describe as ''readerly.'' What about all those educational activists who have been—or continue to be—inspired by the writings of Karl Marx, John Dewey, and Michel Foucault? The works of these thinkers do not make for easy reading, and they demand a lot from readers.

Whether in the public school classroom or university lecture hall, educational reformers need to work at multiple levels where they feel they have the most expertise and can effect the kind of change they see as necessary. Some choose to advance educational change through theoretical advances, others through community and teacher advocacy, and still others through direct classroom innovation. It would be unproductive and imprudent to accord some efforts as by definition more important than others. All such efforts need to be seen as important and urgent, provided they are undertaken as part of a genuine project of social and educational transformation and not some self-serving effort to gain personal recognition, promotion, or advantage outside of the collective struggle itself and the ultimate goals of the project.

At the level of community activism we need to recognize the work of people such as Bill Bigelow, Stan Karp, and *The Rethinking Schools* group that publishes a newspaper out of Milwaukee, Wisconsin, not to mention the *Radical Teacher* collective. Ideally, critical theorists working in the academy and school and community activists establishing networks between schools and neighborhoods should forge stronger bonds in the future in order to establish more locally and nationally coordinated efforts at school reform, something that Ira Shor has helped to accomplish.

The task of reconceptualizing the nature of theory and the role of the educator is currently being undertaken in a very conceptually exciting and politically important field known as "postmodern education." Postmodern education draws upon new insights from recent French social theory, such as the work of Julia Kristeva, Jacques Derrida, and Michel Foucault, in an attempt to critique "transcendent" or universal theories of human agency and those Western theoretical narratives that developed out of the Enlightenment and humanist traditions. Readers may wish to consult the work of Stanley Aronowitz and Henry Giroux, Barry Kanpol, Patti Lather, or my own efforts in this area. Recent books such as *Postmodern Education* by Stanley Aronowitz and Henry Giroux, *Border Crossings* by Henry Giroux, *Between Borders* edited by Henry Giroux and Peter McLaren, *Towards a Theory and Practice of Teacher Cultural Politics* by Barry Kanpol, and *Politics of Liberation* edited by Peter McLaren and Colin Lankshear are representative of some of this new work.

Feminist pedagogy is an important new direction in education. Various strands of feminist pedagogy attempt not only to criticize limitations that exist in critical pedagogy (which has primarily been advanced by white male writers) but also to articulate a vision of emancipation that addresses the needs and concerns of women. Madeline Grumet's work *Bitter Milk* and JoAnne Pagano's *Exiles and Communities* are representative of this new direction. Of course, recent work in feminist pedagogies by women of color has offered important criticisms of both the patriarchal framework of some strands of critical pedagogy and feminist pedagogies developed by white bourgeois women. In addition, this work has advanced new understandings of the role of race, class, gender, and sexuality in the context of postcolonial criticism. The works of bell hooks, Michele Wallace, Gloria Anzaldúa, and Chandra Mohanty signal some of the most important contributions in this area.

Another recent direction of educational theory has been in the area of popular culture and mass communication and includes an emphasis on media literacy. Henry Giroux and Roger Simon's *Popular Culture: Schooling and Everyday Life* is an excellent example of this work as well as *Black Looks* by bell hooks. *Media Knowledge* by Susan Reilly, James Schwoch, and Mimi White, and a forthcoming work by McLaren, Hammer, Reilly, and Sholle, *A Critical Pedagogy of Representation,* address the themes of student identity as they are constructed through the discourse of popular representations in news media and advertising.

Multicultural education is not a new development but has assumed a leading role in educational reform over the last five years. Important exponents in this field outside of those critical educators already discussed include Christine Sleeter, James Banks, Antonia Darder, Cameron McCarthy, Carl Grant, Ira Shor, Stephen Haymes, Sonia Nieto, Cathy Walsh, and others. My own work in multicultural education draws more from a cultural studies perspective, and here the works of Henry Louis Gates, bell hooks, Michele Wallace, Henry Giroux, Anthony Appiah, and Cornel West are signally important. A work that should be required reading by all prospective teachers interested in multicultural education is *The IQ Mythology: Class, Race, Gender, and Inequality* by Elaine and Harry Mensh.

The work of Jim Cummins and Donaldo Macedo in the area of bilingual education has assumed a new urgency in this era of conservative restoration, as has the work of George Wood and Jesse Goodman in the domain of democratic education. The sociology of education has made important contributions to our understanding of schooling in the context of social and cultural relations and includes work by Dennis Carlson, Tom Popkewitz, Barry Kanpol, and Lois Weis. At the same time, critical ethnographies and case studies of teachers' lives continue to enrich our understanding of schools and communities, such as those by Michelle Fine, Lois Weis, Jay McLeod, Deborah Britzman, Bill Tierney, and Dan McLaughlin. One should not forget work being done in sexuality education, especially the work on gay students pioneered by Jim Sears.

The area of higher education has also been examined from a critical perspective by such researchers as Bill Tierney and William Foster. Critical pedagogy and teacher evaluation has recently been reexamined brilliantly by Andrew Gitlin and John Smyth and has revolutionized the way we understand evaluation and classroom teaching.

The work of Joe Kincheloe has moved critical pedagogy in new and expanded directions. Examining what happens when critical pedagogy encounters the unquestionable assumptions of educational orthodoxy, Kincheloe has sabotaged the shibboleths of educational research in *Teachers as Researchers: Qualitative Paths to Empowerment,* the homilies of critical thinking in *Toward a Critical Politics of Teacher Thinking: Mapping the Postmodern,* and the clichés of educational reform in *Toil and Trouble: Good Work, Smart Workers, and the Integration of Vocational and Academic Education.* Epistemologically grounding his work on what he calls a critical constructivism, Kincheloe argues that all aspects of education must be reconceived in light of critical pedagogical and postmodern analysis. With Shirley Steinberg, Kincheloe rethinks the social foundations of education in *Thirteen Questions: Reframing Education's Conversation* and *The Stigma of Genius: Einstein and Beyond Modern Education.* Maintaining the value of critical pedagogy in a myriad of public conversations, Kincheloe engages readers' social imagination in a "post-formal reconceptualization of the workplace"—an analysis which induces teachers and workers to examine their work from a new angle. Kincheloe's work reminds us of the power and possibility of the critical discourse. Bill Pinar's work cannot be ignored.

The foregoing has been just a short summary of only several of the many important new directions undertaken by critical educators over recent years. A few of these will be discussed in more detail in the postscript to this volume.

CHAPTER 9

Conclusion to Parts Three and Four

I have tried to provide educators and prospective educators with a theoretical framework that defines schools as sites of possibility, in which classrooms provide conditions for student empowerment. I've tried to suggest that particular forms of knowledge, social relations, and values can be taught in order to educate students to take their places in society from a position of empowerment, rather than from a position of ideological and economic subordination. I have tried to construct a language of analysis and to liberate the concept of education from the realities of present-day schooling.

For critical pedagogy to become viable within our schools, teachers must learn to employ critical analysis and utopian thinking. Henry Giroux refers to this as combining the language of critique with the language of possibility. Educators must develop forms of analyses that acknowledge the spaces, tensions, and opportunities for democratic struggles and reforms within the day-to-day activities and events of the classroom. Similarly, educators must develop a language that allows teachers and others to view schooling in a critical and potentially transformative way. Two important directions for reforming contemporary school practices put forward by Aronowitz and Giroux involve viewing schools as democratic public spheres and teachers as transformative intellectuals.

Viewing schools as democratic public spheres means regarding schools as sites dedicated to forms of self and social empowerment, where students have the opportunity to learn the knowledge and skills necessary to live in an authentic democracy. Instead of defining schools as extensions of the workplace or as frontline institutions in the battle for international markets and foreign competition, schools as democratic public spheres function to dignify meaningful dialogue and action and to give students the opportunity to learn the language of social responsibility. Such a language seeks to recapture the idea of democracy as a *social movement* grounded in a fundamental respect for *individual freedom* and *social justice.* As Giroux argues, viewing schools as democratic public spheres provides a rationale for defending them, along with progressive forms of pedagogy and teacher work, as institutions that perform public service essential to the democratic state.

By politicizing the notion of schooling, we also illuminate the role that educators may play as transformative intellectuals performing a particular social and political function. The term *transformative intellectual* is important here for analyzing the particular social practices in which teachers routinely engage. I follow Aronowitz and Giroux in using it to describe one who attempts to insert teaching and learning directly into the political sphere by arguing that schooling represents both a struggle for meaning and a struggle over power relations.[35] I also refer to one whose intellectual practices exhibit concern for the suffering and struggles of the disadvantaged and oppressed. Here the traditional view of the intellectual as someone who is able to analyze various interests and contradictions within society is extended *to refer to someone capable of articulating emancipatory possibilities and working toward their realization.* Teachers who assume the role of transformative intellectuals treat students as critical agents, question how knowledge is produced and distributed, utilize dialogue, and make knowledge meaningful, critical, and ultimately emancipatory.

Henry Giroux notes that if schools are to be linked to the imperatives of radical democracy and civic courage, educators must examine how the schools themselves reproduce those aspects of the wider society that contribute to gender, class, and racial injustices. Democracy in this case begins in the school itself, and this suggests the need for educators to question both the formal and the hidden curricula of public schooling so as to identify those ideologies and social practices that operate both for and against the imperatives of democracy. Teachers must be willing to develop and use a critical language in order to structure school experiences around a public vision of self and social empowerment, both in and outside of schools. Giroux argues that this struggle not only dignifies teachers in their capacity as intellectuals and social critics; it also links their work to those practical pedagogical concerns that make the preconditions for critical learning, social empowerment, and democracy possible.

An excellent example of liberating education can be seen in the efforts of students and teachers at Dr. Pedro Albizu Campos Puerto Rican High School in West Town, Chicago. Here, the staff use critical pedagogy in their collective work with the Puerto Rican community. They try to help students acquire a sense of humanity and purpose in their lives after an often brutal and dehumanizing colonization within the United States, where the material conditions of their labor are controlled and their dreams, desires, hopes, and visions are often ideologically subjugated. Teachers at Pedro Albizu Campos are committed to equality and social justice and demonstrate an unyielding dedication to the empowerment of the Puerto Rican people. The accomplishments of the school are profound; students (many of whom are former street gang members) have not only gained access to university programs, but have also acquired a resistance to the socially manufactured dreams of consumer wealth and a desire to become social and moral agents dedicated to transforming the structural injustices that threaten their community.

The pedagogy of the teachers, which has evolved from the historical plight of a colonized people, is linked to wider social problems outside the school and is grounded in the ongoing struggle of community members to secure jobs, to reform repressive legislation, and to redefine the concept of education.

Of course, liberating education runs its risks. Dr. Pedro Albizu Campos Puerto Rican High School has been invaded by FBI agents wielding shotguns and searching for evidence of FALN (Armed Forces for National Liberation) terrorist activity; an award from the U.S. Department of Education citing it as an exemplary private school was rescinded because of allegations that the school teaches revolution and sedition. What the school does, in fact, teach is a revolution in consciousness and in understanding; students and teachers learn to see schooling as a transformative agency of social change.

Liberating education hopes to develop a new kind of critical discourse, one that will inspire us to play a more active role in school and classroom life. In my view, such a discourse is vital in order for educators and others to understand the specifics of oppression and the possibilities for democratic struggle and renewal in our schools. Of course, such a discourse always presents a risk to those who use it, but one that is worth taking if we believe that democracy itself is worth fighting for.

The development of an incipient critical consciousness on the part of students must be followed by its transformation to social action through public engagement and participation. Guiding this transformation must be a commitment to authentic democracy and social justice, a commitment that is undertaken in solidarity with the subordinated and the disenfranchised. A language of possibility must be spoken in public spaces such as schools, where authentic dialogue can take place between teachers and students about decisions that affect the quality of human life.

THE TEACHER AS SOCIAL AND MORAL AGENT

Nowhere does the challenge of shaping social history, fashioning new cultural narratives, and rethinking the nature and purpose of schooling become more urgent than in the struggle to define the civic responsibility of the teacher.[36] The dialectics of hope expounded by early twentieth century writers such as Walter Benjamin and Ernst Bloch now appear silenced and forgotten. New forms of social theory and educational practice that are profoundly antiutopian in character have, in their propensity to retreat from both history and a politics of commitment and struggle, helped to forge a new generation of intellectuals who have failed to take seriously Benjamin's maxim that freedom requires that we brush history against the grain.

Abandoning the project of political engagement and human possibility, educators and professional critics alike have promoted despair at the expense of analyzing the fundamental relationships of power that characterize existing forms of cultural and political hegemony. They have jettisoned a consideration for the realities of suffering, pain, and torture, not to mention the barrenness of everyday life, in favor of mastery learning techniques and the "teacher-proof" curriculum.

Current reform efforts demonstrate an unwillingness to construct and sustain a clearly articulated political project, in which pedagogy can be linked to the creation of social practices and moral referents necessary for the construction of a democratic public sphere.

Teaching always takes place in relation to a particular regime of truth or dominating logic. Acquiring knowledge does not provide students with a reflection of the world; it creates a specific rendering of the world that is only intelligible within particular ideological configurations, social formations, or systems of mediation. Teaching itself functions to produce students and teachers as social and cultural subjects. How we, as subjects, are positioned by various pedagogical discourses and classroom practices constitutes an ideological process that often provides us with an illusion of autonomy and self-determination and helps us to misrecognize ourselves as free agents. Although it may be true that we can never escape ideology, the teacher must both *reveal how subjectivity gets constructed and legitimated through dominant pedagogical discourses and eventually challenge the imaginary relations that students live relative to the symbolic and material conditions of their existence.*

The teacher's task must take the form of a critical pedagogy. That is, the teacher must do more than simply further legitimate shared assumptions, agreed upon proprieties, or established conventions. He or she must make classrooms into critical spaces that truly endanger the obviousness of culture—i.e., the way reality is usually constructed—as a collection of unalterable truths and unchangeable social relations. Within such critical spaces, he or she must excavate the "subjugated knowledges" of those who have been marginalized and disaffected, whose histories of suffering and hope have rarely been made public. Thus, we must point to the histories of women, people of color, economically disadvantaged groups, and others whose banished legacies challenge the moral legitimacy of the state. The stories and struggles of the oppressed are often lodged as "dangerous memories" in the social system's repressed unconscious.[37] As teachers of "dangerous memory," we are called to rub these narratives against the more normative frames of reference which give dominant knowledge its meaning and legitimacy.

The teacher performs a social function that is never innocent. There is no neutral, nonpartisan sphere into which the teacher can retreat to engage student experience. Giroux maintains that, as one who takes seriously the link among language, knowledge, and power, the teacher must first dignify his or her position by recognizing that the foundation for all human agency as well as teaching is steeped in a commitment to the possibilities for human life and freedom.

Finally, I would argue that teachers must function as more than agents of social critique. They must attempt to fashion a language of hope that points to new forms of social and material relations attentive to the principles of freedom and justice. And they must actively intervene in the conduct of human affairs. Critical discourse must be more than simply a form of cultural dissonance, more than a siphoning away of the potency of dominant meanings and social relations. It must function instead to create a democratic community built upon a language of public association and a commitment to social transformation. Critical discourse must call for a new narrative through which a qualitatively better world can be both imagined and struggled for. We must be united in the face of overwhelming odds, and the pedagogy we use must be capable of inflating the human capacity to vie with the forces of domination at a scale that makes us reject despair and refuse capitulation to the status quo. Teaching is anticipatory, rooted in a dialectical logic that makes critique and transformation its central challenge. The perilous and immense task ahead of us is to engage the real needs of the oppressed and to foster an unending commitment to their empowerment. We must work hard to reverse the current decline of moral passion and the socially induced depletion of the human spirit. The anger and sullen outrage that fills the gap between need and fulfillment for many of our youth must be met in the classroom, in the courts, in the legislature, and in the streets with a redemptive pedagogy of commitment and compassion. Only in this engagement can we, as agents of transformation and hope, begin to both feel and understand the suffering and alienation of the world and also be provided with the will, the purpose, and the understanding to overcome it.

NOTES TO PART FOUR

1. John Ogbu, "Class Stratification, Racial Stratification, and Schooling," in L. Weis (Ed.), *Race, Class, and Schooling* 17 (1986), 22. Special Studies in Comparative Education, Comparative Education Center, Faculty of Educational Studies, State University of New York at Buffalo.
2. Ibid., 25–26.
3. Peter McLaren, *Schooling as a Ritual Performance: Towards a Political Economy of Educational Symbols and Gestures* (London and New York: Routledge and Kegan Paul, 1986).
4. Paul Willis, *Learning to Labor* (Lexington: D.C. Heath, 1977).
5. For further discussion, see The Open University (1981): *The Politics of Cultural Production;* Whitty, "Ideology, Politics, and Curriculum," 9–49; and Davies, "Popular Culture, Class, and Schooling," 53–108.
6. Robert Everhart, *Reading, Writing, and Resistance: Adolescence and Labor in a Junior High School* (New York: Routledge and Kegan Paul, 1983).
7. Michelle Fine, "Silencing and Nurturing Voice in an Improbable Context: Urban Adolescents in Public School," in H. A. Giroux and P. McLaren (Eds.), *Critical Pedagogy, the State, and Cultural Struggle* (New York: State University of New York Press, 1989).
8. See Peter McLaren, "'Bein' Tough': Rituals of Resistance in the Culture of Working-Class Schoolgirls," *Canadian Woman Studies* 4, 1 (1982, Fall): 20–24.
9. See Paul Willis, *Learning to Labor.*
10. See Angela McRobbie and Jenny Garber, "Girls and Subcultures," in S. Hall and T. Jefferson (Eds.), *Resistance through Rituals* (London: Hutchinson, 1980), 209–222. I am indebted throughout this section to the work of Angela McRobbie for her insights on working-class girls. See especially A. McRobbie, "Working Class Girls and the

Culture of Femininity," in Centre for Contemporary Cultural Studies Women's Group, *Women Take Issue* (London: Hutchinson, 1978).

11. William Ryan, *Blaming the Victim* (New York: Vintage Books, 1976).

12. R. Boudon, *Education—Opportunity and Social Inequality: Changing Prospects in Western Society* (New York and London: Wiley Interscience, 1974). As cited in Davies, "Popular Culture, Class, and Schooling," 91–92.

13. See Davies, "Popular Culture, Class, and Schooling," 91–92.

14. For a fuller discussion of this point, see Peter McLaren, "The Technocratic Classroom," *Ontario Public School Teachers' Federation News* (1982, April 1): 11.

15. See Peter McLaren, "Education as Myth," *Ontario Public School Teachers' Federation News* (1981, October 15): 17.

16. Paul Olson, "Methods, Interpretations, and Different Views of Aspirations," *Interchange* 17, 1 (1986): 78.

17. Noam Chomsky, "I.Q. Tests: Building Blocks for the New Class System," in B. Casin et al. (Eds.), *School and Society* (London: Routledge and Kegan Paul, 1971), 244–299, as cited in Olson, "Methods, Interpretations," 78.

18. Walter Feinberg and Jonas F. Soltis, *School and Society* (New York: Teachers College Press, 1985), 34–35.

19. This category was first developed by Giroux and expanded in his *Schooling and the Struggle for Public Life* (Minneapolis, MN: University of Minnesota Press, 1988). This section is based on Henry A. Giroux and Peter McLaren, "Teacher Education and the Politics of Engagement: The Case for Democratic Schooling," *Harvard Educational Review* 56, 3 (1986): 234–235.

20. Robert W. Connell, Dean J. Ashenden, Sandra Kessler, and Gary W. Dowsett, *Making the Difference: Schools, Families, and Social Division* (Winchester, MA: Allen and Unwin, 1982), 199.

21. David Lusted, "Why Pedagogy?" *Screen* 27, 5 (1986, September/October): 4–5.

22. Henry A. Giroux, *Schooling and the Struggle for Public Life: Critical Pedagogy in the Modern Age* (Minneapolis, MN: University of Minnesota Press, 1988), 164.

23. Sharon Welch, *A Feminist Ethic of Risk* (New York: Fortress Press; and South Hadley, MA: Bergin and Garvey Publishers, 1989).

24. Michelle Fine, "Silencing and Nurturing Voice," 26.

25. See Henry A. Giroux, "Radical Pedagogy and the Politics of Student Voice," *Interchange* 17, 1 (1986, Spring): 48–69. The three categories used in this section are taken directly from Giroux's work.

26. As quoted in Harold Rosen, "The Importance of Story," *Language Arts* 63 (1986): 234.

27. Pierre Bourdieu, "Symbolic Power," *Critique of Anthropology* 13/14 (1977, Summer): 77–85.

28. Philip Corrigan, "State Formation and Classroom Practice." Paper delivered at the Ivor Goodson Seminar, University of Western Ontario, Canada.

29. Fine, "Silencing and Nurturing Voice," 16.

30. Ibid., 18.

31. Ibid., 17.

32. See Giroux, *Schooling and the Struggle for Public Life,* 21.

33. See the discussion of "Chorus Line: Women in Production," in Tony Wilden, *The Rules Are No Game* (New York: Routledge and Kegan Paul, 1987).

34. Roland Barthes, *The Grain of the Voice: Interviews,* Trans. Richard Miller (New York: Hill, 1977), 149. As cited in Joseph Harris, "The Plural Text/The Plural Self: Roland Barthes and William Coles," *College English* 49, 2 (1987, February): 158–170.

35. The term "transformative intellectual" comes from Stanley Aronowitz and Henry A. Giroux, *Education Under Siege: The Conservative and Radical Debate Over Schooling* (South Hadley, MA: Bergin and Garvey Publishers, 1985), 40–43. See Giroux and McLaren, "Teacher Education and the Politics of Engagement," 215.

36. This section is adapted from Peter McLaren, "The Writer as Social Agent," *University of Toronto Review* 11 (1987): 24.

37. For a discussion of "dangerous memory" see Sharon D. Welch, *Communities of Resistance and Solidarity: A Feminist Theology of Liberation* (New York: Maryknoll, 1985).

PART V

Other Voices

I have added Part Five to the second edition of *Life in Schools* to reveal several important criticisms of the first edition and to clarify further the concept of critical pedagogy as I developed the idea throughout the first edition. In this part I respond to two reviews of the first edition, one by Ursula Kelly and the second by John Portelli, who have graciously permitted me to reprint their commentaries. Some readers may find it unusual for an author to reprint an extended criticism of his or her work in a new edition of the same book that was the focus of the criticism. I feel that self-criticism and criticism by others are vital to the spirit of critical pedagogy, and I believe that by sharing some criticism of my own work I am enhancing the pedagogical mssion of this volume. I am also aware that the comments by Kelly and Portelli are made in a spirit of solidarity with such a mission. Their criticisms are not mean-spirited or unfair. On the contrary, they have been undertaken in order to fill existing gaps in the project of critical pedagogy in general and, in particular, in the way I have advanced such a project in *Life in Schools*. This is not to say that I agree with all of their criticisms, or those reported by their students. I simply wish to acknowledge that they have done my project a service by drawing attention to certan fault-lines in the ongoing development of my work and that of other educators working in the field of critical pedagogy.

However, the most important reason for including Part Five in the new edition is that it provides me with a context for exploring new ideas that were only tangentially addressed in the initial volume. Since the initial publication of *Life in Schools,* I have focused to a much greater extent on the themes of multiculturalism and postmodernism. These are themes that are currently at the center of the debate over educational reform and democratic citizenship and in my estimation will be themes that will occupy educators for the foreseeable future, especially given the worsening economic and social conditions in our urban centers. Since the first publication of *Life in Schools,* I have been fortunate to have worked with progressive educators in Mexico, Argentina, Brazil, Cuba, Eastern Europe, and other parts of the world. As a result, I have a better sense of situating the struggle over conditions in our schools and in the larger society in a geopolitical perspective—one that I have tried to share in the pages that follow.

CHAPTER 10

From Text to Textuality: "Reading" McLaren's *Life in Schools**

Ursula A. Kelly
Saint Mary's University, Halifax, Nova Scotia

That the publication of *Life in Schools* and the first offering of my introductory graduate course in Critical Pedagogy coincided, I initially thought quite fortuitous. McLaren presents, through his title, the argument that *Life in Schools* is "an introduction to critical pedagogy in the foundations of education" and, through his preface, the hope that it "might prove to be not just a book about education, but an *educational book* that will promote an understanding of teaching in cultural, political and ethical terms" (p. xi).

Upon reviewing *Life in Schools* for adoption in my course, I found much that pleased me. I also experienced real emotional-theoretical difficulties, both with the presentation of the material and with the material presented. Nevertheless, seeing texts as sites of struggle, I felt the struggles I encountered with *Life in Schools* could be valuable. I felt they could make the project of critical pedagogy, itself a quagmire of struggle, more explicit, more deeply lived. Further, given my own strong responses to the book, I was interested in how the students in the course, most of whom are practicing public school teachers in and from Nova Scotia, would struggle with it. I wondered how their readings and my reading might converge and diverge.

The course to which I refer is a seminar course which I attempt to structure in ways consistent with Freirean philosophy—the "dialogical method" (Shor & Freire, 1989) in particular. We begin, in the course, with our mutual formulations of our lived histories and experiences, with a focus on our work as educators. Students struggle out their perspectives as they are challenged, denied, and/or affirmed through collegial comments and critique and through assigned readings.

---

* This article first appeared in the Boston University *Journal of Education* (Volume 173, Number 3, 1991), pp. 8–14. Reprinted with permission of the publisher and the author.

Students are also expected to lead critiques of assigned readings and encourage their own atmosphere of interrogation and critique in the seminar context.

My own responsibility is to pose critical questions and perspectives which represent, affirm, or oppose the tenets of the arguments made by the students or by the author. In this atmosphere, many "readings" are simultaneously produced: of the printed texts, of the context, and of one another. In this latter respect, as actual and perceived "authority" in the classroom, I attempt to remain as conscious as possible of the ways in which this particular relation of power impacts on readings made. I make this point to take responsibility, immediately, for the ways in which my own politics may be reinscribed in those of the students in the class. Yet, aspects of our readings, my own and the students', reflect certain shared historical configurations which work concretely in the production of common meanings.

As did I, then, students experienced *Life in Schools* as provocative, contentious, inspiring, elating, frustrating, and, in the final analysis, a "must read" for teacher workers in North American public schools. However, in no case was any of these emotions exclusive. Students, regardless of their predominant response to *Life in Schools*, did experience the text as problematic. Their articulations of their struggles with *Life in Schools*, as partial and contradictory as they must necessarily be, are rich data for the project of critique as promoted by critical pedagogues.

For the purposes of this paper, I have chosen to focus specifically on the "resistant readers" (Fetterley, 1978), particularly those whose readings challenge McLaren's interpellation of their subjectivities through nation and gender. I, like my students, believe these readings represent fundamental contradictions between the project of *Life in Schools* and the projects (or, at least two of them) of critical pedagogy; to contextualize, to place experience in the politics of its history; and to resist the reproduction of social inequalities, in this case, those surrounding gender. In each of these senses, I will argue, as did many of the students, that McLaren's book in some ways belies his project, leaving both the book and the project of critical pedagogy in need of transformative critique.

These resistant readings of *Life in Schools* are offered here in the spirit of that transformative critique and hope which McLaren himself expresses. These readings are also offered as political moments in the "circuits of culture" (Johnson, 1983, p. 26), moments which are, at once, affirming and disrupting. Ultimately, the readings are aimed at promoting "the possibility of transforming tradition," the intellectual tradition on which both my course and McLaren's book draw.

STRUGGLING WITH "PLACE"

> The critical educator endorses theories that are, first and foremost, *dialectical*. . . . Dialectical theory attempts to tease out the histories and relations of accepted meanings and appearances, tracing interactions from the context to the part, from the system inward to the event. (McLaren, 1989, p. 166)

While McLaren's book is used as an introductory text in my co[...] pedagogy, it does not constitute the introductory readings of the c[...] after detailed discussions with students about what they see as crucial p[...] in schooling and pedagogy, I usually proceed with shorter introductory articles which raise similar issues in the context of the tradition of critical pedagogy. In this initial section of the course, we often read and discuss writings by Maxine Greene (1986), Ira Shor (1987), Roger Simon (1983, 1987), William Bigelow (1990), Jane Gaskell and colleagues (1988), Linda Briskin (1990), John Smyth (1989), myself (Kelly, 1990), and others. I make this point in order to emphasize that, by the time students encounter McLaren's book, they have already formu-lated a partial set of assumptions about what critical pedagogy is and what it should be about. These assumptions they take into their readings of *Life in Schools*.

I believe it is altogether likely that, even without such a sketchy background as these readings provide in the foundations of critical pedagogy, these mainly Nova Scotia students would still have difficulty accepting two aspects of McLaren's book: the relevance and applicability to their work lives of the inner-city school journal accounts; and the blendng of data collected in Central Canada into the socio-historical context of the United States.

The resistance to acceptance of the relevance and applicability of the inner-city teaching accounts, quite strong in the initial responses to the book, is usually fairly quickly overcome as denial turns to recognition and then to attempts at change. This teacher's comment is fairly representative:

> As I began to read Peter McLaren's diary entries, I first felt a general
> feeling of his days as being unbelievable. To me, they were very removed
> from my own experiences at the junior high level in rural Nova Scotia.
> Never having experienced teaching in an inner city school as he describes,
> I was completely taken aback by his day-to-day entries. However, the
> more I read, the more I could see that although his situation was a far
> cry from any of my experiences, there are many things that are common,
> although more blatant in his case. . . . The incidents of violence, sexism
> and racism he writes about are in our schools, too. (Karen O'Toole, 1990)
> [Unpublished comment by Kelly's student.]

This response, as well, indicates the extent to which McLaren's text works to disrupt teachers' understandings of their own worker contexts and the social realities of their own lives and those of their students.

However, the resistance to the "blending" of Canadian data and American context, if anything, intensifies as students continue to reflect on their reading of *Life in Schools*.

> Everywhere we turn, in newspapers, on television, in movies, magazines,
> in textbooks, we [Canadians] are expected to make sense of our experi-
> ences through American interpretations. As a former(?) Canadian, I
> would have expected Peter McLaren to understand this, especially given
> what he says about culture and history. There is a real hypocrisy here.

It angers and disappoints me. (Anonymous) [Unpublished comment by Kelly's student.]

I disliked the fact that McLaren assumed that statistics about American society and its history could translate directly to Canadian culture. . . . The question in the back of my mind about this book is "did McLaren write this American/Canadian hybrid to sell more copies or to get the book published?" McLaren states that "the appropriateness of incorporating my Canadian journal in this volume has been favorably gauged by reactions I have received from audiences in the United States" (p. 26). One wonders why McLaren did not check this "appropriateness" out with the reading audience north of the border. Or maybe we just are not the intended reading audience. I do grant McLaren that many social problems are endemic to both cultures, especially in inner city schools, but I find it curious in a book about empowering members of a society and recognizing particular backgrounds and realities, that the Canadian Jane-Finch Corridor schooling experience is only validated through an American perspective. (Maxine Evans, 1990) [Unpublished comment by Kelly's student.]

I have elsewhere discussed the importance of "place" as a dimension of social relations as they are lived out in Canada. I have argued: "If, in the classroom, we are to take seriously people's life experiences, the personal and social histories out of which these experiences come must be where we begin . . . [with] what it means, socially, historically, culturally, to be 'here'" (Kelly, 1990, p. 40). When these students resist McLaren's use of data gathered in inner-city Toronto schools and then couched in the socio-historical context of the United States, I see this not as a misguided protectionism but, rather, as a refusal to accept what they have come to see as inappropriate ethnography and displaced historicism.

While some of this resistance comes out of aspects of subjectivities formed through dominant discourses of Canadian nationalism and regionalism, still more of it, I believe, comes from a growing radicalism of the sort formed through exposure to the objectives of critical pedagogy. It is not a denial of the "perilous course of history" (p. 3) which McLaren sees in contemporary American life, nor of the "frontiers of despair" (p. 33) he names as the Canadian Jane-Finch Corridor. Nor is it even a denial of the global interconnectedness of the two. It is, however, a serious challenge to McLaren to be faithful to the situated, critical pedagogy he declares is so desperately needed in both these contexts.

STRUGGLING WITH GENDER

Within such critical spaces, [the critical teacher] must excavate the "subjugated knowledges" of those who have been marginalized and disaffected, whose histories of suffering and hope have rarely been made public. (McLaren, 1989, p. 241)

The tradition of critical pedagogy has been criticized elsewhere for its insufficient attention to feminist critiques of knowledge, power, and schooling (Brookes and Kelly, 1989; Ellsworth, 1989; Lewis and Simon, 1986; Maher, 1987). Indeed, more recent writings attempt to redress the historical male bias of this tradition (Giroux, 1991; McLaren, 1989, 1991; Shor, 1990; Simon, in press; Weiler, 1988). Early in my course, students question the differences between a critical pedagogy and a feminist pedagogy. Through readings which sensitize them to questions of race, class, and gender, they begin to recognize bias, both in themselves and in the texts. *Life in Schools* is no exception [as these unpublished comments from my students show].

When I read the preface to McLaren's book, I noticed he mentioned many of the writers we had previously looked at through articles, et cetera. Having especially enjoyed the articles written by women, I was glad to see their names show up here. Women like Maxine Greene and Jane Gaskell had been important to McLaren, too! When I got to Chapter Seven and saw that he mentioned all male critical educators, I wondered what had happened. Were their works not that important after all? Or was McLaren's own male bias showing through? (Anonymous)

Perhaps McLaren feels that he and men like him must lead. Indeed, in Chapter Seven, "Critical Educators: Some Examples", he makes reference only to men. Work by women, such as Michelle Fine and Maxine Greene, is briefly mentioned elsewhere but they don't rate the special status of the men nor is their work listed in recommended reading. (Shirley Hambrick, 1991)

In many ways, I relived my own working class life as a student, both in McLaren's "front line" experience in the school and in his theory and analysis. It is hard to imagine this man to be middle-class because of the sensitivity he gives to working-class experience. My best gauge for this is in not being offended by anything he said about us. . . . . A couple of times he referred to women by how attractive they were—so nobody's perfect, and he may have had time to reflect on this sexist behavior since writing the book. (Muriel Houston, 1991)

Other students were upset with the effect of objectification by the male "voice" in McLaren's analysis of working-class girls in his classes in the Jane-Finch Corridor. Many students insisted that, while gender analysis is clearly present in parts of *Life in Schools,* the gendered perspective of the researcher is evident in the research. This criticism, I agree, points, in particular, to a gaping hole in the "Bein' Tough: Bein' Female" essay in Chapter Eight [now Chapter 6] of the book.

CELEBRATING THE STRUGGLE

There is no mediation of text, of course, which is a mediation of the text, per se, the text, only. In reading McLaren's *Life in Schools,* students are, at once, reading the social structures, their relationships to schooling, and (through reflecting on their own lived experiences) their own role in reproducing these structures. They are also reflecting on the ways in which these structures are reproduced in them. In these senses, I would argue for McLaren's book as being the most positively disruptive and flawed text I've yet used in Critical Pedagogy. Invariably, comments of this sort are made by students:

> I have been aware for some time that one does not "pull oneself up by one's bootstraps," but that is just the beginning of what I now consider to be a lifetime task of searching my white, middle-class soul, embedded as it is in liberal-humanist assumptions. . . . I find, personally, it is difficult to look at self. McLaren, I believe, has done an admirable job in this regard. I believe I have to be very clear as to what a transformative vision of society means for me in terms of the power (which I do not always experience myself as having) relative to many others, that I have to give up. I am feeling very much alone and agitated with what I am learning in the area of feminist and critical pedagogy and theories, and I know it will be necessary to search out others in order to live with some of the resulting ambiguities and tensions. (Diane Furnell, 1991) [Unpublished comment by my student.]

I mentioned earlier that, initially, I thought it quite fortuitous that McLaren's book was published the same year my course in Critical Pedagogy was first taught. I still feel that way. Despite the problems I and my students encounter in our mediations of the book, we agree that it is, as McLaren hoped, an educational book. Through provocation, through identification, through omission, and through clearly articulated and well-written theory, *Life in Schools* makes possible the very critique it suggests is a healthy and vital ingredient to good teaching. Part of that project is accomplished, ironically, by the book's partial undermining of its own project. That students can see this, name this, and demand more is exciting testimony of what Simon (1987) calls a "pedagogy of possibility."

REFERENCES

Bigelow, W. (1990). Inside the classroom: Social vision and critical pedagogy. *Teachers College Record, 91*(3), 437–446.

Briskin, L. (1990). *Feminist pedagogy: Teaching and learning liberation.* Ottawa: CRIAW/ICREF.

Brookes, A. L. and Kelly, U. A. (1989). Writing pedagogy: A dialogue of hope. *Journal of Education, 171*(2), 117–131.

Ellsworth, E. (1989). Why doesn't this feel empowering? Working through the repressive myths of critical pedagogy. *Harvard Educational Review, 59*(3), 297–324.

Fetterley, J. (1978). *The resisting reader: A feminist approach to American fiction.* Bloomington: Indiana University Press.

Gaskell, J., Novogrodsky, M., and McLaren, A. (1988). *Claiming an education: Feminism and Canadian schools.* Toronto: Garamond Press.

Giroux, H. A. (1991). Modernism, postmodernism and feminism: Rethinking the boundaries of educational discourse. In H. A. Giroux (Ed.), *Postmodernism, feminism and cultural politics: Redrawing educational boundaries* (pp. 1–59). Albany: SUNY Press.

Greene, M. (1986). In search of a critical pedagogy. *Harvard Educational Review, 56*(4), 427–441.

Johnson, R. (1983). What is cultural studies anyway? *Anglistica, 26*(1–2), 7–81.

Kelly, U. A. (1990). "On the edge of the eastern ocean": Teaching, marginality and voice. In D. Henley and J. Young (Eds.), *Canadian perspectives on critical pedagogy* (Canadian Critical Pedagogy Network Occasional Monograph No. 1). Winnipeg: University of Manitoba.

Lewis, M., and Simon, R. I. (1986). A discourse not intended for her: Learning and teaching within patriarchy. *Harvard Educational Review, 56*(4), 457–472.

Maher, F. (1987). Toward a richer theory of feminist pedagogy: A comparison of "liberation" and "gender" models for teaching and learning. *Journal of Education, 169*(3), 91–100.

McLaren, P. (1989). *Life in schools: An introduction to critical pedagogy in the foundations of education.* Toronto: Irwin.

McLaren, P. (1991). Schooling the postmodern body: Critical pedagogy and the politics of enfleshment. In H. A. Giroux (Ed.), *Postmodernism, feminism, and cultural politics: Redrawing educational boundaries* (pp. 144–173). Albany: State University of New York Press.

Shor, I. (Ed.). (1987). *Freire for the classroom: A sourcebook for liberatory teaching.* Portsmouth: Boynton/Cook.

Shor, I. (1990). Liberation education: Interview with Ira Shor. *Language Arts, 67*(4), 342–352.

Simon, R. I. (1983). Critical pedagogy. *International Encyclopedia of Education, 2,* 1119–1120.

Simon, R. I. (1987). Empowerment as a pedagogy of possibility. *Language Arts, 64*(4), 370–382.

Simon, R. I. 1992. *Teaching against the grain.* South Hadley, MA: Bergin and Garvey.

Smyth, J. (1989). A critical pedagogy of classroom practice. *Journal of Curriculum Studies, 21*(6), 483–502.

Weiler, K. (1988). *Women teaching for change: Gender, class and power.* South Hadley, MA: Bergin and Garvey.

CHAPTER 11

From Text to Textuality: Using McLaren's *Life in Schools* *

John P. Portelli
Mount Saint Vincent University, Halifax, Nova Scotia

In a very general sense this paper is an analytical reflection on some aspects of a graduate seminar called "Knowledge and the Curriculum," which I have conducted every year during the last four years. It is a required foundations course for teachers in the graduate program in elementary education. This paper concerns some of the contradictions and tensions the teachers and I have encountered/experienced, as well as the possibilities and hope that have emerged. It concerns the "exquisite and awful tension" (Farber, 1991, p. 78) that teachers face, and the painful yet possibly rewarding process of resolving such tension. In a more specific sense, the paper focuses on why I included Peter McLaren's book *Life in Schools* (1989) as a required reading, and how the teachers reacted to the book. My contention is that, notwithstanding the book's limitations (Karp, 1991; Kelly, 1991; Novack, 1989; Portelli, 1991; Werner, 1989), it has helped bring us closer to achieving the purpose of the seminar. That is, it has helped to provide a foundation for investigating curriculum issues that arise from the school context by critically discussing selected curriculum issues from a philosophical and socio-political aspect. My general aim, as I state it in the outline of the seminar, is to encourage the teachers to formulate or at least start formulating their views about these issues, with the hope that this will help them reexamine their classroom practice and school context and act accordingly.

Before focusing on the reasons why I selected *Life in Schools* as a required text and the teachers' reactions to it, I will identify some issues and concerns I have had to struggle with either prior to or while conducting this seminar. I hope this will provide a better context to the rest of this paper.

---

* This article first appeared in the Boston University *Journal of Education* (Volume 173, Number 3, 1991), pp. 15–27. Reprinted with permission of the publisher and the author.

THE CONTEXT: THE ROOTS OF THE STRUGGLE

I became interested in curriculum almost by chance. Or perhaps not, because I was an elementary school teacher for a while. At any rate, some time in October of 1977, while I was doing graduate work in philosophy at McGill University, Montreal, I read in a newspaper about the rapid educational changes at the tertiary level that were demanded by the government of Malta (I was born and lived in Malta until August 1977). These changes were referred to as "radical *curriculum* changes." Almost overnight the University of Malta was expected to function on new principles: students became "worker-students," while "usefulness" became the catch-word. As a result the Faculties of Arts and Sciences and the Faculty of Theology were closed notwithstanding the opposition from students and faculty. This event made me inquire into the nature of the concept "curriculum" as well as ethical justifications of plausible curriculum perspectives or visions. This became my project for the next five years or so. Since my background was primarily in mainstream analytic philosophy, I was encouraged to read in the area of curriculum theory. My first surprise was the discovery that the question of justification, ultimately a crucial ethical question, was almost completely disregarded. In other words, I discovered that the majority of the work in curriculum was almost exclusively focusing on matters of curriculum construction and implementation, that is on matters of *how* rather than *why*. And so I asked: But are we interested in a plausible curriculum perspective or vision? Or are we "submerged in the social reality that prevails" (Greene, 1973)—a technocratic reality that makes us not care? Nonetheless I persisted in my philosophical investigation of the nature of curriculum and philosophical approaches to the question of justification.

Conducting "Knowledge and the Curriculum" has positively forced me to attempt to combine issues in philosophy of education with issues in sociology of education, although for a while the two areas have been kept separate even when both focused on the curriculum. Although when venturing this route I was initially almost fearful, I now believe that the two aspects are not necessarily in opposition. Questions of meaning and justification ultimately are not isolated from questions about power relations. Was not Aristotle making a similar point by including his major thought on education in *The Politics*? And is not the same point reflected in Plato's work given that some of his major concerns on education are discussed in *The Republic*? Can we, then, separate education from power relations? Philip Steedman (1988) contends:

> Aristotle knew that "What should be taught?" is a question that epistemology cannot answer but rather must find its answer in politics. Contemporary curriculum theory has returned to this truth. It is one which should not be feared. The schools are sites of personal creation and development, on the one hand, and social reproduction on the other. It is fitting that democratic people understand that both what their children learn and how they learn it must involve the most subtle and powerful questions of legitimation. To debate such issues is not to betray a heritage, but rather to act democratically. (p. 135)

A similar plea was made by Jane R. Martin a decade ago when she argued that a new paradigm of liberal education is needed—one that goes beyond the limitations of basing curriculum issues solely on an epistemological theory. Martin (1981) refers to the older approach as an ivory tower view.

But will not teachers refer to all of this as ivory tower talk? Will they be interested in discussing different conceptions of curriculum and knowledge? And conflicting approaches to the justification of the curriculum? And what about social class, race, and gender issues in the curriculum? And the control of the curriculum? Can I argue that the relevance of these issues will become obvious if they really come to understand what the issues imply? Or must I now, having selected the subject matter, simply make it interesting? And Dewey's reply that he knows of "no more demoralizing doctrine" than this (Dewey, 1913, p. 23) haunts me.

Without meaning to sound insensitive to the needs of teachers, I do have to admit that one of the problems I face in the beginning stages of a foundations course is how to reduce or diminish some of the anxieties and negative impressions that teachers have about foundations courses. Initially, most teachers do come with what Susan Ohanian (1985) refers to as a "stir-and-serve" attitude toward teaching. They do expect professors to give them solutions to their daily, practical concerns. As the group gathers for the first time the tense and almost anguished looks seem to cry out: How will this help me in my practice? What has this to do with my classroom? Will I really be a better teacher after taking this required course? Will it not be better for us to take another course in some subject area? The concern of the teachers about the theory–practice dichotomy becomes once again a concern for me: Will I be able to show the difference between an impossible one-to-one relationship between theory and practice and a healthier role of theory, i.e., "to consciously question (the practical) interrupting the predictable with analyses that point to other possibilities" and "to restore the contemplative moment in which we interrupt our taken-for-granted understandings . . . and ask again the basic questions practical activity silences" (Pinar and Grumet, 1988)? At least initially, most teachers still expect a "skills-related approach" even though it has "repeatedly been shown to be educationally bankrupt" (Smyth, 1989, p. 484). My intention is not to criticize teachers. To do so in this instance would be unfair, for our culture promotes "the myth that . . . teaching is or should be detached, neutral, objectivist and a value-free activity" (Smyth, 1989, p. 484). Teachers are still either influenced by or put in situations wherein they are made (usually by administrative personnel) to feel inadequate unless they emphasize "the technical as distinct from the intellectual nature of the pedagogical enterprise" (Smyth, 1989, p. 499). Of course, I do feel morally obliged to seriously consider the day-to-day context in which teachers have to survive. And should I not heed Kierkegaard's advice that "instruction begins when you, the teacher, learn from the learner, put yourself in his (her) place so that you may understand what he (she) understands and in the way he (she) understands it" (quoted in Greene, 1967)? Yet, at the same time, I feel equally morally obliged to resist the emphasis that has been put on "the economical rationalization of educational systems, with the requirements that teachers attend to the business management canons of "standardization," "efficiency," and "effectiveness"—

canons that provide "a form of ideological control" (Smyth, 1987b, p. 161) and encourage, albeit implicitly, a deskilling of teachers and a silencing of the teacher's voice. Resisting this view implies "rejecting the instrumentalist transmission view of education in which experts determine content which is then relayed to passive students" (Smyth, 1987b, p. 164). So, how do I encourage them to look at the theoretical issues without silencing them, since "an education that creates silence is not an education" (Simon, 1987, p. 375)? Or is this merely risking "ahistorical and depoliticized abstractions" (Ellsworth, 1989, p. 307)? And in order to take control of our teaching don't we need to go beyond what we have taken for granted?

INTERMEZZO: A RATIONALE

Why did I select this book as a required reading? I will offer three reasons.

1. Teachers need to be aware of and to discuss ideological stances other than that which reflects mainstream ideology in education— namely, a predominantly conservative perspective which, among other things, assumes the following:
   • that formal schooling is the best way to achieve educational aims;
   • that if we introduce new programs and fix minor things here and there, then schools will be able to achieve their educational aims in a democracy;
   • that if students do not succeed, it is usually their fault—they are either not able or lazy;
   • that schooling offers equal opportunity to all;
   • that teachers ought to present themselves as omniscient—if they do not, then they should not be teaching;
   • that teachers ought not to introduce controversial issues such as those dealing with power relations, and should take a neutral stance if such issues do arise;
   • that there is and ought to be a real correspondence between the formally prescribed curriculum and the actual curriculum.
   Life in Schools provides a healthy contrast by outlining the assumptions of critical pedagogy, highlighting issues related to power relations in education (for example, race, gender, and social class issues), and inviting us to discuss them openly.
2. The combination of a journal about real life in schools in conjunction with a clear explication of a theoretical framework makes it easier to show the need for basing our educational practice in theory. It also helps encourage the development of "grounded theories." In other words, *Life in Schools* provides an opportunity to understand and see the practical relevance of engaging in the kind of questions raised in the foundations of education.

3. McLaren, in his own analysis of his teaching experiences, provides a very good example of someone who has formed a theoretical framework based on critical pedagogy and who engages in self-criticism—which, in my view, is crucial if one aims to improve one's practice. McLaren is not afraid to reflect critically and publicly on his earlier naivete. And this contrasts with the implications of either of the following two extremes: (a) an extreme but popular subjectivist view in education that encourages or implies a laissez-faire attitude in teaching—this is what Henry Giroux (1988b) refers to as "the free-floating antifoundationalism" and Rachel Sharp and Anthony Greene label "an extreme form of subjective idealism where the external objective world is merely a constitution of the creative consciousness, the subject-object dualism disappears in the triumph of the constituting subject" (quoted by Giroux 1988c, p. 26); and (b) a conservative attitude toward "professionalism" in education which implies that the teacher, at face value, is always right and therefore it is *im*proper to raise critical questions about teaching because these kind of questions raise problems, identify contradictions and possible hidden agendas, and are divisive.

"LASCIATE OGNI SPERANZA VOI CHI ENTRATE"?

In the concluding chapter of *Popular Culture, Education and Everyday Life,* Giroux and Roger Simon (1989) warn us against hopelessness:

> Sometimes when students and teachers engage in a critique of existing social practices or forms of knowledge, a feeling of powerlessness comes over the group. Doing critical pedagogy can turn an educational setting into a council of despair. How can we guard against the production of hopelessness when taking up an agenda of critique and social analysis? Given all the limitations of teaching and schooling, how can we effectively empower people?
>
> Working with students to make clear the social contradictions we all live is an important aspect of critical pedagogical practice. However, will not raising contradictions in students' lives simply threaten them? Will not pointing to social contradictions lead to cynicism and despair? Furthermore, if the value of understanding ideology is to stress that what is often taken as natural and inevitable is historically constructed and morally regulated, will not ideology critique destabilize identity and paralyse action? If we start questioning the given of everyday life, won't this simply be overwhelming? (1989, p. 232)

And Giroux (1988a) insists that "hope is very important . . . we have to be able to dream . . . we can't always operate in the logic of resistance. We must be able to speak the language of possibility as well" (p. 100). While *Life in Schools* has enabled most of the teachers to examine seriously the assumptions that under-lie their own teaching—a major aim of the book—has it really inspired hope? It surely evoked several mixed feelings: anger (at McLaren, the kids, and the system), sadness, admiration for McLaren, despair, guilt, amusement, depression, shock, helplessness, frustration, disbelief, and hope. For a few the book did not inspire hope. Surely the teacher who found McLaren at times somewhat patroniz-ing and entitled her reaction-analysis to the book "*Lasciate ogni speranza voi chi entrate,*" that is "Abandon all hope you who enter" (a quote from Dante's *Inferno,* Canto 3), found no hope at all. And I was left uttering to myself Dante's own reply to the narrator: "Teacher, for me their meaning [that is, of the words quoted] is too hard." However, the majority of the teachers' reactions progressed from anger and despair to hope and possibilities. And this time I am reminded of the concluding verses of Dante's *Inferno*:

> My guide and I took that dark path in order to return to the world of light, and without thought of any rest we climbed, he first and I second, until, through a round opening, I saw the beautiful things that the sky holds; and we came out from there to look again at the stars.

Yet, our process, like Dante's, was not easy. The following are some of the conflicting views the teachers expressed in the discussion as documented in their written reactions to the book.[1]

Truthfulness? Fabrication?

SHIRLEY: There is the question to which extent the situations he describes are an accurate account of the actual events. I am puzzled with his ability to recall detail. McLaren's choice of words throughout the book is very powerful and their actual source should not go unquestioned in my view.

CAROLYN: There is a rumour the diary is untrue—for whom the account might seem false is unclear, but Harold Entwistle notes of school staff-room ". . . rednecks, racists, sexists and chauvinists are not unknown, nor are practitioners who expect nothing of children. . . ." So con-ceivably there are even myopic teachers, if it is they who regard the diary as a fabrication.

JILL: We have wondered how McLaren could have recorded his entries with such detail. Each anecdote captures the feeling (of humour, hope-lessness, frustration, anger, despair) that he wishes to convey. When I grab a moment during the day or sit down at the end of a school day I find it difficult to record an incident with any degree of description or feeling. McLaren was not only a teacher, he was a writer.

WENDY: I try to envision myself in McLaren's world. It was not a world where he could write about himself as being a hero. I find a lot of educa-tional documents on classroom activities are always written with the teacher appearing, at times, as a "superhero"! McLaren appears to write the *facts* and *true* happenings in his classroom, without adding sugar and spice. His daily writing of the accounts makes the point clear that this type of life does exist. McLaren recognizes that the lives of his students are FAR removed from the formal curriculum he thought he should teach. I appreciate his honesty to write the true story.

CONNIE: I found McLaren's book to be a strong statement about the inherent inequalities in society, and especially in schools. His diary of his experiences [does] not make for a pleasant read; they make many feel uncomfortable. I do not feel that he used sensationalism to promote his book or his point of view. . . . He feels very strongly that this social dilemma and its effect on children and their future lives is so debilitating, that it takes powerful, but REAL images to convince, or inform the people who may make the difference. This problem requires action by all participants or actors if the vicious and endless cycle . . . is to be halted or redirected.

Too Negative?

CAROLE: McLaren's method of describing his experiences in his diary has served to shock the reader into an awareness of the problem. A part of his purpose in writing the diary was to make others aware of the severity of the problem. He also states he hopes to promote change by encouraging people "to confront structures of oppression." I feel that he may have gone too far in his attempts to point out the difficulties he encountered. The result could be that his readers feel despair and see no hope for change. It is difficult to see even a glimpse of hope for these children and their families. I can imagine people reading the diary and assuming that these children are incorrigible, since he tried everything and the children did not appear to respond. If he had included some of his successes (which I am sure he had judging from the attachment that some of the children and parents had for him), the readers of his diary might see these children in a more positive light.

MARIE: I believe he *had* to record these incidents as he did in order to make an impact with readers, authorities and society. If he had told too much, his diary would have lost some of the focus. By "too much" I mean if he had related his teaching methodologies, reactions to reactions, and follow-up procedures, we would be tempted to evaluate the extended circumstances and lose focus of the initial events. When experiences are written down, *dated,* and recorded day after day, a clear, definite message is sent. A pattern emerges. Relationships can be seen, connections can be made.

BEV: I particularly enjoyed when he wrote about actual learning activities and the response of the students to them. I found there were not enough of these kinds of entries.

CAROLYN: A "safer" account could not as vividly depict the plight of these students.

Not Here in Nova Scotia or Canada!? This Is for the Yankees!?

JOANNE: His experiences are far removed from my own both as a student and a teacher in rural Nova Scotia, relatively untroubled by racial prejudice and extreme poverty.

CAROL: I think McLaren's concerns are more pertinent to the situation in the U.S. I feel that in Canada, especially in Nova Scotia, we have come a long way towards addressing some major problems in philosophy (is this naive of me?). The Whole Language movement and those who have promoted it deserve a great deal of credit. I feel we, as teachers, are taking back the power, and passing it on to the students. I believe this is part of the feminization of our society. Unfortunately, the success of Operation Desert Storm and the dawn of President Bush's New World Order are going to slow down this process in the U.S. and give the prevailing technocratic paradigm some fuel to sustain it. I think we are going to see a growth in the gap between what is happening in the U.S. and what is happening in Canada.

CAROLYN: It was a relief to have you point out, at the outset, that the content and context of the diary are not peculiar to a particular locality or country. While you note there are differences between teaching in the U.S. and Canada, you undoubtedly realize that Canadians, generally, prefer to believe that accounts of events occurring in American schools and society could not, or would not, happen in Canada so they are often inclined toward self-congratulatory smugness. Unfortunately, events and studies in our own city, suburbs and province indicate the opposite. Subsequent reading of your diary gives one cause to ponder and reflect upon the similarities between the two countries lest back-patting become a basic in the divine Beaver Pelt Curriculum.
[From a reaction written in letter form to McLaren]

What About Sexism and Patriarchy?

JULIE: I believe that he allowed a great deal of sexism to exist within his classroom. Much of his writing is related to males and their problems. He does not allow for any differences related to gender. It is quite likely that the females in his room were receiving very different messages from the curriculum. On more than one occasion, their oppression appeared to be linked as much to gender as any other thing. How often did he inadvertently allow girls to be put down by their male peers? He really didn't understand that to be poor and female is not easy. I don't recall any instances where he purposely sought out experiences related to females. Perhaps as the father of a young daughter, he is not able to look beyond how he feels females should act and be treated. Perhaps being poor and being feminine are not compatible!

LINDA: I wonder if a feminist researcher would have named patriarchy as one of the major concepts. While McLaren gives reference to it, he does not NAME it the way he names culture and class. There is a difference. Nevertheless, his research into the educational system does encourage thinking that ought to make a difference. It is up to the reader however to do that thinking.

Desertion!? Chickened Out!? Betrayal!?

JILL: McLaren ends his diary saying "The battle to save our children will never be won as long as we sit back comfortably and let history take its course instead of actively taking part in creating history." I wonder if McLaren can be considered to be taking an active role or is he simply asking others to do so. He left the system and became a recorder of events, pointing out problems but no longer participating in trying out solutions. He was drained and frustrated *but* he was helping in a small way in his own practice. Isn't that important? It is better to be involved and work for change in the situation than to withdraw and blame others. If we all take on the responsibility for making the small changes we are capable of then could we not change the system slowly from within rather than looking for outside intervention and change from the top down. The parents in the Jane-Finch Corridor were beginning to organize and to fight for their children's rights. Couldn't McLaren have helped them by offering his strengths and knowledge? We are reading the words he wrote but what impact will this have on our practices? We have to personally make the decision to make changes.

In a way I feel McLaren has failed his kids. He left them, left the daily struggle and although he became active on another level, by writing his books, he is no longer an active participant in his own cause. Instead of being a big part of a smaller struggle he has become a small part of a huge struggle. Which is more effective?

BEV: I can see how McLaren's decision to go back to graduate school came about. It wasn't just his day to day frustrations with the system, but rather his concern with the bandaid approach to the problem rather than a complete first-aid treatment. I think he felt there had to be a better way to educate his kids. He wanted to be a part of the cure, rather than the cover-up.

NORMA: In consideration of what he began to accomplish regarding his students, the community, and in reflecting upon his own values and assumptions in education, I find it surprising that he chose to leave the school to embark upon graduate studies in order to do research and possibly effect change from "outside the system." I wonder if McLaren ever really let go of his middle class values as they emerged in his teaching experience in the inner city schools (if this is possible). I also wonder if McLaren suffered from "burn out" and took an opportunity to escape. Regardless of his motives, his writing caused reflection on my part, on many issues in my own teaching experience and in my own education.

Where Are the Practical Suggestions?
No, Don't Reproduce His Moral Superiority?

JILL: I find I am feeling a little frustrated. It seems the advocates of radical education are very good at pointing out where our educational system is failing and that changes need to be made. *But* there don't seem to be any practical suggestions as to *how* these changes are to be implemented. It sounds very simple to say: "Begin with your own practice." But it is not that easy.

CAROL: We spent a lot of time during our previous two courses discussing the idea of "voice." Everyone writes with his own voice. I don't like McLaren's. He sounds like he is addressing us from the heights of moral superiority. Take this statement, for example: ". . . it is reasonable to argue that education programs are designed to create individuals who operate in the interests of the state, whose social function is primarily to sustain and legitimate the status quo." I, as an educator, take exception to that statement. I don't feel the programs in my school reflect this at all. [And later on she concludes:] . . . I don't disagree with McLaren as I thought, but I definitely don't like his tone.

Empowerment? Hope?

JILL: I believe *Life in Schools* is an important book as it has caused me to think, to examine issues that are relevant to education today. . . .

I am beginning to believe that teacher education is crucial and action is necessary. I was happily cocooned in my classroom, secure in the knowledge that I was a "good" teacher and I loved my job. When school politics rocked my world my feeling was "this will pass," or "it's not my concern," or "really, what can I do?" I am being forced to see that I can do something—indeed I am doing something. I am becoming aware, I am asking questions and I am changing the way I view my practise. Through the readings and the class discussions I am being challenged and supported in my beliefs. I am feeling overwhelmed but also alive and important. I can make a difference. This is the impact that McLaren's book has had on me.

MARIE: After I read Chapters 1, 4, 5 and 6 I felt quite low and wondered: Do we as teachers do anything right? We impose curriculum, we impose our views, whether hidden or explicit; we don't respect the individual culture and deep feelings of others. Then I read Giroux. I'm glad I did. We do *some* things right.

BEV: The diary made me more aware of the terrible inequalities of educational systems and how the poverty cycle is perpetuated. He brought out the part politics and economics play in this cycle, too. More important, he made me realize the cycle won't be broken until a lot more affirmative action is taken such as teachers respecting the disadvantaged students as individuals with potential and different values, greater social planning and smaller class sizes.

MABEL: McLaren's diary has opened yet another avenue in my teaching career. It has made me realize how destructive our culture can sometimes be to our children.

BETH: Why has it taken 20 years of practice for me to discover that schools merely perpetuate the myth that education and hard work will create an equality of opportunity?

JULIE: Since first reading his journal during my Christmas vacation, I couldn't help but think he was a sensationalist trying to justify his own shortcomings in the classroom. I also accused him of trying to make a quick buck by only describing every negative and demeaning experience he ever had within his teaching career in the public school system. In fact, I was angry! I believed he was exploiting the students he had taught. What I suppose affected me the most was my final admission that what he said was true and what he really wanted to do is make me angry enough to think about what schooling does and does not do for the underprivileged and impoverished in our country. I was not naive enough to deny the existence of these schools, I just didn't think about them in terms of a critical pedagogy. How could I be so middle-class?

So, Shall We Hide and Forget?

LORNA: When I understood what his real purpose was I realized he was attempting to make his audience confront the hard realities of what our society is very good at hiding. Many students are disadvantaged in the most unjust ways. We can take a hard look at this and strive for change, or view it as sensationalism and sweep it under the carpet along with the other unpleasant aspects of modern day society.

HAVE WE REALLY SEEN "THE BEAUTIFUL THINGS THAT THE SKY HOLDS"?

The answer to this question inevitably depends on one's conception of "the beautiful things." Since as Ursula Kelly (1991) has clearly reminded us, the notion of struggle is crucial to critical pedagogy, "itself a quagmire of struggle," the voices of the teachers ought to indicate some progress toward the realization of this project. Amy Gutmann (1990) has observed that competing philosophies try "to *dissolve*" the conflicts between individual freedom and civic virtue by offering us strong philosophical solutions and as a result we disregard "the political problems" that arise from such tensions. And she wonders whether "the most distinctive feature of a democratic theory of education is its *simultaneous* refusal to dissolve these tensions philosophically and its insistence on finding a principled, rather than simply a pragmatic, way of living with the tensions" (p. 8). And in a sense, Gutmann's position reminds me of "the tragic sense of education" that Nicholas Burbules (1990) offers us in order to be able "to continue our efforts without deceiving ourselves about the complications and contradictions inherent in the endeavour" (p. 478)—an endeavor that of its very nature reflects "the inseparability of success and failure" (p. 469). Faced with such tensions and the realization of them, some of the teachers, perhaps even more than I am able to recognize, have moved, to use Smyth's framework (1987a), beyond describing and informing to confronting and reconstructing:

LYNN: Although I had, what I thought to be, a good theoretical grounding in "holistic learning" and considered myself a learner-centered teacher interested in "empowering" students, I would have to admit that I had, what I now consider to be, a limited sense of the political nature of education. I had a personal sense of the importance of "empowering" students to negotiate a curriculum in a personally meaningful way. What Kathleen Weiler, Freire and McLaren, in particular, are making me examine are new meanings to the term "empowerment." As I continue to read I feel like I've been living without critical consciousness of the politics of schooling. That's a frightening revelation. . . . It makes me wonder why I have never been aware of these authors and their ideas before! They certainly were not required reading in any previous education courses. Nor were they available in the reading material of any staffroom I've been privy to! . . . The toughest part of all this exploration is knowing that I cannot go back to teaching with these new beliefs and not teach differently. Yet only I can find my own way to interpret how this can be done. I'm both excited about the possibilities and overwhelmed by the realities that face me.

Is this not part of the possibilities the limitless sky can offer?[2]

NOTES

1. These selections represent a sample representation, though quite a wide one, of the issues raised by the teachers in our discussions. I kept record of these issues as the seminar unfolded but I prefer to quote directly from the teachers' writings as their writing on these issues is more articulate than my notes. To give a better sense of the development of the discussions, the selections are grouped under subheadings and the issues are presented, more or less, in the order in which they were raised. In a sense, of course, the subheadings may seem to be arbitrary or artificial. I wanted to use the subheadings, however, to indicate how I have interpreted the reactions. While at times, I may still be uncertain where I stand, in other cases, I hope, my stance emerges quite strongly. Moreover, the selections are arranged in a way to provide the reader with alternating, though recurrent, teachers' voices about the issues, for this is the way I heard them in the seminar.

   I should also note that *Life in Schools* is usually discussed (in conjunction with other readings) in the first part of the seminar and for about 6 weeks (out of the entire 12 weeks of the seminar duration).

2. I would like to thank Ursula Kelly for suggesting the title for this paper, the teachers for allowing me to quote from their reactions, and Blye Frank, Ursula Kelly, Allan Neilsen, Glynis Ross, and Rhoda Zuk for finding time to patiently discuss parts of this paper.

   A version of this paper was presented at the CSSE (SERC) annual meeting, Queen's University, Kingston, Ontario, in June 1991.

REFERENCES

Burbules, N. C. (1990). The tragic sense of education. *Teachers College Record, 91*(4), 469–480.

Dewey, J. (1913). *Interest and effort in education.* New York: Augustus M. Kelly.

Ellsworth, E. (1989). Why doesn't this feel empowering? Working through the repressive myths of critical pedagogy. *Harvard Educational Review, 59*(3), 297–324.

Farber, P. (1991). The politics of teacher authority. *Educational Foundations, 5*(1), 75–88.

Giroux, H. (1988a). The hope of radical education: A conversation with Henry Giroux. *Journal of Education, 170*(2), 91–101.

Giroux, H. (1988b). *Schooling and the struggle for public life: Critical pedagogy in the modern age.* Minneapolis: University of Minnesota Press.

Giroux, H. (1988c). *Teachers as intellectuals.* Granby, MA: Bergin and Garvey.

Giroux, H., and Simon, R. I. (1989). *Popular culture, education and everyday life.* Granby, MA: Bergin and Garvey.

Greene, M. (1967). *Existential encounters for teachers.* New York: Random House.

Greene, M. (1973). *Teacher as stranger.* Belmont, CA: Wadsworth.

Gutmann, A. (1990). Democratic education in difficult times. *Teachers College Record, 92*(1), 7–20.

Karp, S. (1991, Winter). Review of *Life in Schools. Radical Teacher,* No. 39, pp. 32–34.

Kelly, U. (1991). *From text to textuality: "Reading" McLaren's Life in Schools.* CSSE (SERC) annual meeting, Queen's University, Kingston, Ontario.

Martin, J. R. (1981). Needed: A new paradigm for liberal education. In J. F. Soltis (Ed.), *Philosophy of education* (pp. 37–59). Chicago: National Society for the Study of Education.

McLaren, P. (1989). *Life in schools: An introduction to critical pedagogy in the foundations of education.* New York: Longman.

Novack, J. (1989). Constructing life in schools. *Journal of Education, 171*(2), 150–154.

Ohanian, S. (1985, June). On stir-and-serve recipes for teaching. In K. Ryan and J. M. Cooper (Eds.), *Kaleidoscope* (5th ed.).

Pinar, W., and Grumet, M. (1988). Socratic *Caesura* and the theory-practice relationship. In Pinar (Ed.), *Contemporary curriculum discourses* (pp. 92–100). Scottsdale, AZ: Gorsuch Scarisbrick.

Portelli, J. (1991). Review of *Life in Schools. Reflections on Canadian Literacy, 9*(1), 54–57.

Simon, R. I. (1987). Empowerment as a pedagogy of possibility. *Language Arts, 64*(4), 370–382.

Smyth, J. (1987a, Winter). Teachers theorising their practice as a form of empowerment. *The Educational Administrator, 30,* 27–37.

Smyth, J. (1987b). Transforming teaching through intellectualizing the work of teachers. In Smyth (Ed.), *Educating teachers: Changing the nature of pedagogical knowledge* (pp. 155–168). Philadelphia: Falmer Press.

Smyth, J. (1989). A critical pedagogy of classroom practice. *Journal of Curriculum Studies, 21*(6), 483–502.

Steedman, P. H. (1988). Curriculum and knowledge selection. In L. E. Beyer and M. W. Apple (Eds.), *The curriculum: Problems, politics and possibilities* (pp. 119–139). Albany: State University of New York Press.

Werner, W. (1989). Review of *Life in Schools. Phenomenology + Pedagogy, 7,* 271–277.

CHAPTER 12

Critical Pedagogy, Multiculturalism, and the Politics of Risk and Resistance: A Response to Kelly and Portelli*

> *As the history of Orientalist education demonstrates, a curriculum may incorporate the systems of learning of a subordinate population and still be an instrument of hegemonic activity. . . . Until curriculum is studied less as a receptacle of texts than as activity, that is to say, as a vehicle of acquiring and exercising power, descriptions of curricular content in terms of their expression of universal values on the one hand or pluralistic, secular identities on the other are insufficient signifiers of their historical realities.*
> *Gauri Viswanathan,* Masks of Conquest, *p. 167*

When I was invited to respond to the essays by Ursula Kelly and John Portelli, both by the editors of the *Journal of Education* and by the authors themselves, I was glad to accommodate the request. Many of the comments included by Kelly and Portelli in their essays cast severe doubts on certain aspects and characteristics of *Life in Schools*. But the overall form of criticism in no way resembles what might be called "desperate criticism"—a politics of malice that too often appears in journal reviews these days (see, e.g., Bowers, 1991a). The questions raised by Kelly and Portelli (and by their students), while trenchant and demanding, appear refreshingly free of the self-aggrandizement and mean-spirited quest for power and influence that so often blur the critical imagination and poison the integrity of critics on both the left and the right. Furthermore, I felt that a response was necessary in order to establish an ongoing dialogue among teachers and students who share a common interest in liberatory struggle and democratic social transformation—the kind of dialogue that I have referred to elsewhere as constructing "an arch of social dreaming."

---

* This article appeared in slightly different form in the Boston University *Journal of Education* (Volume 173, Number 3, 1991), pp. 109–139. Reprinted with permission of the publisher. Some similar sections can be found in other recent writings.

sexism

:lly and Portelli have created space for critical pedagogy in their essays. It is an interpretive space in which educators are called on to explore the dialectic tensions generated by pedagogical texts as part of the teacher's own pedagogical practices.

Having said this, I am left to express a feeling of disappointment in what appear to have been missed opportunities in both reviews. In my mind, Kelly's paper suffers from her failure to discuss her own role in establishing the hermeneutic grounds from which a critical reading of *Life in Schools* is possible. She obviously did not teach *Life in Schools* in a vacuum, but I am given only a fleeting glimpse of Kelly's own politics of location—her situatedness—as a cultural worker actively and pedagogically present in her graduate class. Although there is some indication of what readings were assigned in the course, there is little indication of how the course was taught, how the issues in the book were taken up pedagogically. We do not know how the students' engagement with critical/feminist pedagogy enabled them to challenge the taken-for-granted realities of the students—what Kelly refers to as "the position of bias [the students] begin to recognize as working in themselves."

NEVER MIND THE BOLLOCKS

Kelly is obviously sympathetic to the overall project of critical pedagogy, and is knowledgeable about recent writings by male social theorists that attempt to redress the historical male bias of critical pedagogy. In this regard, she and her students may be interested in the way that my more recent work has addressed some of the issues that they feel were not adequately addressed in *Life in Schools,* specifically gender (see Hammer and McLaren, 1991; McLaren, 1988; McLaren and Hammer, 1989; McLaren and Lankshear, 1993). These writings, meant for a graduate-level readership, deal fairly explicitly (although still inadequately) with the colonization of women, the construction of the gendered body, the political formation of desire, and the abuses of phallocentric and Eurocentric economies of power and privilege in the construction of subjectivity. I draw attention to this material because I agree with Kelly and her students (and some of Portelli's students) that my discussion of gender in *Life in Schools* lacked theoretical depth compared to the other sections of the book. Although I summarized ideas generated by feminist researchers such as Angela McRobbie, I overgeneralized many of the arguments and made little attempt to use feminist theory to criticize my own practices as a classroom teacher.

In my own description of female students, I obviously failed to escape the sexist formations in which so many male teachers are invited to be situated through mainstream institutional, cultural, and social discourses and practices. My own positionality as a male was not immune to sexist social and cultural practices—practices that are still reproduced in teacher education programs as well as in most spheres of public and private life. That I should have intervened in incidents of sexual harassment among students is painfully obvious to me now, and I would hope to all readers. *Life in Schools* is an attempt not just to come to terms with my own subjective formation in colonialist and neocolonialist discourses and social practices structured in patriarchal social relations, but also to invite readers to question presuppositions that inform their own identities and behaviors as social agents.

Even though reviewers of *Life in Schools* have frequently held the teaching practices described in my diary to be progressive, critical, and liberating, I would be the last to argue that my formation as a social agent escaped the dominant discourses of white patriarchal privilege and racist formations that unwittingly position so many white Anglo teachers like myself as custodians of Western rationality. Often my teaching patronized my students; often it was condescending. My descriptions of both minority and working-class parents frequently failed to situate their behavior in the wider context of oppressive capitalist social relations and cultural, political, and institutional constraints.

Several readers and colleagues felt that I was not deliberate enough in my invitation to readers to recognize my own behavior as complicitous with the interests of the dominant society. Of course, this was the whole purpose of the book—to invite a critical reading of my early ideological formation as a teacher. Perhaps I should have made the link between my diary and the theoretical sections of the book clearer—but, in truth, it is part of the pedagogical design to encourage readers to make these links for themselves. In retrospect, however, I should have been clearer as to where those links might be found: in my descriptions of parents and students; in my failure to intervene successfully in racist and sexist student practices; in my failure to become sufficiently involved in the grassroots movements that were organizing the community to struggle for social justice.

I am not arguing that critical theory is an antidote to sexism and racism, but it can help us take the first important step toward analyzing our own complicitousness in those very practices that we as teachers so assiduously condemn. Accepting one's own complicitiousness in oppressive social relations is not easy, and this is perhaps even more true for teachers who are looked upon as examples for the rest of society. Each time I read through my diary, I am painfully struck by the power of discourses to seduce and seize the mind and to colonize the will. But the private disappointment following an examination of one's history is nothing compared to the social and political consequences of one's history left unexamined in terms of its real and potential effects on the lives of others. Myles Horton said that "you only learn from experiences that you learn from." One way I've learned and continue to learn from my experiences is to find a language that challenges their embeddedness in white, male, Eurocentric, and patriarchal systems of domination. This book constitutes a critical examination of my teaching practices and values within such a context.

This response is a further examination of the ideological practices that escaped my awareness in my attempt to provide a critical framework for understanding my classroom diary published in 1980 (Part Two of this present volume). Perhaps at a later date I'll be invited to reflect upon the limitations of this revised edition, and to develop a language that is even better equipped to question the presuppositions that inform our practices as teachers but unveils the hope out of which possibility is born.

When my publisher organized a seminar at the University of Cincinnati on the topic of revising *Life in Schools,* all of the participants agreed that there should be more mention of feminist researchers and women of color. For instance, the book would have benefited from references to the contributions of people such as bell hooks, Maxine Greene, Jo Anne Pagano, and Christine Sleeter. The contributions of Black female intellectuals such as Hazel Carby, Patricia Williams, Michele Wallace, and Beverly Guy-Sheftall would also considerably strengthen the sections on race and gender. Participants also agreed that there should be reference to sexuality education, and the struggle against homophobic school practices found in the excellent work of Jim Sears.

Other issues immediately come to mind in reading through Kelly's and Portelli's essays that relate to some objections I have to their analysis. Despite current theoretical prohibitions against reducing social texts to the intentions of the author, Kelly chose to focus on relationships of texts and authors rather than texts and readers. Why are there no attempts to explore the reading formations that students (and the teacher, for that matter) bring to their engagement of the text? Had she established the intertextual dynamics of her students' engagement with *Life in Schools,* I think it would have made for a more powerful analysis. Texts are not independent or discrete objects of analysis.

The same criticism could be applied to John Portelli's essay, although Portelli manages to be a bit more self-reflective about locating his own reading of *Life in Schools* within a pedagogy of possibility. Yet Portelli misses an opportunity to engage the voices of his students critically and to analyze the forces and relations that shaped them—that is, to analyze the social histories and cultural dynamics of their constitutive discourses and their extratextual significance in relationship to *Life in Schools.* In both essays the student responses (both favorable and unfavorable) to *Life in Schools* are presented as supposedly transparent, self-articulating, and self-authenticating commentary. I am more interested in knowing why the students responded the way they did: why they chose to raise certain issues surrounding the text and not others, why they took into account certain contexts yet ignored others. After all, the internal psychological states of students are not constructed in some neutral matrix outside the exigencies of culturally generated codes and conventions which impose particular constraints on the perceptions of the students. What is remarkable is the tension embodied in the responses by the students, the passion that often speaks louder than their words, the contradictory nature of their comments, and the bipolar characteristics of their viewpoints.

Given these reservations surrounding the essays, I think that both Kelly and Portelli raise some important issues and uncover some genuine fault lines in my attempt to introduce critical pedagogy to teachers. And I appreciate their care, their concern, and their erudition in raising them.

FILLING IN SOME BIOGRAPHICAL GAPS

Before I respond to the specific charges made in these essays, I would like to expand a bit on the context surrounding my decision to leave teaching, to study critical pedagogy, and to write and teach within this tradition in a university setting in the United States. Many of the questions (especially those raised by student readers in both essays) at least implicitly call for such a historical and biographical accounting. Similar questions are almost invariably raised by my own students with respect to *Life in Schools,* and by audiences during speaking engagements.

I did not resign from my teaching position as an inner-city classroom instructor before entering graduate school. I resigned after I read comments that school board officials had made to newspaper reporters. These stated that I would not be permitted to work in the inner city if I chose to return to classroom teaching after completing my doctoral degree. I had seen how board officials had treated other teachers who had made the plight of their students public, and I knew that more than likely I would be shepherded to some isolated school in an affluent suburb.

Once I graduated, I was more fortunate than many of my fellow graduates during those tough economic times. I managed to secure a one-year contract as a special lecturer in a Canadian university where I had earned my master's degree. Since I had met some wonderful colleagues there, and worked with some excellent students, I planned to stay there if I could—if the dean saw fit to create a job line for me beyond my one-year position.

NO MORE NORTHERN EXPOSURE

Circumstances during my first year of college teaching (as a sabbatical replacement) were not in my favor. Students who were ideologically inhospitable—and in some instances leeringly hostile—to the idea of language arts being taught from the perspective of critical pedagogy tried to organize the student body to have my contract terminated on the grounds that my approach was "Marxist-inspired." Another group who mobilized in my defense (fortunately I had the support of many students on the student council) caused such a stir among some administrators that I was not surprised to learn that the job line I had hoped for at that university did not materialize. My efforts to secure a position in other Canadian institutions also bore no fruit. It should come as little surprise to the readers of *Life in Schools* that I decided to accept an invitation by Henry Giroux, one of the leading educational critics in the United States, to establish a Center for Education and Cultural Studies as part of a graduate education program at Miami University of Ohio.

Consequently, the audience for *Life in Schools* is primarily—although not exclusively—U.S. teachers and students. My inner-city diary, *Cries from the Corridor,* which comprised over a third of the contents of *Life in Schools,* had already been published in Canada and was still provoking considerable interest eight years later but the prospects for publishing a revised Canadian edition seemed dim. As a matter of fact, the Canadian publisher who owned the Canadian rights to *Cries from the Corridor* stipulated in my contract with my U.S. publisher that *Life in Schools* could not be sold in Canada (it might diminish sales of *Cries from the Corridor*). Later, after the contract was taken over by another Canadian publisher, I managed to acquire permission for *Life in Schools* to be purchased in Canada.

I do not want to take up further space defending the historical circumstances that led me to teach in higher education in the United States. I would rather address concerns raised by some students related to my "abandoning" my elementary students and providing an "American" interpretation—criticisms that exemplify what I call "dead essentialism." I also want to take up the charge that *Life in Schools* runs into serious methodological deficiencies as an example of critical ethnography.

THE CASE OF THE MISSING ETHNOGRAPHY

Let me begin with the latter criticism. As far as I am concerned, the only book published under my name that could be called a critical ethnography is *Schooling as a Ritual Performance,* my study of Azorean and Italian students at an inner-city Catholic junior high school in Toronto's Portuguese community. If I had claimed that *Life in Schools* embodied critical ethnographic analysis, then I could support Kelly's charge that my analysis is in places "inappropriate" and in part constitutes a form of "displaced historicism." Yet as the outset of the book I explicitly say that it is not meant to represent a critical ethnographic study. It certainly contains some interesting empirical data that could serve to generate various types of qualitative analysis. And I would not object to researchers describing some of the journal entries as "ethnographic data." But I would never presume to call *Life in Schools* a generalizable ethnographic study. This is clearly stated in the introduction to Part Four (now Part Three). Here I remark:

> I want to make clear from the outset that my own elementary school teaching experiences are not offered as evidence that in some way "proves" the theories that follow. This book is not meant to be read either as an empirical study or as a devout acolyte's conversion journal to the critical tradition. A concern with the validity and verifiability of theory is beyond the scope of this book; those wishing for empirical studies are encouraged to consult my book, *Schooling as a Ritual Performance,* or the numerous other books within the critical education tradition listed at the back of this volume. (p. 157; now p. 165)

Having made this point I would still argue that the vignettes that I have written in a largely journalistic style can certainly serve—and indeed are meant to serve—as polyvalent heuristic narratives that work as a kind of "signing system." These narratives may or may not be generalizable in certain school contexts in the United States or Canada—or Britain or Ireland, for that matter. For instance, in the context of postmodern cultures and their often shifting centers and margins in present-day North America, inner-city schools in Cleveland and Toronto may have more in common than those in Halifax and Toronto.

I have suggested that the vignettes in the diary section of *Life in Schools* do indeed reflect some general conditions of poverty and strife that exist in U.S. schools. When I wrote them I had read Jonathan Kozol and Herbert Kohl and journalistic accounts by other inner-city teachers. Later, during my work here in the United States, I continued to read ethnographic studies of U.S schools as well as visit inner-city schools in various U.S. cities. I also had the privilege of working with some inner-city teachers at the Center for Education and Cultural Studies. I knew we had the same challenges with respect to the structural dynamics of our classroom experiences. I believed I could put my classroom diary into the service of an emancipatory project that would cross national/geographic/geopolitical as well as disciplinary boundaries. I was not seeking explanatory criteria specific to my journal entries (as an ethnographic study would demand), but rather inviting readers to engage in new perspectives in critical social theory. I hoped to provide a more meaningful vocabulary with which to address the issues of why some students are systematically oppressed within capitalist schools in an age of commodity imperialism and the valorization of image-perfect people.

Life in Schools attempts to describe to readers why I find the radical literature more helpful in understanding the education of the powerless and the poor than I do explanations provided by conservative and liberal critics. The question I am asking the student reader is: Does the theoretical vocabulary provided in *Life in Schools* do a more convincing and ideologically emancipating job in explaining the current crisis in our schools than those which are presently available to you through your local board of education, your in-service workshops, your graduate seminars, or your undergraduate teacher education classes? For those readers who might be interested in ethnographic analysis as part of the available radical literature, I suggested that they read *Schooling as a Ritual Performance.* Paul Willis's *Learning to Labor* was discussed in Parts Three and Four. And Kathleen Weiler's feminist ethnography, *Women Teaching for Change,* was listed as a further reading.

TEACHER EDUCATORS: GUARDIANS OF THE STATUS QUO OR CULTURAL WORKERS FOR SOCIAL CHANGE?

Let me address briefly the issue of teachers who leave the classroom to pursue a vocation in colleges of education. Student teachers especially might consider it a betrayal when a teacher decides to leave the classroom and work in a teaching capacity in higher education, even if the new job involves working with inner-city teachers and developing programs and research projects to foster liberatory education. There is a perception that professors of education are always one or two steps removed from the real work of school reform. And one can hardly blame students for entertaining such a view, given the current state of affairs in many colleges of education. But this prevailing view establishes an invidious ranking system based on physical proximity to those most oppressed in our system: our youth. While classroom teaching in my mind is one of the most noble and important projects in our society, proximity to the oppressed does not carry with it any guarantees that social change will be most effectively carried out in that site. Here it becomes important to break through the captivity of binarisms such as "insiders/outsiders" and "top/down" and understand that school reform involves crossing and sometimes collapsing the multiple borders that separate "public/private," "personal/political," "local/global," "schooling/politics," "power/knowledge," and "subjectivity/objectivity." The view that school change can only occur at the site of classroom resistance—a binaristic view that resonates both with simple-minded left-wing populism and with certain strands of neo-conservative school reform measures—needs to be rejected as we envision new forms of collective solidarity in a multiplicity of social and cultural spheres of struggle. As Jonathan Rutherford (1990, p. 22) remarks,

> Binarism operates in the same way as splitting and projection: the centre expels its anxieties, contradictions and irrationalities onto the subordinate term, filling it with the antithesis of its own identity; the Other, in its very alienness, simply mirrors and represents what is deeply familiar to the centre, but projected outside of itself. It is in these processes and representations of marginality that the violence, antagonisms and aversions which are at the core of the dominant discourses and identities become manifest—racism, homophobia, misogyny and class contempt are the products of this frontier.

It is this type of binaristic thinking that also *others* class, racial, gendered, and sexual subjects.[1]

Working outside the classroom (in university settings or in settings within the domain of the popular such as artistic production or community activism or governmental agencies) should not necessarily be pathologized. Such settings may be used as constitutive sites of school reform. The politics of hegemonic refusal and educational transformation ascribes to us—as teachers, students, parents, activists—a multiplicity of subject positions and potential roles as historical agents. School reform can (and does) take place on multiple levels and in a variety of political and social sites that involve classroom teachers, administrators, parents, community activists, and social theorists. Each of us must try to discover where we can be most effective. Critical pedagogy is not exhausted in inner-city classrooms nor is it restricted to public school settings, though such sites are admittedly of extreme importance in any wider project of social reform. I think cultural workers in universities who work in the area of critical pedagogy (and they need not be restricted to colleges of education) should be encouraged to speak to multiple audiences. In an age in which right-wing watchdog groups monitor scholarship for leftist "bias," and purvey a "political correctness" canard, it behooves us as radical scholars not to retreat from the politics of theory into a particularist politics of the personal. Teachers who are critical, oppositional intellectuals should not stand silent, especially in these present times. We must also rise to protect those under attack. For instance, the noted literary scholar Edward Said, has recently received death threats for his support of Palestinian rights as well as verbal assaults from reactionary scholars such as Edward Alexander. We should work in solidarity with scholars such as Said and not allow him, and others like him, to stand alone.

In addition, I would like to point out that cultural workers in the university should not be limited to teaching and writing but should also attempt to establish political networks with groups both inside and outside of education who share a common interest in social justice. Since critical pedagogy is largely marginal within most colleges of education, there is a dire need for teacher networks to be established. Many teachers with whom I work resent the fact that they were unaware of critical pedagogy until very late in their careers. In my own case, not until my last year as a doctoral student did I become aware of most of critical pedagogy's notable texts. So there is a real need here to break the stereotypical role of the professor of education and invest it with a discourse of possibility.

NUESTRA AMERICA: PEDAGOGICAL ENCOUNTERS WITH ALTERITY

Life in Schools was published in 1989, and my thinking since that time has shifted in emphasis. I have become more interested in questions of identity and race, gender and sexuality, language and the production of desire, and the politics of popular culture and popular pleasures. Let me summarize some recent thoughts on some of these issues as a way of indicating where I think critical educational scholarship should be headed.

First of all, we should stop seeking a language that will provide educational researchers with access to either epistemological or moral truth. Teachers need to acknowledge that we live in an era of rival, contradictory, and conspicuously diverse truths. Every era has more or less shared this trait, but the difference now is that we cannot escape into a world devoid of interpretation where purposes can be substantiated monologically through one single authority.

Let me speak here briefly on the direction my work has taken with respect to postmodernist trajectories within the social sciences. I have space only to punctuate and not elaborate on recent turns in my work. Let me begin with some heat that I have taken from fellow educators in my so-called abandonment of Marxism as a central theoretical and political orientation in my work. While I would characterize my work as a non-Marxist democratic socialist project, by no means have I abandoned Marxism *in toto*. In fact, I have been drawn in recent years to what Cornel West (1991) describes as Marx's "metaphilosophical move" and his "radical historicist viewpoint" which, in many ways, prefigures the work of antifoundationalists. Perhaps Marx did, after all, anticipate Derrida and was really the first deconstructionist (Rosenau, 1992). This is more than merely an effort to be cute—especially if one examines Marx's rejection of philosophy as a quest for certainty (see West, 1991), which refutes contrary claims made by Engels, Kautsky, and Lukács.

Further, my interest in postmodernism has not led me to embrace what Teresa Ebert (1991, p. 115) terms "ludic postmodernism," in which reality is constituted by "a theater of simulation marked by the free play of images, disembodied signifiers, and the heterogeneity of differences." Postmodern social theory is exemplary in revealing how empiricism (as preached by the New Right, for example) seeks vainly to transcend the political, ideological, and economic conditions that render the world into cultural and social formations. At most we can employ new vocabularies of meaning that will enable us to uncover a semiological landscape of densely packed signifiers hidden beneath modernist surfaces of meanings. But ludic postmodernism (e.g., Lyotard, Derrida) really constitutes only a moment of self-reflectivity in deconstructing Western metanarratives. Here, irony and playfulness is put in the service of smudging representations of the world that were thought to be accurately mappable. I believe that educators should move in a different direction because, as Ebert notes, this form of postmodernism, while serving a limited role as ideology critique, ultimately reinscribes the status quo and "reduces history to a free-floating trace of textuality" (p. 115). Ludic postmodernism is akin to what Scott Lash (1990) calls "spectral postmodernism" that deals with the de-differentiation and blurring of disciplinary knowledge and genres (e.g., literature and criticism) and involves the implosion of the real into representation, the social into the mediascape, and exchange-value into sign-value. That is, the social is sucked up and dissolved into the world of signs and electronic communication; depth is imploded into superficiality. Pauline Marie Rosenau (1992) calls this "skeptical postmodernism"—a strand of postmodernism that reflects not only an ontological agnosticism that urges a relinquishing of the primacy of social transformation but also an epistemological relativism that calls for a tolerance of a range of meanings without advocating any one of them.

The kind of postmodern social theory I'm encouraging is what Rhonda Hammer and I have called "critical postmodernism" (McLaren and Hammer, 1989) and what Ebert calls "resistance postmodernism." It is not based on a textual theory of difference but rather on one that is social and historical. In this way it serves as an interventionist and transformative critique of U.S. (and Canadian) culture. Following Ebert, it attempts to show that "textualities (significations) are material practices, forms of conflicting social relations" (p. 115). The sign is always an arena of material conflict and competing social relations as well as ideas. Viewed from this perspective, difference is situated in social conflicts.

This practice of postmodern social theory is similar to what Scott Lash (1990) calls "organic postmodernism." Organic postmodernism avoids epistemistic skepticism and explanatory nihilism; it is concerned with the commodification of labor and not just the commodification of language. It re-integrates the cultural into the natural environment. From this perspective, rationality is always situated in particular communities of discourse. It also embodies an ecological criticism of high modernism where reality is a cover for validating a Cartesian universe that collapses difference into the uneasy harmony we know as white patriarchal privilege—a privilege inextricably bound up with nationalism, imperialism, and the state. We can speak from a multiplicity of locations, within a variety of experiential domains, without calling any one of these "home." I have always advocated for restless identities that are never contained by the categories and representations that they generate. Consequently, as teachers we need to interrogate how we have developed and sustained specific pedagogical discourses that have demonized Others who are different (through transforming them into absence or deviance) within particular geopolitical and epistemic conjunctures.

I am calling attention to the dominant meaning systems available to students—most of which are ideologically stitched into the fabric of Western imperialism and patriarchy. Instead of directing all our efforts to understanding ethnicity as "Other than white," we need to interrogate the culture of whiteness itself. This is crucial because unless we do this we naturalize whiteness as a cultural marker against which Otherness is defined. As an educator I am provoked, if not obliged, to raise the following questions: Do we have instruments for such an interrogation within our teacher education programs? Do we have curricula that can unsettle Western patriarchal and imperialist discourse on women and minorities? Do we have approaches for understanding Otherness without making white immigrant experience the benchmark for such an understanding? These are truly perplexing questions but unfortunately we avoid them at our peril. We no longer, as Richard Kearney (1991, p. 180) reminds us, seek ontological foundations to serve as transcendental subjects. But this does not mean the postmodern imagination is without purpose. This is a key point and few people have expressed it as well as Kearney. So what is the purpose, the task, of the postmodern imagination? In Kearney's own words, it is "to interpret the images of the other and to transfigure one's own image of the world in response to this interpretation" (p. 180).

What does this mean? It means, "transforming others' needs into felt ones"; it means moving beyond Buber's liberal "I-thou" ethic; that is, moving outside the realm of face-to-face encounters and into the realm of the public by "introducing the other as *third* alongside the other as *thou*" (Kearney, 1991, p. 226). It means engaging in a critical hermeneutics that "advances a discourse of semantic interaction between different kinds of meaning—subjective and systematic, surface and hidden, obvious and indirect, conscious and unconscious, literal and figurative, emancipatory and distorting" (p. 179). It seeks furthermore to dethrone the autonomous human imagination and humanist ego without surrendering "to nihilism and anarchism but to discern an alternative poetics of imagining capable of responding to the post-modern crisis of culture" (p. 181). Kearney (1988, p. 362) writes that "an other in need makes the ethical demand upon me—'where are you?' before I ask of the other the epistemological question—'who are you?'" Kearney follows this with the astute proclamation: "We are responsible for the suffering of the other before we know his or her credentials" (p. 362). He makes the profound utterance: "When a naked face cries 'where are you?', we do not ask for identity papers. We reply, first and foremost, 'here I am.'" Solidarity is prior to questions of epistemology. Students need to know we are there for them before we ask them to identify themselves. We are not there to speak for them, but to work in solidarity with them, within a discourse of mutuality and respect. We are not there to narrativize their reality but to engage their world and ours and in doing so forge a language of social criticism and also a language of social dreaming.

PARTICIPATION IN BODY AND IN SPIRIT

Part of the solution to understanding the politics of educational reform, it seems to me, is to move beyond a politics of representation to a politics of transformation. This means a politics that can move beyond representation to participation, by recognizing meaning outside a language of linguistic signification alone, that is, by recognizing the body as the primary site of meaning and resistance. I have referred to this notion of meaning as "enfleshment." Joel Kovel articulates a perspective similar to "enfleshment" when he writes:

> Flesh is matter which is also the presence of subjectivity. It is matter as subject-object: the subject that feels, the object that is felt and at the same time the place of the feeling. Flesh is more than the "physiologically" describable organism, though it is that as well. Flesh is that body as it enters and constitutes the subject. (Kovel, 1991, p. 154)

Teachers often forget that the flesh is as much the seat of subjectivity—of individual and collective identity—as language. In fact, I would go as far as Kovel in naming the flesh—the body—as spiritual. Kovel notes that "flesh is inherently spiritual and open to the Other, and only ceases being spiritual through repression" (p. 156). Therefore, liberation of the mind and spirit first and foremost means liberation of the flesh and those material and linguistic constraints that form practices of domination. When we forget how our identities are enfleshed, we ignore the domain of popular culture and popular pleasures and the way in which students invest their identities in everyday social practices. And we then fail to understand how popular culture forms can rupture the oppressive conventions of the social order. Since schools are part of this order, this means that we fail to understand the desire of students to construct their identities outside of or in opposition to the *doxa* (the *déja-dit* or *already said* of public conventions) in order to forge a narrative identity that is more positive and enabling. We need to ask ourselves how it is possible to live under the concrete gaze of others. How is it possible to counter politically and ethically undesirable constructions of the Other?

In my view, the project of transformation also requires what Ramon Saldivar (1990, p. 175) calls a "dialectics of difference." He refers to the formation of subjectivities of resistance, that is, subjectivities that are able to resist "the absolutizing tendencies of a racist, classist, patriarchal bourgeois world that founds itself on the notion of a fixed and positive identity and on specified gender roles based on this positive fixation."

I want to add that we foreshorten the possibility of self- and social transformation by our failure to see our own reflection in the eyes of others. That is, in failing to recognize the Other we take flight from our own being, our own spirit. Joel Kovel (1991, p. 214) takes up the issue of self- and social transformation by recognizing that liberation of the subject also requires a liberation of the spirit. By spirit, I am not referring to a bodiless essence or an oceanic yearning to merge with a transcendental source of truth but to what Kovel (p. 108) describes as "a commitment to a philosophy of becoming, in which the self can become Other to itself, and from that position either remain alienated or transcend itself"; it is "to speak of a practical wish to be free." Kovel expands on this idea by proclaiming:

> I am a subject, not merely an object; and I am not a Cartesian subject, whose subjectivity is pure inwardness, but rather an expressive subject, a transformative subject; I am a subject, therefore, who needs to project

my being into the world, and transform the world as an expression
of my being; and finally, I will appropriate my being rather than have
it expropriated. (p. 108)

Critical pedagogy must be spiritually restorative as well as politically transformative. Human spirit, according to Kovel, is not an abstract universal principle
but is expressed as a desire for being, that is, as a "spirit being." Spirit being must
be understood as a desire to "dissolve the self toward the Other, because it sees
in the Other an opening toward being" (p. 133); spirit is determined by concrete,
historically determined Otherness in which a person lives in the sensuous
specificity of her or his lived social relations through a "concretely unfolding
historical dialectic" (p. 132). Consequently, spirit "requires emancipation, and
this implies not only political and economic revolution but a total revolution in
all spheres of domination" (p. 214). There is no liberation of the spirit without
material liberation (p. 159). According to Kovel, we recognize the presence of
the soul in human action by "the appropriation of the Other, according to our
understanding; which is to say, by an overcoming of Egoic relations of being"
(p. 215). As educators, we need to push and strain the boundaries that hold us
conceptually captive to reading the world through words alone; we need to read
the world as well through our situatedness in a sea of emotions and desires and
through our location as body/subjects and as spiritual beings.

THE IMPORTANCE OF LANGUAGE AND THEORY

In the space that remains I can only offer a scattershot of directions that my present
work is taking. My current concerns involve the way in which identities are
constituted within the seamless persistence of regimes of brutality and an insidious
and frenzied panopticism. The enemy can no longer be characterized by the
vestigial cliché "the ruling class." Systems of influence and economies of power
and privilege are not so neatly characterized or identified in the complex process
that makes schooling for the marginalized an inevitable allegory of loss. Postmodernism's contemplative reflection on the torn limbs of desire's body needs
to imagine a new war of position that ruptures capitalist social relations that
reproduce the subalternity of racial and gendered groups. New questions emerge
as new vocabularies are brought into play in the critical social sciences (Giroux,
1992). When I say that we must move beyond the jargon of Sunday barbecue
naturalism, I am not suggesting that we should start dressing up our vocabularies
in ostentatious or gaudy terms but rather recognize that our educational language
needs to be capable of glancing sideways at itself in order to reflect upon its
own socially constitutive nature. In order that pedagogy may become more self-
reflective, we need a revisionist literacy consisting of new terminologies to help
educators see beneath the surface structure of our everyday classroom practices.
Trinh T. Minh-ha (1991, p. 228–229) issues a very telling warning against
calls for accessibility of language. She writes that resistance to the language of
complex theory can reinstitute "common sense" as an alternative to theory—that

is, it can usher in a new dictatorship of pre-theoretical nativism in which experience supposedly speaks for itself. To be "accessible," writes Trinh, often suggests

> one can employ neither symbolic and elliptical language, as in Asian, African, or Native American cultures (because Western ears often equate it with obscurantism); nor poetic language (because "objective" literal thinking is likely to identify it with "subjective" aestheticism). The use of dialogical language is also discouraged (because the dominant world-view can hardly accept that in the politics of representing marginality and resistance one might have to speak at least two different things at once). (p. 228)

Trinh additionally notes, after Isaac Julien, that resistance to theory is embodied in white peoples' resistance to the complexity of black experience. Not only is this to remain mystified by the illusion that there exists a natural, self-evident language but such a call for accessibility can also lead to forms of racism and intolerance and the politics of exclusion. The "diversely hybrid experiences of heterogeneous contemporary societies are denied" by such a form of binary thinking that would reduce language of analysis to white, hegemonic forms of clarity (p. 229).

TEACHERS AS CULTURAL WORKERS

While my work has moved away from trying to investigate psycho-social ways of behaving in favor of understanding socially constituted rituals, this doesn't mean that I am not interested in normative values. In fact, I feel that such values are important in determining what is worth keeping in the social order and what is worth struggling for. But values do not determine their own instantiation: they are forged in the domain of the conflictual and contingent and are continually fought over. As cultural workers we need to work toward the detotalization and deterritorialization of global corporatist and phallocentric patriarchy. How do we begin to index the vectors of this new global regime of paranoia? Or challenge the vending machine mentality that is carried across the globe through the profusion of commodity desire and the narcissistic aggrandizement of the social will? How are we coded for desires in specifically cultural and historical ways—desires encapsulated and encysted in the logic of commodity fetishism?

How have subjectivities become marginalized and desire policed in ways that encourage us to court homophobia, white supremacy, sexism? Why do women remain ominously uninscribed in the annals of critical educational research? How do we deal not only with patrilineage in the academy (under the gaze of the mega-fathers of Marx, Dewey, Foucault, Derrida, Lyotard) but also with systems of differences without creating oppositions—male vs. female, white vs. black, subjective vs. objective? These are oppositions reaffirmed by commentators such as Allan Bloom, E. D. Hirsch, and William Bennett, whose works constitute the new reactionary cabal of white male literacy evangelists. We need to restructure colonized reality by taking the risk of bringing such reality into our classrooms so it can be interrogated and transformed into new paradigms of ethical and political revolt. That's why I encourage teachers to study both "high" culture and "popular" culture: the cultural forms of opera, classical music, rap, house music, digital sampling, TV news, soap operas, sports events, and the like.

THE IMPORTANCE OF METACRITICAL NARRATIVES

But our mode of critical analysis must move beyond the tropological displacement of discursive familiarity or a highjacking of meaning in the back alleys of theory. We need narratives of liberation that serve a *metacritical* function—that can metaconceptualize social relations of everyday life—yet do not succumb to the allure of the transcendental unity of subject and object or their transfiguring coalescence (Saldivar, 1990, p. 173). We must pry open a new vision of the future that is latent in the present, immanent in this very moment of reading, in the womb of the actual. Subjective intentions do not constitute the archaic site of truth. Subjectivities and identities of students and teachers are always the artifacts of discursive formations; that is, they are always the products of historical contexts and language games. We are all actors in narrative configurations that we did not develop but which are the products of historical and discursive struggles. It is true, most of us act with good intentions and under the cover of universal principles that evoke the importance of justice, fairness, and equality. However, what concerns me most is not so much the reiteration of abstract universal principles but their historical applications and the contradictions that emerge. Teachers need to recognize not only the discourses that inform their teaching practices, but those that organize their vision of the future and their politics of the everyday both within and outside of the sphere of the classroom or school.

There is a serious issue in the debates surrounding critical pedagogy that needs to be addressed at this point in the discussion. Many educators and cultural workers in the schools and in other social and cultural sites whose approach to understanding and transforming the conditions of everyday life falls under the rubric of "critical pedagogy" have been accused—often viciously and imperiously—of trying to speak *for* the oppressed. Many of the attacks, often directed at but not limited to male social theorists within the academy, bear sloganeering-type titles that protest the apparent presumptuousness of critical pedagogy as a practice of liberation. They translate into something like: "Who Do Those Intellectuals in Critical Pedagogy Think They Are When They Assume That They Can Empower the Oppressed?"

A standard argument is that many of us in the academy don't acknowledge our own positionality or politics of location (as white Anglo heterosexual males or females) in trying to work for social justice. This argument has merit in drawing attention to the fact that one's location as a critical educator in terms of race, class, gender, and sexual orientation certainly informs one's liberatory praxis, often undercutting good faith and emancipatory intent. But too often critics treat gender or class or ethnic location as a universal generalization. Such critics usually try to make their case against critical social theorists by taking one or two quotations out of the context of the corpus of their works and then following this with a series of unsupported assertions that conveniently avoid the qualifications that the authors have made regarding the complex issues of speaking for others. This contributes to the often unfair assumption that critical educators haven't struggled with the problem of positionality, place, and politics of location when working with oppressed groups and suggests that the critics of critical pedagogy are the only ones who have seriously struggled with this issue. This is criticism at a low ebb that is as mean-spirited as it is lacking in substantive critique.

In my own work I have tried to stress the importance of narrating the contingency of one's own authority and social location in developing a critical approach to teaching and working with oppressed groups. This is not to argue that my own politics and practice of pedagogy is always transparent to my own engagement with it or that I am always able to articulate my own best interests or those of the people with whom I am working. But too often critics of critical pedagogy retreat into the problematic position of claiming that teachers can and should only speak for themselves. This, in my mind, undermines political praxis and constitutes the erasure of what I have called "historical agency." Notice that I am claiming that social location *informs* one's praxis. However, to claim that positionality and the specificity of one's social location informs one's practice is not the same thing as saying that it *predicts* it. This is a crucial distinction that is worth elaborating. Linda Alcoff (1991–1992, p. 16) has recently framed this issue slightly differently but with a similar analysis. She argues: "To say that location *bears* on meaning and truth is not the same thing as saying that location *determines* meaning and truth." Location does not determine meaning and truth. Location or positionality is not a "fixed essence." Alcoff's analysis deserves serious attention. In Alcoff's (p. 20) terms, the attack on critical researchers who advocate taking a stand on social justice alongside oppressed minority groups often "presumes an ontological configuration of the discursive context that simply does not obtain." That is, such a view assumes that it is actually possible for one to speak simply and unproblematically from one's own position. This perspective, as Alcoff notes, falls into the liberal trap of assuming the existence of the autonomous ego.

I have argued, along with other critical social theorists, that one cannot hold a purely personal desire or attitude since the technologies of the social structure and cultural formations always mediate our world of representations. Agency doesn't exist in a vacuum, prior to representation. We can never escape from the social into the purified ether of the self. Reality is always in the process of negotiation through forms of enfleshment or embodiment. We engage social life through systems of intelligibility and forms of affective investment that legitimate or disable certain forms of agency. Folded into the unconscious through repression as well as through identification are the collective symbol systems and material practices that make up the larger social order. Oppressive social systems demand certain forms of autonomy (unreflective) and liberatory and democratic systems require forms of automony that are able to interrogate their discourses of desire.

So-called autonomous agency has to be seen in the context of how subjectivity is produced through constitutive forms of social and cultural translation that never escape the influence of the symbol system and structural configurations of the larger social order. Pure, self-directed agency is a bourgeois illusion. But this does not necessarily make us "pawns" of dominant discursive regimes. What this illusion does achieve (at least in the work of many critics of critical pedagogy) is to permit many individuals to retreat from assuming a responsibility for the way their actions affect others. Those who claim that teachers can and should only speak for themselves—a claim that is at the very least implied by many critics of critical pedagogy—forget that "When I 'speak for myself' I am participating in the creation and reproduction of discourses through which my own and other selves are constituted" (p. 21).

Alcoff further notes, citing Gayatri Chakravorty Spivak, that "to promote 'listening to' as opposed to speaking for essentializes the oppressed as non-ideologically constructed subjects" (p. 22). Spivak's position is that we should adopt a "'speaking to,' in which the intellectual neither abnegates his or her discursive role nor presumes an authenticity of the oppressed but still allows for the possibility that the oppressed will produce a 'countersentence' that can then suggest a new historical narrative" (p. 23). This, of course, stresses the importance of dialogue rather than an unproblematic "speaking for" others. True, we need to listen to the other's voice, even if such a voice is not ideologically innocent. But for too many critics of critical pedagogy this means falling back on essentializing and romanticizing the voice of the other as if that voice automatically speaks for itself.

I have always argued against privileging concrete experience and stressed the importance of developing a critical language for analyzing and transforming experience. This language will not be, of course, necessarily the language of the academy. This is because critical educators must take into consideration the contextual specificity of the groups they are working with. Freire's work with peasants didn't draw upon the same language he used in *Pedagogy of the Oppressed*. That's a tough and demanding book to engage with a highly specialized vocabulary. Both Freire's work with disenfranchised peoples and his scholarly publications in which he tries to make the case for philosophy and pedagogy as forms of liberation are indeed two important moments in the struggle for liberation. Critics of critical pedagogy often confuse these two moments.

Alcoff (p. 26) suggests that "in order to evaluate attempts to speak for others in particular instances, we need to analyze the probable or actual effects of the words on the discursive and material context." This is crucial. We need to ask how our own discourse as an *event* positions us as authoritative and empowered speakers in ways that unwittingly reinscribe the discourse of colonization, of patriarchy, of racism, of conquest—"a reinscription of sexual, national, and other kinds of hierarchies" (p. 29).

RETHINKING MULTICULTURALISM AS "DIFFERENCE" AND NOT JUST "DIVERSITY"

There are some important new works in the field of education dealing with multiculturalism and the politics of difference (Giroux, 1992; McCarthy, 1988; Nieto, 1992; Sleeter, 1991). I think it's important to continue the dialogue around the meaning of difference, especially in the light of conservative assaults on multi-culturalism from academics, politicians, and growing public constituencies in the "colonial theater" known as the United States. The growing presence of Black people and Latinos in our cities—the constituently different and the subaltern—has unsettled the patronizing complacency and politics of avoidance and exclusion that has marked previous approaches by the nation state to the "problem" of "Them." I did not adequately address the concept of multiculturalism in *Life in Schools* although its theme is implicit throughout. In the section that follows, I want to develop the concept of multiculturalism in the context of discussions of colonialism and post-colonialism.

For me, the key question that teachers need to address is how to develop a multiculturalism that is attentive to the specificity (historical, cultural) of differ-ence (in terms of race, class, gender, sexual orientation etc.) yet addresses the commonality of diverse Others under the law with respect to global principles of equality and justice. How do we develop an understanding of difference that avoids an essentializing of Otherness? We can take a look at the struggle of femi-nists of color, for instance, who have long resisted a definition of femaleness constructed by white bourgeois feminists, claiming that the voices of Black, Asian, and Latino females do not appear in such a definition.

The view of multiculturalism articulated by conservative critics such as William Bennett and Diane Ravitch suggests that minorities unwilling to adopt a consensual view of social life are stubbornly separatist and ethnocentric. This view of multiculturalism carries with it the assumption that American society fundamentally constitutes social relations of uninterrupted accord. This view of society furthermore assumes that American society is largely a forum of consensus with different minority viewpoints accretively added on. Of course, this is funda-mentally a Cartesian viewpoint. It presupposes a harmonious space in which differences can coexist undisturbed by conflict. In this highly ideological view, the state is populated by transhistorical, metaphysical, and autonomous citizens.

Speaking from a "critical multiculturalist" position, Chandra Talpade Mohanty (1989/90) notes that difference cannot be formulated as negotiation among cultur-ally diverse groups against a backdrop of presumed cultural homogeneity. Differ-ence is the recognition that knowledges are forged in histories that are riven with differentially constituted relations of power; that is, knowledges, subjectivities, and social practices are forged with "asymmetrical and incommensurate cultural spheres" (p. 181).

The conservative view assumes that justice already exists and needs only to be evenly apportioned. However, both teachers and students need to realize that justice does not already exist simply because laws exist. Justice needs to be continually created, continually struggled for. This is especially urgent in a world which has recently been granted, in the words of Vincent Pecora (1991, p. 130) "one grandly obfuscating vision of global harmony and interdependence policed by Conan the American—the 'new world order,' a phrase whose historical resonance alone demands the keenest suspicion of all that it attempts to name." Against what Donaldo Macedo (in press) describes as a "landscape of violation of international laws and aggression perpetrated by the United States or other countries with the support of the United States," how can we develop the "postmodern literacies" necessary to educate a citizenry not as phallomilitary imperialist warriors but rather as capable of struggling for social justice? At a time in which the United States is focusing on the concept of "benevolent domination" in place of collective internationalism, how can we develop a concept of global citizenry that avoids the trappings of fascism? The question I want to pose to teachers is this: Do we have a language of analysis necessary to create democracy or simply to preserve the status quo in which the illusion of democracy "covers" injustice and inequality—an illusion that blinds democracy to its constitutive Outside. Democracy, in the terms I use to teach its meaning to my students, means continually suspending the habitual. It means undoing associations that bring closure to—that "quilt"—the subject/citizen within the discourse of racial/cultural apartheid and other forms of domination (Žižek, 1989; Laclau, 1990).

One of the crucial distinctions teachers need to explore is that made by Homi Bhabha (1990) between "difference" and "diversity." The latter is a mainstream liberal notion that speaks to the importance of plural, democratic societies. But with diversity comes a "transparent norm" constructed and administered by the "host society" that creates a consensus. A normative grid locates cultural diversity while at the same time *containing* cultural difference. The "universalism that paradoxically permits diversity masks ethnocentric norms" (p. 208). Differences, on the other hand, do not always speak to consensus but are often incommensurable. Culture, as a system of difference, as a symbol-forming activity, must be seen as "a process of translations" (p. 210). Cultures in this view never really exist fully formed in the sense that they possess "a totalized prior moment of being or meaning—an essence" (p. 210).

Otherness in this sense is often internal to the symbol-forming activity of that culture and it is best to speak of the hybridity of culture. There exists a "third space" that enables other positions to emerge. This opens up possibilities for new structures of authority, and for new political vistas and visions. Identity in this sense is always an arbitrary, contingent, and temporary suturing of identification, of meaning. Bhabha's distinction makes it clear to me why people such as Ravitch, Bloom, Hirsch, and Bennett are so dangerous when they talk of the importance of a common culture. Who has the power to exercise meaning, to create the grid from which Otherness is defined, to create the identifications that invite closures on meanings, on interpretations and translations? Once we begin to think about this, the question of power and democracy invariably arises.

How can we further conceptualize the concept of democracy and difference? I want to move away from defining difference within liberal strands of meaning, which often simply translates into the "smoothing over" of supposedly irreconcilable and permanently divisive identity politics revolving around race, gender, ethnicity, sexual preference, and nationality—all through the opportunistic agenda of constructing a common culture. This form of liberal multiculturalism is, of course, what the politics of assimilation is all about. It assumes we really do live in a meritocracy. Such a definition of difference implies, as Iris Marion Young (1990) notes, "coming into the game after the rules and standards have already been set, and having to prove oneself according to those rules and standards"

(p. 164). These standards are not culturally and experientially specific, as one would hope, because within a pluralist democracy privileged groups have occluded their own advantage by invoking the ideal of an unsituated, neutral, and universal common humanity of self-formation in which all can happily participate without regard to differences in race, gender, class, age, or sexual preference.

Difference needs to be understood, as Teresa Ebert (1991) points out, not as clearly marked zones of auto-intelligible experience or a unity of identity within a cultural pluralism. Rather, difference needs to be seen as produced through a politics of signification, that is, through signifying practices that are both reflective and constitutive of prevailing economic and political relations. Our current ways of seeing and acting are, according to Ebert, being disciplined for us through forms of signification, that is, through ideological frames of sense-making. Ebert illustrates that just as the term "Negro" became an immutable mark of difference and naturalized the political arrangements of racism in the 1960s, so too is the term "Black" being refigured in the white dominant culture to mean criminality, violence, and social degeneracy—as in the Willie Horton campaign ads and in the George Bush and David Duke position on "hiring quotas." Carlos Munoz, Jr. (1989) has revealed how the term "Hispanic" in the mid-1970s became a "politics of white ethnic identity" that de-emphasized and in some cases rejected the Mexican cultural base of Latin Americans. Munoz writes that the term "Hispanic" is derived from "Hispania" which was the name the Romans gave to the Iberian peninsula, most of which became Spain, and "implicitly emphasizes the white European culture of Spain at the expense of the nonwhite cultures that have profoundly shaped the experiences of all Latin Americans" (p. 11). Not only is this term blind to the multiracial reality of Mexican Americans through its refusal to acknowledge "the nonwhite indigenous cultures of the Americas, Africa, and Asia, which historically have produced multicultural and multiracial peoples in Latin America and the United States," it is a term that ignores the complexities within these various cultural groups. Here is another example of the melting pot theory of assimilation fostered through a politics of signification. So that we might ask ourselves what signifieds (meanings) will be attached to certain terms such as "welfare mothers." I think we know what government officials mean when they refer derisively to "welfare mothers." They mean Black and Latino mothers, even though most women on welfare happen to be white.

Differences, therefore, may be seen as forms of social signification in which certain groups and certain characteristics are produced as different through the economic and ideological organization of signification. As Mas'ud Zavarzadeh and Donald Morton (1990, p. 156) point out, "signs are neither eternally predetermined nor pan-historically undecidable: they are rather 'decided' or rendered as 'undecidable' in the moment of social conflicts." Difference is not "cultural obviousness" such as Black vs. white or Latino vs. European; rather, differences are historical and cultural constructions (Ebert, 1991).

You can see the politics of signification at work in special education placement when you notice that Black students are more often than not placed in "behavioral classrooms" whereas white students are categorized as "learning disabled.'' French sociologist Pierre Bourdieu captures what is meant by the ''politics of signification'' in the following quotation:

> Struggles over ethnic and regional identity—in other words, over the properties (stigmata or emblems) linked with the *origin* through the *place* of origin and its associated durable marks, such as accent—are a particular case of the different struggles over classifications, struggles over the monopoly of the power to make people see and believe, to get them to know and recognize, to impose the legitimate definition of the divisions of the social world and, thereby, to *make and unmake groups.* What is at stake here is the power of imposing a vision of the social world through principles of division which, when they are imposed on a whole group, establish meaning and a consensus about meaning, and in particular about the identity and unity of the group, which creates the reality of the unity and the identity of the group. (1991, p. 221)

Critical educational theorists recognize that teachers and students are all subject to ideological inscriptions and multiply organized discourses of desire through a politics of signification. They are subjects produced by a discursive ventriloquism in that they are creatures of the languages and knowledges that they have inherited and which unconsciously exert control over their thinking and behavior. And, of course, they are prisoners of a ''male monopoly on the production and reception of knowledges'' and the ''overwhelming masculinity of privileged and historically dominant knowledges'' (Grosz, 1990, p. 332). At the same time such theorists recognize that students are also active agents who are capable of exercising deliberate historical actions in and on the world. The point, of course, is that conscious knowledge is not exhaustive of identity. We need to acknowledge what is *not so obvious* about difference.

Unfortunately, students become too often attached to those versions of themselves advocated by Hollywood and the culture industry. Or else they adhere to versions of themselves which have been produced by the discursive practices of state power. Since identities are produced in such a polyvalent nexus of competing discourses and social practices, it is important that as teachers we help students consider the ways that are available for rendering the self into thought and structures of meaning. In other words, what are the structures of understanding, the structures of feeling, available for disclosing and transforming the technology of self?

Of course, the point is that we need to find ways of talking outside the totalizing systems of modernist understanding by creating border identities, what I have called ''restless subjectivities.'' We need to get outside the admixtures and remnants of languages—the multiplicity of voices that already populate our vocabulary and suffocate all the available linguistic spaces—in order to find different ways of appropriating or mediating reality. We need to escape the terminal despair brought on by the logic of identity and liberal versions of social engineering that fall under the banner of ''liberal pluralism.'' We need to cross borders into zones of cultural difference (Giroux, 1992) rather than construct subjectivities that simply reassert themselves as monadic forms of totality facilitated by a consumerist ethics and marketplace logic that saturate subjectivity in the corporatist discourses of market regulation.

The point that is worth emphasizing is not to define difference from a pre-given patriarchal norm but as pure difference with no identity. In the case of defining gender difference, difference is not seen as a distinction that implies the pre-evaluation of one of the terms from which the difference of the other is drawn, but rather necessitates a rejection of existing definitions in order to redefine oneself in the world according to women's perspectives (Grosz, 1990, p. 340).

In speaking about minority groups, I want to follow the advice of Iris Marion Young (1990) and suggest that we need to assert the positivity of group difference in a politics that "asserts that oppressed groups have distinct cultures, experiences, and perspectives on social life with humanly positive meaning" (p. 166). Difference, in this view, ruptures the sacerdotal status of universalist claims to unity that demonize certain groups as baleful Others. Difference situates groups *in relation to,* not in binary opposition to, other groups and thereby avoids the translation of difference to mean exclusion or dominance. Young is worth quoting at length on this issue:

> Asserting the value and specificity of the culture and attributes of oppressed groups, moreover, results in a relativizing of the dominant culture. When feminists assert the validity of feminine sensitivity and the positive value of nurturing behavior, when gays describe the prejudice of heterosexuals as homophobic and their own sexuality as positive and self-developing, when Blacks affirm a distinct Afro-American tradition, then the dominant culture is forced to discover itself for the first time as specific: as Anglo, European, Christian, masculine, straight. In a political struggle where oppressed groups insist on the positive value of their specific culture and experience, it becomes increasingly difficult for dominant groups to parade their norms as neutral and universal, and to construct the values and behavior of the oppressed as deviant, perverted, or inferior. (p. 166)

This perspective calls for a politics of refusal that challenges the institutionalization of formal equality based on the prized imperatives of a white, Anglo male heterosexual world. It puts the oppressed in a position to investigate how the dominant institutions must be transformed so that they no longer reinforce asymmetrical relations of power and privilege.

Lucy R. Lippard (1990) makes the astute observation that protesting the universal as dismissive of differences (which often promotes provincialism) can be as ideologically problematic as erasing differences in the name of the homogeneous dominant culture. She notes:

> Part of the crippling bias of ethnocentrism in this country comes from the fact that we learn geography mostly from imperialism, discovering

other nations when our government chooses to interfere in their sovereignty. . . . Some of our national imperviousness can be blamed on the manic pace at which we absorb culture; on the inadequate, biased information we receive from the trade media; and on the invisible process of hegemony itself, which blinds us to the unfamiliar by conflating all "otherness." (p. 156)

To abandon all vestiges of the dominant culture that is informed by the discourse of modernism can lead to a futile search for pre-modern roots, which, in turn, leads to a narrow nationalism as in the "old ethnicity." On the other hand, to abandon the search for identity in the midst of the prevailing ideological and cultural hegemony can serve as a capitulation to assimilation and the loss of forms of critical historical agency. Needed is a view of multiculturalism and difference that moves beyond the "either-or" logic of assimilation and resistance. To make a claim for multiculturalism is not, in the words of Trinh T. Minh-ha,

to suggest the juxtaposition of several cultures whose frontiers remain intact, nor is it to subscribe to a bland "melting pot" type of attitude that would level all differences. It lies, instead, in the intercultural acceptance of risks, unexpected detours, and complexities of relation between break and closure. (1991, p. 232)

Critical pedagogy does not work toward some grandiose endpoint of an ideologically perceived world history. It works toward the specificity of struggle and then expands the margins of hope to include all peoples. We need to resist the idea that forms of minority group representation are just some type of special interest. Young writes:

The test of whether a claim upon the public is just or merely an expression of self interest is best made when those making it must confront the opinion of others who have explicitly different, though not necessarily conflicting, experiences, priorities, and needs. . . . As a person of social privilege, I am more likely to go outside myself and have regard for social justice when I must listen to the voice of those my privilege otherwise tends to silence. (p. 186)

DEMOCRACY AS PARADOX: RESISTING
IDEOLOGICAL CLOSURE

As teachers, we need to refigure the concept of difference with democratic social life but we also need to understand the paradoxes sustaining democracy—i.e., the undemocratic foundations of democracy itself. There is a space between the universal and the specific that needs to be apprehended dialectically. We don't want to endorse a monistic or monocultural view of democracy that speaks to a crippling transcendentalism. Nor do we want to elevate contingency and provisionality to the status of an ontological, foundational necessity. For instance, the notion of the particular, specific, concrete subject often disappears under a concern with the universal subject. If we are concerned about bringing a critical multiculturalism to the United States, then we need to see it in regard to the context of constructing democratic practices. Democracy is not only a set of procedural practices, but also signifying practices.

Impartiality is, in effect, the enemy of democracy because such a position assumes a privileged decision-making status from some transcendental reference point that can best serve all people—some glowing centrist place in the sun whose light exposes counterfeit values and counterfactual positions. But do not for a moment think that this is the light of detached, impartial reason; rather, it is more likely the reason of the privileged and powerful whose sense of power is purified and strengthened and whose advantage is masked by the myth of the ideal of impartiality. Where is this privileged space that an observer can stand and claim to be impartial? It is definitely not the space of science, or religion, or sociology, or, for that matter, critical pedagogy. Meaning is always created within a heterogeneous public space of conflictual, competing discourses. The view that society is really a benign balance of social tensions provides an opening for the reprivatization of social ethics and social services. It gives some weight to the corporatist claim that, say, if a plant closes down in a working-class community it's simply the law of market imperatives and not a question of social justice.

If you want to know how the "impartial" democracy of "consent and consensus" has scarred the identities of marginalized and exploited minorities, ask the students and teachers who work in African-American ghetto schools. Go into Puerto Rican neighborhoods and ask social activists what happens to *independentista* youth; ask the teachers and students of Dr. Pedro Albizu Campos Puerto Rican High School in West Town, Chicago, about raids on their classrooms by the FBI, who suspected the school was teaching terrorism. Ask the Canadian government about its policies and practices directed at the Mohawks. Or ask the Canadian oil companies about their appropriation of lands of the Lubicon Cree. Go to an art gallery and behold the powerful works of Mel Edwards, Martha Jasckson-Jarvis, Elizam Escobar, Joe Lewis III, Luis Jimenez, Juan Sánchez, Ron Noganosh, Guillermo Gómez-Peña, Mario Torero, and Yolanda M. López and you will see a politics of refusal written over the imperial and sovereign narratives of state citizenship.

Educators need to ask themselves what it means to be "impartial" while living in a complex of dehumanizing realities of nightmare metropolises and small towns that have lost their soul, where everyday life consists of living narratives of exile, victimage, racism and marginalization. What is the implication of speaking as a teacher from the citadels of the center when your students live out their lives in the margins, in the barrios of hope?

Joan Copjec (1991) points out that modern democracy creates through the mass media a "referential illusion" of consensus (just as the idea of "pluralism" creates a referential illusion of domestic harmony). Democracy in the United States defines itself through its leadership not necessarily in terms of creating a transcendental signifier in the form of a George Bush or Bill Clinton. Rather, it defines itself by emptying out the characteristics of its citizens. As Copjec notes:

> Democracy is the universal quantifier by which America—the "melting pot," the "nation of immigrants"—constitutes itself as a nation. If *all* our citizens can be said to be Americans, this is not because we share any positive characteristics, but rather because we have all been given the right to *shed* these characteristics, to present ourselves as disembodied before the law. I divest myself of my positive identity, therefore I am a citizen. This is the peculiar logic of democracy. (1991, p. 30)

In other words, democracy allows you to commit racial suicide and become an invisible person of whiteness.

In the peculiar brand of democracy in the United States, the relationship that citizens have to their leaders is not one based on the Cartesian notion of the transparent referentiality of truth (i.e., the president of the United States as the Universal Father who embodies sovereign control of the New World Order). Rather, we often require our leaders to accredit our singularity, our difference, more than our commonality. But since every sign universalizes what it represents "by making difference communicable to another," our singularity or difference is automatically abolished (Eagleton, 1990). So if we want to remain loyal to pluralism we need leaders who do not stand for transcendental truths and who ultimately fail to deliver the accreditation we seek. Some of the paradox of this situation has been described by Terry Eagleton. He writes:

> Any emancipatory politics must begin with the specific, then, but must in the same gesture leave it behind. For the freedom in question is not the freedom to "be Irish" or "be a woman," whatever that might mean, but simply the freedom now enjoyed by certain other groups to determine their identity as they may wish. Ironically, then, a politics of difference or specificity is in the first place in the cause of sameness and universal identity—the right of a group victimized in its particularity to be on equal terms with others as far as their self-determination is concerned. This is the kernel of truth of bourgeois Enlightenment: the abstract universal right of all to be free, the shared essence or identity of all human subjects to be autonomous. In a further dialectical twist, however, this truth itself must be left behind as soon as siezed; for the only point of enjoying such universal abstract equality is to discover and live one's own particular difference. The *telos* of the entire process is not, as the Enlightenment believed, universal truth, right and identity, but concrete particularity. It is just that such particularity has to pass through that abstract equality and come out somewhere on the other side, somewhere quite different from where it happens to be standing now. (1990, p. 30)

Very little work in multiculturalism directly addresses the fundamental tension between structure and agency, between the universal and the particular, and how identities are formed across zones of difference. Much of this work has already privileged the perspective of the white, male colonizer to set the terms of the debate and the definitions of the terms to be used. Yet in the struggle over the meaning of liberation within U.S. democratic life, I am struck by the dignity and strength of the marginalized, the vanquished, and disenfranchised people of color in the face of Anglo patriarchy's phallocentric call for transformation. By this I mean that the vision of liberation that informs such a call, that serves as an invisible (because it is all too visible) backdrop against which liberation struggles are waged, judged, and legitimated, is framed by concerns that are marked by intransigence and exclusion, and which do not stress the particularities and needs of different ways of knowing of women, people of color, and other oppressed groups. Discourses of liberation articulated by males need to avoid universalizing liberation and must pay more attention to the specificities of race and gender. This point is not made to simply invert relations between oppressors and oppressed so as to merely demonize all that is white, male, and Euro-American through a crude essentialism that would make white patriarchy the universal receptacle of social pathology but to recognize how gender, class, race, and sexual orientation inform meaning (but never exhaust it) even when one is trying to construct new strategies of contesting oppression.

In our struggle we need to take up the issue of "difference" in ways that don't replay the monocultural essentialism of the "centrisms"—Anglocentrism, Eurocentrism, phallocentrism, androcentrism, and the like. We need to build a politics of alliance-building, of dreaming together, of solidarity that moves beyond the condescension of, say, "race awareness training" that really keeps forms of institutionalized racism intact. We need to build a solidarity that is not informed by market imperatives but is built around the notion of critical citizenship.

The notion of the citizen has been pluralized and hybridized, as Kobena Mercer notes, by the presence of a diversity of social subjects. Here we discover the most uncommon people of all—the common people. Mercer (1990, p. 68) points out instructively that "solidarity does not mean that everyone thinks the same way, it begins when people have the confidence to disagree over issues because they 'care' about constructing a common ground." Solidarity is not solid and depends to a certain degree on antagonism and uncertainty. Simone (1989, p. 191) calls this type of multiracial solidarity "geared to maximizing points of interaction rather than harmonizing, balancing, or equilibrating the distribution of bodies, resources, and territories." We need to stand back from our search for identity politics and grassroots struggles and create a space to ask ourselves: What is our politics of the human spirit? We need to sound our voices from the tombs of history where educators have been stationed in their roles as custodians of dead knowledge and curators of empty dreams. While cautioning against the privileging of a false universalism, a false unity that denies the internal rifts of bodily desire, we need to open ourselves to the possibility of Otherness so that the particularity of individual being can become visible. We need to devise different assemblages of the self by understanding and dismantling the different kinds of discursive segmentarity that make us up, by subverting the stratified and hierarchized forms of subjectivity that code our will, and by developing nomadic forms of individual and collective agency and democratic community that opens up new assemblages of desire and modes of being-in-the-world.

What I am calling for is not an outright rejection of modernity nor an embrace of cultural relativism. Rather, I seek a history that is not afraid to remove its mask of deception so that we can see the ambivalences, instabilities, and contingencies that inform it. This would enable us to trace its collaboration with regimes of intelligibility known as patriarchy, imperialism, empiricism, and triumphalist forms of Enlightenment rationalism. I join Dipesh Chakrabarty (1992) in asking:

> I ask for a history that deliberately makes visible, within the very structure of its narrative forms, its own repressive strategies and practices, the part it plays in collusion with the narratives of citizenships in assimilating to the projects of the modern state all other possibilities of human solidarity . . . that . . . lays bare to its readers the reasons why such a predicament is necessarily inescapable. This is a history that will attempt the impossible: to look toward its own death by tracing that which resists and escapes the last human effort at translation across cultural and other semiotic systems, so that the world may once again be imagined as radically heterogeneous.

The current arena in which school reform is being struggled over is filled with new conceptual and practical issues that can no longer be ignored by teachers and researchers. There has been an explosion of theoretical approaches to social life over the last few decades. Yet underlying my own work is a recurring theme which could be described as problematizing our encounters with difference. I believe that our understanding of the meaning of difference will largely determine the future of our educational projects. Our approach to multiculturalism and democracy is inextricably tied to understanding how difference signifies, and what role it plays in the politics of representation. It is my belief that the themes of multiculturalism and democracy need to be at the heart of all our present and future educational endeavors if we are to successfully defeat domination and oppression. It is my conviction that we need to forge new identities as educators. To construct an identity is to negotiate among a polyvalent assemblage of competing discourses that vie for our allegiance. To what discourses do you wish as a teacher to become allied? Imperialist discourses of the Anglo, Eurocentric, and patriarchal metropolitan center? Or do we wish to deterritorialize such discourses and occupy identities in what I call a "border culture"—a culture that is multicultural, multilingual, and multiconceptual. We need to become familiar with multiple sets of referential codes from other languages, histories, and cultures. In this way we can become border educators as well border intellectuals (Giroux, 1992). Ultimately, we need to reinvent ourselves.

As an introductory text, *Life in Schools* did not adequately address all of these issues. But at least some of the terms of the debate were set forth in ways that attempted not simply to reverse the master/slave relation between the oppressors and the oppressed but to reconstitute the very meaning of difference in a democratic society. Dialogues such as those set up by Kelly and Portelli are vitally important. They open up the project of transformation to new criticisms, new readings, and new ways of making a difference in a world of differences.

NOTE

1. You can clearly see this binaristic thinking in the sovereign power of naming reality undertaken by Diane Ravitch and Arthur Schlesinger's Committee of Scholars in Defense of History. Here Western Enlightenment knowledge is opposed to the knowledge of the unredeemed non-Western populations. Whose history is being defended here? Whose histories are being displaced to the vanishing point of the cultural present? The kind of culture that these hegemonic defenders of tradition wish to preserve calls itself pluralistic but this term is just used as an ideological cover for an exclusionary politics of sedimented dreams of white superiority that have crusted over the terrain of the social since the days of the old empire. In this view, the objective necessity of history privileges the white race as the vanguard of moral, social, and economic redemption.

   Another type of crude binarism is set up by some educators aspiring to the label of progressive. For instance, C. A. Bowers (1991b) has situated critical pedagogy as a mode of Western rationality that is set in binaristic terms against nonanthropocentric cultures. He does this through the crudest form of reductionism by asserting that a pedagogy that sets out to question the assumptions of Eurocentric, patriarchal, and universal master narratives is really just reinforcing such narratives unless it explicitly adopts a Batesonian language of ecosystems and biotic communities. Unless you adopt "plant" metaphors and the like to describe the social system, you are immediately falling into the trap of the mythic part of the Eurocentric belief system. This ignores the fact that critical pedagogy has always recognized the multi-layered constraints of the social/environmental order and has never equated transformation simply with forms of rationality. Here I would follow Laclau's (1990) assertion that while we can criticize the "fundamentalism of the emancipatory projects of modernity" we do not need to engage (as Bowers implies) in "an abandonment of the human or political values of the project of the Enlightenment" (p. 188). Rather, what is needed is "a different modulation of its themes." In other words, "It is not the specific demands of the emancipatory projects formulated since the Enlightenment which have gone into crisis; it is the idea that the whole of those demands constituted a unified whole and would be realized in a single foundational act by a privileged agent of historical change" (p. 215). Bowers completely misses the implications of organic forms of critical pedagogy, preferring instead to reduce its arguments so that he can assert the superiority of his own reactionary claims.

REFERENCES

Bhabha, H. (1990). Interview with Homi Bhabha. In J. Rutherford (Ed.), *Identity: Community, culture, difference* (pp. 207–221). London: Lawrence and Wishart.

Bourdieu, P. (1991). *Language and symbolic power.* Cambridge: Harvard University Press.

Bowers, C. A. (1991a). Critical pedagogy and the "arch of social dreaming": A response to the criticisms of Peter McLaren. *Curriculum Inquiry, 21*(4), 479–487.

Bowers, C. A. (1991b). Some questions about the anachronistic elements in the Giroux-McLaren theory of a critical pedagogy. *Curriculum Inquiry, 21*(2), 239–252.

Chakrabarty, D. (Winter 1992). Postcoloniality and the artiface of history: Who speaks for "Indian" pasts? *Representations, 37,* 1–26.

Copjec, J. (1991). The unvermogender other: Hysteria and democracy in America. *New formations,* No. 14, pp. 27–42.

Eagleton, T. (1990). Nationalism: Irony and commitment. In T. Eagleton, F. Jameson, and E. Said, *Nationalism, colonialism, and literature* (pp. 23–39). Minneapolis: University of Minnesota Press.

Ebert, T. L. (1991). Political semiosis in/of American cultural studies. *American Journal of Semiotics, 8*(1/2), 113–135.

Giroux, H. (1992). *Border crossings.* New York: Routledge.

Greene, M. (1988). *The dialectic of freedom.* New York: Teachers College Press.

Grosz, E. (1990). Conclusion: A note on essentialism and difference. In S. Gunew (Ed.), *Feminist knowledge: Critique and construct* (pp. 332–344). London: Routledge.

Hammer, R., and McLaren, P. (1991). Rethinking the dialectic. *Educational Theory, 41*(1), 23–46.

Kearney, R. (1988). *The wake of imagination.* Minneapolis: University of Minnesota Press.

Kearney, R. (1991). *Poetics of imagining.* London: Harper Collins Academic.

Kovel, J. (1991). *History and spirit.* Boston: Beacon Press.

Laclau, E. (1990). *New reflections on the revolution of our time.* London: Verso.

Lippard, L. (1990). *Mixed blessings.* New York: Pantheon Books.

Lash, S. (1990). Learning from Leipzig—or politics in the semiotic society. *Theory, Culture and Society, 7*(4), 145–158.

Macedo, D. (in press). Literacy for stupidification: The pedagogy of the big lies. *Harvard Educational Review.*

McCarthy, C. (1988). Rethinking liberal and radical perspectives on racial inequality in schooling: Making the case for nonsynchrony. *Harvard Educational Review, 58*(3), 265–279.

McLaren, P. (1988). Schooling the postmodern body: Critical pedagogy and the politics of enfleshment. *Journal of Education, 170*(3), 53–83.

McLaren, P., and Hammer, R. (1989). Critical pedagogy and the postmodern challenge: Towards a critical postmodernist pedagogy of liberation. *Educational Foundations, 3*(3), 29–62.

McLaren, P., and Lankshear, C. (Eds.). (1993). *Critical literacy: Politics, praxis, and the postmodern.* Albany: State University of New York Press.

Mercer, K. (1990). Welcome to the jungle: Identity and diversity in postmodern politics. In J. Rutherford (Ed.), *Identity: Community, culture, difference* (pp. 43–71). London: Lawrence and Wishart.

Minh-ha, T. T. (1991). *When the moon waxes red: Representation, gender, and cultural politics.* New York: Routledge.

Mohanty, C. (1989/90). On race and voice: Challenges for liberal education in the 1990s. *Cultural Critique,* Winter, pp. 179–208.

Munoz, C. (1989). *Youth, identity, power.* London: Verso.

Nieto, S. (1992). *Affirming diversity: The sociopolitical context of multicultural education.* White Plains, NY: Longman.

Pecora, V. P. (1991). Nietzsche, genealogy, critical theory. *New German Critique,* No. 53, pp. 104–130.

Rosenau, P. M. (1992). *Post-modernism and the social sciences: Insights, inroads, and intrusions.* Princeton: Princeton University Press.

Rutherford, J. (1990). A place called home: Identity and the cultural politics of difference. In J. Rutherford (Ed.), *Identity: Community, culture, difference* (pp. 9–27). London: Lawrence and Wishart.

Saldivar, R. (1990). *Chicano narrative: The dialectics of difference.* Madison: University of Wisconsin Press.

Simone, T. M. (1989). *About face: Race in postmodern America.* Brooklyn: Autonomedia.

Sleeter, C. (Ed.). (1991). *Empowerment through multicultural education.* Albany: State University of New York Press.

Viswanathan, G. (1989). *Masks of conquest: Literary study and British rule in India.* New York: Columbia University Press.

West, C. (1991). *The ethical dimensions of Marxist thought.* New York: Monthly Review Press.

Young, I. M. (1990). *Justice and the politics of difference.* Princeton: Princeton University Press.

Zavarzadeh, M., and Morton, D. (1990). Signs of knowledge in the contemporary academy. *American Journal of Semiotics,* 7(4), 149–160.

Žižek, S. (1989). *The sublime object of ideology.* London and New York: Verso.

CHAPTER 13

Conclusion to Part Five

What I would like to emphasize in concluding this section of the second edition of *Life in Schools* is the importance of developing a pedagogy that brushes history against the grain of its enforced amnesia, that challenges the fabulous amalgamation of emptiness that constitutes our identities as citizens, that refuses to genuflect before the churchy advocates and praise-singers of the new world order. Teachers need to become warriors against certainty, to contest the interrogative monopoly of standardized tests and texts, and to intensify the obvious until it becomes strange while accelerating the unfamiliar until it becomes mundane. *...and set fired.*

This means that we must keep students connected to the power of the unacceptable, we must plague normalcy, and help to make students more comfortable with the unthinkable (*impensable*) possibilities of hope. We can do this, I believe, by stressing in our work the indissociability of language, power, and subjectivity and by emphasizing that all teaching constitutes a realm *not in but of politics.* We can achieve a pedagogy of transformation if we turn our teaching into an outrageous practice and a practice of outrage. If we can invent our pedagogies anew such that they are based on recovering dangerous memories from society's structural unconscious, from the Eurocentric archives of dead reason, then perhaps we can begin to build a project of recovering the lost particles of our dreams, dreams shattered in modernity's thralldom to the tight-fisted logic of consumer capitalism.

We need to teach dangerously, but to live with optimism. We need to be outrageous, but to temper our outrage with love and compassion. We need to be warriors for social justice, yes, but warriors whose ethical bearings and praxis are informed by the best that critical thought has to offer. Although the term "critical pedagogy" has admittedly become too vague, there are still crucial issues to be engaged in its vicinity. We need to remember that our students are not bodiless wraiths to be blown about the corridors by pedagogical rhetoric and sophistry; rather, students are complex historical agents and they need to be able to read the multiple texts of their own lives. That is, they need to read the languages and discourses in which they find themselves in order to reinvent themselves. Consequently, critical pedagogy must not become a "privileged space" for academics but must be forged amidst the daily struggle of the oppressed themselves. The spirit of the pedagogy I have been describing throughout this book can be summarized best by Paulo Freire who recently described his pedagogy of liberation in an interview with Moacir Gadotti as "a bohemian pedagogy of happiness . . . a pedagogy of laughter, of questioning, or curiosity, of seeing the future through the present, a pedagogy that believes in the possibility of the transformation of the world, that believes in history as a possibility."[1]

It is not an exercise to enhance the ability of citizens to survive in a world of market-driven logic. It is not designed to create loyal servants of tradition, beneficiaries of progress, and disciples of perpetual novelty in a world of endless commodities and renewable identities. Rather, critical pedagogy is designed to agitate over-confidence and ideological comfort, to establish roadblocks to modernity's search for the natural sublime, to render as unsuitable a consensus of ideas and practices that permit anyone to suffer needlessly. Critical pedagogy is at odds with inaction and disembodiment. It is a project that is a rage against enforced silence and confrontation with indifference, against the mindless Pepsi generation optimism of marketplace ideology.

NOTE

1. Moacir Gadotti, *Reading Paulo Freire: His Life and Work* (Albany, New York: State University of New York Press, in press).

Critical Educators: Some Examples

BELL HOOKS

The works of bell hooks have enjoyed an enormous following, especially in recent years. An African-American cultural critic, she is an academic and cultural worker who writes with power and passion in a prose style that is at once accessible and profound. I have heard students—both black and white—describe their engagement with her writings as a type of "religious experience." One of the best descriptions of hooks that I've read comes from Cornel West, who comments:

> [hooks] has preserved her intellectual integrity alongside her personal rage at [the rules of the academy] which devalue Black women. She has insisted on doing her intellectual work—grappling with questions and issues usually eschewed by the academy—in her own style and in the interests of Black people. It is no accident that certain academics (both White and Black), with their fashionable jargons and hierarchical pecking orders, shy away from her writing while nonacademic writers and artists devour them. She threatens the prevailing notions of what it means to be an "acceptable" academic and professional intellectual in our time.[1]

The intellectual contributions of hooks are vast,[2] and range from her first volume on feminist theory, *Ain't I a Woman: Black Women and Feminism* to her book on sexual politics, *Feminist Theory: From Margin to Center*, to *Talking Back: Thinking Feminist, Thinking Black*, a powerful book about, among other issues, pedagogy and the practice of freedom, to *Yearning: Race, Gender, and Cultural Politics* in which hooks examines the politics of race and gender in the context of an analysis of postmodernism, to her powerful exegesis on the politics of representation, *Black Looks: Race and Representation.* Her most recent work to date is a book of poems entitled *A Woman's Mourning Song.*

She has also coauthored a book-length critical dialogue with African-American philosopher and social critic Cornel West, entitled *Breaking Bread: Insurgent Black Intellectual Life.* Some of the themes she addresses include representations of whiteness in popular culture, film, and everyday life; the political status of French social theory within African-American insurgent intellectual life; whiteness as a culture of terror; the films of Oscar Micheaux; the obstacles that face African-American women intellectuals; the struggle to construct a feminist pedagogy; revolutionary black women; and the reconstruction of black masculinity.

The work of hooks represents a constant call to educators and academics not to get lost in the fashionable apostasy of certain strands of postmodern criticism such that concrete relations of oppression are not seriously challenged by a politics and strategy of critical insurgency. The project of bell hooks is to construct critical subjectivities. Her political project is guided by a decolonized vision of what empowered communities might become. She attempts to work often through a reflection on her own lived experiences and an analysis of the complexities of African-American cultural life. One of her most poignant and powerful reflections on education is expressed in a dialogue she has with herself (Gloria Watkins) about the Brazilian educator Paulo Freire.[3] Her work enables students, educators, and cultural workers to reflect on their own emotional, spiritual, and cultural dismemberment and to refuse those modes of analysis and social relations that serve to foster and reproduce an entrapment in spiraling economies of racism, hatred, suffering, and oppression.

MAXINE GREENE

Maxine Greene's books,[4] *Teacher as Stranger, The Public School and the Private Vision,* and *Landscapes of Learning* have become landmark texts in the critical tradition. For me, however, her recent book, *The Dialectic of Freedom,* is the most important in terms of developing the social vision I have tried to construct in *Life in Schools* and my subsequent work. Here she emphasizes with singular clarity the idea of being in the world together—as social beings within diverse communities of difference and solidarity. For people who are always embedded in memory and history, it appears a fruitless endeavor to search only for "inner freedom," because such a search denies praxis and a public space.[5] Meanings need to enter into the exercise of the imagination and should never occur outside the conditions of a praxis capable of remaking democratic community. What is so powerful about Greene's work is the way it cogently draws upon existential phenomenology, literature, and the arts, and the best insights from the sociology of knowledge to develop a vision for education reform that always goes hand in hand with a reconstruction of the larger social order in which schools are embedded and reproduced.

To be self-reflective about how one chooses to ground one's pedagogical project is, of course, in keeping with one of the central themes in *Life in Schools*—

a theme that suggests that critical analysis is an ongoing project. Critical pedagogy, Greene points out, is necessarily in a state of flux and discontinuity; early ideas and practices have to be continually placed in dialectical tension with more current ones. Educators and cultural workers need to follow Greene's lead by vigilantly redressing the structured exclusions that inform their projects of transformation.

JONATHAN KOZOL

Reading Jonathan Kozol has been, for many educators, the first step toward entering the domain of radical schooling and the world of educational outlawry. Perhaps more than anyone else, Kozol has resurrected the study of education on a popular level from the grave of political neutrality where it had wasted away for decades. Once considered the educational correlative of such well-known "sixties" guerrillas as Abbie Hoffman, Eldridge Cleaver, and Timothy Leary, Kozol deserves tribute because his passionate concern with social and educational reform has scarcely diminished over the decades. Kozol continues to do what he has been doing for years: demythologizing our classrooms and influencing the development of ethical rebels and warriors of social change.

When Kozol's first book, *Death at an Early Age,* appeared in 1968, it was decried by school board officials throughout America as a work of major heresy.[6] It is fortunate for the cause of school reform, however, that some people's heresies become other people's orthodoxies, and *Death at an Early Age* quickly became established as the bible of education's radical left. Needless to say, there are always bureaucrats astute enough to diffuse through the school setting some of the ideas of the radical heretics, usually in modified form. It's like vaccinating the schools against radical revision by injecting them with a watered-down version of the "virus"—hence the proliferation in the early 1970s of self-consciously progressive open classrooms, learning modeled on encounter groups, existential classroom curricula, and "emancipated" free schools.

Kozol's initial struggle to liberate the classroom from its death-like miasma involved deconstructing the codes drawn up so rigidly by the board's knowledge-brokers, codes which frequently invoked the culturally sterile and politically laundered writing preserved in antiquated classroom texts and basal readers. Such codes were often embalmed with the accompanying hazards of the modern Western mind-set: mechanistic thinking, technocratic teaching styles, and Skinnerian behavior modification.

Even today, state mandates require our colleges of education to ordain teachers as guardians and mediators of the world's "facts," necessary mystagogues who possess the power and sacrosanct narrowmindedness not only to legitimize students as people but also to define their cultural reality: *this is the way the world is, and there's not much you can do to change it.*

For me, Kozol's work throws into relief the gap between critical educational theory and classroom practice. For students uninitiated into critical educational theory, the immediate attraction of Kozol's work is that it avoids both theoretical labyrinths and the often simplistic revisionist rhetoric of the sixties.

The issues Kozol addresses are no less urgent today than they were three decades ago. The poor continue to be exploited by the rich, and the educational system still serves the interests of those with money and power.

I agree with Kozol when he says that we still need today

> a generation of hard-working, ethically motivated and effective rebels: people who do not choose to leave the skills of numbers and of scientific competence to the engineers of Westinghouse and I.B.M., who do not choose to leave the competence of words and word persuasion to the managers, scriptwriters, and producers of the major television networks.[7]

Kozol questions the infallibility of the teacher and emphasizes ways in which students and teachers can disagree on significant political and moral issues while still retaining respect for one another. His *On Being a Teacher* is a call for teachers to return to students the license to say *no*. The book, among other things, reveals the racist views of Abraham Lincoln and describes how the traditional portrayals of Martin Luther King and Henry David Thoreau in school texts mask the extent of their original political radicalism. It also informs the reader how, for generations, women have been treated with contempt or relegated wholly to oblivion within the public schools. Kozol discusses the important but generally ignored contribution of the late Dorothy Day, cofounder of the Catholic Worker Movement in the thirties, to the civil rights movement, and later to the anti-Vietnam War movement and the antinuclear movement.

More recently, Kozol's work on the problem of illiteracy in America has captured the attention of the general public. Kozol is one of a small number of critical educators whose work is increasingly featured by the mainstream American media. Examples of his recent works that have received widespread publicity include *Rachel and Her Children*[8] and *Savage Inequalities.*[9]

In summary, the work of Jonathan Kozol provides teachers with a provocative conceptual pick for chipping away at the ideological bedrock that fortifies most of what goes on in our classrooms today. But his work is more than just a useful tool for splintering cornerstones of moribund educational thought: It is also a practical guide for what to do should the walls come tumbling down.

PAULO FREIRE

The work of Brazilian educator Paulo Freire places him in the front ranks of that "dying class" of educational revolutionaries who march behind the banner of liberation to fight for social justice and educational reform.[10] Freire's pedagogy, which started out as a means of empowering oppressed Brazilian peasants, has, over the years, assumed legendary status. Few educators have strode so knowingly and with such determination along the boundaries of language and culture.

Freire's internationally celebrated teaching began in the late 1940s and continued until 1964, when he was arrested in Brazil, imprisoned by the military government for seventy days, and exiled for his work in the national literacy campaign, which he had served as director. Freire's years of exile were tumultuous and productive: a five-year stay in Chile as a UNESCO consultant with the Agrarian Reform Training and Research Institute; an appointment in 1969 to Harvard University's Center for the Study of Development and Social Change; a move to Switzerland in 1970 as consultant to the office of education of the World Council of Churches, where he developed literacy programs for Tanzania and Guinea-Bissau; the establishment of the Institute of Cultural Action in Geneva; and his eventual return to Brazil in 1981 to teach at the Pontificia Universidade Catolica de Sao Paulo and the Universidade de Campinas in Sao Paulo. These years also produced numerous works, most notably *Pedagogy of the Oppressed, Education for Critical Consciousness,* and *Pedagogy in Process: Letters to Guinea-Bissau.* His work to date has culminated in a brilliant and moving volume on literacy coauthored with Donaldo Macedo.[11]

Freire's work has been cited by educators throughout the world and constitutes an important contribution to critical pedagogy not simply because of its theoretical refinement, but because of Freire's success at putting theory into practice. Based on a recognition of the cultural underpinnings of folk traditions and the importance of the collective construction of knowledge, Freire's literacy programs for disempowered peasants are now employed in countries all over the world. Freire believes that poverty and illiteracy are directly related to oppressive social structures and the unequal exercise of power in society. His adult literacy campaigns were designed to transform these oppressive social structures by empowering individuals to engage in social analysis, in political activism, and in reading the world in order to reshape it. By linking history, politics, economics, and class to the concepts of culture and power, Freire has developed both a language of critique and a language of hope that together have proven successful in liberating the lives of generations of disenfranchised peoples.

For Freire, speech and language always exist within a social context; and context, in turn, is the reference point for the transformative possibilities of his work. For Freire, the social context is comprised of the social relations resulting from the material conditions of oppression, the exigencies of daily life, critical consciousness, and social transformation. Freire's sensitive grasp of the contradictions and tensions that emerge from such a volatile context is what eventually leads him to posit the need for a radical politics of liberation. As Florence Tager puts it:

> Freire's pedagogy insists on a deep connection between the culture of everyday life and radical politics. For Freire, critical consciousness and the dissection of themes from daily life is an ongoing process that grows out of praxis and leads to further praxis (Freire's term for action with reflection). Ultimately, education for critical consciousness leads to revolutionary politics. For Freire, radical pedagogy integrates culture and politics.[12]

Freire defines culture as a field of struggle over meaning, a many-sided conversation that is never neutral. For Freire, language and culture always reflect a plurality of values, voices, and intentions which generate dialogue. Such a perspective draws attention to the intensity of social contradictions within linguistic and symbolic systems. *Culture is never depoliticized; it always remains tied to the social and class relationships that inform it.*

For Freire, human beings do not float aimlessly in a sea of abstractions; they are firmly rooted in historical struggle and never lose their capacity for suffering or their resoluteness for effecting social transformation. The Freirian man and woman are very much alive; they are anchored in a multiplicity of social relations that provide the "stuff" out of which Freire fashions his cultural politics.

Freire is strong in his analysis of literacy and learning as an underlying political process—which he frequently refers to as "conscientization"—a process that invites learners to engage the world and others critically. Freire posits a "recognition of the world, not as a 'given' world, but as a world dynamically 'in the making.'" The ultimate goal of such a process is for learners to "exercise the right to participate consciously in the sociohistorical transformation of their society." Human beings "have the sense of "project," in contrast to the instinctive routines of animals."[13] And, of course, it is Freire's attentiveness to the scope and quality of his political "project" that illuminates the emancipatory dimensions of his work.

Freire's work begins and ends with the individual subject. His work is linked to the cultural capital of the oppressed; he uses their own vocabularies, ideas, and values in the teaching encounter. His work also attempts to promote forms of consciousness that will eventually lead people to cultural action and cultural revolution. Freire's theories grow out of a "culture of silence," where people are victimized and submerged in "semi-intransitiveness;" they become realized as a "revolutionary project . . . engaged in a struggle against oppressive and dehumanizing structures."[14]

To be committed to cultural action for *conscientization* means not only to engage in a vigorous form of ideology criticism but also to take part in a praxis (action based on reflection), which Freire unabashedly refers to as "utopian." Freire's utopian project addresses *the need for a fundamental faith in human dialogue and community. Becoming literate is not just a cognitive process of decoding signs, but of living one's life in relation to others.* Literacy becomes empowerment. "To undertake such a work," writes Freire, "it is necessary to have faith in the people, solidarity with them. It is necessary to be utopian."[15] The utopian dimension is natural to any revolutionary project dedicated to transforming and recreating the world.

Freire's work is primarily directed at helping students become critically literate as distinct from functionally literate or culturally literate. Functional literacy refers primarily to the technical mastery of particular skills necessary for students to decode simple texts such as street signs, instruction manuals, or the front page of a daily newspaper. Some definitions of functional literacy include the ability to read somewhere between fourth- and fifth-grade levels. Cultural literacy refers to the acquisition of a broad range of factors which accompany functional literacy, such as a familiarity with particular linguistic traditions or bodies of information. More specifically, it means acquiring a familiarity with selected works of literature and historical information necessary for informed participation in the political and cultural life of the nation. Two radically different positions characterize cultural literacy. The first advances the establishment of a cultural canon of literary works prescribed for all students and also insists upon a required form of English usage; the second advocates using the language standards and cultural information students bring into the classroom as legitimate and important constituents of learning. Critical literacy, on the other hand, involves decoding the ideological dimensions of texts, institutions, social practices, and cultural forms such as television and film, in order to reveal their selective interests. The purpose behind acquiring this type of literacy is to create a citizenry critical enough to both analyze and challenge the oppressive characteristics of the larger society so that a more just, equitable, and democratic society can be created.

Suffering and the historical memories of those who have suffered under the heels of the power elite are, for Freire, the reference points that ground his revolutionary text. The task of liberating others from their suffering compels us to affirm our humanity in solidarity with victims. Freire's work does not aspire to create a frictionless world that exists outside of human engagement and struggle; it speaks to an unequivocal and sovereign concern: everyday human suffering that must be alleviated and transformed.

Freire emphasizes pedagogical practices designed to create what he terms *dialogical communication.* His pedagogical structures are designed for liberation by providing individual and collective possibilities for reflection and action. Dialogical communication should prompt educators to draw upon the cultural capital of the oppressed in order to allow the oppressed to "read" the world in both immediate and wider contexts. For Freire, educators who ignore the cultural capital, language, and life-style of the oppressed practice a form of cultural invasion.

Henry Giroux makes the important observation that, given the sophisticated capacity of advanced North American technology and science to administer and manipulate individuals and to conceal class-specific interests and systems, the existence of forces of domination must be *proven* to many North Americans. To apply Freire's pedagogy in a North American context, we must examine how specific forms of science and technology work to empower and reward select groups over others, while hiding the true nature of the interests they serve.

Freire understands that a pedagogy of liberation has no final answers: change must always emerge from continuous struggle within specific pedagogical sites and among competing theoretical frameworks. History is, for Freire, always "becoming" and is, furthermore, "a human event."

Recent volumes about the contribution of Freire's work to school reform throughout the Americas include *Paulo Freire: A Critical Encounter,* edited by Peter McLaren and Peter Leonard (1993), *Politics of Liberation: Paths from Freire* (1993), edited by Peter McLaren and Colin Lankshear, and *Empowering Education* by Ira Shor.[16]

JOHN DEWEY

John Dewey, the famous American philosopher and educator who wrote in the early part of this century, is often referred to as the father of progressive education.[17] In the 1960s and early 1970s, progressive educators frequently invoked Dewey's name in their attempts to develop a pedagogy of experience, sometimes called "learning by doing." The reactionary nature of present day educational policy-making and the essentially conservative ethos that infuses much of contemporary school instruction should in no way be interpreted as a failure of Dewey's impact on our schools; rather, it underscores the pervasive and unremitting stranglehold that social, political, and economic constraints have always placed on the educative process, especially during times of falling profitability and corporate malaise. In 1971, Richard Bernstein noted

> The social conflicts that even Dewey perceived have not been ameliorated, they have been worsened. Where in American society can one find evidence of the growth of "creative intelligence" and the realization of the ideal of a democratic community of shared experience? Despite the influence of Dewey, our school system is even more chaotic and confused in its practices, aims, and objectives than it was during Dewey's lifetime.[18]

The situation has become even more tragic over the last decade. Government cutbacks, declining enrollment, and a worldwide economic crisis have provoked a heightened sense of anxiety among the public over the state of our educational system, and we are reluctantly embracing a return to a core curriculum, management by behavioral objectives, a stress on discipline and accountability, and a move toward more objective forms of evaluation.

At the same time, critical theorists have moved beyond the limits of Dewey's analysis and are gaining currency and recognition among some educators. Though many of their conclusions remain unpalatable to liberal humanists and pragmatists, critical theorists have made important advances in the attempt to understand and recompense existing educational inequality. In their analyses of how students are subjugated by the industrial mode of capital accumulation, however, critical theorists have largely sidestepped Dewey's understanding of, and commitment to, social reconstruction. They have curiously underestimated the salutary influences of Dewey's work, especially Dewey's understanding of human nature based on the moral norms of associative interactionism (communication, mutuality, respect, and positive regard for human potential).

The eschewal of Dewey by many critical theorists is surprising, since both Dewey and Marx share, upon close examination, an epistemology that claims to unite theory and practice. Furthermore, the pragmatism of Dewey is not that far removed in spirit from the social praxis of Marx: each believed that a freer and more just society could be achieved only through the transformation of existing social institutions, and both agreed that social action must necessarily be informed by correct understanding. However, it is certainly no secret that Marxist critics regard the similarities between Marx and Dewey as a basis not for a shared understanding but for the condemnation of Dewey's philosophy. For the Marxist critic, Dewey's faith in creative intelligence is eminently naive, because he underestimates the powerful social, political, and economic forces that mediate against equality and justice.

Despite Dewey's unrealistic optimism about the direction of social reform through the schools, there is much he still has to offer the new critical theorists. Regrettably, the tendency of some critical theorists to tag him as a liberal (whose reforms do not go far enough and therefore help perpetuate social injustice) is often a product of what Bernstein has called a degeneration into uncritical dogmatism. It remains to be seen whether or not critical educational theorists will develop a renewed interest in Dewey's pragmatist theory of inquiry, which still has much to offer critical pedagogy in its ability to evaluate and appropriate new ideas.

I do not have the space or opportunity to offer here an extensive review or even a brief recapitulation of Dewey's major social and political writings.[19] Nor can I rescue his radical temper and insights from conservative or liberal theorists and pedagogues who wish to appropriate his works for their own purposes. Notwithstanding Dewey's propensity to minimize power divisions within society, his denial of partisan political activity, his occasional incipient positivism and instrumental thinking, and his restricted approach to widespread social transformation, Dewey's social vision still in many ways approximates the critical theorists' approach to pedagogy and social change. His commitment to the norms of mutuality and reciprocity and his call for a renewal of democracy, a reconstitution of public life, and a revitalization of the concept of community, offer much to the critical educator of today.

We need to reexamine Dewey's important distinction between "education as a function of society" and "society as a function of education" in our attempt to create a citizenry concerned with struggling for equality and social justice. At issue here is whether schools are to serve and reproduce the existing society or to challenge the social order so as to develop and advance its democratic imperatives.

Dewey's thought is consistent on certain issues, particularly in his attempt to link the notion of individual and social (cooperative) intelligence with the discourse of democracy and freedom. Dewey may have been wary of ideological constructs, but he was unwavering in his support for the ideology of democracy as both an historical construction and a referent for dignifying politics, human efficiency, and social struggle.

Dewey's emphasis on democracy provides a language of possibility for educators while remaining sensitive to the radical impulses in American history, and educational theorists working within the critical tradition would be wise to incorporate some of that language into their work. For critical educators, the pressing task is to develop a political project combining the best insights of Dewey and new critical theory in linking education to the imperatives of democracy and social reconstruction. Such a task needs to be carried out in the spirit of self- and social criticism, on the one hand, and social transformation, on the other. Neither impulse was alien to Dewey.

The search for a creative democracy, undertaken at the turn of the century by Dewey and others, is presently in retreat—abandoned by liberals and radicals alike. Nevertheless, it may be more important now than in any previous era that we learn from the "radical" legacy of Dewey while at the same time attempting to extend his democratic project.

MICHAEL APPLE

The work of Michael Apple constitutes a formidable advance in conceptualizing the relationship between schools, the arena of culture, and the economy.[20] At the center of Apple's analysis of schooling and the wider society are the relationships of class, gender, race, and cultural forms of resistance. Schools, Apple argues, are both productive and reproductive apparatuses of the state. We may conceptualize school culture not only as a product (technical and administrative knowledge needed to keep capital and power circulating in the hands of the dominant order) but also as a relatively autonomous sphere of "lived experiences" and "everyday patterns of interaction" of students and teachers, including class and gender related cultural forms. In *Education and Power,* Apple offers a convincing critique of *theories of reproduction* (e.g., theories about the reproduction through the schooling process of existing structures and ideological conditions of the dominant social order). This work moves beyond the rather mechanical conception of reproduction that informed his earlier work, *Ideology and Curriculum.*[21]

Apple's original contribution to critical pedagogy is his ability to articulate clearly how curricular form, the transmission of various knowledges, and teaching as a labor process are linked to the logic of capital and capital accumulation. In Apple's view, successful educational reform must include a number of dynamics: outside struggles over modes of production; reforms in the workplace; the democratization of decision-making procedures and social practices in the schools; and the efforts of classroom teachers to make multiclass coalitions with progressive social movements in the wider society. Michael Apple's most recent work is *The Politics of Official Knowledge.*[22]

HENRY GIROUX

The work of Henry Giroux has affected both modern social theory and major trends in critical pedagogy.[23] Giroux assumes that schools must be seen not simply as instructional sites, but as complexes of dominant and subordinate cultures, each ideologically linked to the power they possess to define and legitimate a particular construction of reality. As cultural sites, schools are contested terrains in which different values, conventions, and knowledges variously intersect, juxtapose, and exclude one another. Teachers and others interested in education must understand how the dominant culture at all levels of schooling functions to disconfirm and, less frequently, to legitimate or celebrate the cultural experiences of students who inhabit subordinate cultures.

Giroux points out that one of the central weaknesses of classical Marxist conceptions of schooling is its tendency to view teachers and students primarily as victims or collaborators, operating in pedagogical factories where domination and Manichean gloom is all but total. Rather than view schools as sites of struggle over meaning and social relations, orthodox Marxist educators have provided an oversimplified version of domination in which an oppressive hegemony is virtually inescapable. Giroux suggests that critical analyses of schools have not given sufficient emphasis to schools' potential as sites of social transformation. He argues that schools are more than a machinery of domination; they are also places where particular forms of knowledge, social relations, and values can be taught to educate students to take their place within society from a position of self and social empowerment, rather than from a position of ideological and economic subordination.

Giroux, along with Michael Apple and others, argues that schools are partially autonomous sites. Students can therefore resist the dominating logic and restrictions embodied in school rules and conventions. For Giroux, however, schooling does more than reproduce inequality, give or take various acts of resistance and oppositional behavior exhibited by truculent students. Rather, schooling is a form of cultural production through which a number of processes are set into motion: the selection and legitimation of school knowledge and student subjectivities; the organization and sanctioning of particular forms of experience; and the development of forms of subjugation resulting from the enforcement of particular forms of authority.

Giroux's work to date can certainly be described as both politically courageous and theoretically pathfinding. Because of his attempts to redefine the terrain of radical social theory, Giroux remains vulnerable to attacks by both the right and the left. Yet he has steadfastly refused to allow his work to become fettered by any particular brand of orthodoxy that might compromise the theoretical advancement of his political project. Recent works by Giroux include *Schooling and the Struggle for Public Life, Border Crossings,* and *Living Dangerously.*[24]

NOTES TO APPENDIX

1. Cornel West, in bell hooks and Cornel West, *Breaking Bread: Insurgent Black Intellectual Life* (Boston: South End Press, 1991), 60.
2. These include (all by bell hooks): *Ain't I a Woman: Black Women and Feminism* (Boston: South End Press, 1981); *Feminist Theory: From Margin to Center* (Boston: South End Press, 1984); *Talking Back: Thinking Feminist, Thinking Black* (Boston: South End Press, 1989); *Yearning: Race, Gender, and Cultural Politics* (Boston: South End Press, 1990); *Black Looks: Race and Representation* (Boston: South End Press, 1992); and *A Woman's Mourning Song* (New York: Writers and Readers Publishing, Inc., 1993, and New York and London: Harlem River Press, 1993). Also bell hooks and Cornel West, *Breaking Bread: Insurgent Black Intellectual Life* (Boston: South End Press, 1991).
3. bell hooks, "bell hooks Speaking about Paulo Freire: The Man, His Work," in Peter McLaren and Peter Leonard (eds.), *Paulo Freire: A Critical Encounter* (London and New York: Routledge, 1993), 60.

4. All by Maxine Greene: *Teacher as Stranger* (Belmont, California: Wadsworth, 1973); *The Public School and the Private Vision* (New York: Random House, 1965); *Landscapes of Learning* (New York: Teachers College Press, 1978); and *The Dialectic of Freedom* (New York: Teachers College Press, 1988).

5. Maxine Greene, *The Dialectic of Freedom* (New York: Teachers College Press, 1988).

6. Jonathan Kozol, *Death at an Early Age* (New York: Bantam Books, 1968). This section first appeared in Peter McLaren, "Jonathan Kozol: Practical Rebel," *Orbit* 63 (1982, October): 24–26 and Peter McLaren, "Jonathan Kozol: Practical Rebel," *Ontario Public School Teachers' Federation News* (1983, February 1): 13–14.

7. Jonathan Kozol, *On Being a Teacher* (New York: Continuum, 1981), 116.

8. Jonathan Kozol, *Rachel and Her Children: Homeless Families in America* (New York: Fawcett, 1988).

9. Jonathan Kozol, *Savage Inequalities: Children in America's Schools* (New York: Crown Publishers, 1991, and New York: Harper Collins Publications, Inc., 1992).

10. The source for this section is Peter McLaren, "Postmodernity and the Death of Politics: A Brazilian Reprieve," *Educational Theory* 36, 4 (1986): 389–401. See also Peter McLaren, "Paulo Freire e o Pós-Moderno," *Educação E. Realidade* 12,1 (1987): 3–13.

11. See the following works by Paulo Freire: *Pedagogy of the Oppressed* (New York: Seabury Press, 1973); *Education for Critical Consciousness* (New York: Seabury Press, 1978); *Pedagogy in Process: Letters to Guinea-Bissau* (New York: Seabury Press, 1978); and with Donald Macedo, *Literacy: Reading the Word and the World* (South Hadley, MA: Bergin and Garvey Publishers, 1987).

12. Florence Tager, "The Relation between Politics and Culture in the Teaching of Working-Class Students," *Curriculum Inquiry* 12, 2 (1982): 214.

13. Paulo Freire, *The Politics of Education: Culture, Power, and Liberation* (South Hadley, MA: Bergin and Garvey Publishers, 1985), 44, 50, 83.

14. Freire, *The Politics of Education,* 106.

15. Ibid., 63.

16. Peter McLaren and Peter Leonard, eds. *Paulo Freire: A Critical Encounter* (London and New York: Routledge, 1993); Peter McLaren and Colin Lankshear, eds. *Politics of Liberation: Paths from Freire* (London and New York: Routledge, 1993); Ira Shor, *Empowering Education* (Chicago and London: University of Chicago Press, 1992).

17. The sources for this section are: Peter McLaren, "The Pursuit of Educational Excellence," *Insights* 21 (1985): 1–2; Peter McLaren, "Radical and Pragmatic Politics of Education," *Insights* 21, 1 (1985): 2–3; Henry A. Giroux and Peter McLaren, "Resurrecting the Spirit of John Dewey and the Challenge of Critical Pedagogy," *Insights* 22, 2 (1986): 1–2; and Henry A. Giroux and Peter McLaren, "Response to Webb and Sherman," *Insights* 22, 2 (1986): 3.

18. Richard J. Bernstein, *Praxis and Action* (Philadelphia: University of Pennsylvania Press, 1971), 228.

19. See John Dewey, *Liberalism and Social Action* (New York: G. P. Putnam's Sons, 1980); *Experience and Education* (New York: Collier Books, 1971); *Democracy and Education* (New York: Free Press, 1966); and *Freedom and Culture* (New York: G. P. Putnam's Sons, 1963).

20. This section is taken from Peter McLaren, "Critical Pedagogy and the Egalitarian Dream," *Social Education* 51, 2 (1987): 146–150.

21. See Michael Apple, *Education and Power* (London and Boston: Routledge and Kegan Paul, 1982); and *Ideology and Curriculum* (Boston: Routledge and Kegan Paul, 1979).

22. Michael Apple. *The Politics of Official Knowledge* (New York and London: Routledge, 1993).

23. This section is taken from a number of my reviews of Giroux's work which include the following: "Critical Pedagogy and the Egalitarian Dream," *Social Education;* "Essay Review: *Education under Siege,*" *Educational Studies* 17, 2 (1986): 277–289; "Education as Counter-Discourse," *Review of Education* 13, 1 (1987, Winter): 58–68; "Review of *Education under Siege,*" *Forum* 12, 14 (1986): 40.

24. Henry A. Giroux: *Schooling and the Struggle for Public Life: Critical Pedagogy in the Modern Age* (Minneapolis: University of Minnesota Press, 1988); *Border Crossings: Cultural Workers and the Politics of Education* (New York and London: Routledge, 1992); *Living Dangerously* (New York: Peter Lang Publishers, 1993).

Further Readings

Adorno, T. W. (1967). *Prisms* (Samuel and Sherry Weber, Trans.). London: Neville Spearman.

Adorno, T. W. (1973). *Negative Dialectics.* New York: The Seabury Press.

Adorno, T. W., and Horkheimer, M. (1972). *Dialectic of Enlightenment* (John Cumming, Trans.). New York: The Seabury Press.

Althusser, L. (1969). *For Marx.* New York: Vintage Books.

Althusser, L. (1970). *Reading Capital.* London: New Left Books.

Althusser, L. (1971). Ideology and the Ideological Slate Apparatuses. In L. Althusser, *Lenin and Philosophy and Other Essays.* New York: Monthly Review Press.

Anyon, J. (1980, Winter). Social Class and the Hidden Curriculum of Work. *Journal of Education, 162* (1).

Anyon, J. (1981). Elementary Schooling and Distinctions of Social Class. *Interchange, 12,* 2–3.

Anyon, J. (1981, Spring). Social Class and School Knowledge. *Curriculum Inquiry, 11* (1), 3–42.

Anzaldúa, G. (1987). *Borderlands/La Frontera: The New Mestiza.* San Francisco: Aunt Lute Books.

Apple, M. W. (1979). *Ideology and Curriculum.* Boston: Routledge and Kegan Paul.

Apple, M. W. (1982). *Education and Power.* Boston: Routledge and Kegan Paul.

Apple, M. W. (1988). *Teachers and Texts.* New York and London: Routledge and Kegan Paul.

Apple, M. W. (1993). *The Politics of Official Knowledge.* New York and London: Routledge.

Arnot, M. (1981). *Class, Gender, and Education.* London: Open University Press.

Aronowitz, S. (1973). *False Promises.* New York: McGraw-Hill.

Aronowitz, S. (1980). Science and Ideology. *Current Perspectives in Social Theory, 1,* 75–101.

Aronowitz, S. (1980, Spring). Technocratic Rationality and the Politics of Schooling. *Social Practices.*

Aronowitz, S. (1981). *The Crisis in Historical Materialism: Class, Politics, and Culture in Marxist Theory.* New York: Praeger Press.

Aronowitz, S., and Giroux, H. (1986). *Education Under Siege.* London: Routledge and Kegan Paul.

Aronowitz, S., and Giroux, H. (1991). *Postmodern Education.* Minneapolis, MN: University of Minnesota Press.

Baron, S., Fink, D., Grant, N., Green, M. and Johnson, R. (1981). *Unpopular Education.* London: Hutchinson and Co. Publishers.

Bates, R. (1980). New Developments in the New Sociology of Education. *British Journal of Sociology of Education, 1,* 67–79.

Bennett, T. (1980, Spring). Popular Culture: A Teaching Object. *Screen Education, 34.*

Berlak, A., and Berlak, H. (1980). *The Dilemmas of Schooling.* London: Methuen.

Bernstein, B. (1971). On the Classification and Framing of Educational Knowledge. In M. F. D. Young (Ed.), *Knowledge and Control.* London: Collier Macmillan.

Bernstein, B. (1977). *Class, Codes, and Control. Vol. 3. Towards a Theory of Educational Transmission* (2nd edition). London: Routledge and Kegan Paul.

Bernstein, B. (1981). Codes Modalities and the Process of Cultural Reproduction: A Model. In M. Apple (Ed.), *Cultural and Economic Reproduction in Education.* Boston: Routledge and Kegan Paul.

Bisseret, N. (1979). *Education, Class Language, and Ideology.* Boston: Routledge and Kegan Paul.

Bobbitt, F. (1918). *The Curriculum.* Boston: Houghton Mifflin.

Borman, K., and Spring, J. (1984). *Schools in Central Cities.* New York: Longman.

Bourdieu, P. (1962). *The Algerians.* Boston: Beacon.

Bourdieu, P. (1967). Systems of Education and Systems of Thought. *International Social Science Journal, 19* (3).

Bourdieu, P. (1968). Outline of a Theory of Art Perception. *International Social Science Journal, 20* (4), 589–612.

Bourdieu, P. (1968). Structuralism and Theory of Sociological Knowledge. *Social Research, 5* (4), 681–706.

Bourdieu, P. (1971). Intellectual Field and Creative Project. In M. F. D. Young (Ed.), *Knowledge and Control.* London: Macmillan.

Bourdieu, P. (1971, October 15). The Thinkable and the Unthinkable. *Times Literary Supplement.*

Bourdieu, P. (1973). Cultural Reproduction, and Social Reproduction. In R. Brown (Ed.), *Knowledge, Education, and Social Change.* London: Tavistock.

Bourdieu, P. (1973). The Three Forms of Theoretical Knowledge. *Social Science Information, 12* (1), 53–80.

Bourdieu, P. (1974). The School as a Conservation Force: Scholastic and Cultural Inequalities. In J. Eggleston (Ed.), *Contemporary Research in the Sociology of Education.* London: Methuen.

Bourdieu, P. (1975). The Specificity of the Scientific Field and the Social Conditions of the Progress of Reason. *Social Science Information, 14* (6), 19–47.

Bourdieu, P. (1976). Marriage Strategies as Strategies of Social Reproduction. In R. Forster and Orest Ranum (Eds.), *Family and Society: Selections from the Annales.* Baltimore: Johns Hopkins University Press.

Bourdieu, P. (1977). Cultural Reproduction and Social Reproduction. In J. Karabel and A. H. Halsey (Eds.), *Power and Ideology.* New York: Oxford University Press.

Bourdieu, P. (1977). *Outline of Theory and Practice.* Cambridge, England: Cambridge University Press.

Bourdieu, P., and Passeron, J. C. (1977). *Reproduction in Education, Society, and Culture.* Beverly Hills, CA: Sage.

Bourdieu, P., and Reynaud, J. D. (1974). Is a Sociology of Action Possible? In A. Giddens (Ed.), *Positivism and Sociology*. London: Heinemann.

Bourdieu, P., and Saint-Martin, M. de (1974). Scholastic Intelligence and the Values of the Educational System. In J. Eggleston (Ed.), *Contemporary Research in the Sociology of Education*. London: Methuen.

Bourdieu, P. (1979, Summer). Symbolic Power. *Critique of Anthropology, 4*, 13–14.

Bowles, S., and Gintis, H. (1976). *Schooling in Capitalist America*. New York: Basic Books.

Britzman, D. P. (1991). *Practice Makes Practice: A Critical Study of Learning to Teach*. Albany: State University of New York Press.

Burbules, Nicholas (1993). *Dialogue in Teaching*. New York: Teachers College Press.

Carby, Hazel (1987). *Reconstructing Womanhood*. New York: Oxford University Press.

Carlson, D. (1992). *Teachers and Crisis: Urban School Reform and Teachers' Work Culture*. New York: Routledge.

Connell, R. W., Dowsett, G. W., Kessler, S., and Ashendew, D. J. (1981). Class and Gender Dynamics in a Ruling-Class School. *Interchange, 12*, 2–3.

Corrigan, P. (1974). *Schooling the Smash Street Kids*. London: Macmillan Press, Ltd.

Darder, A. (1992). *Culture and Power in the Classroom*. South Hadley, MA: Bergin and Garvey.

Davies, B. (1976). *Social Control and Education*. London: Methuen.

Davies, D. (1981). *Popular Culture, Class, and Schooling*. London: Open University Press.

DeMaggio, P. (1979). Review Essay: On Pierre Bourdieu. *American Journal of Sociology, 84* (6), 1460–1474.

Drier, P. (1980, Sept./Oct.). Socialism and Cyncism: An Essay on Politics, Scholarship, and Teaching. *Socialist Review, 10*, 5.

Durkheim, E. (1956). *Education and Sociology*. Boston: Free Press.

Erben, M., and Gleeson, D. (1977). Education as Reproduction: A Critical Examination of Some Aspects of the Work of Louis Althusser. In G. Whitty and M. Young (Eds.), *Society, State, and Schooling*. Sussex, England: Falmer Press.

Feinberg, W. (1975). *Reason and Rhetoric: The Intellectual Foundations of Twentieth Century Liberal Reform*. New York: Wiley.

Feinberg, W. (1980, Winter). Educational Studies and the Disciplines of Educational Understanding. *Educational Studies, 10* (4).

Fine, M. (1991). *Framing Dropouts: Notes on the Politics of an Urban Public High School*. Albany: State University of New York Press.

Freire, P. (1970, May). The Adult Literacy Process as Cultural Action for Freedom. *Harvard Educational Review, 40* (2), 205–225.

Freire, P. (1973). *Education for Critical Consciousness*. New York: Seabury Press.

Freire, P. (1974). *Pedagogy of the Oppressed*. New York: Seabury Press.

Freire, P. (1978, November). *Cartas a Guinea-Bissau: Apuntes de una Experiência en Proceso*. Mexico: Siglo Veintiuno.

Freire, P. (1985). *The Politics of Education: Culture, Power, and Liberation*. South Hadley, MA: Bergin and Garvey Publishers.

Freire, P., and Macedo, D. (1987). *Literacy: Reading the Word and the World*. South Hadley, MA: Bergin and Garvey Publishers.

Foucault, M. (1977). *Discipline and Punish: The Birth of the Prison*. New York: Pantheon.

Foucault, M. (1979). *Power, Truth, and Strategy*. Sydney, Australia: Feral Publication.

Foucault, M. (1980). In C. Gordon (Ed.), *Power/Knowledge: Selected Interviews and Other Writings*. New York: Pantheon.

Giddens, A. (1970). *Central Problems in Social Theory: Action, Structure, and Contradictions in Social Analysis.* Berkeley: University of California Press.

Giroux, H. (1980). Critical Theory and Rationality in Frankfurt School Thought. *Curriculum Inquiry, 10* (4).

Giroux, H. (1983). *Theory and Resistance: A Pedagogy for the Opposition.* South Hadley, MA: Bergin and Garvey Publishers.

Giroux, H. (1988). *Teachers as Intellectuals: A Critical Pedagogy for Practical Learning.* South Hadley, MA: Bergin and Garvey Publishers.

Giroux, H. A. (1980). Beyond the Correspondence Theory: Notes on the Dynamics of Educational Reproduction and Transformation. *Curriculum Theory, 10* (3), 225–247.

Giroux, H. A. (1988). *Schooling and the Struggle for Public Life: Critical Pedagogy in the Modern Age.* Minneapolis: University of Minnesota Press.

Giroux, H. A. (1992). *Border Crossings.* New York and London: Routledge.

Giroux, H. A. (1993). *Living Dangerously.* New York: Peter Lang Publishers.

Giroux, H. A., and McLaren, P. (1986). Rejoinder to Rodman Web and Robert Sherman. *Insights: The John Dewey Society for the Study of Education and Culture, 22* (22), 3.

Giroux, H. A., and McLaren, P. (1986). Resurrecting the Spirit of John Dewey and the Challenge of Critical Pedagogy. *Insights: The John Dewey Society for the Study of Education and Culture, 22* (22), 1–2.

Giroux, H. A., and McLaren, P. (1986, Spring). Reproducing Reproduction: An Essay Review of *Keeping Track* by Jeanie Oakes. *Metropolitan Education, 1,* 108–118.

Giroux, H. A., and McLaren, P. (1987). Teacher Education as a Counterpublic Sphere: Notes Toward a Redefinition. In T. Popkewitz (Ed.), *Critical Studies in Teacher Education: It's Folklore, Theory, and Practice* (266–297). Philadelphia: Falmer Press.

Giroux, H. A., and McLaren, P. (1987, Spring). Teacher Education as a Counterpublic Sphere: Radical Pedagogy as a Form of Cultural Politics. *Philosophy and Social Criticism, 12* (1), 51–69.

Giroux, H. A., and McLaren, P. (1987). Review of *The Management of Ignorance* by Fred Inglis. *Canadian Journal of Sociology, 12* (3), 290–292.

Giroux, H., and McLaren, P. (Eds.) (1989). *Critical Pedagogy, the State, and Cultural Struggle.* Albany: State University of New York Press.

Giroux, H., and McLaren, P. (Eds.) (1993) *Between Borders: Pedagogy and Politics in Cultural Studies.* New York and London: Routledge.

Giroux, H., and McLaren, P. (in press). Teacher Education and the Politics of Democratic Life: Beyond the Reagan Agenda in the Era of "Good Times." In C. C. Yeakey and G. S. Johnston (Eds.), *Schools as Conduits: Educational Policy Making During the Reagan Years.* New York: Praeger Press.

Giroux, H. A., and Simon, R. I. (Eds.) (1989). *Popular Culture: Schooling and Everday Life.* Granby, MA: Bergin and Garvey Publishers.

Gitlin, A., and Smyth, J. (1989). *Teacher Evaluation: Educative Alternatives.* London, New York, and Philadelphia: The Falmer Press.

Goodman, J. (1984). Reflection and Teacher Education. *Interchange, 15* (3), 9–26.

Goodman, J. (1992). *Elementary Schooling for Critical Democracy.* Albany: State University of New York Press.

Goodson, I. (1987). *School Subjects and Curriculum Change.* London, New York, and Philadelphia: The Falmer Press.

Grace, G. (1978). *Teachers, Ideology, and Control: A Study in Urban Education.* Boston and London: Routledge and Kegan Paul.

Gramsci, A. (1971). In Q. Hoare and G. Smith (Trans. and Ed.), *Selections from Prison Notebooks.* New York: International Publishers.

Grossberg, L. (1992). *We Gotta Get Out of This Place.* New York and London: Routledge.

Grumet, M. (1988). *Bitter Milk: Women and Teaching.* Amherst: University of Massachusetts Press.

Hakken, D. (1980, Winter). Workers Education and the Reproduction of Working Class Culture. *Anthropology and Education Quarterly, 11,* 4.

Hall, S. (1981). Cultural Studies: Two Paradigms. In T. Bennett, et al. (Eds.), *Culture, Ideology, and Social Process.* London: Batsford Academic and Educational Ltd.

Hall, S. (1991). Ethnicity: Identity and Difference. *Radical America, 23* (4), 9–20.

Hall, S., and Jefferson, T. (1976). *Resistance through Rituals.* London: Hutchinson and Co.

Hargreaves, D. (1967). *Social Relations in a Secondary School.* London: Routledge and Kegan Paul.

Harty, S. (1979). *Hucksters in the Classroom: A Review of Industry Propaganda in Schools.* Washington, D.C.: Center for Study of Responsive Law.

Haymes, S. (forthcoming). *Race, Culture, and the City: A Pedagogy for Black Urban Struggle.* Albany: State University of New York Press.

Hebidge, D. (1979). *Subculture: The Meaning of Style.* London: Methuen.

hooks, b. (1981). *Ain't I a Woman: Black Women and Feminism.* Boston: South End Press.

hooks, b. (1984). *Feminist Theory: From Margin to Center.* Boston: South End Press.

hooks, b. (1989). *Talking Back: Thinking Feminist, Thinking Black.* Boston: South End Press.

hooks, b. (1990). *Yearning: Race, Gender, and Cultural Politics.* Boston: South End Press.

hooks, b. (1992). *Black Looks: Race and Representation.* Boston: South End Press.

hooks, b. (1993). *A Woman's Mourning Song.* New York and London: Harlem River Press.

hooks, b., and West, C. (1991). *Breaking Bread: Insurgent Black Intellectual Life.* Boston: South End Press.

Horkheimer, M. (1947). *Eclipse of Reason.* New York: Oxford University Press.

Horkheimer, M. (1972). *Critical Theory.* New York: The Seabury Press.

Kanpol, B. (1992). *Towards a Theory and Practice of Teacher Cultural Politics: Continuing the Postmodern Debate.* Norwood, NJ: Albex Publishing.

Keddie, N. (1971). Classroom Knowledge. In M. F. D. Young (Ed.), *Knowledge and Control.* London: Collier Macmillan.

Kincheloe, J. L. (1991). *Teachers as Researchers: Qualitative Inquiry as a Path to Empowerment.* London, New York, and Philadelphia: The Falmer Press.

Kincheloe, J. L. (1993). *Off to Work We Go: Social Foundations of Vocational Education.* Boulder, CO: Westview Press.

Kincheloe, J. L. (1993). *Toil and Trouble: Good Work, Smart Workers, and the Integration of Vocational and Academic Education.* New York: Peter Lang Publishers.

Kincheloe, J. L. (1993). *Toward a Critical Politics of Teacher Thinking: Mapping the Postmodern.* South Hadley, MA: Bergin and Garvy Publishers, Inc.

Kincheloe, J. L., and Pinar, W. F. (1991). *Curriculum as Social Psychoanalysis: The Significance of Place.* Albany: State University of New York Press.

Kincheloe, J. L. and Steinberg, S. (1991). *Thirteen Questions: Reframing Education's Conversation.* New York: Peter Lang Publishers.

Kincheloe, J. L., with Steinberg, S. R., and Tippins, D. J. (1992). *The Stigma of Genius: Einstein and Beyond Modern Education.* Wakefield, NH: Hollowbrook.

Kliebard, H. M. (1975). Re-appraisal: The Tyler Rationale. In W. Pinar (Ed.), *Curriculum Theorizing: The Reconceptualists.* Berkeley, CA: McCutchan.

Kozol, J. (1978, August). A New Look at the Literacy Campaign in Cuba. *Harvard Educational Review, 48* (3), 341–377.

Kozol, J. (1991). *Savage Inequalities: Children in America's Schools*. New York: Crown Publishers.

Kreisberg, S. (1992). *Transforming Power: Domination, Empowerment, and Education*. Albany: State University of New York Press.

Labov, W. (1969). The Logic of Non-standard English. In N. Keddie (Ed.), *The Myth of Cultural Deprivation*. Middlesex, England: Penguin Books.

Lacey, C. (1970). *Hightown Grammar: The School as a Social System*. Manchester, England: Manchester University Press.

Laclau, E. (1977). *Politics and Ideology in Marxist Theory*. London: New Left Books.

Lankshear, C., and McLaren, P. (Eds.) (1993). *Critical Literacy: Politics, Praxis, and the Postmodern*. Albany: State University of New York Press.

Lather, P. (1991). *Getting Smart: Feminist Research and Pedagogy with/in the Postmodern*. New York and London: Routledge.

Lukács, G. (1968). *History and Class Consciousness*. Cambridge, MA: M. I. T. Press.

Marx, K. (1967). In F. Engels (Ed.), *Capital. Vol. 1* (S. Moore and E. Aveling, Trans.). New York: International Publishers.

McCarthy, C., and Apple, M. (1988). "Race, Class, and Gender in American Educational Research." In L. Weis (Ed.), *Class, Race, and Gender in American Education*. Albany: State University of New York Press.

McLaren, P. (1980). *Cries from the Corridor*. Toronto: Methuen.

McLaren, P. (1982). *Cries from the Corridor: The New Suburban Ghettos,* revised with new Afterword and Foreword by Laurier LaPierre. Markham, Ontario, Canada: PaperJacks.

McLaren, P. (1982, Fall). Bein' Tough: Rituals of Resistance in the Culture of Working-Class Schoolgirls. *Canadian Woman Studies, 1,* 20–24.

McLaren, P. (1984). Rethinking Ritual. *Etc.: A Review of General Semantics, 41* (3), 267–277.

McLaren, P. (1984, January). Victor Turner: In Memoriam 1920–1983. *International Semiotic Spectrum, 1.*

McLaren, P. (1985). Contemporary Ritual Studies: A Post-Turnerian Perspective. Review Article, *Beginnings in Ritual Studies* by Ronald L. Grimes. *Semiotic Inquiry, 5* (1), 78–85.

McLaren, P. (1985). From Ritual to Reasoning: A Prolegomena Towards Linking Ritology and Schooling. In J. Kase-Polisini (Ed.), *Creative Drama in a Developmental Context*. Washington, D.C.: University Press of America. (pp. 209–251).

McLaren, P. (1985). The Politics of Student Resistance. In R. Common (Ed.), *New Forces in Educational Policy-Making*. Brock University Occasional Publications. (pp. 94–107).

McLaren, P. (1985). The Ritual Dimensions of Resistance: Clowning and Symbolic Inversion. *Boston University Journal of Education, 167* (2), 84–97.

McLaren, P. (1985, May). Radical and Pragmatic Politics of Education: The Possibility of Rapprochement. *Insights: The John Dewey Society for the Study of Education and Culture, 21* (1).

McLaren, P. (1985, December). The Concept of Excellence in Education: A Reaction. *Insights: The John Dewey Society for the Study of Education and Culture, 21* (1).

McLaren, P. (1986). Education as Counter-Discourse. An Essay Review of *Education Under Siege* by Stanley Aronowitz and Henry Giroux. *Educational Studies, 17* (2), 277–289.

McLaren, P. (1986). Interrogating the Conceptual Roots of Invitational Education. An Essay Review of *Inviting School Success* by William Watson Purkey and John Novak. *Interchange,* 17 (4), 90–95.

McLaren, P. (1986). Making Catholics: The Ritual Production of Conformity in a Catholic Junior High School. *Boston University Journal of Education, 168* (2), 55–77.

McLaren, P. (1986). Postmodernism and the Death of Politics: A Brazilian Reprieve. An Essay Review of *The Politics of Education* by Paulo Freire. *Educational Theory, 36* (4), 389–401.

McLaren, P. (1986). *Schooling as a Ritual Performance: Towards a Political Economy of Educational Symbols and Gestures.* London: Routledge and Kegan Paul.

McLaren, P. (1987, Winter). Review of *Theory and Resistance* by Henry Giroux and *Education Under Siege* by Stanley Aronowitz and Henry Giroux. *Review of Education, 13* (1), 58–68.

McLaren, P. (1987). The Writer as Social Agent. *University of Toronto Review, 11,* 24. Reprinted in *Que Ondee Sola,* (1987), 20 (12).

McLaren, P. (1987, February). Radical Pedagogy and the Dream of Emancipation. *Social Eduation, 51* (2), 146–150.

McLaren, P. (1987). The Anthropological Roots of Pedagogy: The Teacher as Liminal Servant. *Anthropology and Humanism Quarterly,* 12 (3 and 4), 75–85.

McLaren, P. (1987). Ideology, Science and the Politics of Marxian Orthodoxy: A Response to Michael Dale. *Educational Theory,* 37 (3), 301–326.

McLaren, P. (1987). Schooling for Salvation: Christian Fundamentalism's Ideological Weapons of Death. Review of "God's Choice: The Total World of a Fundamentalist Christian School" by Alan Peshkin. *Boston University Journal of Education, 169* (2), 132–139.

McLaren, P. (1988). The Liminal Servant and the Ritual Roots of Critical Pedagogy. *Language Arts, 65* (2), 164–179.

McLaren, P. (1988). Culture or Canon? Critical Pedagogy and the Politics of Literacy. *Harvard Educational Review, 58* (2), 213–234.

McLaren, P., Ed. (in press). *Postmodernism, Postcolonialism, and Pedagogy.* Albert Park, Australia: Jame Nicholas Publishers.

McLaren, P. and Leonard, P., Eds. (1993). *Paulo Freire: A Critical Encounter.* New York and London.

McLaren, P., and Lankshear, C., Eds. (1993). *Politics of Liberation.* New York and London: Routledge.

McLaren, P., and Smith, R. (1989). "Televangelism as Pedagogy and Cultural Politics." In H. Giroux, and R. Simon (Eds.), *Popular Culture: Schooling and Everyday Life.* Granby, MA: Bergin and Garvey.

McRobbie, A. (1980, Spring). Settling Accounts with Subcultures. *Screen Education,* 34.

Mensh, E., and Mensh, H. (1991). *The IQ Mythology.* Carbondale and Edwardsville: Southern Illinois University Press.

Mohanty, C. (1989/90). On Race and Voice: Challenges for Liberal Education in the 1990's, *Cultural Critique,* Winter, 179–208.

Mohanty, C. T., Russo, A., and Torres, L. (1991). *Third World Women and the Politics of Feminism.* Bloomington and Indianapolis: Indiana University Press.

Mouffe, C. (1979). Hegemony and Ideology in Gramsci. In C. Mouffe (Ed.), *Gramsci and Marxist Theory.* London: Routledge and Kegan Paul.

Murphy, R. (1982). Power and Autonomy in the Sociology of Education. *Theory and Society, 11,* 179–203.

Nieto, S. (1992). *Affirming Diversity: The Sociopolitical Context of Multicultural Education.* New York and London: Longman.

Olson, P. (1981). Laboring to Learn: How Working Theory Gets Down to Classrooms and Kids. *Interchange, 12,* 2–3.

Pagano, J. (1990). *Exiles and Communities: Teaching in the Patriarchal Wilderness.* Albany: State University of New York Press.

Pinar, W. (1975). The Analysis of Educational Experience. In W. Pinar (Ed.), *Curriculum Theorizing: The Reconceptualists.* Berkeley, CA: McCutchan.

Pinar, W. F. (Ed.) (1988). *Contemporary Curriculum Discourses.* Scottsdale, AZ: Gorusch Scarisbrick, Publishers.

Popkewitz, T. (1978, December). Educational Research: Values and Visions of Social Order. *Theory and Research in Social Education, 6* (4).

Popkewitz, T. (1981). The Social Contexts of Schooling, Change, and Educational Research. *Journal of Curriculum Studies, 13,* 3.

Popkewitz, T., et al. (1982). *The Myth of Educational Reform.* Wisconsin: University of Wisconsin Press.

Reilly, S., Schwoch, J., and White, M. (1992). *Media Knowledge.* Albany, NY: State University of New York Press.

Rist, R. C. (1970, August). Student Social Class and Teacher Expectations: The Self-Fulfilling Prophecy in Ghetto Education. *Harvard Educational Review, 40* (3), 411–451.

Sears, J. (1990). *Growing Up Gay in the South: Race, Gender, and Journeys of the Spirit.* Binghamton, NY: Haworth Press.

Shapiro, H. S., and Purple, D. E. (1993). *Critical Social Issues in American Education.* New York: Longman Publishing Group.

Shapiro, S. (1990). *Between Capitalism and Democracy: Educational Policy and the Crisis of the Welfare State.* New York: Bergin and Garvey.

Sharp, R. (1980). *Knowledge, Ideology, and the Politics of Schooling: Towards a Marxist Analysis of Education.* Boston and London: Routledge and Kegan Paul.

Shor, I. (1992). *Empowering Education.* Chicago and London: University of Chicago Press.

Sieber, R. T. (1981, Winter). The Politics of Middle-Class Success in an Inner City School. *Journal of Education, 164,* 1.

Sleeter, C. E. (Ed.) (1991). *Empowerment through Multicultural Education.* Albany: State University of New York Press.

Sleeter, C., and McLaren, P., Eds. (forthcoming). *Multiculturalism and Critical Pedagogy.* Albany: State University of New York Press.

Smyth, J. (1987). *A Rationale for Teachers' Critical Pedagogy: A Handbook.* Victoria, Australia: Deakin University Press.

Smyth, J. W. (1988). *A "Critical Pedagogy" of Teacher Evaluation.* Geelong Victoria, Australia: Deakin University.

Stinchombe, A. (1964). *Rebellion in a High School.* New York: Quadrangle Books.

Spring, Joel (1972). *Education and the Rise of the Corporate State.* Boston: Beacon Press.

Spring, Joel (1975). *A Primer of Libertarian Education.* New York: Free Life Editions.

Spring, Joel (1985). *American Education: An Introduction to Social and Political Aspects.* New York: Longman.

Sulkunin, P. (1982). Society Made Visible: On the Cultural Sociology of Pierre Bourdieu. *Acta Sociologica, 25* (2), 103–115.

Swartz, D. (1977). Pierre Bourdieu: The Cultural Transmission of Social Inequality. *Harvard Educational Review, 47* (4), 545–555.

Thompson, E. (1966). *The Making of the English Working Class.* New York: Vintage Press.

Tierney, W. G. (Ed.) (1991). *Culture and Ideology in Higher Education: Advancing a Critical Agenda.* New York: Praeger Publishers.

Torres, C. A. (1990). *The Politics of Nonformal Education in Latin America.* New York: Praeger Publishers.

Volosinov, V. V. (1973). *Marxism and the Philosophy of Language.* New York: Seminar Press.

Vygotsky, L. S. (1962). *Thought and Language.* Cambridge, MA: M.I.T. Press.

Vygotsky, L. S. (1978). In M. Cole, V. John-Steiner, S. Scribner and E. Soubrman (Eds.), *Mind in Society*. Cambridge, MA: Harvard University Press.

Walkerdine, V. (1981, Spring). Sex, Power, and Pedagogy. *Screen Education, 30*.

Wallace, M. (1979). *Black Macho and the Myth of the Superwoman*. New York: Dial Press.

Wallace, M. (1990). *Invisibility Blues: From Pop to Theory*. London and New York: Verso Press.

Weiler, K. (1988). *Women Teaching for Change: Gender, Class, and Power*. South Hadley, MA: Bergin and Garvey Publishers.

Weiler, K., and Mitchell, C. (Eds.) (1992). *What Schools Can Do: Critical Pedagogy and Practice*. Albany: State University of New York Press.

Weis, L. (1990). *Working Class Without Work: High School Students in a Deindustrializing Society*. New York: Routledge.

Williams, P. (1991). *The Alchemy of Race and Rights*. Cambridge, MA and London: Harvard University Press.

Williams, R. (1963). *Culture and Society, 1790–1950*. London: Penguin.

Williams, R. (1965). *The Long Revolution*. London: Penguin.

Williams, R. (1973). Base and Superstructure in Marxist Cultural Theory. *New Left Review, 82*.

Williams, R. (1977). *Marxism and Literature*. London: Oxford University Press.

Willis, P. (1976). The Class Significance of School Counter-Culture. In M. Hammersley and P. Woods (Eds.), *The Process of Schooling*. London: Routledge and Kegan Paul.

Willis, P. (1977). *Learning to Labor*. Lexington: D. C. Heath.

Willis, P. (1978). *Profane Culture*. Boston and London: Routledge and Kegan Paul.

Willis, P., and Corrigan, P. (1980). Cultural Forms and Class Mediations. *Media Culture and Society, 2*.

Willis, P. (1981). Cultural Production Is Different from Social Reproduction Is Different from Reproduction. *Interchange, 12, 2*.

Woods, P. (1979). *The Divided School*. London: Routledge and Kegan Paul.

Woods, P., and Hammersley, M. (1977). *School Experience*. London: Croon-Hilm.

Young, M. (1971). *Knowledge and Control*. London: Collier Macmillan.

Young, M. (1973, June). Taking Sides Against the Probable Problems of Relativism and Commitment in Teaching and the Sociology of Knowledge. In R. Meighan (Ed.), Sociology and Teaching. *Educational Review, 25,* (3).

Young, M. (1975, Summer). Sociologists and the Politics of Comprehensive Education. *Forum for the Discussion of New Trends, 17* (3).

Young, M., and Whitty, G. (1977). *Society, State, and Schooling*. Sussex, England: Falmer Press.

Zinn, H. (1980). *A People's History of the United States*. New York: Harper and Row.

Index